BETWEEN WORLDS: THE RHETORICAL UNIVERSE OF
PARADISE LOST

WILLIAM PALLISTER

Between Worlds

The Rhetorical Universe of *Paradise Lost*

UNIVERSITY OF TORONTO PRESS
Toronto Buffalo London

© University of Toronto Press Incorporated 2008
Toronto Buffalo London
www.utppublishing.com
Printed in Canada

ISBN 978-0-8020-9835-1

Printed on acid-free paper

Library and Archives Canada Cataloguing in Publication

Pallister, Will, 1967–
    Between worlds : the rhetorical universe of Paradise lost / William
    Pallister.

    Includes bibliographical references and index.
    ISBN 978-0-8020-9835-1 (bound)

    1. Milton, John, 1608–1674.   Paradise lost.   2. Milton, John,
    1608-1674 – Literary style.   I. Title.

PR3562.P24 2008   821'.4   C2008-902278-5

University of Toronto Press acknowledges the financial assistance to its
publishing program of the Canada Council for the Arts and the Ontario
Arts Council.

This book has been published with the help of a grant from the Humanities
and Social Sciences Federation of Canada, through the Aid to Scholarly
Publications Programme, using funds provided by the Social Sciences and
Humanities Research Council of Canada.

University of Toronto Press acknowledges the financial support for its
publishing activities of the Government of Canada through the Book
Publishing Industry Development Program (BPIDP).

Contents

Acknowledgments

Sir Francis Bacon wrote that fortune is like the market, where many times, if you can stay a little, the price will fall. Without Lohren Green, who saw to it that I was able to stay long enough at a critical time, Fortune wouldn't have permitted me to finish this book. I also thank Ron Bond and Jill Kraye and gratefully acknowledge Shadi Bartsch for her wise counsel and cheerful support in the later stages of preparing the manuscript. Special thanks are due to John Baxter, whose remarks on Aristotle suggested one of the central themes of this project. My greatest debt is to my parents, and I dedicate this book to them.

Notes on the Text

Translations of classical works in this study are by other hands, with occasional slight changes to translations from Latin where the meaning of a technical term has been obscured or where I wish to highlight an alternative meaning. Neo-Latin translations, unless otherwise noted, are my own; the original Latin for these translations (in which I have expanded scribal abbreviations and removed accent marks) may be found in the endnotes. Milton's Latin prose is quoted from the English translations of the Yale *Complete Prose Works*, with occasional references to the Latin text from the Columbia *Works*. In quoting from English Renaissance texts, I have normalized spelling, changing *is* to *js* and *us* to *vs* (and vice versa). *CWE* stands for *The Collected Works of Erasmus*; *PL* for *Paradise Lost*; *PR* for *Paradise Regained*; *ELLMA* for *European Literature in the Latin Middle Ages*. The Yale *Complete Prose Works* are cited as *YP*, followed by volume and page numbers. No other abbreviations are used.

BETWEEN WORLDS: THE RHETORICAL UNIVERSE OF
PARADISE LOST

Introduction

In January of 49 BC Julius Caesar, enacting one of the most famous events in history, crosses the Rubicon, a violation of senatorial decree that precipitates the series of events leading to the battle of Pharsalus and the extinction of the Roman republic. Once on the river's south bank, Caesar as portrayed in Lucan's *Bellum Civile* delivers one of the poem's many apostrophes: 'Here I abandon peace and desecrated law; / Fortune, it is you I follow' (I. 225–6). Caesar rises in Fortune's favour as Pompey falls, pressing on to military victory and imperial power (Fortune eventually abandons him, as she does all her followers, five years later on one of the most famous dates in history, which Lucan did not live long enough to write about). Impersonal forces, not the gods or the wills of men, dispose Lucan's universe: either immovable Fate or random Chance seems to control earthly affairs (II. 9–13); Fortune wreaks havoc at Pharsalus while Fate rushes on (VII. 504–5); Fortune at length reduces Pompey, having formerly supported him (VIII. 21–3, 701–8). Here the future is trammelled by necessity, not shaped by the contingent play of alternative outcomes. Fortune, Fate, or Chance, or some combination thereof, denies free agency to human beings, cancels out autonomy and self-assertion, hinders the will of even the most driven and able of men to achieve their aims independently. Similar forces influence human affairs in Greek epic. Agamemnon and Achilles fall prey to Até, the state of mind leading to disaster, against which men are powerless. The modern judicial plea of temporary insanity – I didn't know what I was doing – contains a trace of this old idea. Judges sometimes believe it, just as Achilles believes Agamemnon's declaration that Até had impelled him to steal Briseis.

Are human actions committed freely? The Greek concept of human destiny gradually became more self-deterministic, culminating in Heraclitus's maxim, 'Man's character is his daemon' – that is, man's character, over which he has some control, determines his personal destiny, not the external and often capricious powers at work in Lucan or Homer. Yet the Stoics later acknowledged the efficacy of those powers and urged resignation to their ineluctable currents: 'Everything is fitting for me, my Universe, which fits thy purpose,' writes Marcus Aurelius. Examples from all periods, arguing both sides, determinism and voluntarism, could be endlessly multiplied. But these arguments are better comprehended subjectively, by reflecting on your own approach to the perennial questions they attempt to answer. Consider the matter, as everyone has, whether you believe your station in life, your portion of happiness, your day-to-day actions, and the management of your affairs lie within your own power to direct and determine, or whether those things are influenced to any degree, even settled, by some inscrutable power, be it God, Fortune, or Fate. Is there a divinity (or other force) that shapes your ends, rough-hew them how you will? Or is it in yourself that you are thus or thus? The question of personal agency, including whether the future is necessary or contingent, is central to the concept of rhetoric and to the rhetorical reading of *Paradise Lost* that occupies this book.

Milton admired Lucan for his politics, not his theology; the divine machinery of epic that Lucan discarded and replaced with Fortune, Chance, and Fate is of course reintroduced in *Paradise Lost*. God presides once again over the epic scene, and His relationship to narrative events as they unfold differs distinctly from that of the pagan forces that control human life in *Bellum Civile*. Pagan determinism gives way to Christian voluntarism, free will being an essential condition of human existence within Milton's theodicy. The presence and attributes of God are the most critical determinants of future contingency in *Paradise Lost*; therefore, they also bear directly on the nature of rhetoric, which is conventionally bound up with the properties of contingent statements and events. It was a first principle of classical and Renaissance rhetoric that persuasive arguments were based on probability, with no claim to be absolutely true or correct at all times, and that the decisions that those statements prompted an audience to make could have been made differently – future contingency meant that another choice or course of action was almost always open for consideration. This freedom to weigh the relative merits of an argument and to act accordingly was the essence of rhetorical persuasion as it was conceived from its earliest beginnings down to the seventeenth century.

In light of future contingency, which I judge to be the central rhetorical issue of *Paradise Lost*, I interpret Milton's epic as comprising three discrete rhetorics, one for each of heaven, hell, and the Garden of Eden. The division is called for because in Milton's epic cosmos, the expansion of the rhetorical arena to heaven and hell, especially the inclusion of God in the poem's *dramatis personae*, complicates the standard rhetorical model predicated on contingency and probability. Questions arise concerning the omniscience of Milton's God and the implications of a providentially disposed universe. Does God's foreknowledge of events mean that they must necessarily come to pass, regardless of what other characters say and do? To what extent does providence, whereby all things happen according to God's plan, restrict the contingent outcome of decisions and actions? A normative conception of rhetoric does not account for divine foreknowledge or the certain fulfilment of Christian providence, or for situations in which supernatural characters, from heaven and hell, visit earth and speak to its human inhabitants. These circumstances exert different effects on the rhetorics of heaven, hell, and Eden; the main result is that the degree of future contingency varies from one plane of reality to another, and so, therefore, does the nature of rhetoric, which depends so much on the existence of possibility and uncertainty in order to accommodate persuasion and be genuinely 'rhetorical.'

The title of this book recalls the flight of the angel Raphael, who, charged with warning man of the impending crisis, 'Sails between worlds and worlds' (V. 268) on his journey to Paradise, a journey that mirrors the course to be taken in the following pages. We too will travel, with a rhetorical eye, between the worlds of *Paradise Lost*, between heaven, hell, and the Garden of Eden, noticing how Raphael and his fellow travellers negotiate that same journey as users of rhetoric. This course will also shuttle us between the worlds of Greece, Rome, and Renaissance Europe, as well as the spheres of history (secular and Christian), moral philosophy, politics, theology, biblical hermeneutics and homiletic theory, poetics, and, finally, poetry and rhetoric, the book's two main subjects. Rhetoric is aptly suited for conducting such a tour; according to a long-standing objection, it has, so to speak, no fixed address. Taught by the itinerant sophists of ancient Greece, rhetoric is inherently portable, having neither a rational account of what it is (at least before Aristotle) nor an ontological grounding in what is true or good. It deals with opinion, not knowledge, values expediency, not justice, strives for victory, not demonstration. By the time of rhetoric's revival, however, fully under way in the fifteenth century, these qualities were considered either positive virtues or, if defects, ones that could be reformed with a due leavening of ethics: an eloquent man must be a good man, ran the standard theory. Moreover, rhetoric had found a home in the Renaissance arts curriculum and regained its high stature in both education and public life. Its days of wandering were over.

By the time Milton returned to poetry in earnest after a long hiatus of writing polemical prose, the identity that had been defined for rhetoric since approximately Petrarch's time was changing in a number of ways. The undifferentiated body of knowledge that rhetoric (and grammar) had subsumed or bordered on during the Renaissance was becoming compartmentalized during the seventeenth century, divided into specialized subjects. Rhetoric remained influential, for by it all subjects were bodied forth in words. It was itself, however, caught between worlds. It continued to figure significantly in English political argumentation during the upheavals from the 1620s to the post-Restoration period, but its role as a discipline implicated in the discovery of knowledge changed with the advent of the New Science, and it attracted particular interest for its long-acknowledged powers of moving the emotions and influencing the will. For Milton, rhetoric retained in full measure the universal importance accorded it by Renaissance humanists, who established it as an ethical and political instrument as well as the cornerstone of the cultural and literary pursuits that formed the chief areas of humanistic interest. Milton has been called 'the last great exponent of humanism in its historical continuity,'[1] and insofar as his allegiance to rhetoric is concerned, the designation is an appropriate one. He learned it as a student, later would have taught it as a tutor, practised it expertly – contemporaries acknowledged the vigour of his Latin prose – and explored it thematically throughout his literary career.

Rhetoric, in the technical tradition,[2] is the art of speaking or writing in order to persuade a given audience, based on a model of composition that unifies all the material of an argument: *inventio* finds what is to be said; *dispositio* organizes it; *elocutio* determines the proper words with which to express the subject; lastly, in the case of a spoken oration, there is *memoria*, or memory, and *actio*, the tones and gestures of delivery. During the Middle Ages, a myopic concentration on *elocutio*, particularly the tropes and figures, had stripped rhetoric of its characteristic persuasive capability, which was not revived until the Renaissance.[3] As handed down from both Latin and Greek classical sources, rhetoric claimed eminence during the Renaissance partly from its central position in the curriculum of European humanists, the *studia humanitatis*, which comprised the linguistic arts of grammar, rhetoric, and poetry, as well as history and moral philosophy and later other areas of philosophy and the various sciences.[4] The cultural and educational priorities of humanism ensured that rhetoric was substantially a literary enterprise, concerned with the language of expressing ideas at least as much as the ideas themselves. This engagement with form meant that lettered men of the time were preoccupied with the ideal of eloquence, defined by the sixteenth-century French educator Peter Ramus (echoing the Roman rhetorician Quintilian) as 'the power of expressing oneself well' (*vis est bene dicendi*).[5] Eloquence was more than fluency in style, however much, as we shall see, style held a key place in humanist rhetoric. It was, in its true pursuit, a harmonious union between wisdom and style, with an emphasis on persuasion that often stressed the efficacy of moving the emotions. The art of rhetoric, replete with precepts to guide literary composition at all stages, constituted the methodological infrastructure of eloquence. It is this status as the technical machinery of eloquence in all its forms, from letters to historical and philosophical treatises, that allowed rhetoric to play a major role in the development of Renaissance culture. Of all the disciplines to which rhetoric imparted form and a consciousness of expressive intention, none was more closely connected with it, virtually since the inception of both arts, than poetry.

'Poetry has a history; ideas-in-poetry (which are not the same as ideas) have a history too; and the historian's task is a delicate and creative one.'[6] Frank Kermode raises a provocative question: why are 'ideas-in-poetry' not the same as ideas? Stanley Fish has recently explained this distinction by way of criticizing the historicist trend in Milton studies. Ideas-in-poetry (he does not use Kermode's term) need to be discussed in relation to the poetic form that expresses them, always in consideration of what the poem is intended to do. He judges this consideration to be absent from some of the best contemporary Milton scholarship, which often wrenches ideas out of their local context '-in-poetry' – the context that gives them meaning and significance – and discusses them in isolation simply as 'ideas,' forgetting or ignoring that Milton the poet pressed those ideas into service as part of a specific poetic (not political or historical) agenda. In order to perform the historian's task effectively, 'you have to attend to the specificity of the discourse that has solicited your attention, and that means attending to its history, not to history in general (there is no such thing) but to the history of a form'; consequently, the history 'appropriate to the description and evaluation of literary works ... is the history of literary forms.' With form as a touchstone for critical inquiry, it is evident that 'historical and political matters matter chiefly as the material of an aesthetic achievement. Describing and evaluating that achievement, which while it is often inconceivable apart from historical and political concerns cannot be identified with them, is the proper business of literary criticism.'[7]

One of rhetoric's virtues as a method of critical inquiry is that it *is* the material of an aesthetic achievement. Its very nature is form, and as such it keeps critical attention tightly focused there. Rhetoric's inherent association with form makes it the ultimate idea-in-poetry; it has always been valued as an instrument of both composition and criticism, a means both of making a text, as the material of an aesthetic achievement, and of seeing how a text was made, describing and evaluating it in terms of its form. In studying rhetoric, the critic examines the formal constituents of the literary artefact – the bricks and mortar of which the cathedral is made, to borrow from C.S. Lewis's famous opening sentence, which Fish cites in his injunction to a realigned critical approach. Lewis is similarly concerned with the history of literary forms. Having stated that 'every poem can be considered in two ways – as what the poet has to say, and as a *thing* which he *makes*,' he directs himself to the second consideration.[8] This book will proceed along similar lines, turning to rhetoric for the insights it provides into the making of a poem written at a particular time, for a particular audience, under a particular set of laws and conventions. Poetry has a history. Its conventions are of material interest, as Quentin Skinner reminds us: 'We need to focus not merely on the particular text in which we are interested but on the prevailing conventions governing the treatment of the issues or themes with which the text is concerned.'[9] Rhetoric is one of a number of prevailing conventions, formal and otherwise, that governs Milton's treatment of themes in *Paradise Lost* (what the poet has to say) and also the process of composing the poem (the thing which he makes). As an essay on the history of literary forms, the present study will consider *Paradise Lost* in both ways, but it will stress the application of rhetoric to evaluating the poem's formal elements, especially those that individuate the discourses of heaven, hell, and Paradise.

A history of literary forms presupposes a historical context in which we may interpret form. Establishing that context puts us in touch with the rhetorical tradition behind *Paradise Lost*, acquaints us with the material of Milton's aesthetic achievement, and lets us inspect the joinery that went into its construction. Familiarity with tradition enables the literary analysis of the epic to proceed with informed awareness. The present work seeks it from two sources. One is examining rhetoric as it was historically understood and practised in ways that bring the formal conventions of *Paradise Lost* into full view, the other is Milton's concept of rhetoric – itself, of course, derived significantly from that complex of historical precedents. According to John Hale, we see 'huge advantages in principle as well as practice when we try to stand first where Milton himself, composing, had placed himself.'[10] I agree with this view in part (hesitating at 'huge' and 'in principle') and think that rhetoric goes some way towards attaining this shared standpoint. Milton used rhetoric, and speculatively tracing his usage of rhetorical structure and technique, much as Hale has done with Milton's languages and classical allusions, can reveal important features of his poetic practice. I believe, however, that in addition to trying to gain the standpoint of Milton composing, complementary and greater advantages may be gained from trying to establish a hermeneutic precondition of understanding, that of identifying with the original reader rather than the author and from there acquiring a more thorough *formal* understanding of *Paradise Lost* than Milton himself, unconscious of much of his art, could have possessed.

Bridging this temporal distance from contemporary reader to original reader calls for elaborating the set of rhetorical conventions that lies behind *Paradise Lost* and its age, including rhetoric's classical heritage, its close ties with theology and poetry, and its relationship to other humanist pursuits. Describing the Renaissance emphasis on *elocutio*, to give one example, is the surest way of appreciating the dedication to form, the hypersensitivity to matters of genre and style, that are manifested in the works of Renaissance writers and that live and breathe in every line of *Paradise Lost*. By gaining the standpoint of Milton's original addressee through an immersion in relevant areas of the rhetorical tradition, we can situate *Paradise Lost* in the context of the history of literary form. Milton's poetic construction may thus be reconstructed and illuminated through rhetorical analysis, with an objective formal consciousness greater than the state in which the author made the poem. For he neither had nor needed such a consciousness when he made it. Ingrained in him from boyhood, rhetoric early became second nature, one standby option in an artistic repertoire that, fully stocked though it was, he believed to contribute less to his ability to write poetry than divine inspiration. Things that Milton did by reflex, we must apprehend – do over again – by concerted application. The advantage gained is explicit, anatomical understanding of artistic expression. Rhetoric, then, described historically and applied technically, affords a better critical standpoint from which to view the literary production of *Paradise Lost* than does the standpoint of Milton composing. Having arrived at that point, we may establish the terms for literary analysis with some confidence, discriminating the rhetorical features of the poem that mark it as distinctive and that raise particular interpretive questions. The main question of this kind that emerges from historical excavation, the central rhetorical problem of *Paradise Lost*, is that of future contingency. It will function as a topic or commonplace, as it were, which I will draw my arguments through as a means of gathering material for evaluating the rhetoric(s) of the poem. For that reason, the book begins by defining contingency and probability and examining their relationship to rhetoric, their articulation in classical theory, and their role as defining features of Milton's epic universe.

In an attempt to retrieve the prevailing rhetorical conventions of *Paradise Lost*, the book's early chapters explore Milton's dialogic relationship with the history of rhetoric. Chapter 1 describes contingency and probability as the epistemological basis of a fully functional rhetoric and identifies free will as the agent that sustains them in the face of divine foreknowledge. Chapter 2 surveys the classical rhetoricians whom Milton cites in *Of Education* as constituting the authoritative pedagogical foundation of the subject. There follows in chapter 3 a discussion of Renaissance rhetoric – its focus on style; its association with eloquence; its prescribed uses in relation to politics, moral philosophy, poetry, and theology. This outline of the humanist rhetorical tradition sets the stage for a discussion of Milton's concept of rhetoric in chapter 4, which takes into account statements about rhetoric in Milton's prose and reveals his humanistic faith in the power of eloquence to captivate its audience and compel them to embrace Christian values, a faith that is reflected everywhere in his own writing and that ties in with his definition of rhetoric as a love of the truth.

Since the variable nature of rhetoric in *Paradise Lost* depends on the unique properties of Milton's God, it is necessary to consider the long-standing association of rhetoric and Christian theology. In chapter 5, I explore the history of their relationship in terms of the Bible as a rhetorical text, preaching as a rhetorical art, God as a rhetorical speaker, and, of special relevance to *Paradise Lost*, the poetic dimension of God's speech. In much the same manner, chapter 7 delves into the history of Satan's use of rhetoric. Here I demonstrate that satanic eloquence inverts the humanist model of eloquence and show, with reference to some literary antecedents of Milton's Satan, that the Devil employs oratorical strategies and that the temptation of Eve (and of Jesus) was a rhetorical act. The tripartite scheme of rhetoric mentioned earlier is discussed in depth as each rhetoric, that is, each rhetorical environment, receives its own analysis: heaven in chapter 6, hell in chapter 8, and Paradise in chapters 9 and 10. Our exploration of the rhetorical universe of *Paradise Lost* concludes in the Garden of Eden, which contains the discourse of all three locations and is, in consequence of fully realized future contingency, the most vibrantly rhetorical of the three planes of creation.

One objective of this book will be to give the reader a sense of rhetoric's versatility, of the range of activities and pursuits in which it was involved during the Renaissance. Its linguistic and literary applications are readily apparent: drama, poetry, literary criticism, essays, theological tracts, sermons, political speeches, even scientific descriptions, all drew in various ways on the principles and techniques of this art, most noticeably with respect to style. But rhetoric, as a cultural institution, also had a moral philosophical dimension that extended the terms of its operation – that is, probability and contingency – to everyday life. Personal decisions amounted to the persuasion of oneself to do one thing or another. These choices, uncertain by nature, were matters for probabilistic speculation, for the weighing of arguments on two (or more) sides of the question at hand. Rhetoric's utility, then, was twofold: it was a method both for expressing oneself eloquently in speech and for living virtuously. For this reason, decorum was similarly double-sided, covering what was appropriate in both areas – in saying the right thing at the right time with a view to the character of one's audience, in order to be persuasive and elegant, and in doing the right thing in response to a situation that called for a moral choice. The interaction of these varieties of rhetoric composes the central narrative event of *Paradise Lost*, for it is rhetoric as persuasion, most pivotally that practised (and abused) by Satan, that perverts the rhetoric of moral choice in Eve. The conventions of Renaissance rhetoric inform many themes, including temptation, obedience, deliberation, regeneration, and prophesy, and find voice in the performative registers of proclamation, teaching, warning, intimidation, judgment, and supplication (a summary by no means exhaustive). Milton's portrayal of rhetoric's scope and power, as it shapes the outcome of momentous affairs, establishes its signal importance in *Paradise Lost*. In this, the poem is a microcosm of the Renaissance, when beliefs and theories about rhetoric elevated it to similar prominence. By first looking into some of these beliefs and theories, we shall better understand the sources from which Milton's original reader acquired a concept of rhetoric's identity, capabilities, and different uses.

1 Contingency, Probability, and Free Will

In order to approach the subject of rhetoric in *Paradise Lost*, it is first necessary to establish the standing of Milton's epic cosmos, especially the created world of man, in relation to the basic rhetorical principles of contingency and probability. Initially, we must narrow the context in which they, and rhetoric as a whole, will be treated in the four chapters that analyse the poem. To do so we must refer to the principle, first recorded in Aristotle's *On Rhetoric*, that rhetoric is divisible into three kinds, distinguished by their purpose in relation to the orator's audience: the political or deliberative, which is used to urge others either to do or not to do something; judicial or forensic, which is used to accuse or defend somebody; and epideictic or demonstrative, by means of which someone or something is praised or blamed. Although each of these three will enter the discussion at various points, it is the deliberative or political strain, concerned with advising and deciding upon future actions, that will receive the most attention. This branch of the art, which addresses the moral and prudential questions that were especially meaningful to Renaissance humanists, defines and shapes the poem's central theme of the human decision to commit the original sin. *Paradise Lost* is essentially about ethics, and the rhetoric of ethics is the deliberative mode. Milton shows how the disaffected angels and the first human pair are persuaded to make improper ethical choices, examples that, in line with a primary function of Renaissance poetry, warn his readership to choose more wisely in their own lives. Here we must narrow the rhetorical stage further. It is rhetoric within the narrative structure, as the characters use it and are persuaded by it, that will occupy these pages, not the rhetoric of Milton the poet-orator speaking to his audience. With the focus now set on deliberative rhetoric and on its internal dramatization, we may proceed to discuss contingency and probability. First, I shall identify their integral relationship with rhetoric, then discuss in detail the main agent of their preservation in *Paradise Lost*: the theological concept of free will.

Aristotle's *On Rhetoric* will continue to direct the discussion. This section will be framed by a pair of observations from that text, each to the effect that rhetoric's epistemological foundation lies in the contingent and the probable. That Renaissance scholars and rhetoricians understood the centrality of these principles may be inferred from the relatively late but subsequently steady interest in *On Rhetoric*. In fact, the work's emphasis on probability in rhetorical argument may have contributed to an initial lack of Renaissance enthusiasm for it, since that emphasis 'proved a stumbling block to those committed to deriving infallible doctrines from scripture and the Church Fathers.'[1] In any case, *On Rhetoric*, a set of lecture notes that Aristotle never intended for publication, eventually passed through many editions, commentaries, and translations, the most frequently reprinted of the latter being the Quattrocento's first Latin translation (1445) by George of Trebizond.[2]

The first of our two key statements from *On Rhetoric* denies that necessity impinges on the human actions that rhetoric is used to influence: 'Since few of the premises from which rhetorical syllogisms are formed are necessarily true (most of the matters with which judgement and examination are concerned can be other than they are; for people deliberate and examine what they are doing, and [human] actions are all of this kind, and none of them [are], so to speak, necessary) and since things that happen for the most part and are possible can only be reasoned on the basis of other such things, and necessary actions [only] from necessities ... it is evident that [the premises] from which enthymemes are spoken are sometimes necessarily true but mostly true [only] for the most part.'[3] Human decisions and actions are not objects of knowledge; they have a contingent character and are rarely determined by necessity. Each decision presents us with alternative possibilities from which we may choose. In the uncertain world of human affairs there are only probabilities, 'things that happen for the most part' but that may happen other than they do. In constructing enthymemes, the abbreviated syllogisms used for rhetorical proof, a speaker must take into account this open-ended quality of human existence and accordingly derive his arguments from probability (τὸ εἰκός). In deliberative rhetoric, an audience may conclude, with reasonable assurance, that an argument from probability recommends the most judicious course of action. This is not always so, however, sometimes for reasons related not to the inherent lack of unconditioned truth in probable argument but to the motive of the arguer, who may 'persuade what is debased' in order to deceive his audience. 'One should,' therefore, 'be able to argue persuasively on either side of a question ... in order that ... we ourselves may be able to refute if another person uses speech unjustly. None of the other arts reasons in opposite directions; dialectic and rhetoric alone do this, for both are equally concerned with opposites.'[4]

Rhetoric reasoned and argued in opposite directions not only for the tactical purpose of refuting unjust speech, but also on philosophical grounds related to the ideas of contingency and probability. On account of the uncertainty of knowledge in day-to-day life, adherents of both sophism and Academic scepticism recognized the need to argue *in utramque partem* (on both sides of a question). The sophists treated subjects in this way because their epistemology sanctioned it and their goal of persuasion dictated it: truth was temporary and relative to the individual, so that a skilful orator might argue one side or another and conceivably make either opinion appear true at a given time. The sceptical objective behind this procedure was similarly persuasive – Carneades was renowned for stating each side of a question in turn with overwhelming eloquence – but it was also heuristic, rooted in the search for truth. Academic scepticism, especially as developed by Cicero, held that certain truth was elusive, but that probable truth could be attained from arguing on both sides: 'the sole object of our discussions is by arguing on both sides to draw out and give shape to some result that may be either true or the nearest possible approximation to the truth. Nor is there any difference between ourselves and those who think that they have positive knowledge except that they have no doubt that their tenets are true, whereas we hold many doctrines as probable, which we can easily act upon but can scarcely advance as certain.'[5] Discoursing *in utramque partem* is a rhetorical technique for assessing the kinds of contingencies inherent in the uncertain realm of human experience. Although nothing might be known positively, rhetorical debate could nevertheless draw out and give shape to answers warranted by probability. 'The method which I pursued in other volumes,' Cicero writes elsewhere, 'was that of setting out a continuous discourse both for and against, to enable each student to accept for himself the view that seems most probable.'[6] He refers as well to Plato, 'in whose books nothing is stated positively and there is much arguing both *pro* and *contra*, all things are inquired into and no certain statement is made.'[7] Plato believed that practical reasoning involved fewer degrees of certitude than speculative reasoning, as did Aristotle, whose treatise on rhetoric instantiates this; their Renaissance interpreters, however, portrayed them as more dogmatic and prescriptive than they really were,[8] and the sceptical leanings of the two most important Greek philosophers consequently disappeared from critical view.

Sophism, to be discussed in greater detail in chapter 9, plays a critical role in the rhetorical universe of *Paradise Lost*. During the temptation Satan's eloquence invites comparison with the classical orators of Athens and Rome; more specifically, it is the sophists whose rhetorical strategy and relativistic approach to knowledge he most closely imitates. Satan denies the absolute authority of God's prohibition, reducing it to a *dissos logos*, a double argument of eristic debate in which he and God voice opposing sides. God's case in favour of obedience is, fittingly, simple and direct: obey or die. In the face of this, Satan's exhortation to disobedience is anything but direct and is advanced with a combination of rhetorical fallacy and sophistic ingenuity that takes every advantage of the deceptive potential of probable argumentation. For the present, however, scepticism goes some way towards explaining how probability and contingency rose to prominence in fifteenth- and sixteenth-century intellectual life and came to influence the practice of rhetoric up to Milton's day (not to mention scepticism's influence on philosophy, which was much more significant than its effect on rhetoric).

Scepticism became an important source of probabilistic thinking during the Renaissance, first through authors including Cicero and later through its most important exponent, Sextus Empiricus. It gained a limited foothold early in the period, informing the writings of some fifteenth-century humanists in dialectic and ethics, until widespread popularity came with the printed Latin translations of Sextus Empiricus in the 1560s. 'Truth is difficult to discover,' admits Petrarch, describing himself as 'a proselyte of the [New] Academy'; 'I do not believe in my faculties, do not affirm anything, and doubt every single thing, with the exception of what I believe is a sacrilege to doubt.'[9] Academic rhetorical method could be helpful in allaying sceptical doubt, 'for the truth is customarily brought out by debating on both sides of a question,' as Poggio Bracciolini notes.[10] Humanists valued the heuristic properties of rhetoric in bringing out probable truth, for the ideal of eloquence included an allegiance not only to classical studies, where rhetoric's critical assistance was essential, but also to the practical realities of the contemporary world, where rhetoric provided the deliberative skills to acquire moral knowledge and to act prudently. An acknowledgment that the truth was difficult to discover and that certainty, in reasoning and arguing alike, could not be attained characterized the thinking of Rudolph Agricola, Lorenzo Valla, Juan Luis Vives, and John Rainolds; the most notable exception to this trend was Peter Ramus. Ramistic reform notwithstanding, Renaissance dialectic generally moved away from a scholastic focus on syllogistic inference towards developing controversialist techniques of argument and debate, techniques directed at inventing and generating probable arguments and at communicating persuasively on particular subjects rather than confirming the validity of universal propositions. Dialectic became, in short, more like rhetoric, whose province had always been the probable and the contingent, coordinates that reflected the uncertainties of common experience and opened them to deliberation. Rhetoric's compatibly contingent view of human activity provided a useful framework for working out moral and prudential questions along probabilistic lines. As a mode of inquiry into any number of subjects, it permitted the free play of contrasting opinions, often in the form of dialogues that, in Academic fashion, argued different sides of an issue without obviously endorsing one opinion over another.[11] For Agricola, the uncertainty of knowledge licensed his rhetoricized dialectic to construct arguments on opposite sides of a given question, either as a method of inquiry directed towards clearer understanding or as a means of securing conviction by arguing forcefully and appropriately: 'It appears that this system of places is useful ... in the majority of the liberal arts, because most subjects therein are controversial and require the encounters of disputants for clarification. After all, only a very few of the things we learn are certain and established, so much so that if we believe the Academy we know only this, that we know nothing. Certainly many subjects are interpreted now this way now that way, in accordance with some individual's ingenuity in devising an appropriate argument.'[12] In *De libero arbitrio*, Erasmus denied the necessity of human actions in favour of freedom and future contingency, while defending a rhetorical posture of sceptical, tentative deliberation, willing to consider different opinions, against the dogmatic assertiveness of his opponent: 'For even though I believe myself to have mastered Luther's argument, yet I might well be mistaken, and for that reason I play the debater, not the judge; the inquirer, not the dogmatist: ready to learn from anyone if anything truer or more scholarly can be brought.'[13]

The sceptical eloquence of Erasmus was exceptional in the field of religious dispute, where rhetoric was most often used – by Luther, for example – to proclaim the truth authoritatively.[14] Reformation polemicists in both camps maintained the certain truth of their respective opinions, Catholics staking their claim of orthodoxy in tradition, Protestants in the complete conviction afforded by individual conscience.[15] Truth claims were debated within the scientific community, especially with respect to the validity of experiment; and initial hopes for certain knowledge in scientific enterprises eventually gave way to a concession that here, too, results were more or less probable.[16]

Moral decisions were also held to rely on probability, partly because, in reaching them, one could rarely tell virtue apart from vice with conclusive assurance. Montaigne, applying relativism to ethics, writes that standards of acceptable behaviour vary so much from one society and one age to another that the confident identification of virtue and vice, in absolute terms, becomes all but impossible: 'Subjects have divers lustres, and severall considerations, whence the diversitie of opinions is chiefly engendred.'[17] Diversity of ethical opinion may stem not only from cultural conditioning, as Montaigne believed, but from rhetorical interpretation as well. According to Valla, the moral character of an act may be variously interpreted as good or bad, since 'the virtues and vices are so close together that it is not easy to distinguish them.' Is Cato, for example, to be praised for strictness or, rather, condemned for cruelty? The answer is either, depending on one's rhetorical motive: 'Sometimes one says not what one feels, but what his side of the argument requires; thus a prosecutor calls a harsh judge properly strict, and a defendant calls a strict one inhumane. Since, then, there is so much uncertainty in the judgement of men's actions, it is inequitable to put the worse interpretation on doubtful matters, as to call someone avaricious instead of thrifty, inquisitive instead of zealous, buffoonish instead of humorous, stubborn instead of firm.'[18] Doubt usually arises over the moral designation of an action, and individuals deserve the benefit of that doubt. Rhetorical argument has the power to align a moral act with virtue at one time and with vice at another, further complicating our knowledge of what constitutes proper ethical conduct. In seventeenth-century England, the rhetorician's ability to redescribe virtues as vices or the reverse was regarded with frustration, and even fretfulness for political stability, which contributed to a growing suspicion of rhetoric in that period.[19]

Like Valla and Montaigne, Milton believed that virtue and vice were not easy to distinguish: 'Good and evil we know in the field of this World grow up together almost inseparably; and the knowledge of good is so involv'd and interwoven with the knowledge of evill, and in so many cunning resemblances hardly to be discern'd, that those confused seeds which were impos'd on *Psyche* as an incessant labor to cull out, and sort asunder, were not more intermixt. It was from out the rinde of one apple tasted, that the knowledge of good and evill as two twins cleaving together leapt forth into the World.'[20] Just as the attempt to discern good from evil is fraught with perplexities, so too are the moral decisions based on that difficult process. Consequently, probability rules in both seeing what is truly good and acting accordingly, as Agricola makes clear: 'Everyone agrees that there is nothing of what pertains to life and morals – and the same is so for ideas about the nature of things – which has not been disputed, and about which we cannot find every position proposed by some great mind. In all these matters, therefore, probabilities are examined, since necessities cannot be.'[21] In this climate of dispute and moral uncertainty, deliberative rhetoric, concerned with generating probable arguments, advises us about those courses of action most likely to resolve ethical quandaries.

One point must be emphasized with respect to the ethical decisions prompted by rhetoric: they are contingent, unconstrained by any necessity, and may be decided otherwise. This is the nature of human actions in general, as Aristotle states in the passage cited above on page 14, and is also characteristic of the truth content of speech, as recognized in 'the philosophical clarification of the contingent as an event (what might or might not happen) and of the contingent as a property of statements (what might or might not be true).'[22] In the second of two key statements on future contingency from *On Rhetoric*, Aristotle more specifically identifies future contingency as the one essential prerequisite for deliberative rhetoric: 'First, then, one must grasp what kinds of good or evil the deliberative speaker advises about, since [he will be concerned] not with all, but [only with] those which can both possibly come to pass and [possibly] not. As to whatever necessarily exists or will exist or is impossible to be or to come about, on these matters there is no deliberation ... But the subjects of deliberation are clear; and these are whatever, by their nature, are within our power and of which the inception lies with us.'[23] Cicero praises Aristotle's recognition of this basic fact: 'for all debate is at once cut short by the realization that a thing is impossible or it is proved to be inevitable, and the philosopher who taught this truth, which others did not discern, showed the greatest insight.'[24] Quintilian agrees that necessity cancels out deliberation and political oratory: 'where necessity exists, there is no room for deliberation ... For deliberation is always concerned with questions where some doubt exists. Those therefore are wiser who make the third consideration for deliberative oratory to be τὸ δυνατόν or "possibility."'[25] A possible alternative is usually available to us; we are rarely compelled to do anything by necessity. Rhetorical debate, and the deliberation that it seeks to influence, can occur only in an environment of possibility, doubt, and contingency, where an individual can decide a matter freely, one way or another, having considered arguments on different sides of a question.

Contingency and probability are the constitutive elements of political rhetoric, being the characteristic properties of argument, deliberation, and decision. Knowledge about most subjects – including ethics – is uncertain, ensuring that arguments may be true or may advise well only for the most part, that deliberation therefore must be conjectural and tentative, and that the matters with which judgment and examination are concerned can be other than they are: 'The subjects of deliberation are clear; and these are whatever, by their nature, are within our power and of which the inception lies with us.' It is within our power to judge probable arguments and to reach an ethical decision on that basis; this power, the faculty whose operation justifies rhetoric's existence, is free will: 'Persuasion involves choice, will; it is directed at a man only insofar as he is free.'[26] The exercise of prudence, by which we deliberate wisely, 'is inseparable from the ideal practice of the orator' and 'is itself contingent upon the essential paradox of Christian humanism: the coexistence of divine foreknowledge and human free will.'[27] Rhetoric depends on that same paradox. Free will preserves the future contingency and the range of alternative possibilities that must be in place for rhetoric to function as persuasion. For when man is not free, when necessity rather than human will or choice directs a decision, alternatives are taken away, debate is cut short, there is no deliberation and hence no rhetoric – none, at any rate, as understood here, by the classical authorities and by humanists such as Milton. The first step in my rhetorical analysis of *Paradise Lost* will therefore be to show that the foreknowledge of Milton's God implies no such necessity; and that Milton's concept of free will strengthens rhetoric's epistemological underpinnings of contingency, probability, debate, and deliberation. The following sections on free will outline the theological position, backed by Milton, that our actions are entirely within our power despite God's foreknowledge of them. Being subject to our deliberation, they are, by extension, amenable to the persuasive pressure of rhetorical arguments. Having established that no necessity or external compulsion informs moral decisions, we may subsequently treat deliberative rhetoric as a force central to the shaping of those decisions, capable of advocating either good or evil, with the choice between them left to the God-given discretion of human beings and angels in Milton's epic.

'I confess,' wrote Walter Charleton in 1652, 'that the apparent discord betwixt the infallibility of God's Prenotion, and the indetermination of Man's Free will to the actual election of good or evil, hath been the rock, against which many of the greatest wits of all Ages and Religions have bin shipwrackt.'[28] The crux of this discord, a long-standing theological debate, is whether divine foreknowledge in any way impairs human free will: does God's infallible knowledge of the outcome of every future event, including every human decision, make those decisions necessary? Though the implications of this question are clear enough, since the freedom of human actions hinges on it, the problems encountered in trying to solve it show that it admits of no easy answer.

Yet there had to be an answer – at least for seventeenth-century English commentators – because the theological stakes of the issue were so high, involving the accountability of man for sin and consequently for his own salvation or damnation. For Milton, the answer had to affirm unequivocally the complete freedom of human choice in the face of divine foreknowledge, and it had to do so for reasons not only theological, but poetic as well. By examining the seventeenth-century English debate concerning foreknowledge and free will, the construction of Milton's own uncompromising voluntarism, and the ideas behind it, can be better understood.

The debate itself had a long history. As background to its seventeenth-century expression, a few post-classical highlights should be briefly touched on. The free will question lies at the heart of Christian doctrine: the Church Fathers advocated human freedom as a means of establishing moral responsibility for human actions that might otherwise be perceived as governed by pagan notions of fate.[29] St Augustine asserted free will, yet he reconciled it with divine foreknowledge: 'we Christians declare both that God knows all things before they happen, and that it is by our own free will that we act, whenever we feel and know that a thing is done by us of our own volition ... Even if there is in God's mind a definite pattern of causation, it does not follow that nothing is left to the free choice of our will. For in fact, our wills are also included in the pattern of causation certainly known to God and embraced by his foreknowledge. For the wills of men are among the causes of the deeds of men ... He [God] foresaw that these wills are the causes of our deeds.' Embracing the truth of God's foreknowledge 'is required for correct belief,' embracing the truth of man's free will 'for right living,'[30] which binds the will with moral responsibility.

Boethius examined the dispute more closely than Augustine. He concluded, from analysing the epistemology of God's foreknowledge and its relationship to future contingent events, that free will determined the future decisions that God had empowered it to make. Boethius's affirmation of free will sprang from the idea that God's foreknowledge (*praescientia*) was more accurately perceived as 'knowledge of a never-failing present' (*scientia numquam deficientis instantiae*). Whereas man's knowledge is perpetual, a linear unfolding in time, God's eternal knowledge transcends time, 'embracing the infinite extent of past and future, and in its simple act of knowing considers all things as if they were happening now.' The conclusion drawn from this was crucial for asserting free will: foreknowledge was interpreted simply as knowledge, and knowledge itself could not cause the outcome of the thing known. Boethius writes: 'This divine foreknowledge does not change the nature and character of things, and sees things present to itself in the same way as they are going to come to be in time at some future time ... if Providence which is present sees anything, it is necessary that that thing be, even though it has no natural necessity ... And so all the things which God knows beforehand will happen do without doubt come about, but some of them proceed from free choice; and these ... before they came about, they were also able not to come about.'[31] The belief that God's foreknowledge did not cause future events – which remained dependent on human will even though, foreknown, they would certainly come about – became an important and closely argued consideration in seventeenth-century defences of free will.

Medieval discussions of the free will problem are numerous[32] and, once again, usually affirm contingency and human freedom despite God's foreknowledge. 'It is impossible to express clearly,' wrote William of Ockham, 'the way in which God knows future contingents. Nevertheless it must be held that he does so, but contingently.'[33] Of this position Frederick Copleston remarks, 'By saying that God knows future contingent facts "contingently," Ockham means that God knows them as contingent, and that His knowledge did not make them necessary.'[34] Likewise, God's knowledge does not make future contingents necessary for St Thomas Aquinas, who relates the two concepts in terms of causation: 'A first cause can be necessary and yet its effects contingent because of a contingent proximate cause ... things known by God are contingent because of their contingent causes [i.e., the will], though the first cause, God's knowledge, is necessary.'[35] Thomas assertes future contingency, and thereby free will, on the grounds that the will is a contingent or proximate cause, subordinate to, though independent of, the necessary first cause of God's knowledge. It can choose freely among possible courses. But by imputing necessity to God's knowledge, however mitigated by a causal hierarchy, Thomas veers into what Milton called compulsory necessity, a concept inimical to free will. Its details will be more fully examined below in a seventeenth-century context.

Fifteenth- and sixteenth-century discussions of foreknowledge and free will were more variable concerning the degree of liberty afforded human decisions. Although Lorenzo Valla restricted human freedom by positing that 'inborn character' largely determined how people would act, and by attributing significant determinacy in human affairs to the will of God, the foreknowledge of God remained neutral, as it had for Boethius, with respect to future events. Yet Boethius's method of proving this fact, philosophy, was repudiated by Valla as a means of comprehending divine attributes; he thus reproached Boethius for philosophical presumption, and, invoking St Paul on the inscrutability of God's nature, he exhorted humility in a fideistic rebuttal of discussions directed at bridging the unfathomable gap between man and God: 'We stand by faith, not by the probability of reason.'[36] For Valla, precisely why divine foreknowledge was neutral could not be comprehended, since he included the question among the Christian mysteries ultimately impenetrable to any kind of human inquiry.

Instead of dismissing philosophy out of hand, as Valla claimed to do,[37] Pietro Pomponazzi sought answers both from philosophy, based on the probability of human reason, and from faith, whose scriptural foundation furnishes certain knowledge. When he addressed the immortality of the soul, Pomponazzi first left 'aside revelation and miracles' and remained 'entirely within natural limits' in order to subject the matter to philosophical scrutiny. In the end, however, this method having generated inconclusiveness and doubt, Pomponazzi turned for a definitive answer to faith, a concession – which would have pleased Valla – to the vanity of philosophy as an instrument for elucidating

Christian mystery: 'Of the truth of [the soul's immortality] there is for me no doubt at all, since the canonical Scripture, which must be preferred to any human reasoning and experience whatever, as it was given by God, sanctions this position ... I think that this [position] can be made certain only through God.'[38]

On the doctrinal question of free will, God's scriptural word is much less certain than it is concerning the immortality of the soul. This ambiguity engenders controversy and doubt, whereby probable argument gains the purchase that faith, and its attendant certainty, loses. Perhaps having sensed this rhetorical realignment, Pomponazzi held to philosophy alone in maintaining, by way of Aristotelian logic, that God's knowledge of things does impose necessity on them: 'Seeing that God now knows all future things and has known them for a millennium, and since that a thing is follows logically from the knowledge of the thing, since there is no knowledge of what is not ... consequently it follows, if God has known all things that will be, those things will be ... Therefore, it is necessary that all things that will be, will be because they will be unable not to be. Thus, when human actions will occur, and of necessity, free will is snatched away; for necessity and such freedom are mutually exclusive.'[39] That which is known by God, in short, must necessarily come to pass as it is thus known.

Scriptural contradictions concerning free will occasioned the famous debate between Erasmus (arguing *pro*) and Martin Luther (*contra*), each of whom seized on the biblical passages that corroborated his own position. The question of foreknowledge was only a minor skirmish in the their battle. Erasmus said, 'they sufficiently explain the difficulty about foreknowledge by saying that it does not impose necessity on our will ... For prescience is not the cause of things which happen'[40] (the best discussion of this point, for Erasmus, was Valla's). Luther, conversely, opposed Ockham on the contingent nature of divine foreknowledge, which, he said, argued necessity: 'God foreknows nothing contingently, but that he foresees and purposes and does everything by his immutable, eternal, and infallible will. He is a thunderbolt by which free choice is completely prostrated and shattered.'[41]

Free choice had regained its feet and rallied by the seventeenth century, even against the authoritativeness of Luther and of Calvin's Reformed orthodoxy. Milton himself was apparently a Calvinist in 1645, but by the time he wrote the *Christian Doctrine*, probably 1660 or thereafter, he held Arminian beliefs. In the following section of this chapter I will introduce various seventeenth-century commentators on foreknowledge and free will within the framework of Book I, chapter 3, of the *Christian Doctrine*, in which 'Milton lays down the foundation stone of his Arminianism: his belief that from eternity God bestowed on man a freedom of choice.'[42] Milton defended this belief on several counts, one of which was that its truth is in no way impaired by God's foreknowledge. As we shall see, Milton insists on an airtight compartmentalization of human will from God's prescience, which leaves man completely free and self-determining.

Early in the first book of the *Christian Doctrine*, Milton proffers a telling definition: 'God's foreknowledge is simply his wisdom under another name' (*YP*, 6: 154). Foreknowledge and wisdom are the same thing, an important similarity in light of Milton's observation on wisdom in chapter 4 that 'God's supreme wisdom foreknew the first man's falling away, but did not decree it' (*YP*, 6: 174). If God's wisdom had no part in decreeing Adam's fall, then neither did his foreknowledge. This recalls the proposition, stated by Boethius and echoed by Valla and Erasmus, that knowledge, divine or otherwise, does not cause what it knows. Pomponazzi, we recall, argued that what God knows must necessarily be, thereby destroying contingency. Some seventeenth-century theologians espoused the same belief. William Perkins claimed that 'the fall of Adam was necessary ... by reason of the foreknowledge of God, for that which hee foreknew would come to passe, must needs of necessity come to passe.'[43] And for John Owen, contingency became an Arminian idol opposed to God and the necessity attendant on his foreknowledge: 'if [God] foreknow all things that shall hereafter come to passe, it seemes to cast an infallibilitie of event, upon all their [the Arminians'] actions, which encroaches upon the large territory of their new goddesse contingencie, nay it would quite dethrone the Queen of Heaven, and induce a kind of necessitie of our doing all, and nothing but, what God foreknows ... [His] praescience is destructive to the very nature of [contingency].'[44]

Others, however, particularly those whose conception of free will approximated the Arminian position excoriated by Owen, declared the passivity of foreknowledge along the lines of Boethius, whom Thomas Pierce, an Anglican pamphleteer, echoes and acknowledges: 'the knowledge of the Eternal far transcending all motion and succession of time, does abide in the simplicity of its present being, beholding all past and present things in his simple knowledge ... And therefore Boethius will have it called not Praescience, but Science ... which doth not change the natures and properties of things future, but considers them as they are, in respect of himself, which is as they shall be, in respect of Time. For as the knowledge of things present doth import no Necessity on that which is done, so the foreknowledge of things future lays no necessity on that which shall be.'[45] 'To know is not to make either the cause or the effect,' he says elsewhere; God's foreknowledge 'doth not *ponere quicquam in objecto*, being an action within itself ... it works not anything upon the creature.'[46] 'Prevision' and predetermination, which Perkins and Owen conflated, are distinct concepts, notes the Anglican minister Henry Hammond, 'predetermination having a visible influence and causality on the object, but eternal vision, or prevision, being so far from imposing necessity on a thing to be, that it supposes it to be already, *from the free choice of the Agent* ... God's seeing, or foreseeing hath no ... operation or causality of any kind on the object.'[47] Free choice alone determines the course of human action, the tenet at the core of Milton's Arminianism. God's prevision only sees, as other seventeenth-century writers attest.[48]

Milton, too, held this view. His argument by now sounds familiar: 'Divine foreknowledge can no more effect the action of free agents than can human foreknowledge, that is, not at all, because in both cases the foreknowledge is within the mind of the knower and has no external effect. Divine foreknowledge cannot itself impose any necessity' (*YP*, 6: 164). Knowledge of any kind, foreknowledge included, cannot itself impose any necessity because, according to Renaissance psychology, the will (in conjunction with reason) is the faculty that causes actions to be done. 'To know is properly an act of the intellect,' observed Pierce, 'but to decree or determine is an Act of the Will.'[49] Knowledge is not a faculty; it does not decree. But the will does do so, and once God's will decrees, Milton writes, it becomes the primary efficient cause: 'I do not deny that God's will is the first cause of everything. But ... God's will is no less the first cause of everything if he decrees that certain things shall depend upon the will of man, than if he had decreed to make all things inevitable' (*YP*, 6: 163–4). God's will is the first cause, but it is not a necessary cause, since it decrees contingency, transferring to human reason complete freedom of choice unfettered by any kind of necessity: 'Only those causes act freely *ex hypothesi* which do things through reason and deliberation, as angels and men – on the hypothesis, to be sure, of the divine will, which in the beginning gave them the power to act freely' (*YP*, 8: 227). Not only, then, is God's foreknowledge by nature no cause, and thus neutral with respect to human freedom, but God's will decrees that no external force whatsoever should impair the human will from acting freely. This decree thus preserved '*Futura Contingentia*, which,' notes Charleton, 'hang suspended *in aequilibrio* upon the Free Will of their Efficients, so that they may, or may not, come about.'[50]

A closely related strategy that Milton employs to protect free will and future contingency is to distinguish certainty from necessity, definitions that go hand in hand with the neutrality of God's foreknowledge and the divine decree that liberates human will: 'Though future events will certainly happen, because divine foreknowledge cannot be mistaken, they will not happen by necessity, because foreknowledge, since it exists only in the mind of the foreknower, has no effect on its object. A thing which is going to happen quite freely in the course of events is not then produced as a result of God's foreknowledge, but arises from the free action of its own causes, and God knows in what direction these will, of their own accord, tend. In this way he knew that Adam would, of his own accord, fall. Thus it was certain that he would fall, but it was not necessary, because he fell of his own accord and that is irreconcilable with necessity (*YP*, 6: 165).' Everything God knows, whether necessary or certain, must come to pass infallibly, 'because divine foreknowledge cannot be mistaken.' William Pemble also remarks on the infallibility of all events and connects contingency to God's permissive decree: 'It comes to passe necessarily, because God ordered it should come to passe necessarily. And [a contingent thing] therefore contingently, because he would have it be [i.e., decree it] contingently ... It is one thing to come to passe necessarily, another contingently, another infallibly: these two note an order between the cause and the effect, but this is common, inasmuch as both contingent things and necessary doe come to passe infallibly, but those contingently, these necessarily,'[51] according to God's decree. For Milton, this decree left a future contingent thing to 'the free action of its own causes.' John Goodwin concurs: 'no decree of God that is purely and barely permissive ... doth any ways interesse to God any manner of interposal ... towards the effecting or bringing to passe of what is so decreed. So that such events ... are in the same posture of contingency, in the same possibility of being, or not being ... had there been no such decree of all concerning them.'[52] What is certain must, by virtue of divine infallibility, come to pass, but contingently, by permission of divine decree. Hammond links certainty and contingency: 'what is contingently come to pass, being done, is certain, and God sees it, as it is, therefore he sees it as done, and so certain, yet as done contingently.'[53]

Pierce's distinction of necessity from certainty indicates with which coordinate divine foreknowledge is aligned: '1. What God decreed to effect, will come to pass unavoidably, and by necessitation, because his absolute will and his power cannot possibly be rejected. 2. But what he onely decreed to permit, will contingently come to pass; yet with a certainty of event, because his foreknowledge is infallible, and cannot possibly be deceived.'[54] Necessity, then, emanated from God's will; infallible foreknowledge was simply what must unfold in accord with 'what God onely decreed to permit,' so it once again stood detached from any kind of necessity. What a person would do, he would certainly do, but he would do it freely.

Milton's insistence on God's having bestowed total liberty on the human will informs his statement: 'No place must be given even to that shadowy and peripheral idea of necessity based on God's immutability and foreknowledge' (*YP*, 6: 161–2). Such kinds of necessity might arise in the context of Milton's definition of compulsory necessity, which comprised any attempt to equate divine foreknowledge with necessity, or to set it up as a first cause above free will:

> The result of the compulsion of some external force ... is called compulsory necessity ... Now any necessity operating externally upon a given cause either makes it produce a certain effect or limits it from producing other effects. *In either case it is clear that the cause loses all freedom of action* ... But it is said that divine necessity, or the necessity of a first cause, does not bring any compulsion to bear upon the liberty of free agents [as Thomas Aquinas argues]. I reply that, if it does not compel, then it either restricts liberty within certain limits, or assists it ... If it restricts or assists then it is either the only or the joint and principal cause of every action, good and bad, of the free agent. (*YP*, 6: 159–60; my italics)

A necessary first cause always exerts some measure of compulsion – or restriction, or assistance – over a proximate cause, thereby precluding its free, contingent, independent operation. This is why Thomas Aquinas's claim, that God's knowledge as a necessary first cause leaves the will free as a contingent or proximate cause, falls into compulsory necessity. 'Freedom,' Thomas adds, 'does not require that a thing is its own first cause.'[55] Milton argues here that freedom *does* require that a thing is its own first cause. If the human will is causally ranked beneath any kind of divine necessity, its freedom is at best impaired, at worst obliterated. This is what happened when William Perkins, like Thomas

Aquinas, held out divine foreknowledge as a first cause over contingency: 'God his foreknowledge, is conjoyned with his decree ... The same decree of God is the first and principall working cause of all things ... This first and primary cause, howbeit in it selfe it be necessarie, yet it doth not take away freedom of will in election, or the nature and property of second causes, but onely *brings them into a certaine order*, that is, it *directeth them to a determinate end*. Whereupon the effects and events of things are contingent or necessarie, as the nature of the second cause is.'[56] The contingency Perkins claims to be at work here is undercut by a divine foreknowledge that, as a 'cause of all things,' cannot leave contingent any cause secondary to it; since, as Milton says in his own theory of remote and proximate causes in the *Art of Logic*, 'whatever is the cause of the cause is also cause of what is caused' (*YP*, 8: 225). This means, in short, that anything enacted by the will in such a scheme really has been enacted by its first or remote cause, divine foreknowledge. And having an effect on its object, we recall, is something that knowledge cannot do.

Milton's case for reconciling contingency and free will with divine foreknowledge is mainly traditional. Its foundational idea, that divine foreknowledge by nature does not cause or act at all upon the objects it knows, reaches back to Boethius, and this idea's adjunct, that the certainty of an event – based on the infallibility of God's foreknowledge and his permissive decree – implies no necessity, was current around the time Milton was writing the *Christian Doctrine*. Milton's unusually thoroughgoing theory of compulsory necessity was perhaps artificial and laboured – he himself cautioned against too strictly observing causal theory[57] – but the example of William Perkins shows how it could effectively discover concepts of divine foreknowledge that damage free will by cloaking prescience in necessity.

Yet whatever criticism might be levelled against Milton's defence of free will in the *Christian Doctrine*, a remark he makes elsewhere, in the *Areopagitica*, is especially difficult to take issue with: 'many there be that complain of divin Providence for suffering *Adam* to transgresse, foolish tongues! when God gave him reason, he gave him freedom to choose, for reason is but choosing; he had bin else a meer artificall *Adam*, such an *Adam* as he is in the motions' (*YP*, 2: 527) – that is, in puppet shows. Without free will, man is a puppet, not a man at all. Freedom to choose is fundamental to man's being, the *sine qua non* of his humanity and the definitive expression of his soul. Milton's image is appropriately poetic; for his line of argument lays aside the logical, theological, and epistemological approaches of writers examined in this chapter to argue human freedom from a more intuitive, rhetorical side. What does man amount to without free will? Part of Erasmus's defence of free will is that 'almost the whole of Scripture speaks of nothing but conversion, application, and striving after better things. All these go for nothing if once you admit that doing good or bad comes by necessity.'[58] These kinds of activity, like the free will on which they are predicated, define humanity. Any necessity that would obviate them, Erasmus implies, is anti-human. It may be added, as Victoria Kahn observes in the context of Valla's *De libero arbitrio*, that 'the very fact of [rhetorical] debate can be evidence for the freedom of the will – which can never be known but which can be practiced.'[59] Earlier in this chapter we saw Aristotle explain that necessity has no place in rhetoric, 'for no one debates things incapable of being different either in past or future or present.'[60] He sets poetry on a similar footing: 'it is ... the poet's function to relate ... the kinds of events that might occur and are possible in terms of probability.'[61] Aristotle's poet fashions a rhetorical environment in which contingency and probability inhere as a matter of course because they are characteristic of the human activities that poetry imitates. And it is, of course, through poetry that Milton would make his most famous use of – and have the greatest need of – a viable defence of human freedom in the face of God's immutable foreknowledge.

The free will defence, as gradually developed in the course of *Paradise Lost*, may be regarded from one perspective as an exercise in *copia*, moving through stages of confirmation, restatement, and refinement in the speech of various characters at various important moments. Its most forceful expression, not only for the clarity but for the authority of its utterance, arrives during God's theodical oration, which at one point relates free will to divine foreknowledge just as we have come to understand that relationship on the preceding pages. The will of man is free, says God, not

> dispos'd by absolute Decree
> Or high foreknowledge; they themselves decreed
> Thir own revolt, not I: if I foreknew,
> Foreknowledge had no influence on their fault,
> Which had no less proved certain unforeknown.[62]

Milton's God dissociates human free will from the influence of divine prescience and later from the influence of the entire providential order –

>   no Decree of mine
> Concurring to necessitate his Fall,
> Or touch with lightest moment of impulse
> His free Will, to her own inclining left
> In even scale   (X. 43–7)

– so that man alone is responsible for the Fall. The rhetorical implications of Milton's voluntarism are readily apparent. Necessity having been cleared away, the human moral universe in *Paradise Lost* becomes solidly grounded in the contingent and hence the probable. If, in such a world, foreknowledge or a divine decree of any sort had no influence on man's fault, what did? 'Man falls deceiv'd,' says God, by Satan (III. 130); and the instrument of satanic deception – as we shall see in chapters 7 through 9 – is rhetoric, exploited in order to enhance the already perplexing resemblance between virtue and vice. In Eden, as in the humanistic milieu, deliberative rhetoric has the power to affect man's ability to discriminate virtue and vice. It can thereby influence the acceptance of a given course of action, making an audience believe that doing one thing is better than doing another. In this contingent world, another choice is always available, though whether it is better or worse can be known for certain only by God, and thus it becomes a subject of debate through probable arguments. With probability established as the criterion of human judgment, a judgment that God has left entirely free to determine human actions, rhetoric finds solid purchase in Milton's Paradise, where, as chapter 9 in particular will show, it exerts a material effect on ethical decisions. Before turning earthward, however, our critical attention will focus on those regions of the poem where rhetoric's foundation is less stable: on the circumstances in heaven that colour probability with a tinge of certainty and on those in hell that impose necessity on the existence, and the speech, of the fallen angels. It will be especially important to explain the relationship of rhetoric to God, whose presence and powers must be accounted for in any attempt to understand rhetoric in *Paradise Lost* as it functions both within the Garden of Eden and outside it.

Now that we have qualified the rhetorical nature of Milton's epic universe, founded in the key ideas of probability, contingency, and free will, a more detailed exposition of rhetoric is in order. If we hope to read *Paradise Lost* as received by its original audience, comprehending rhetoric in seventeenth-century terms, we must try to reconstruct a historically accurate portrait of rhetoric that will both add to our general knowledge of the subject and clarify the relevance of the ideas discussed in this chapter. Rhetoric's purpose, scope, and ancient origins, as well as its acquisition, points of emphasis, and many areas of disciplinary influence during the Renaissance, must be examined for the sake of retrieving the formal conventions of *Paradise Lost* through the practice of historically aware criticism. The best place to start is where Milton the humanist would have us start, for this or any other topic of cultural significance: classical literature.

2 Milton's Classical Rhetoricians

To quote a Moderne Dutchman where I may use a Classick Autho^r; is as if
I were to Justifie my reputačon; And I neglect p[er]sons of note and quality
that know me; and bring ye Testimoniall of ye Scullion in ye kitchien.

John Selden, *Table Talk*

Exchanging ancient wisdom for modern novelty was held by many to
be a dubious enterprise. Though challenged from several quarters, classical authority, along with the humanist beliefs and practices that sustained it, continued to thrive during the seventeenth century.[1] It exerted
considerable influence on writers such as Milton, whose attitude concerning a variety of topics remained anchored in the *bonae litterae*, the
writings of ancient Greece and Rome. When he listed the most valuable
writers on rhetoric to be studied in the scheme of his ideal curriculum,
he included none of the many pedagogical texts that had been published in his own or in the preceding two centuries. His choice reflects
the humanistic preferences of his time, when, with regard to all grammar school subjects, including rhetoric, 'no one doubted that the works
principally worth recommending were all composed in antiquity,' and
at Oxford and Cambridge, 'the statutes stipulate[d] no modern textbooks of rhetoric.'[2] There were a few exceptions at the grammar school
level, mainly the principal 'Moderne Dutchman,' Erasmus, and other
humanist authors who paid special attention to the tropes and figures
judged so important for both critically aware reading and elegant writing. School reading lists, however, overwhelmingly supported Milton's
curricular slant.[3] Since relatively new books on rhetoric were derived
from ancient Greek and Roman treatises, Milton's classicizing sensibil-

ity advocated a return directly to those sources themselves. The recovery of most of the extant works from antiquity had long since been completed. Milton's proposal for 'a graceful and ornate Rhetorick taught out of the rule of *Plato, Aristotle, Phalereus, Cicero, Hermogenes, Longinus*' (*YP*, 2: 402–3) points to this completion and traces a history of rhetoric from its earliest beginnings to late antiquity. Along with Isocrates, 'that Old man eloquent,'[4] whose school of oratory near the Lyceum in Athens was one of the models for Milton in *Of Education*, these writers represent the classical tradition that Milton knew so thoroughly and that informed the humanist conception of rhetoric.

This group of classical writers can be loosely categorized to show where Milton's humanistic emphases lay. Plato and Isocrates stressed the ethical imperative behind true eloquence: that a speaker's character was of the utmost importance and that speaking with wisdom (which each writer defines very differently) could be accomplished only by a good man. This idea, more than any other, governed Milton's concept of rhetoric. Demetrius (mistakenly believed to have been Demetrius Phalereus, who headed Ptolemy Soter's great library at Alexandria), Hermogenes, and Longinus represent the abiding concern with style in both Greek and Latin antiquity, which Renaissance writers adopted with equal if not greater enthusiasm. Aristotle took up the moral concerns of his teacher Plato, although less urgently, and also prescribed a formal method of rhetorical composition. Cicero, combining all these elements, stressed the interrelationship of wisdom and eloquence, treated rhetoric as an art, and discussed style fully, if not with the attention to detail it would receive in later antiquity. Richard DuRocher has studied the ten authors of Milton's Latin curriculum, which the poet taught from 1640 to 1646, as 'major precursors for Milton's art'[5] whose influence he traces through reference to a range of subjects discussed in the Roman texts, from botany and zoology to architecture and astronomy. The works of Isocrates and the six classical rhetoricians grouped together in *Of Education* also influenced Milton's work, not as material for allusion and imitation, as DuRocher reads the Romans, but rather as a collective *ratio* or method for the framing of that material. Their rhetorical principles constituted an art, that is, 'a reasoned habit of mind in making'[6] by which Milton made *Paradise Lost* and that required formal guidance in order to become habitual. These writers handed down to Milton a system of rhetoric that considered everything from its moral and philosophical bases to the minutiae of style, and that early on had established rhetoric's contribution to the writing and interpretation of literature.

The long quarrel between philosophy and rhetoric was initiated by Plato. Rhetoric stood at the periphery of Plato's concerns, and it drew his attention not so much as a subject of genuine interest as an accident of his dispute with the sophists, whom he deprecated for raising expediency above due consideration of what was right and good. Plato valued inquiry through dialectic far more highly than persuasion through rhetoric, associating the teaching of rhetoric with the ethical irresponsibility of sophistic instruction and its practice with the attendant degeneration of Athenian society. This is the context of the *Gorgias*, in which Plato disparaged rhetoric as being detached from a knowledge of the truth about its subject (459B–C). Its amoral practitioners, concerned with securing their own advantage, pander to popular opinion, merely convincing their audience, not teaching them, in an enterprise that could make the worse appear the better reason (502D–503B, 454E, 458E). 'The man who is to be an orator in the proper sense,' by helping others find the best way to live, 'must be upright and understand right and wrong' (508C) as the philosopher does, which would allow rhetoric to emerge from the shadow of opportunistic misuse under which it typically laboured. In Plato's estimation even reputedly great orators of the past, such as Themistocles and Pericles, satisfied the immediate desires of the populace for personal gain and failed to put eloquence to its best possible use of moral edification (503C–D).

Plato moderated his criticism in a later dialogue, the *Phaedrus*. Rhetoric now becomes a legitimate pursuit, provided that a student follows the method, undergirded by dialectic, that would furnish a complete knowledge of the subject, audience, and techniques of persuasion.

> Until someone knows the truth of each thing about which he speaks or writes and is able to define everything in its own genus, and having defined it knows how to break the genus down into species and subspecies to the point of indivisibility, discerning the nature of the soul in accordance with the same method, while discovering the logical category which fits with each nature, and until in a similar way he composes and adorns speech, furnishing variegated and complex speech to a variegated and complex soul and simple speech to a simple soul – not until then will it be possible for speech to exist in an artistic form in so far as the nature of speech is capable of such treatment, either for instruction or persuasion, as has been shown by our entire past discussion.[7]

Above all, the rhetorician must know the truth – defining 'the exact nature of a subject' by dialectical combination and division (265D–266B) – as thoroughly as the philosopher, with the result that 'speakers and writers have become philosophers along the way.'[8] This transformation, an alignment of oratorical purpose with philosophical wisdom, ensures that rhetoric will be safeguarded against potential misuse. A knowledge of the truth, in relation to both the matter at hand and the souls of men, imparts a wisdom that invariably guides the philosopher-orator to say and to encourage what is ethically right. Moral accountability, not public success in winning over an audience, is the primary index of rhetoric properly applied: the wise man speaks 'not with the object of addressing and dealing with human beings but in order to be able to the best of his power to say and do what is acceptable in the sight of heaven' (273E). Milton pledged himself to the same ideal, particularly as his eventual disillusionment with the republican cause led him to turn his attention away from politics and towards the grand project that all eyes, heavenly and human, might look upon with favour. Plato's ideas about the relationship between truth and rhetoric reverberate in Milton's prose, as chapter 4 will show.

Plato's contemporary rival, Isocrates, similarly insisted on good character as an oratorical attribute. Isocrates' canon comes down to us virtually intact (the sole exception cited in ancient literature being an *Art of Rhetoric*, of which nothing remains). His extant writings outline a theory of rhetoric as a way of conducting life, not simply of speaking, which combines wisdom and eloquence in the most judicious and most philosophically comprehensive formulation of the discipline as received from antiquity. Praised during the Renaissance for both their politics and their elegant style, his orations were translated into Latin by many humanists from the fifteenth century on, and Milton embraced Isocrates as a proponent of liberty (both intellectual and civil) and the liberal education necessary to obtain and preserve it.[9] This chapter is devoted to *Milton's* classical rhetoricians; unfortunately, Milton's knowledge of Isocrates precludes his having read the most thorough discussion of rhetoric that Isocrates left us, the *Antidosis*, a defence of his life and teachings that was mostly lost until the nineteenth century and that therefore will not be discussed here. However, on account of his profession on the one hand (he was a teacher) and his remarkable longevity on the other (he completed his final oration in 339 BC at the great age of ninety-seven), Isocrates repeated the central themes of his philosophy and pedagogy throughout the course of his career, so that we can construct a nearly complete picture of his rhetorical ideas from other texts that would have been available to seventeenth-century readers.

Isocrates almost entirely passes over the theoretical particulars of composition, attending instead to the nature of the art of discourse and to its status as a cultural institution of central importance to both the moral life of the educated citizen and the flourishing of the Hellenic state. One critic notes that 'the ideal rhetoric sketched in the *Phaedrus* is as far from the possibilities of mankind as his Republic was from Athens.'[10] In contrast stands the practical rhetoric of Isocrates, readily deployable by anyone who was properly educated. Isocrates clearly defines the attribute that distinguishes the educated person: 'whether men have been liberally educated from their earliest years is not to be determined by their courage or their wealth or such advantages, but is made manifest most of all by their speech, and ... this has proved to be the surest sign of culture [σύμβολον τῆς παιδεύσεως] in every one of us.'[11] The art of speaking was the centrepiece of an Athenian gentleman's liberal education.

The one thing Isocrates has in common with Plato is that he often discusses rhetoric in the context of declaiming against unscrupulous sophists. He criticizes mainly their pretension to exact knowledge and their teaching of eristics, captious disputation for its own sake that has no practical application in daily affairs. Isocratean rhetoric emerges from an epistemological matrix at variance with that of Plato; in it, the Platonic universe of Forms, and the possibility of knowledge of them, does not exist. Human speech and action, Isocrates' main concerns, defy such an understanding, given the manifold circumstances in which they arise and are carried out. As he states repeatedly, 'in dealing with matters about which [men] take counsel, they ought not to think that they have exact knowledge of what the result will be,' as the sophists mistakenly do, but rather ought 'to be minded towards those contingencies as men who indeed exercise their best judgement, but are not sure what the future may hold in store.'[12] The future is always uncertain: 'foreknowledge of future events is not vouchsafed to our human nature ... for mankind this power lies within the realms of the impossible. But these professors have gone so far in their lack of scruple that they attempt to persuade our young men that if they will only study under them they will know what to do in life and through this knowledge will become happy and prosperous.'[13]

It is an empty promise. Isocrates stresses that human existence is based on contingency and that, since no knowledge or science can account for the uniqueness and open-endedness of every occasion, a person must try to assess each one, on its own terms, according to a 'standard of what is best.' Thus, in the realm of speech, 'perfect eloquence must be the individual expression of a single critical moment, a *kairos*, and its highest law is that it should be wholly appropriate.'[14] The concept of *kairos*, essential to the art of oratory, will recur in my rhetorical reading of *Paradise Lost*. It means 'the right moment' or 'the opportune,' and it dictates that the orator, to be persuasive, must consider the various elements of a speech situation, especially timing and audience, and adapt his words appropriately. The skill is clearly a part of decorum and so, as a similarly intuitive 'sense,' was never developed as a formal art.[15] In order to understand what rhetorical abilities the *kairos* emphasizes, 'speech' should be thought of in terms of 'speaking,' since engaging an audience is an act, an event, one complicated on each occasion by a new set of demands on a speaker's ingenuity and responsiveness. The fruit of these abilities is a knack for saying the right thing, which is determined solely by whatever seems likely to persuade an audience.[16] A liberal education teaches the faculty of sound judgment, of apprehending the *kairos* by speaking the right words at the right moment, so that what is said will be persuasive. For Isocrates, adapting oneself to the moment in this way constitutes the wisdom of the educated man: 'Whom, then, do I call educated? First, then, those who manage well the circumstances which they encounter day by day, and who possess a judgement which is accurate [δόξαν ἐπιτυχῆ] in meeting occasions as they arise and rarely misses the expedient course of action.' Claiming to possess this attribute, Isocrates characterizes himself as 'better able to form a correct judgement [δοξάσαι] of the truth of any matter than are those [sophists] who claim to have exact knowledge.'[17] One reason that Isocrates passes over rhetorical theory is that formal knowledge is of little use in helping one to speak effectively on the fly. The 'analogy of an art with hard and fast rules' does not apply 'to a creative process' such as the art of discourse. 'For what has been said by one speaker is not equally useful for the speaker who comes after him,'[18] since that speaker will always encounter a different situation that he must manage differently, relying on a combination of good judgment and natural talent in order to win the assent of his audience.

Isocrates scorns speculative wisdom, detached from the exigencies of political life. For him wisdom is prudential, the application of reason to discerning the best thing to do or say, the ability to take the right decision as often as possible – philosophy is the acquisition of this skill. Practicality is continually urged: 'likely conjecture about useful things is far preferable to exact knowledge of the useless' inculcated by teachers of eristics, who 'care nothing at all for either private or public affairs, tak[ing] most pleasure in those discourses which are of no practical service in any particular.'[19] Rhetoric, on the other hand, is eminently practical, and not just in speech or debate. In a letter to Philip of Macedon's young son Alexander, Isocrates contrasts eristics, which Alexander was likely learning at that time from his tutor Aristotle, with 'the training which rhetoric gives, which is useful in the practical affairs of everyday life and aids us when we deliberate concerning public affairs. By means of this study you will come to know how at the present time to form reasonably sound opinions about the future ... how to form correct judgements about the right and the just and their opposites.'[20] Rhetorical training is as valuable for teaching prudence and discriminating right from wrong as it is for speaking persuasively. The similarities between the two processes come out in another letter. In rhetoric, 'the first question to be considered is – what is the object to be accomplished by the discourse as a whole and by its parts? And when we have discovered this and the matter has been accurately determined, I say that we must seek the rhetorical elements whereby that which we have set out to do may be elaborated and fulfilled. And this procedure I prescribe with reference to discourse, yet it is a principle applicable not only to all other matters, but also to your own affairs. For nothing can be intelligently accomplished unless first, with full forethought, you reason and deliberate how you ought to direct your own future.'[21] Isocrates gave this kind of advice to powerful rulers, especially those whom he spent decades trying to enlist in realizing his cherished dream of uniting the factious Greek states against the overlordship of the Persian monarchy. National policy, as it would be for Milton, was the noblest service in which he could invest his own eloquence. Civic duty called the rhetorically trained to the service of the state, an occupation that put the liberal education to its most important use and that had always been most ably assumed by men of both eloquence and wisdom.[22]

The foundation of rhetoric for Isocrates lies in what he took to be the symbol of education and culture, speech. The classic statement of this idea occurs first in *Nicocles* (and later in the *Antidosis*). 'There is no institution devised by man,' he claims, 'which the power of speech [λόγος] has not helped us to establish':

For this it is which has laid down laws concerning things just and unjust, and things base and honourable; and if it were not for these ordinances we should not be able to live with one another. It is by this also that we confute the bad and extol the good. Through this we educate the ignorant and appraise the wise; for the power to speak well is taken as the surest index of a sound understanding, and discourse which is true and lawful and just is the outward image of a good and faithful soul. With this faculty we both contend against others on matters which are open to dispute and seek light for ourselves on things which are unknown; for the same arguments which we use in persuading others when we speak in public, we employ also when we deliberate in our own thoughts; and while we call eloquent those who are able to speak before a crowd, we regard as prudent those who most skilfully debate their problems in their own minds. And, if there is need to speak in brief summary of this power, we shall find that none of the things which are done with intelligence take place without the help of speech, but that in all our actions as well as in all our thoughts speech is our guide, and is most employed by those who have the most wisdom.[23]

It would be difficult to formulate a more inclusive definition of rhetoric than Isocrates proposes here. All of the concepts signified by *logos* fall under the purview of the art of discourse, since everything beneficial depends for its expression on *logos* in its office as the power of persuasive speech, or eloquence. The word connects eloquence with virtually every intellectual pursuit, with justice, civil concord, moral philosophy, even inquiry into the unknown; moreover, it binds eloquence to two other meanings of *logos*, reason and wisdom.[24] Rhetoric as wisdom is the prudential art of judging variables such as subject and audience and then *speaking* correctly: appropriate, well-weighed, persuasive speech is effectively a cardinal virtue. Those who exhibit this type of wisdom are called eloquent. For the individual, *logos* is also the ethical process of making a moral choice and then *acting* correctly, since the public persuasion of others and private deliberation, Isocrates tells us, are the same process, employing the same arguments. Deliberate choice (*proaireis*) is rhetorical, a persuasion of one's own will to act a certain way. Those who do so skillfully, that is, virtuously, are regarded as prudent: 'in all our actions as well as in all our thoughts speech is our guide.' That rhetoric can be internal and deliberative, a method of reasoning as well as speaking, will be an important consideration in examining the rhetorical universe of *Paradise Lost*. Isocrates' system accounted for a very human trait whose gravity Milton would amplify to the full – that people do not always succeed in finding the proper course of action.

Isocrates believed that a liberal education, the cultivation of the art of discourse, could make men good, a characteristic that was both an end in itself and a key means of persuasion. Pursuing the ambition to speak well and to convince one's hearers enabled a person to become better and worthier: 'those who desire to follow the true precepts of this discipline may, if they will, be helped more speedily towards honesty of character than towards facility in oratory.'[25] The orator so trained will necessarily choose great and honourable subjects, devoted to the welfare of man and the common good. Apart from its intrinsic desirability, the good character instilled by studying the art of discourse has the added benefit of persuading an audience. This idea is implicit in many of his writings – as in his telling Philip, 'I do lay claim to sane judgement and good education'[26] – and is discussed most fully in the *Antidosis*. Good character, *ethos*, is a rhetorical attribute as well as an ethical one. Isocrates would hardly have made the distinction, since a good man's intention in persuading others is to exhort them to virtuous courses of action. In *ethos*, the art of speaking well and the complementary art of living prudently are fused, on the understanding that such a union of eloquence and wisdom justifies itself in the man who wisely instructs and seeks to improve his fellow citizens.

Like Isocrates, Aristotle aimed to make men good, but he omitted that concern (taken up in his ethical works) from his rhetorical writings. In *On Rhetoric*, Aristotle continued the Greek tradition of philosophical rhetoric. He brought to it – unlike Plato, who considered it merely a knack[27] – the systematic treatment specific to an art (*techne*), a designation he assigns to rhetoric at the outset.[28] He begins by defining it as the faculty, not of persuasion, but of observing in any given case the available means of persuasion, and of doing so on either side of a question. He goes on to cover in detail the *pisteis*, or artistic means of persuasion: *logos*, proof, or apparent proof, provided by the words of the speech itself, mainly by enthymeme and example; *ethos*, the speaker's character; and *pathos*, playing on the emotions of the hearers, a technique that Aristotle recognizes as expedient for persuading an audience less sophisticated than that addressed by dialectic, the counterpart of rhetoric. There are three major considerations in a speech situation – speaker, subject, and audience – and the three types of oratory previously discussed: political or deliberative, used to urge others either to do or not to do some future action; judicial or forensic, to accuse or defend somebody's past actions; and epideictic or demonstrative, to praise or blame someone or something in the present. He also gives a list of twenty-eight valid topics (and ten invalid ones) that an orator may draw on in establishing arguments for the three types of speech. These topics, like Aristotle's whole scheme of rhetoric, are based on what is probable, and one may be readily counter-argued by another; they make no claims to be truthful, their priority being expediency and what seems likely to persuade at a given moment.[29] The parts of Aristotle's entire rhetorical system may be discerned in *Paradise Lost*, especially the qualities of political rhetoric that define the poem's central event, man's disobedi-ence, as Adam and Eve are encouraged both to obey and to disobey and to choose a course of action based on those exhortations.

A long section in Book II of *On Rhetoric* covers types of character and the nature of various emotions, so that a speech may be adjusted to per-suade a particular audience. This reduces to method Plato's injunction in the *Phaedrus* that a speaker should know the souls of his listeners.[30] But Plato's moral censure of rhetoric is not repeated by his pupil. Rhet-oric, Aristotle observes, may be put to just or unjust purposes;[31] but the prescriptions and cautions he might be expected to issue concerning its uses and the duties of the orator are not stated. The third book of *On Rhetoric*, on style, is not exhaustive, but some of Aristotle's remarks in-fluence later treatments of the subject. Clarity, he writes, should be the sole virtue of style,[32] a prescription that his successor Theophrastus later expanded into the four stylistic virtues of clarity, correctness, appropri-ateness, and ornamentation.[33] Aristotle's remarks on appropriateness, that style should correspond in dignity to its subject and should express emotion and character, constitute one of the first programmatic state-ments regarding decorum. Similarly, what he says about the need to hide rhetorical art recurs frequently in succeeding ages: a speaker or writer's style should be natural, not artificial so as to arouse an audi-ence's suspicion.[34]

Much of the classical Greek rhetorical tradition passed into Roman currency through the works of Cicero. Agreeing with Aristotle that rhet-oric was an art,[35] Cicero adopted the Aristotelian divisions of political, forensic, and epideictic oratory, and the three artificial means of persua-sion,[36] *logos*, *ethos*, and *pathos*. His own highly influential innovation was that to these *pisteis* he linked what he saw as the three duties of the ora-tor, who needs to teach (*docere*), delight (*delectare*), and move (*movere*) the emotions of his audience. Furthermore, Cicero matched to these duties the three *genera dicendi*, or levels of style: the low for teaching, the middle for delighting, and the lofty or grand for swaying the emotions. But a speech in the grand style, for example, neither aimed exclusively at *movere* nor exclusively employed *pathos*. An orator should modulate all the styles and persuasive techniques, mixing them in whatever proportions a particular rhetorical situation might call for. Cicero's spokesman in *De oratore*, Crassus, states that a dignified and graceful style is the prime concern of the orator, since this is what arouses an audience's emotions, the most effective channel of persuasion. Although an orator required a full understanding of his subject, and although form and content were interdependent, Cicero held that eloquence was less a matter of invention and thought than of style.[37] That idea was enthusiastically received during the Renaissance. Cicero exerted enormous influence on Renaissance rhetoric, partly on account of his theoretical treatises, to which many volumes of commentary were devoted. His orations and letters, moreover, served many Renaissance humanists as practical models of correct Latin composition. Ciceronianism, which established Cicero's diction and style as the gold standard of neoclassical Latin, met with opposition that questioned whether it was desirable or even possible to adhere to such a standard given the changes in current linguistic usage from Cicero's time to the Renaissance. The Ciceronian controversy, which involved cultural and linguistic issues whose treatment would lead us beyond the boundaries of the present discussion, shows how seriously Renaissance humanists took the pursuit of elegant literary expression, however conceived. It also explains in part, along with Cicero's emphasis on style in his definition of eloquence, why a general shift towards a stylistic concept of rhetoric occurred during the Renaissance, a subject that I will examine in the next chapter.

A style composed of words that are correct, lucid, ornate, and suitably appropriate to the matter under consideration has great power, if delivered with artistic flair, to seize assemblies of men and bend their collective will to the intent of the skilled orator. Persuasion was the orator's first priority, but Cicero also defined eloquence more inclusively as a literary and aesthetic quality: 'What in hours of ease can be more pleasant or more characteristic of culture [*proprium humanitatis*], than discourse that is graceful and nowhere uninstructed?' Cicero derived his cultural understanding of speech from Isocrates, to whom Crassus refers as 'the master of all rhetoricians.'[38] In assessing the nature of discourse, Cicero similarly observes that the power of speech had civilized humanity, bringing people together in communities, and that it subsequently shaped laws and social institutions.[39] The ethical foundation of

Ciceronian rhetoric stems from the writings of Isocrates as well. The proficient orator should be not only naturally talented but also good,[40] a trait that would benefit the whole community and that Quintilian would later expand into the definition of the orator as a good man skilled at speaking (*vir bonus dicendi peritus*).[41] Cicero explicitly recognizes as Greek, and as essential to the character of his own ideal orator, the undertaking to live rightly and speak copiously.[42]

Education had formerly taught right conduct and good speech under the same system – 'the same masters gave instruction in both ethics and rhetoric.'[43] Cicero continually stressed the union of wisdom and a cultivated rhetorical style; he defined eloquence as 'nothing other than wisdom speaking copiously.'[44] The quarrel between philosophy and rhetoric, he maintained, originated with Socrates, who had 'separated the science of wise thinking from that of elegant speaking, though in reality they are closely linked together.'[45] The orator must study philosophy, while philosophy required for its exposition the ornament and forcefulness of rhetoric.[46] Despite hearing the Socratic voice as anti-rhetorical, Cicero nevertheless regarded Plato's writings as supremely eloquent, the model for a philosophical style that drew profitably on the resources of rhetoric.

Wisdom manifested itself as prudence, an engagement in the moral and political affairs of men. Educated in philosophy, which for the Romans meant primarily ethics, the *vir bonus* could guide the actions of his fellow citizens by both example and precept: 'Who more passionately than the orator can encourage [others] to virtuous conduct, or more zealously than he reclaim [them] from wicked courses of action?'[47] Cicero's orator is a philosopher-orator, a moral instructor, a persuader to virtue. It is a role that would feature centrally in the Renaissance concept of rhetoric, including Milton's. In order to guide public conduct, 'all things relating to the intercourse of fellow-citizens and the ways of mankind, or concerned with everyday life, the political system, our own corporate society, the common sentiments of humanity, natural inclinations and morals must be mastered by the orator.'[48] The summit of eloquence applied to these concerns was the *vita activa*, the civic life, which brought glory to oneself, served one's friends and family, and, most important, benefited the republic.[49] All of the most important attributes obtained from the study of rhetoric and ethics tie into Crassus's description of the orator as a civil servant, advising on public affairs: 'to give advice for or against a course of action seems to me to be a task for a person of the greatest weight of character, for to expound one's advice on matters of high importance calls for wisdom and ability and eloquence, to enable one to make an intelligent forecast, give an authoritative proof and employ persuasive eloquence.'[50] The task of speaking on behalf of the state requires an orator after the pattern of Isocrates, one who embodies and uses *logos* in the numerous connotations previously encountered. Crassus is describing, moreover, the role in which Milton would envisage himself as a disputant in the religious and political controversies of the 1640s and 1650s.

Cicero acknowledged the centrality of style in philosophy and oratory, spoke of it as the motive power behind persuasion, and analysed the three *genera dicendi*; apart from a section on prose rhythm at the end of the *Orator*, however, he passed over close discussion of *elocutio*, including, for example, what he called the orator's 'stock-in-trade,' the *ornatus* of the tropes and figures.[51] Near the end of *De oratore*, Crassus gives a cursory descriptive overview of eighty-seven rhetorical devices and arguments, assuming that his audience is already familiar with their names and functions.[52] Aristotle, too, though he considers metaphor in depth and makes some interesting links between rhetorical figures and psychology, does not accord style the same importance as subject matter and audience. Plato and Isocrates do not discuss it programmatically at all. In proposing a rhetorical curriculum for his ideal school, Milton needed to account much more fully for the technical points of style than these writers had done. To meet this need he suggested the study of Demetrius, Hermogenes, and Longinus.

After Aristotle the study of style became extremely popular, frequently at the expense of the more philosophical or Isocratean aspects of rhetoric. Demetrius, writing probably around 270 BC, is the most formalistic of the three authors Milton recommends. He describes four types of style: the plain, the grand, the elegant, and the forceful. These are not separate levels, but qualities of writing, variously combinable, set out as general guidelines. Clarity, the use of current and usual words, and lucid diction make up the plain style. Under it, 'persuasiveness' is classed as a separate category. The very purpose of rhetoric itself has become merely a subheading of the plain style, which indicates how deeply form engages Demetrius and how he excludes from rhetoric its traditional social functions. His focus on style is reflected in the attention he gives to literature. Frequent citations of literary passages show his four categories being put to critical use and point up his classicizing desire to maintain the excellence of older models through imitation.

Demetrius focuses constantly on rhetorical tropes and figures, which, in the case of the grand style, can greatly impress an audience. Metaphors, in particular, achieve this. He observes of the figure anaphora (beginning successive clauses with the same word) that it contributes to grandeur but can also be elegant and forceful, showing his awareness of the varied rhetorical effects that can be achieved from the same technique.[53] The elegant style, polished and embellished with beautiful words, charms the listener. The forceful style expresses strong emotion, mainly through brevity and rough-sounding clauses, and is heightened by a number of figures, especially asyndeton (the omission of conjunctions). At all times, Demetrius notes, a writer must attend to decorum, 'observ[ing] what is fitting in each case; that is, we must write in the appropriate manner, lightly when our subject is slight, impressively when it is impressive.' He observes particularly that 'we must assign to each style the figures that are appropriate to it.'[54]

There were two schools of thought on style in antiquity.[55] One, already seen in Cicero, acknowledged the three levels of plain, middle, and grand style and was authoritative in the west; the other, almost exclusively Greek, posited an ideal form of style, made up of various virtues or qualities combined in different ways. The most famous exponent of this eastern tradition was Hermogenes, who refined stylistics more precisely than any other classical writer. At the outset of *On Types of Style* (c. AD 180), he claims that his subject is an art and that good speakers and good critics alike must know it. The precepts of art supply critical standards and are necessary as a rational, teachable basis for imitation, since 'imitation and emulation of the ancients that depend upon mere experience and some irrational knack cannot, I think, produce what is correct, even if a person has a lot of natural ability. Natural abilities, without some training ... could in fact go particularly badly.'[56] Aristotle legitimized rhetoric as an art; Hermogenes treats style on its own in the same way. He identifies seven types or *ideai* of style and divides them into thirteen further subcategories. He discusses clarity, grandeur, beauty, rapidity, character, sincerity, and force, all of which are perfectly realized in the orations of Demosthenes, whom Hermogenes continually cites. Although cumbersome and in places overlapping, his categories provided a more sophisticated method both for personal composition and for criticizing the style of others than the tripartite Roman scheme.

The important feature to notice about *On Types of Style* is the organic relationship of *lexis*, style, with *ennoia*, thought or content. Along with the conventional linguistic elements of diction, rhythm, clauses, and rhetorical figures, thought and the approach to thought (*methodos*) also contribute to the creation of a particular style. All the *ideai* are related to the subjects they express. Solemnity, for example, one of the six sub-types of grandeur, addresses thoughts concerning the gods or glorious human affairs. Another division of grandeur, asperity, is for thoughts typical of open reproach directed at people who are more important than oneself. In many cases Hermogenes sensitively evaluates which rhetorical figures convey related thoughts. The diction appropriate to reproach, for instance, includes frequent rhetorical questions. Style in-volves the approach to thought as well as thought itself: distinctness, a subtype of clarity, is mainly organizational. It selects topics to make a speech clear, provides signposts, and uses the logico-rhetorical figures of division and enumeration. In further extending the conventional boundaries of style, Hermogenes makes character (*ethos*), previously seen as an Aristotelian artistic proof, into a lexical category, employ-ing modesty, simplicity, and an unaffected manner. The last type, force (*deinotes*), oversees the entire system and is, in effect, decorum, the proper use of all the styles: knowing when, where, for how long, against whom, and why to use particular types of style will make an oration forceful.

Hermogenean style, then, involves a variety of neighbouring rhetor-ical principles from invention to appropriateness, and its importance for a speaker or writer is firmly established. Yet, unlike Demetrius, Hermo-genes keeps in mind rhetoric's primary goal of persuasion, which stays in the foreground through the continual references to Demosthenes. In addition, Hermogenes generally presents a more rounded concept of rhetoric, especially when two of his other extant works, *On Staseis* and *On Invention*, are taken into account. *On Types of Style* also retains a fuller sense of the cultural importance of words for human beings: 'I should be surprised if there were anything better for men, since we are logical ani-mals, than fine and noble *logoi* and every kind of them.'[57] The works of Hermogenes, especially *On Types of Style*, were popular subjects of com-mentary and literary criticism during the Renaissance.[58]

In *On Sublimity* (first century AD), which is traditionally ascribed to 'Longinus,' the formulaic division of style into levels or ideas disap-pears entirely. The author (who has never been properly identified) is concerned not with a particular kind of style, but rather with the effect of sublimity on a literary audience and with the kind of writing that produces it. Nor is he concerned with persuasion, which he deems weaker than sublimity: 'Sublimity is a kind of eminence or excellence in discourse ... For grandeur produces ecstasy rather than persuasion in the hearer; and the combination of wonder and astonishment always proves superior to the merely persuasive and pleasant. This is because persuasion is on the whole something we can control, whereas amazement and wonder exert invincible power and force and get the better of every hearer ... Sublimity, produced at the right moment, tears up everything like a whirlwind, and exhibits the orator's whole power at a single blow.'[59] The concept is apparently original with this writer; and modern scholars point to his handling of it as the most significant and incisive idea in ancient literary criticism.[60] Sublimity is achieved in part through style, but that is only one of its rhetorical constituents and not the most important. The ability to transport one's audience, a process that may or may not involve evoking an emotional response, is to some extent a natural endowment; however, sublimity is 'not altogether without method,' which 'finds appropriate occasions for everything,' since 'grandeur often needs the curb as well as the spur.'[61] Longinus sketches an art of sublimity by stating five sources of elevated language. The first two – the power to conceive great thoughts and strong, inspired emotion – are natural, while the remaining three involve art: certain kinds of rhetorical figures, both of thought and speech; noble diction; dignified, elevated word arrangement.

Longinus devotes a large portion of *On Sublimity* to the discussion of rhetorical tropes and figures: 'Properly handled, figures constitute ... no small part of sublimity.'[62] His insights regarding both their nature and their use are penetrating and lively, partly because in passages 'where he discusses some rhetorical figure or quality of style, he represents it in his own writing,'[63] as one of his seventeenth-century commentators notes. Longinus recognizes, more than any other classical critic, that figures express feelings of the speaker or writer that are transmitted to the audience. He writes, for example, of hyperbaton (the unusual arrangement of clauses or words within a sentence), that 'it is a very real mark of urgent emotion.' Those who, in real life, are deeply moved by any strong emotion jumble the order of their words: 'thus hyperbaton is a means by which, in the best authors, imitation approaches the effects of nature. Art is perfect when it looks like nature, nature is felicitous when it embraces concealed art.' Just as art is best when it seems to be nature, so 'a figure is therefore generally thought to be best when the fact that it is a figure is concealed. Thus sublimity and emotion are a defence and a marvellous aid against the suspicion which the use of figures engenders. The artifice of the trick is lost to sight in the surrounding brilliance of beauty and grandeur, and it escapes all suspicion.' Longinus has refreshed the Peripatetic maxim about hiding rhetorical art by adding the notion that sublimity is one sure way of achieving this effect. As art, figures must be deployed under the ordering principle of method, which regulates their application and enforces decorum. Figural sublimity depends on place, manner, occasion, and purpose.[64]

Longinus emphasizes the need to account for these contingencies with respect to rhetorical figures, just as Hermogenes observes that achieving force requires knowing when, where, for how long, against whom, and why a particular type of style ought to be applied. Both writers recognize the importance of *kairos*, speaking well at the right moment, the apprehension of which engages the faculty of judging a speech situation correctly. For Isocrates, however, this formal aspect of *kairos* has a moral obverse. Wisdom governs living well, not just speaking or writing well. Judgment embraces ethics as well as stylistics, and true eloquence requires judgment's best effort in both fields. Longinus is unusual in recognizing the same dual sense of prudence. As we have seen, he makes it a formal virtue, in that one must judge the propriety of rhetorical figures in order to check the potential excesses of the sublime style; but he also implies that prudence is a moral virtue when he defines the character of the sublime speaker or writer: 'we must state where sublimity comes from: the orator must not have low or ignoble thoughts. Those whose thoughts and habits are trivial and servile all their lives cannot possibly produce anything admirable or worthy of eternity. Words will be great if thoughts are weighty. This is why splendid remarks come naturally to the proud.'[65] Grave, morally sound character is the most important requirement for sublime oratory. Longinus thus reaffirms the connection between speaking well, in a rhetorically ornamented style reined in by method, and living virtuously.

At this point a brief summary is in order of what each of these seven rhetoricians would have taught the student of Milton's ideal school. From Plato, the pupil learns above all that rhetoric must be based on knowing the truth – although Milton's idea of what it meant to know the truth differed, of course, from Plato's, as I will discuss in chapter 4. Plato also teaches that dialectic helps to comprehend a subject fully, that the orator must understand human nature and that speech must be fitted to the type of person being addressed. Although mentioned in *Of Education* as a teacher, not as a rhetorician, Isocrates sketched an account of eloquence so rooted in the liberal arts, and so consonant with Milton's own ethical concept of it, that the school would certainly draw on his rhetorical authority. Exactly how a student ought to develop the good character that underpins this Isocratean rhetoric, however, had to be left to other writers, since Isocrates does not elaborate on that point. Cicero's rhetorical works unite the Isocratean ideal of *logos* as both wisdom and eloquence; Cicero himself provides a model for imitation in both his written works and his public life. Aristotle's *On Rhetoric* would make a solidly pedagogical contribution to Milton's curriculum, expounding a method that defines rhetoric and that lays down its general principles both for the student's own compositions and for the criticism of other texts. Demetrius and Hermogenes do the same, but for style rather than for rhetoric as a whole. Their treatises, along with that of Longinus, would satisfy one of the primary educational and cultural requirements of the Renaissance, a comprehensive knowledge of style or *elocutio*.

3 Milton's Forerunners: Renaissance Rhetoric

I should declare how for us, of all the arts and teachings, the most out-standing quality of eloquence holds rulership and pre-eminence by virtue of its intrinsic excellence, which, to be sure, adorns and embellishes human or divine affairs of any kind at all, and without which every mode of speaking, every elaboration and refinement of language, is considered poor in expression, indeed miserable and unpleasing. More and more we are awakening to the principles of this art.

> Antonio da Rho, 'Exhortatoria fratris theologi ad scolares'

The premium put on a knowledge of *elocutio* can hardly be overempha-sized. The bias towards it in Milton's education tract is representative of Renaissance humanism as a whole, which embraced mastery of speech as an ornament in letters and in life. Although Milton proposes a rhetorical curriculum whose principle texts combine to present the art in its organic entirety – as it was, in fact, taught and applied across Europe – his basing half of it in authors who deal almost exclusively with style reflects the priorities not only of his age but of centuries past, when verbal techniques of diction, syntax, and amplification had con-sistently risen to distinction as the most useful and prestigious objects of rhetorical study. The Renaissance emphasis on style, especially on these verbal devices, the tropes and figures, is a major episode in the history of literary forms, and we must reacquaint ourselves with the attitudes and terminology surrounding it if we are to gain a truly his-torical understanding of the literature of the period, including *Paradise Lost*. The most significant contribution towards such an understanding has been made by Brian Vickers, who argues that 'modern distaste for stylistic rhetoric ... is wholly unhistorical' and that a critical awareness of rhetorical tropes and figures, parallel to that exercised by the authors who used them, is necessary in order to think ourselves 'back into a Renaissance frame of mind.'[1] The assiduous cultivation of tropes and figures contributed significantly to the Renaissance preoccupation with literary style, which I will establish as a key formal convention governing Milton's composition of *Paradise Lost*. In this respect my goal as a literary critic is to approximate as nearly as possible the technical knowledge and vocabulary possessed by Milton's original reader, the reader whose perspective will supply the most thorough formal understanding of *Paradise Lost*. And so I now turn to the theories of Renaissance humanists who read with a heightened alertness to rhetoric and its stylistic office and who, importantly, taught others to read in the same way. These readers were Milton's audience, 'fit ... though few' as he hoped to find them in *Paradise Lost* (VII. 31), one criterion of fitness being a knowledge of the art of style, which we must come to share if the significance of rhetoric as a Miltonic idea-in-poetry is to become fully apparent.

Rhetorical style, long considered the defining feature of eloquence, had maintained an unbroken hold on the western literary imagination since classical times. 'For to discover and decide what to say is important, to be sure,' wrote Cicero, 'but that is a matter of practical knowledge [*prudentia*] rather than of eloquence ... The very word "eloquent" shows that [the perfect orator] excels because of this one quality, that is, in the use of language [*oratio*], and that the other qualities are overshadowed by this.'[2] Style continued to interest practitioners and critics in late antiquity, having been made a legitimate field of Christian study, owing largely to the influence of St Augustine. It was virtually the only part of rhetoric attended to during the Middle Ages, when the relatively few opportunities for public oratory outside the pulpit limited rhetoric's social context and restricted it to epistolary and notarial applications. Fascination with rhetorical form continued into, and peaked during, the Renaissance. As literature lost its standing as an encyclopedic repository of all knowledge, partly with the publication of reference books for specialized subjects, humanist commentators directed critical attention to areas that set literature apart from other branches of learning, including the methods of elegant expression that fell within the province of rhetoric.[3] Of all the parts of rhetoric, *elocutio* claimed pride of place in a Europe of intensive literary production based largely on classical models. The formalist aesthetic of the period originated in an educational system that engendered an acute sensitivity to all aspects of literary style and to style itself as the first principle of eloquence. 'And so the present work of instruction,' wrote Juan Luis Vives, 'does not discuss what should be said, but rather how to say it. Because choice of language is indeed the source of eloquence, as Julius Caesar used to say, the first thing to consider will be words as the rudiments of this subject.'[4]

Generations of students, taught to handle language with unusual dexterity, sustained an appreciation of style apart from the thought, producing works that showed an exuberant delight in language for its own sake and that appealed to their audiences largely on account of those same verbal displays. Shakespeare, for example, was known early in his career for how he wrote, as an adept stylist, not for what he wrote about.[5] Still, the two elements of composition, *res* and *verba*, were regarded as interdependent, 'for verbal fluency without content,' wrote Jean Sturm, 'is awkward and laughable, while the substance of the content, what it means, cannot be understood unless it is expressed by speech, which must be fashioned not only by the choice of words, but also by their arrangement.'[6] If the Renaissance sensibility was not entirely addicted to form, the consideration was always present. Renaissance readers approached classical texts in two ways: historically, in order to find out specific information about the period or context of the work; and rhetorically, seeing the text as an 'atemporal ideal' from which a reader could extract practical advice and stylistic instruction.[7] Rudolph Agricola expounded the rhetorical approach in a letter referred to as *De formando studio*: 'In reading we must chiefly try to understand, as much as possible, what we read, and possess completely not only the clearly perceived idea which is taught but also the force of expression, decorum, structure, and ornament in eloquent writers. We must try to see clearly what elegance there is, what weight of sentiment, what power of explaining and setting forth hidden things with words, and of bringing them forth as it were into light and view.'[8] Whatever else they taught, the ancients were always teachers of eloquence. In their own writing as well, humanist scholars intended to be read by posterity not only for the content of their works, but also for the elegance of their style.[9] Everywhere, from the classroom to all genres of writing, rhetoric as style captivated the Renaissance mind. As Lorenzo Valla remarked, 'there is no one who does not wish to speak gracefully and eloquently.'[10]

Related to this universal desire was a universally acknowledged first principle, voiced by Peter Mosellanus: 'no one who is even tolerably learned is unaware that all the ornaments of the Latin language depend above all upon the figures and tropes.'[11] These were the elements of style that most interested educators and writers. Definitively systematized by Greek rhetoricians in the first century BC, they had long been the most avidly studied part of rhetoric, and numerous rhetoric-books like that of Mosellanus provided lists of them. Here, as elsewhere, the cultural and linguistic assumptions of humanism should be kept in mind. Schoolboys at St Paul's and Harrow and Westminster did not study English. Renaissance grammar meant Latin grammar, rhetoric Latin rhetoric, as Mosellanus (Peter Schade in his native tongue) assumes in 1519. Later in the sixteenth century rhetoric developed a vernacular side, partly in response to the vogue of *elocutio*. Tudor rhetoricians compiled handbooks defining these flowers of speech – and giving classical, vernacular, and biblical examples of them – that were derived from continental models. Peter Mack contends that these English works by Henry Peacham, Richard Sherry, and George Puttenham were much less popular and influential during the Tudor Age than previously supposed, since each was printed only once (Peacham published two editions). But Mack combines the style handbooks with two works that contained accounts of the tropes and figures within their broader formats: Thomas Wilson's *Art of Rhetoric*, devoted to rhetoric as a whole, and Angel Day's *The English Secretary*, a guide to writing letters. All may be understood 'as versions of a single archtext: the English renaissance style manual.' Which means that 'figurist' rhetoric *was* popular even from this historically adjusted perspective, since Wilson's treatise was printed eight times between 1553 and 1585, Day's nine times between 1586 and 1635, for a total of twenty-one editions of the 'archtext.'[12] Meanwhile, the continental Latin style guides remained strong sellers during the period: the *chef-d'œuvre* of the genre, the *Epitome troporum ac schematum* (1541) by the German schoolmaster Joannes Susenbrotus, was printed seven times in England between 1562 and 1635.

It is easy to understand the appeal of these books. Anyone who is engaged by words and has ever attended closely to literary expression will find that the manuals can still delight, even if what they teach is now of historical rather than practical significance. Their interest extends well beyond lexical matters, for in addition to explaining the tropes and figures they are filled with enthusiasm, wide (if shallow) learning, occasional wit, asides on religious and social issues, and insights into contemporary reading practices. Historians and literary critics ignore the style handbooks to their detriment, passing over rich seams of cultural and historical information that lay within easy reach. Take, as an example, the sixteenth-century book perhaps most widely read today, Erasmus's *Praise of Folly* (*Moriae encomium id est Stultitiae laus*). In discussing it, twenty-first-century teachers expectedly and correctly note that Erasmus personifies Folly. But the sixteenth-century reader had a more codified, disciplined, and tradition-based idea of what Erasmus was doing (as Erasmus himself surely did); he identified the technique more formally, in the artistic vocabulary of *elocutio*, as a rhetorical scheme of amplification. As Susenbrotus explains, 'it is a case of prosopopoeia whenever, for a thing that is mute and without consciousness, we devise a human character proper to that thing. Of such a kind are Folly in the writings of Erasmus, and Virtue and Pleasure, which Prodicus the sophist represents fighting it out between themselves in his composition on Hercules, though the narrator is Xenophon [*Memorabilia*, II. i. 21].'[13] On he goes, multiplying examples of the figure from Ennius (via Quintilian), Lucian, Ausonius, Horace and Quintus Curtius, Aristophanes, Boethius, Prudentius, and others. From this brief passage we observe many things: the definition of prosopopoeia, literary examples that illuminate and reinforce the definition, the humanist's encyclopedic knowledge and recall of classical and post-classical literature, his lively (proud?) eclecticism in moving from Erasmus to Prodicus via Xenophon, his pedagogical leaning towards didactic literature suggested by those two choices, the privileged contemporary status of Erasmus on a par with the classics, and, by inference, the certainty that Erasmus worked consciously within that classical tradition and with the art of rhetoric in composing *Praise of Folly*. We can be confident that Milton read Erasmus and everything else the same way, with extraordinary alertness to stylistic detail and terminology, to a host of precedents for such figures from the literature of the ten languages he acquired, and to the creative potential for those figures in his own writing, based in part on examples culled from his reading.[14] He knew that figures of the kind described here, far from being merely decorative, enabled a work of literature to achieve the purposes an author set for it. Cataloguing his own works in 1523, Erasmus refers to '*Moriae encomium*, a small book full of humour, but it teaches serious lessons, so do not be surprised to find it in this section' of 'works which contribute to the building of character.'[15] Prosopopoeia was the vehicle by which the book taught those lessons, as readers such as Susenbrotus and Milton knew. When faced later with presenting serious lessons of his own, Milton turned to a closely related technique, as the final chapter of this book will show.

The appeal of rhetorical figures is partly explained by a general transformation during the Renaissance when, Paul Kristeller writes, 'the emphasis in rhetoric had shifted from persuasion to style and imitation, and to literary criticism.'[16] Rhetoric left the domain of public oratory, intent on persuasion, and moved into plays, prose fiction, and poetry, concerned with narration. Although rhetoric was significantly concerned with style, the shift from persuasion to style that Kristeller has claimed is disputed by Brian Vickers, who maintains that, for Renaissance rhetoricians, 'the goal of oratory [was] not elegant speaking but persuasion to action.'[17] This persuasive agenda underpinned the theory behind the function of tropes and figures, which were indeed conceived as more than ornamental decking for a literary piece, as Henry Peacham stated in *The Garden of Eloquence*: 'For by Fygures, as it were by sundry streames, that great & forcible floud of Eloquence, is most plentifully and pleasantly poured forth by the great might of Figures which is no other thing then (wisdom speaking eloquently) the Oratour may leade his hearers which way his list, and draw them to what affection he will.'[18] Eloquence draws its power from rhetorical figures, which are able to move the emotions and influence the will in order to convey wisdom persuasively. Peacham is describing the effects of the grand style in a metaphor derived from Cicero and Erasmus. Cicero had defined the grand style, in part, as 'the kind of eloquence that rushes along with the roar of a mighty stream,' a sentiment Erasmus echoed in the opening sentence of his extremely influential *De copia*: 'The speech of man is a magnificent and impressive thing when it surges along like a golden river, with thoughts and words pouring out in rich abundance.'[19] We shall return to this conventional image of eloquence, as an irresistible psychological force, within the framework of Milton's concept of rhetoric in chapter 4.

Rhetorical tropes and figures received widespread attention. As the primary constituents of style, they enjoyed a close relationship with the operational principle behind literary composition in the Renaissance, imitation. In antiquity, imitation had been to a significant extent the imitation of style, and style meant mainly the use of the tropes and figures.[20] The same was true in the Renaissance. Rhetoric's application to both reading and writing was a pedagogical axiom, as in Erasmus's recommendation to 'have at your fingertips the chief points of rhetoric ...

For these are conducive not only to criticism but also to imitation.'[21] He refers to the entire system of rhetoric but especially to *elocutio*, for concentration on smaller formal units was deemed important for anatomizing classical texts to the degree required for imitative mastery, part of which involved a writer's attainment of *copia*, or fullness of stylistic expression. A love of details, captured in notebooks for later reference and use, characterized the humanistic striving after precise imitation. Tropes and figures were among the details of classical form regarded as most useful to a writer; Leonardo Bruni's notebook, for example, shows him identifying them.[22] Susenbrotus noted their utility in both literary criticism and composition. When pointed out and explained in the classroom, 'they are very useful so that we may properly understand both profane and sacred writers' and 'at the same time that we may master formulas of speaking and writing, which one may imitate by incessant practice.'[23] Explaining them was only one of a lecturer's many duties, which obliged him to cover a range of moral, historical, and factual points as well as formal and stylistic ones; but extant pamphlet editions of classical texts, produced specially for classroom use and annotated by their student owners, suggest that such explanation and discussion was routine in the sixteenth century.[24]

Humanist commentators often paid close attention to rhetorical devices, especially in critical editions intended to improve students' comprehension and literary style. In the first and most frequently reprinted Renaissance edition of the *Metamorphoses* (1493), Raphael Regius named and explained Ovid's figures of speech; many subsequent editions by other hands indicated them in the margins. Cicero's style frequently came in for similar treatment, as in the first humanist attempt to analyse the rhetoric of his speeches, by Antonio Loschi (ca. 1390), and in Peter Ramus's extensive annotation of rhetorical devices in his commentaries on *De lege agraria* and *In Catalinam*. Even though Guarino da Verona's commentary on the pseudo-Ciceronian *Ad Herennium* avoids the exquisitely detailed lexical discussions of his scholastic predecessors, he still devotes 40 per cent of his gloss on this central rhetorical text to its fourth book, on stylistic devices.[25] In theology, tropes and figures were regarded as important details of biblical form. The Bible was viewed as a rhetorical text, 'where if you be ignoraunte in the fygurative speches and Tropes, you are lyke in manye greate doubtes to make but a slender solucion.'[26] Understanding the figurative nature of language, especially tropes, was recognized as paramount for scriptural exegesis. Biblical hermeneutics employed the same techniques as secular literary criticism. In homiletics, preachers were enjoined to use rhetorical figures in order to move the spirits of their congregation and to add elegance to the wisdom of Christian doctrine. Bartholomew Keckermann selects eleven rhetorical devices, 'which are wonderfully serviceable for amplification and for moving the affections ... Indeed it is true that there is abundant beauty in those things which the rhetoricians call figures of thought.'[27] Chapters 5 and 6 will more fully discuss the various dimensions of sacred rhetoric, one of the central ideas in the history of literary forms related to *Paradise Lost*.

The primacy of a detailed knowledge of rhetorical style, whether for criticism or composition, is evident in virtually any Renaissance literary exercise. Apart from this technical facet, there were also social and ethical dimensions of style, aspects of its cultural face, which lifted the status of well-crafted discourse, as an ideal of the age, above exclusively lexical concerns. One cultural assumption was that an individual's *oratio* – a word that covered all uses of language, including literary style as well as manner of speech – bespoke the reasoning faculty and moral character of his inner self, his *ratio*. This Isocratean-Ciceronian belief, along with the Socratic injunction, 'Speak, so that I may see you,' appealed to humanists from Erasmus to Robert Burton, and to Ben Jonson, translating Vives: 'Language most shewes a man: speake that I may see thee. It springs out of the most retired, and inmost parts of us, and is the Image of the Parent of it, the mind. No glasse renders a mans forme, or likenesse, so true as his speech.'[28] Certainly, the correspondence between speech and true character was often more complicated, since a keenly developed rhetorical faculty could give a person the appearance of virtue, hiding treachery and duplicity, as Shakespeare shows in a number of instances,[29] or could construct in writing whatever persona an author might wish to project.[30] Style made the man, according to his inclination. Elegant speech, for example, was considered part of a Renaissance gentleman's accoutrement. The word *ornatus* means both rhetorically embellished speech and adornment or clothing, associations that call up the courtly world of etiquette and measured comportment.[31] Language was a badge of social rank. Both Touchstone in *As You Like It* and Berowne in *Love's Labour's Lost* are conscious of their social standing as contingent on their adeptness at witty and colourful forms of speech, particularly the tropes and figures. Sir Philip Sidney wrote *Old Arcadia* with this same socialized view of language in mind. Conventionally, allowances for conscious designs on language aside, *ratio* and *oratio*, inseparably paired under the standard of *logos*, were considered to go hand in hand; therefore, speech, as the voice of right reason, deserved whatever refinements a person might wish to acquire for it: 'For if *oratio* next to *ratio*, speech next to reason, be the greatest gift bestowed upon mortality,' wrote Sidney, 'that cannot be praiseless which doth most polish that blessing of speech.'[32]

'Eloquence,' as Gadamer puts it, 'is not called such simply because what is said is said beautifully, but also because something beautiful is said.'[33] In the concordance of a graceful style and an upright mind, rhetoric and philosophy are united in the humanist tradition. Their compatibility had been the subject of long debate. At Plato's instigation in the *Gorgias*, rhetoric and philosophy had been set at odds on the grounds that the art of speaking – intended to persuade rather than to expound the truth, and prone to value style at the expense of thought – could not give appropriate voice to philosophical discourse. Conversely, the harmony of the two disciplines that Isocrates and Cicero had sought to establish, affirming the interdependence of the *verba* of rhetoric and the *res* of philosophy, became the orthodox position of humanist rhetoricians, who defined true eloquence in Ciceronian terms of wisdom expressed in a copious, appropriate style. The often rehearsed debate between Ermolao Barbaro and Giovanni Pico della Mirandola highlighted the sorts of values and priorities related to the question of rhetorical style as a valid form of philosophical expression. Their views, exchanged in letters in 1485, are predicated on two different opinions of rhetoric. In Pico's condemnation, reminiscent of Plato's, it was suspect and superficial, everything the wisdom of philosophy was not; for Barbaro, it was a glorious fulfilment of the potential of human speech that presented philosophy efficaciously, the attitude that Cicero had propagated and that other humanists would continue to take up for generations. Despite Pico's genuine belief that the wisdom of scholastic philosophy could stand alone, in need of no stylistic adornment, his own rhetorical acumen suggests at least some shading to irony in his wholesale rejection of rhetoric. At any rate, Barbaro's declared position was that of Petrarch, Salutati, Bruni, More, Vives, Melanchthon, Sturm, Nizolio, and Calvin, to name but a few, as well as Erasmus and Valla, who, as we shall see, restructured the affirmative estimation of rhetoric within the matrix of Christian doctrine.

How much the model of a *vir Christianus peritus dicendi* that emerges from the body of Milton's writing may owe to this long humanist tradition is, in the nature of such speculation, too difficult to surmise. Nevertheless, it is noticeable that, for earlier English humanists, the relationship of wisdom to eloquence was a current intellectual issue. In the century preceding the poet's birth, it penetrated educational discourse, including the statutes of St Paul's, established in 1518 as the first grammar school in Europe to institutionalize Latin and Greek literature, where Milton attended from 1615–25. John Colet, the school's founder, laid out a curriculum for studying 'goode auctors sych as have the veray Romayne eliquence joyned withe wisdome specially Cristyn auctours that wrote theyre wysdome with clene and chast laten other in verse or in prose,' for his intent was 'by thys scole specially to incresse knowlege and worshipping of god and oure lorde Crist Jesu and good Cristen lyff and maners in the Children.'[34] Milton was first guided in the humanities under this mandate, a conviction of the inherent correspondence of style and ideas, especially Christian ideas, that, taught day in and day out, could hardly have failed to influence his mature opinion on the subject. Colet's words point up the ethically formative impression, conducive to virtue and piety, that Christian sentiments expressed in a good style were expected to have on young students.

His emphasis on this kind of eloquence found general acceptance among humanist educators in sixteenth-century England. In *The Boke named the Governour* (1531), Thomas Elyot treats the proper education for noblemen and civil servants, part of which consisted in developing a rhetoric that united a fluent style with a command of the facts, essential for persuading one's hearers. A facility in eloquence that was not rooted in wisdom and knowledge, he agrees with Cicero, denoted a madman.[35] Roger Ascham's *The Scholemaster* (1570) gave considerable attention to teaching 'encrease of eloquence,' including a section on imitation. Here, he digresses to affirm that wisdom must be combined with eloquence and that wholesome philosophy, such as Plato's and Aristotle's, naturally generates such expression, while errant doctrines (Stoicism, Epicureanism, scholasticism) are rude and barbarous in their language. Bad style reflects, and reveals, bad ideas sprung from foolish minds (as Milton himself professes in both his defences of the English people). An eloquent style, on the other hand, is the product of a truly philosophical mind, two mutually complementary and indivisible attributes: 'They be not wise therefore that say, "What care I for a mans wordes and utterance, if his matter and reasons be good." ... Ye know not what hurt ye do to learning, that care not for wordes but for matter, and so make a devorse betwixt the tong and the hart.'[36] This divorce, he claims, was responsible for the decline of intellectual life in classical antiquity. Civilization depends on due attention to words, on being both wise *and* eloquent. That this digression occurs at the start of the section on imitation leaves no doubt that Elyot intended its weight to be carried throughout the entire discussion and thereby to inform the stylistic imitation to be practised by his readers. In *The Garden of Eloquence*, published in 1577 and revised in 1593, Henry Peacham, like Sydney, identifies *ratio* and *oratio* as complementary divine gifts and asserts the need to conjoin the refinements of those gifts, wisdom and eloquence, advocating an elegant, pleasing style in philosophy. In *The Art of Rhetoric* (1553), Thomas Wilson paraphrases Cicero's praise of an eloquent style (*Orator* xiv. 44, xix. 61; quoted at the beginning of this chapter), then writes: 'Many are wise, but few have the gift to set forth their wisdom. Many can tell their mind in English, but few can use meet terms and apt order such as all men should have and wise men will use, such as needs must be had when matters should be uttered.' He is judged 'half a god ... that can plainly, distinctly, plentifully, and aptly utter both words and matter.'[37] Generations of English students, Milton among them, had had ingrained into their rhetorical sensibility a belief in the religious, political, and social utility of wisdom united to eloquence. Milton's ideal school in *Of Education*, not to mention his own concept of rhetoric, was founded on the same principle, so important to his sixteenth-century predecessors.

As we have seen, stylistic facility was a perennial humanist priority. The many literary tasks centred in *elocutio* belong to the ideal or cultural plane of rhetoric, identified with elegant discourse, which may be differentiated from a conception of rhetoric as a political instrument.[38] Besides the academic eclecticism that used rhetoric ad hoc in fields such as poetics, criticism, and epideictic oratory, there was a belief, held mainly by Italian humanists, that rhetoric could be revived in its classical integrity and applied, as in ancient Greece and Rome, to civil government. The two outlooks were not rigidly dichotomized: writers such as Bruni and Milton, who balanced careers in letters and in government, cultivated both, and a polished style was no less important a feature of political discourse than of any other. Rhetoric in Italy nevertheless settled into cultural and political divisions, partly on the consideration that 'a rhetoric reduced to style was not the stuff which ruled republics.' Italian humanists have been distinguished from their northern counterparts by 'their broader politico-oratorical conception of rhetoric in the Ciceronian tradition. From [George of] Trebizond to [Bartolomeo] Cavalcanti and Alessandro Piccolomini, the Italian Renaissance witnessed attempts to re-establish the full classical art of rhetoric as vital to civil life.'[39] Yet such awareness was not confined to Italy; English humanists also recognized the virtue of rhetoric in preparing a man for civic life and for pleading and deliberating policy.[40] That rhetoric provided verbal skills that enabled one to take an active hand in such pressing matters and potentially to influence the outcome of state affairs made it an essential accomplishment for anyone who wished to pursue the Renaissance *vita activa*.

The Stoic doctrine that an art should be useful for life, a belief prevalent in the Renaissance, informed the view that rhetoric was practical.[41] In the first place, as noted earlier, rhetoric taught criticism and composition; it could help students both to understand classical and Christian authors and to develop fluency in their own discourse. In his zeal to further these goals, Joannes Susenbrotus exemplifies the practical bent of his age: 'Receive this book eagerly, as they say, read and reread it, and inscribe it in your memory, use it in both speech and writing, because otherwise (as I have often impressed upon you) without exercise and practice every art is completely useless. But if you should do this, the gates of the muses will undoubtedly be opened to you.'[42] Rhetoric could open the gates of the Muses, but it had to do more, as a profitable art, than simply furnish eloquence; that skill, once acquired, had to be deployed in the world of practical affairs. The desire to attain a solely cultural, demonstrative eloquence, writes Erasmus, is 'fair enough, if we are preparing our eloquence for display rather than for practical use. But there's a lot of difference between an actor and an orator. An actor is satisfied with giving pleasure, but an orator wants to be of some use as well, provided he is a good man.'[43] Rhetorical pragmatism obtained both culturally and politically, whether in terms of selecting those elements of rhetoric, mainly stylistic, that would suit contemporary needs in the world of letters or of adapting it in a more complete form to the exigencies of statecraft.

The utility of style, however, reached into politics as well as culture, a fact reflected in Renaissance commentaries on the treatises that figured in Milton's ideal curriculum. Longinus, Demetrius, and Hermogenes were naturally useful in cultural and religious pursuits. Gerard Langbaine introduced *On Sublimity* by arguing that there was no better shortcut to understanding sacred texts than resorting to the techniques of pagan criticism,[44] including rhetoric, on which Longinus was one of the best authorities. Pier Vettori writes of Demetrius's *On Style* that 'the usefulness of this work, and how much benefit it is able to bring to those who read it diligently, is beyond dispute ... It is eloquence, therefore, since it has such force, that the orator ought above all to possess, and possess strong on all sides, embellished and decorated with every method.'[45] Moreover, Vettori everywhere shows by classical examples how Demetrian principles apply to writing poetry. Reading the Byzantine stylists would prove useful to politicians as well. In his commentary on Hermogenes' *On Types of Style*, Gasparus Laurentius claims that a knowledge of style benefits those engaged in state and religious affairs: 'How much force and excellence there is in these two books of Hermogenes will certainly be apparent to those ... who make speeches in court, in the curia, in electoral assemblies, in public meetings, in the senate – and indeed in the very church of God. In short, all those who are engaged in the task of oratory are compelled to use the various [Hermogenean] styles as a method of handling diverse subjects.'[46] Prefaces to editions of Longinus made similar claims for eloquence as beneficial to statesmen, who could find practical guidance in the study of *On Sublimity*. Pietro Pagano dedicated his edition to Aloisio Mocenigo, a Venetian senator who held conference with a variety of high-ranking officials. Pagano testifies to the utility and power of eloquence in telling his patron that, with it, 'you will reply to everyone most authoritatively and wisely, and you will use such grandeur of expression in everything, such skill in discussing affairs of war and peace that it is no wonder if the minds of your senators are so thoroughly moved that they cannot but agree with you in all things.'[47] Gabriel da Petra speaks in a similar vein in his edition of Longinus.[48] The eloquence to be gained partly from rhetoric manuals was viewed as a reliable means of persuasion in Italian politics. The notion that rhetoric lost its political edge later in the Renaissance has been dispelled by Wayne Rebhorn, who associates eloquence with an imperial dynamic of rulership and subjection throughout the period, and by David Norbrook, who traces a strong tradition of republican and royalist rhetoric in seventeenth-century England, including both parties' interest in Longinus. John Hall's preface to his 1652 translation of *On Sublimity* expressed hope for a republican revival of rhetoric in political life, a hope realized in the literary activity of parliamentarians such as Milton, Thomas May, George Wither, and Marchmont Nedham, all of whom adopted the Longinian sublime to contrast the false harmonies of courtly literature.[49] Milton's inclusion of Longinus in his curriculum points to the characterization of rhetoric in this period as a vehicle for stating political ideas forcefully and persuasively.

As a useful art, rhetoric had a hand in guiding the moral life of the individual, since it was closely connected to moral philosophy: 'Who more passionately than the orator can encourage [others] to virtuous conduct, or more zealously than he reclaim [them] from wicked courses of action?'[50] The orator could influence moral action because the psychological channels that determined it – the affections, the imagination, and the will – were the sites on which rhetoric operated. Moving the emotions by rhetorical speech, Vives believed, had an ethical purpose, that of persuading an audience to follow the good and to shun evil. Abolishing evil was the orator's pre-eminent function in this regard.[51] For Bacon, too, rhetoric and moral philosophy were complementary disciplines. Both advanced reason. 'The duty and office of rhetoric,' he wrote, 'is no other than to apply and recommend the dictates of reason to imagination, in order to excite the appetite and will ... the end of rhetoric is to fill the imagination with observations and images' of virtue, so that reason will embrace them and direct the will accordingly: 'Plato said elegantly ... "that virtue, if she could be seen, would move great love and affection"; and it is the business of rhetoric to make pictures of virtue and goodness, so that they may be seen. For since they cannot be showed to the sense in corporeal shape, the next degree is to show them to the imagination in as lively representation as possible, by ornament of words.'[52] Bacon's rhetoric of science rejects verbal ornamentation for the purposes of inquiry. It uses aphorisms that present knowledge in coded fragments, which must be gradually and labouriously assembled in order to reveal nature's secrets intelligibly.[53] In contrast, a rhetoric of ethics requires ornamentation: 'For the method of the Stoics ... who thought to thrust virtue upon men by concise and sharp maxims and conclusions' has 'little sympathy with the imagination and will of man.'[54]

Rhetoric's power to influence the will, Thomas Wilson observes, makes it uniquely suited to persuading people to embrace 'what [is] good, what [is] bad, and what [is] gainful for mankind'; 'such force hath the tongue, and such is the power of eloquence and reason, that most men are forced to yield in that which most standeth against their will.' Rhetoric's power to move the affections, along with 'the sweetness of utterance' that delights, augmented its first function of teaching. Rhetorical techniques of moral instruction include the fable, the example, and the allegory. Richard Rainolde recommends that the orator, 'to perswade [people] in good causes and enterprises, to animate and incense them, to godlie affaires and busines,' use the fable, 'out of which some godlie precepte, or admonicion to vertue is given, to frame and instruct our manners.' Erasmus writes that 'in the development of *copia*, then, illustrations [*exempla*] play a leading role, whether the speech is the sort that debates what action should be taken, or urges to a particular course of action ... or is laudatory or vituperative; in short, whether one is trying to convince one's audience, move them, or give them pleasure.' He writes similarly on extracting a moral didactic kernel from reading allegory and on how scriptural allegories may be used 'to turn men towards piety or from wickedness.'[55]

The connection between rhetoric and moral philosophy was more basic than the fact that the one communicated, and inculcated, the standards for virtuous living prescribed by the other. They were, in fact, similar modes of thinking, as rhetoric exercised the same evaluative and discretionary faculties as ethics.[56] In an idea that went back to Isocrates and the sophists, prudence was a rhetorical virtue as well as an ethical one, proper judgment being characteristic of both speech and moral action. Henry Peacham, son of the Tudor rhetorician, acknowledges this point: 'Under *Prudence* is comprehended, out of generall learning and judgment, that discreete, apt suting and disposing as well of Actions as Words in their due place, time, and manner'[57] – prudence, in both acting and speaking, is predicated on decorum. 'Decorum, ruling the tongue, implies ruling one's actions (*scribere est agere*, as the injunction has it); it is one of the central constituents of *prudentia* ... in early modern England.'[58] George of Trebizond defines prudence mainly as *providentia*, foresight: 'although this is the greatest part of prudence ... it is brought to completion above all by the exact judgement of single circumstances. In which practice, if someone makes significant progress, he will perceive that he has achieved a great deal both in foresight and in expressing himself.'[59] George's prudence encompasses action and speech but lacks a moral imperative of the kind we typically see. The crystallization of this prudence is Trapezuntian *iudicium*, 'the power to grasp the ever-changing, infinitely complex situation, and to adapt to it so as to direct the course of events by the power of speech.'[60] Here again is *kairos*, the situational awareness critical to rhetorical success. In 'demonstrat[ing] the temporal consciousness pervading Tudor Humanist rhetorical and ethical theory,' James Baumlin stresses the importance of *kairos* in relation to decorum and prudence: 'Ciceronian theory combines *to prepon* [decorum] and *to kairos*, at once observing both the formal and the temporal or situational aspects of discourse.' 'In its broadest sense,' he writes, '*kairos* immerses speakers in a moral-intellectual crisis when the choice to speak or act (and what and how one speaks or acts) determines an individual's "fate." Hence, the Humanists' habit of weighing alternatives and occasions, of "looking both ways" and speaking (or acting) accordingly – a habit, in short, of *prudentia*.'[61] Milton's definition of prudence includes *kairos*, and his first prudential maxim concerns the proper timing of speech: 'Prudence is that virtue by which we foresee what ought to be done with respect to the circumstances of time and place. Proverbs 29.11: A fool uttereth his mind: but a wise man keepeth it in till afterwards.'[62]

Rhetoric is a species of prudence, employing the same processes of evaluation: 'For eloquence,' writes Franz Burchard, 'demands the greatest skill [*prudentia*] in investigating and presenting the matter, the fullest abundance of words, the keenest judgment in the selection [of both].'[63] It could also teach prudence: 'I doubt that any study contributes as richly to this practical skill,' writes Thomas More, 'as the study of poets, orators, and histories.'[64] Philipp Melanchthon, an exponent of the practical value of rhetoric in all aspects of life, believes that rhetorical training teaches prudential skills as well as verbal ones: 'For although it is quite useful to be instructed in the copious style, practice in speaking also forms judgments on a wide range of matters ... These considerations are conducive to prudence and advise us concerning many great matters – about morals, about law, about the diversity of actions and judgments, and about the nature of things.'[65] George of Trebizond's relative moral indifference with respect to deciding what to do and say was not typical. On the whole, Renaissance rhetoricians like Melanchthon inherited and christianized the classical belief that speaking well and living rightly were closely related. For Erasmus, the idea that speech was the image of the mind, that *ratio* was mirrored in *oratio*, led to a perception of style as an ethical index; the rhetorical virtue of expressing oneself appropriately (*aptum*) finds a corollary in the moral requirement of living in an appropriate manner.[66] The true orator has to do both, and his speech, writes Jean Sturm, ought to project the Isocratean values of the good man speaking eloquently, both on moral grounds and because good character is persuasive: 'it is necessary that a speech exhibit, one might say, its own spirit, its own cast of thought, its own native quality or character and certain ethical principles peculiar to it; therefore, in a speech there ought to be expressions of morals, wisdom, prudence, fortitude, religion, piety, patriotism towards the state. It is necessary that a speech should be endowed with a specific character, that it contain an *ethos*, which is a way of speaking designed to win over an audience.'[67] The currents of mutual influence passing between rhetoric and ethics naturally means that eloquence will incorporate principles of good character and virtuous living.

Both rhetoric and moral philosophy, in close contact with one another, were related to poetry. Rhetoric and poetry had been allied since antiquity, partly at the level of style. When rhetoric in the Roman Republic lost its original judicial and political functions, it was relegated to study in the schools, where it became a literary discipline: 'Hence it penetrated into all literary genres. Its elaborately developed system became the common denominator of literature in general. This is the most important development in the history of antique rhetoric.'[68] Poetry thus became rhetoricized, acquiring the technical machinery of rhetoric, especially the tropes and figures that constituted virtually the whole of medieval poetics and that Renaissance poets in turn treated as central to their art. A reduction in rhetoric's functions similar to that in Republican Rome, a shift from a political to a mainly literary conception, ensured that poetry and rhetoric maintained a close relation in the Renaissance, merging in their mutual concern for style. As in the Middle Ages, 'one of the ways of considering poetry, which will never lose its popularity in the Renaissance, will be to consider it exclusively in terms of expression or style.'[69] Descartes, who believed that both poetry and rhetoric were gifts of the mind, not acquisitions of study, went so far as to say that if one were skilled in handling the tropes and figures of rhetoric, great poetry would follow as a consequence even without a knowledge of poetics. Vettori regarded this skill as the highest accomplishment, averring that the force generated by rhetorical figures 'lifts the art of the poet to the heavens.'[70] As was the case in mainstream rhetorical theory, however, Renaissance poetics predicated an obligation to *res* as well as to *verba*. The invocation topos, for example, where the poet appeals to a higher power for inspiration, amounts to a wish that thoughts will be expressed in eloquent words. Stylistic ornament, at least for the best poets, was not an end in itself.

Poetic style, moreover, encompassed the wider aims of rhetoric as well. Renaissance poets, unlike their medieval predecessors, accounted for the traditional function of rhetorical devices, that they were meant to move and to persuade an audience.[71] Poetry's acquisition of rhetoric's persuasive dimension was gradual, according to Julius Caesar Scaliger. Early oratory sought only to persuade its hearers, early poetry only to delight; 'afterwards, each borrowed from the other that function in which they were lacking.'[72] Thomas Sébillet maintained that 'sont l'Orateur et le Poète tant proches et conjoints, que semblables et égaux en plusieurs choses, diffèrent principalement en ce, que l'un est plus contraint de nombres que l'autre.'[73] Sidney gave poetry an integrated rhetorical identity by assigning to it the three Ciceronian offices of teaching, delighting, and moving.[74] What poetry often taught, like the rhetoric from which it was hardly distinguished, was moral philosophy. Enthusiastically received in Renaissance poetics, Horace's observation that poets aim either to be useful or to give delight, and ideally do both, contains the idea that poetic instruction contributes to moral integrity. Spenser, aware of how necessary it was to please an Elizabethan audience by rhetorical *copia*, or 'variety of matter,' intended that audience to see patterns for virtuous conduct in the knights of *The Faerie Queene*.[75] Ben Jonson fashioned the poet after Cicero's orator, a man possessed of wisdom and universal knowledge whose ethical instruction shapes the morals and religion of the state: 'I could never thinke the study of *Wisdome* confin'd only to the Philosopher: or of *Piety* to the *Divine*: or of *State* to the *Politicke*. But that he which can faine a *Commonwealth* (which is the *Poet*) can governe it with *Counsels*, strengthen it with *Lawes*, correct it with *Judgements*, informe it with *Religion*, and *Morals*; is all these. Wee doe not require in him meere *Elocution*; or an excellent faculty in verse; but the exact knowledge of all vertues, and their Contraries; with ability to render the one lov'd, the other hated, by his proper embattling them.'[76] Poetry was considered useful, an art that could implant moral precepts with all the efficacy of rhetoric, if not more – at any rate, more than philosophy. Bacon and Sidney saw rhetoric and poetry, respectively, as superior to philosophy in their ability to render virtue attractive through 'pictures' aimed at the imagination. All the major schools of Renaissance poetics, Horatian, Aristotelian, Platonic, and rhetorical, viewed poetry as a vehicle of moral edification.[77] Rhetoric and poetry were intertwined in terms of *sententiae*, by their ethical purposiveness, and again in terms of style, by their shared patterns of figurative language.

Renaissance humanists believed that numerous qualities of rhetoric could stir people to virtuous behaviour, including its didactic function, fortified with the power to delight and move. These features suited rhetoric to a variety of uses in religious matters. Theology was the queen of the sciences, and the very universality that made rhetoric the queen of the liberal arts during the Renaissance ensured that the two disciplines would coalesce. Milton, the representative Christian humanist of the seventeenth century, could take for granted the conjunction of rhetoric and faith, thanks in part to the efforts of two of the leading humanists of the fifteenth and sixteenth centuries, Valla and Erasmus. Both sought to establish the theological relevance of the humanistic disciplines, applying them to illuminating and disseminating religious doctrine, a pragmatism that placed rhetoric in the service of Christianity. In this endeavour, the utility of rhetoric was beyond question. Having made logic a subsection of rhetoric – less expressive and concerned only with teaching, whereas rhetoric teaches, delights, and moves – Valla limns his favourite art in its familiar ethical contours: 'the orator does not only aim at victory or always occupy himself with lawsuits, but also in urging honourable things and those which belong to living well and happily, and in dissuading people from disgraceful and useless things. He praises what merits praise, and condemns what merits disparagement.' The classical image of the legal pleader gives way to a description of the office of the contemporary orator. Zealous to incite his audience to virtue 'because we seem to be born to praise the works of God and the creator himself,'[78] he uses rhetoric to force home a Christian moral philosophy. Ethical persuasion stems from the rhetoric of epideixis, or praise and blame.

For one who would persuade an audience within this paradigm, Valla believes that 'a knowledge of divine things, rectitude of life, and gravity of character are indispensable.'[79] Character receives special emphasis. Valla's orator, in two familiar formulations, must be a good man in order to speak persuasively and must observe decorum in living a grave and dignified life, just as he must do so in the related enterprise, involving similar discretion, of achieving a level of style appropriate for the matter being treated (III. proem, 4). The orator, moreover, should exhibit modesty – apprehension and fear rather than boldness and confidence – in venturing to speak about divine things. Like Augustine, Valla aligns classical rhetorical principles with Christian coordinates, as, for example, the advice of Quintilian (Valla's favourite rhetorician) to kindle in oneself the emotions one would transfer to an audience: 'No one can set other souls on fire with the love of divine things if he himself remains cold to them' (III. proem, 3).[80] It is for this reason also that a person of bad character, who nevertheless speaks well, cannot speak persuasively, since uninspired words fall flat.

An attribute as important as the good character of Valla's orator is his style. The key feature of eloquence is *copia*, 'which makes a matter clear and places it before our eyes ... influences the minds of men, and displays all the ornaments, splendors and riches of eloquence. It carries the listener away and then brings him back to himself, and it gathers around itself almost all other merits of oratory' (II. proem, 1). According to the Renaissance norm, stylistic fluency combined with wisdom was the acme of rhetorical achievement. When that wisdom was the highest of all – the knowledge of divine things – the resources of a copious stylistic grandeur were most necessary. Valla praises the Church Fathers, devoted to the imitation of Paul, for yoking eloquence and theology: 'Such is [Paul's] manner of speaking, such his forcefulness, such his majesty, that those phrases which in others, even the apostles, are flat, are elevated in him, those which in others stand inactive do battle in him, those which in others scarcely glow seem in him to shine out and burn brightly. Hence it is not without reason that he is pictured holding in his hand a sword, which is the word of God. This is the true and, so to speak, the legitimate theology, this is the true norm of speaking and of writing, and those who pursue it are certainly pursuing the best kind of eloquence and of theology.'[81] These pursuits did not occupy medieval scholastics. The ancients had eloquence but lacked true wisdom; the scholastics had the revealed wisdom of Christianity but lacked eloquence. It was now for the Renaissance theologian, mindful of the ideal union of form and content, cognizant of decorum, to lift up the one to the level of the other by imitating the rhetorical example of Paul and the Fathers. A forceful, majestic style has crucial significance; as seen earlier, such a style was traditionally deemed an irresistible means of persuasion, and persuasion in Christian rhetoric is nothing less than turning listeners towards the path of salvation. Thus, Valla writes in De voluptate that he will compose the encomium of heaven 'in the most splendid possible manner, in order to recall the souls of the listeners to the hope of the true good' (I. proem, 7).

These principles of theologia rhetorica are embodied in Antonio da Rho, Valla's authorial spokesman in De voluptate, whose oration in praise of Christian pleasure rebuts Catone Sacco's Stoic viewpoint and the Epicureanism of Maffeo Vegio. The dialogue's structure, composed of three orations, exemplifies the rhetorical strategy of debating a question in utramque partem, which posits nothing as certain but advances competing opinions and compares them in order to reach as close an approximation to the 'truth' as an epistemology grounded in contingency will allow.[82] The rhetorical procedure of De voluptate is heuristic, searching out the truth in relation to virtue and pleasure. The climax of da Rho's oration, the encomium of heaven, itself constitutes a reverently tentative search for the nature of the pleasure to be found in beatitude. This undertaking, he says, 'will serve the double purpose,' rhetorical on both counts, 'of infusing faith in [my audience] and increasing hope and charity in ourselves' (III. xx. 2). Faith is central to da Rho's Christian rhetoric. As the underpinning of Christian virtue and an attendant conception of true pleasure, it is what an audience must be persuaded to embrace, and what the orator himself must possess in order to move them to do so.

Faith is distinguished by a recognition that human inquiry cannot grasp the divine mysteries (III. vii. 7). Yet Valla's pious orator uses rhetoric to make precisely this kind of inquiry, having reproached scholastic philosophy, incapable of reaching into such matters, for presuming to know the unknowable. In the effort to approach elusive truths through language, Valla's attitude recalls Lucretius, 'seeking by what words and what poetry at last I may be able to display clear lights before your mind, whereby you may see into the heart of things hidden.'[83] Eloquent men, to a greater degree than musicians and visual artists, enable their audience to come near to divine things.[84] Their rhetoric forces even the hidden truth to appear by employing a variety of techniques. A few may be quickly noted. An ekphrasis of Jerusalem vividly depicts the empyreal city of Revelation 21. Da Rho then amplifies the desirability of attaining sight of it by arguing *a fortiori*. Men have taken great pleasure in experiencing the cities, customs, foods, and wonders of foreign lands: if all this is so, 'then what marveling, sweetness and joy will fill your senses when this amazing and unexpected structure offers itself glittering to your eyes?' (III. xxv. 5). Da Rho describes heaven by such *a fortiori* analogies on several occasions (III. xxiii. 6, xxiv. 20, xxv. 16). While the rhetorical force of doing so is evident, the technique is nevertheless an acknowledgment that even eyes cleared by faith cannot envision, nor can speech uttered with apostolic eloquence evoke, images sufficient for presenting to man the condition of the ascending soul and the nature of beatitude. A rhetoric of speculation tries to discover inscrutable knowledge, juxtaposing the glories of the familiar world with the unimaginable glories of heaven. By these means mortal listeners are enabled to glimpse the light hidden from full view, their sight, darkened by the Apostle's glass, temporarily illuminated. At times the gulf between heaven and earth overwhelms da Rho's discourse, as when he tries to relate the blessed ascent of the virtuous Christian: 'How could I recall the particulars of all this? ... What may I say here?

What eloquence, what fluency, what genius is needed, not only to cele-brate so great a good but simply to relate it! For this I lack both concepts and words' (III. xxv. 22–3). This type of 'inexpressiblity topos' confesses a perceived failure to address the topic[85] and an attendant failure of lan-guage. It is rhetorically effective, however, in that it invites the listener to use his own imagination in attempting to picture what the orator has declined to express. Moreover, da Rho has given a remarkable depic-tion of what he has said he cannot describe: 'Faith is strengthened greatly if we do get to see what is promised' (III. xx. 2). His listeners, and he himself, have seen, and confess themselves taught, delighted, and moved by da Rho's evocative and poetic eloquence (III. xxvi. 1 – xxvii. 3). Valla's Christian rhetoric simultaneously recognizes its limita-tions, pulling back diffidently where faith dictates while still searching into divine truths in an effort to strengthen faith with all the available resources of eloquence.

Valla's belief that the study of Christian doctrine should abandon its dependence on dialectic and cultivate the ancient languages was taken up by Erasmus, who recognized the importance of rhetoric and rhetor-ical modes of thinking in all fields of learning and who combined phi-lology and rhetoric into the most comprehensive program of humanist theology to emerge from the Renaissance. Erasmus struck a Vallan counterpoise between faith and human learning, maintaining that ratio-nal inquiry into divine mysteries was improper, that the theologian should be content with a partial vision and rely on faith in such matters, but at the same time that grammar and rhetoric applied to sacred texts could elucidate the Word of God, embodied in Christ.[86] Christ is the speech of God, the divine *sermo* who mediates between God and man and whose own rhetorical speech, veiled in parables and allegories, marked him for Erasmus as both an orator and a poet. Christ's speech, it followed, along with that of the prophets, admitted of rhetorical inter-pretation in order to be understood. Erasmus's theologian, therefore, needed a firm grasp of rhetorical tropes and figures, especially allegory, beneath which much of the Bible's meaning was concealed. His exeget-ical rhetoric was a tool of inquiry, a method of discovering scriptural truths. Once understood, the Word had to be disseminated throughout the Christian commonwealth. To this end, the theologian, himself a mediator, should imitate Christ in persuading, reconciling, and saving men, relating the divine eloquence revealed in Scripture by means of the resources of human eloquence, patterned after the rhetoric of Christ, the apostles, and the Fathers. For Erasmus, 'a theologian is a pious man, skilled in speaking of the divine mysteries,'[87] whose role is 'to discourse about piety gravely and efficaciously; to wring out tears, to inflame spirits to heavenly things.'[88] While the theologian's style achieved these effects, it also expressed the purity of his own religious and ethical disposition. As for theological education, a familiarity with the three holy languages (Hebrew, Greek, and Latin) should precede a knowledge of grammar and rhetoric, and Erasmus believed that the classical *bonae litterae* prepared one for the study of *sacrae litterae*.

Imbued with this harmonization of pagan and Christian, the last published treatise of Erasmus's life, *Ecclesiastae, sive de ratione concionandi libri quator*, expounds the utility of rhetoric for both hermeneutics and preaching. I will discuss this pivotal book more fully in chapter 5, as it exerts a major influence on the tradition of religious rhetoric that underlies *Paradise Lost*. For the time being we may note generally that it reflects how Erasmus, like Valla, found in Augustine a model of how to adapt classical principles, such as the *ornatus* of tropes and figures, to Christian needs. The Christian context validated rhetoric and framed its entire purpose: 'Now we will treat the several duties of the orator, but only in such a way that you may remember that we instruct not a legal advocate, but a herald of the word of God.'[89] The same maxim that governed ecclesiastical rhetoric, that the goal of all learning and eloquence was to know and celebrate Christ, covered secular forms as well. Classicism divorced from a Christian outlook at any time was irreverent and myopic, cutting off its practitioners from the true aims of rhetoric, centred in Christ; from a due appreciation of biblical style; and from the practice of true eloquence, which consisted in wisdom expressed copiously and in harmony with decorum: 'There is nothing to stop anyone from speaking in a manner that is both Christian and Ciceronian, if you allow him to be a Ciceronian when he speaks clearly, richly, forcefully and appropriately in keeping with the nature of his subject and with circumstances of the times and of the persons involved. Some people have indeed suggested that the ability to speak well is not a question of skill, but of prudence. Cicero himself neatly defines eloquence in his *Partitiones* as "wisdom speaking copiously," nor is there any doubt that this is the type of eloquence that he himself practised.'[90] Rhetorical prudence here carries its familiar meaning of attention to decorum – to the demands of audience, time, subject, and so forth[91] – and, in the case of Erasmus, the ethical signification necessarily rests alongside it. *Prudentia* also implies another kind of judgment related to the ethical, that which wisely establishes Christianity as the foundation of all oratory.

Whatever the topic, theological or otherwise, the spirit of Christ must animate it. Classical principles of composition, employed in producing a style that is correct, copious, forceful, and ornate, are practised in vain unless that eloquence expresses a speaker or writer's faith, anchored in divine wisdom. An oration that unites faith with a graceful style, tailored to its subject, observes decorum in its fullest sense, for it is appropriate ethically and theologically as well as stylistically – dimensions that always complement one another in the Erasmian conjunction of *ratio* and *oratio*, wisdom and eloquence.

With Erasmus's and Valla's endorsements of classical rhetoric as a suitable infrastructure for articulating Christian themes, our survey of Renaissance rhetoric comes to a close. Its intention has been to orient us in the literary world of the original reader of *Paradise Lost*, a world in which classical tradition and the humanist educational system had established rhetoric as a major convention, amounting virtually to a code of formal laws, in the fields of moral philosophy, politics, theology, and poetry. It was such a world, imported to England by writers such as Thomas Elyot, Roger Ascham, and John Colet, that Milton was born into and educated in and that naturally influenced his own ideas about rhetoric. Next, we will see that Milton's concept of the *ars dicendi* both reflects and refines many of the ideas discussed so far. History will take its place among the rhetorical disciplines, and religion will be shown to be a theme of central importance to rhetoric, particularly to Milton's understanding and application of the rhetorical arts. And so let us prepare to exchange the studious concentration of the classrooms and writing cells of the humanists for a more ardent state of mind, the emotion that so often motivates eloquence in *Paradise Lost*. That emotion is love.

4 Milton's Concept of Rhetoric

And out of his mouth goeth a sharp sword.

Revelation 19.15

What is it to love the truth? In one of hundreds of such cases, John Foxe reports the testimony of five Protestant martyrs who 'refused to recant and deny the received and infallible truth' before their Marian inquisitors in the spring of 1557. '"My lord,"' Henry Ramsey asks Bishop Bonner, '"will you have me go from the truth that I am in? I say unto you, that my opinions be the very truth, which I will stand unto, and not go from them: and I say unto you further, that there are two churches upon the earth, and we," meaning himself, and other true martyrs and professors of Christ, "be of the true church, and ye be not."' His companions stood down inquisition with the same righteous certainty, though they all knew that loving the truth, imitating the Saviour's love, meant giving up everything for it with a joyful heart: 'the sheriff of London ... who being thereunto commanded, the 12th day of the same month of April, brought them into Smithfield, where altogether in one fire most joyfully and constantly they ended their temporal lives, receiving therefor the life eternal.'[1]

The incident raises questions concerning the nature of this truth that many Englishmen, including Milton, loved so completely, questions particularly concerning its relationship with rhetoric. Milton considered true eloquence 'to be none, but the serious and hearty love of truth,' an idea, to be taken up shortly, that breathes life into his concept of rhetoric as a powerful instrument for sowing truth of the kind that the martyrs loved and died for – the kind of truth that would eventually find its fullest voice with the aid of poetry, rhetoric, and, Milton believed, divine inspiration.

England's path to greatness, Milton insisted repeatedly, lay through education. The religious and political reforms necessary to raise up the nation needed to begin in the schools. Central to Milton's pedagogy was 'a noble education not in grammar only, but in all liberal arts and exercises.' Milton believed, like Isocrates, that the idea of a proud and united nation, consolidated in the teaching of these arts, would foster a spiritual rebirth. Such a comprehensive educational system, he wrote on the eve of the Restoration, 'would soon make the whole nation more industrious, more ingenuous at home, more potent, more honorable abroad' and its people 'flourishing, virtuous, noble and high spirited' (*YP*, 7: 460). Milton himself had taken a direct interest in how to teach two arts of the trivium, publishing both a Latin grammar (*Accedence Commenc't Grammar* in 1649) and a recension of Peter Ramus's logic (*Artis logicae plenior institutio* in 1672). To the third, rhetoric, he devoted no formal treatise; yet rhetoric took pride of place in Milton's assembly of the arts. He defined eloquence humanistically – in the manner outlined in the previous chapter – as comprising ethics and oratory. In his career as a polemicist for the Commonwealth, he had envisaged eloquence as the star to which England might hitch the aspirations for greatness and nobility that lay potentially within reach. And in the career of his divine calling, rhetoric was integral to his poetics. His thoughts about rhetoric – what it was and what it was meant to do – can be derived from two sources: first, from his own rhetorical practice, in both the prose and the poetry; second, from remarks in his writings that touch either parenthetically or directly on the nature of oratory. As for his practice, the rhetoric of his poetry, mainly of *Paradise Lost*, will be addressed in later chapters, while his use of rhetoric in his prose works lies outside the scope of this book. Let us turn, then, to the second source of information, Milton's remarks on the subject in his prose, in order to assess the vision of rhetoric that he would bring to *Paradise Lost*.

Milton went to school at a time when rhetoric was flourishing in England. His formal education, first at St Paul's and then at Cambridge, consisted largely of exercises aimed at increasing a student's facility with rhetorical techniques in his own speech and writing. As a boy, for example, he learned a two-step method of literary imitation that moved from analysis, the study of a model to ascertain how its excellences followed artistic rules, to genesis, the composition of imitative exercises.[2] Rhetoric was one of the main features to be emulated – Milton's copy of

John Harrington's translation of *Orlando Furioso* is filled with rhetorical annotations, such as the various tropes and figures he had identified.[3] Milton had a synoptic mastery of the major schools in the classical rhetorical tradition, evident in the full curriculum of writers, Greek as well as Latin, that he proposed in *Of Education* for 'a gracefull and ornate Rhetorick' to be taught alongside poetics. Milton reveals a scholar's knowledge of the art elsewhere from time to time, as when he claims, by way of justifying his own declamatory practice, that he could cite 'the rules of the best rhetoricians, and the famousest examples of the Greek and Roman Orations' to sanction his derisive tone or his arguing *ad hominem* (*YP*, 1: 899–901). In the exordia of his prolusions, academic exercises that demonstrated a university student's command of the orator's craft, Milton occasionally mentions before his Cambridge audience the very art he was engaged in. He refers to the necessity, noted by the ancients, of securing an audience's good will; to the need for an orator to know all arts and sciences; and to Cicero's authority concerning the orator's fundamental duties of teaching, delighting, and persuading or moving an audience (*YP*, 1: 218, 288, 241).

Of these three duties, Rudolph Agricola writes, 'to teach is indeed an easy thing, which anyone who is not exceedingly slow of mind will be able to perform. But to move your auditor through the affections, and to alter his state of mind in whatever way you please, and to win him over; to hold him suspended by the pleasure of listening – that is not possible except by the highest and greatest talents, incited by a certain inspiration of the Muses.'[4] The ability to move an auditor by emotional appeal fascinated humanists such as Milton and gave eloquence the power of persuasion, as Nicholas Caussin wrote in 1630, one and a half centuries after Agricola: 'And indeed the power of this eloquence, which rules in the domain of the passions, is supreme: for it controls assemblies of men, wins over minds, drives wills towards the direction it wishes and leads them away from the direction it wishes; it lends aid to supplicants, raises those who have been struck down, brings salvation to the accused, frees us from dangers; in a word, it establishes a sort of benign tyranny in the hearts of men.'[5] Such comments recall the effects of 'that great & forcible floud of Eloquence,' to be poured forth by rhetorical figures, that we saw Henry Peacham describe in the preceding chapter. The power of eloquence resides in its ability to seize the affections. In one of his Cambridge orations, Milton observes that rhetoric 'so captivates the minds of men and draws them after it so gently enchained that it has the power of moving them to pity, now of inciting them to hatred, now of arousing them to warlike valour, now of inspiring them beyond fear of death' (*YP*, 1: 244). Here he invokes Hercules Gallicus, who, 'being a man of great wisdom, had all men linked together by the ears in a chain to draw them and lead them even as he lusted. For his wit was so great, his tongue so eloquent, and his experience such, that no one man was able to withstand his reason, but everyone was rather so driven to do that which he would, and to will that which he did, agreeing to his advice both in word and work in all that ever they were able.'[6] Hercules Gallicus was a standard Renaissance emblem of the captivating power of eloquence, a power that Milton would later ascribe to his own rhetoric. In the exordium of *A Second Defence of the English People*, he writes of those members of his international audience who, 'conquered at last by the truth, acknowledge themselves my captives' (*YP*, 4i: 555).

Able to lead minds 'enchained' and to make 'captives' of its audience, rhetoric is a capability as great as any that a man could possess. Gerardus Vossius addresses the psychological explanation behind its power; he has already treated demonstrative arguments and proofs, 'but men are incited not only by reason but also by passion – the great part of them, indeed, only by the latter. Therefore we will now come to *pathē* or the passions ... since they are useful for persuading, at one time by arousing the passions, at another by soothing them.'[7] Milton, who may have read Vossius while at St Paul's,[8] similarly believed that rhetoric had to proceed affectively: 'For truth ... hath this unhappinesse fatall to her, ere she can come to the triall and inspection of the Understanding, being to passe through many little wards and limits of the severall Affections and Desires, she cannot shift it, but must put on such colours and attire, as those Pathetick handmaids of the soul please to lead her in to their Queen' (*YP*, 1: 830). Conviction is best secured by appealing to the emotions, owing to the defects of one's hearers. When speaking 'among wise and judicious men,' writes Vossius, 'there is no need to stir up their affections; however, among unsophisticated people, who give little weight to rational considerations, it is absolutely necessary to move their minds, so that they may be more readily led towards virtuous actions ... We are also taught that it is right to do so by the example of Jesus, Paul and other divine prophets, who, not content [simply] to teach, also stir up the affections.'[9] Rhetoric accommodates people 'of a soft and delicious temper who will not so much as look upon Truth herselfe, unlesse they see her elegantly drest' (*YP*, 1: 817–18) in the colours and attire of rhetoric.

Tropes and figures appeal to this kind of temper. Whereas Peacham asserted their power to move by arousing strong emotions, Peter Mosellanus notes their capacity to sway an audience in a gentler manner, by playing on aesthetic sensibilities: 'discourse that is not regular in all respects, but scattered about with appropriate figures and variegated with suitable tropes, enchains the ears of listeners and deserves applause.'[10] *Delectare* can achieve the same persuasive result as *movere*, on a different wavelength of eloquence. Pleasure works affectively as well; delightful rhetorical colours excite emotions that in turn lead truth to 'their Queen,' the soul – the intellective soul of understanding or reason. Considerable critical attention has been given to the ability of rhetorical devices, especially the *figurae sententiarum* (figures of thought) of the grand style, to rouse volatile emotions such as anger, fear, indignation, and pity, with a correspondingly strong persuasive effect. But the state of being charmed by words, of being 'suspended by the pleasure of listening,' as Agricola said, is a dimension of eloquence that has been relatively overlooked. In the Renaissance it was related partly to the literary aesthetic of the age, the pleasure of listening or reading as much for the manner of the discourse as the matter, when the audience recognized the author displaying the verbal dexterity that reflected a linguistic heritage, an appreciation for sparkling rhetorical style, that both parties shared. Mosellanus likened this pleasure to viewing a colourful painting or walking in a flowery meadow. The power of eloquence, from this point of view, is a cultural phenomenon as well as a psychological one, made possible by a humanist educational system that elevated the prestige of the *ars dicendi* in all its detailed formal systems.

Although Milton knew the rules of composition, he downplayed theoretical knowledge as incidental to a true understanding of rhetoric. The hedge against rules was an element of Colet's pedagogy that perhaps rubbed off on Milton when he was at St Paul's: 'For redying of good bokes, diligent informacyon of taught maysters, studyous advertance & takynge hede of lerners, heryng eloquent men speke, and fynally easy imitacyon with tongue and penne, more avalyleth shortly to gete the true eloquent speche than al the tradicions, rules, and preceptes of maysters.'[11] Rules often encumber: 'how many despicable quibbles there are in grammar and rhetoric!' (*YP*, 1: 300) Epic poets, for example, should know when to leave off following rules in favour of cultivating individual talent: 'whether the rules of Aristotle herein are strictly to be kept, or nature to be follow'd, which in them that know art, and use judgement is no transgression, but an inriching of art' (*YP*, 1: 813). Milton understates his own acquaintance with prescriptive rules in order to set off the more inclusive definition of rhetoric mentioned earlier: 'For me, readers, although I cannot say that I am utterly untrain'd in those rules which best Rhetoricians have giv'n, or unacquainted with those examples which the prime authors of eloquence have written in any learned tongue, yet true eloquence I find to be none, but the serious and hearty love of truth' (*YP*, 1:.948–9). In asking what truth is, both here and for rhetoric in general, we may stay for an answer by revisiting Plato. 'There is not nor ever shall be,' wrote Plato, 'a general art of speaking which is divorced from grasp of the truth.'[12] Milton's statement acknowledges this core principle of Platonic rhetoric, yet it goes further: not only must a successful orator grasp the truth, he must also love it. The deeper level of engagement is telling, for it gets at the critical distinction between truth in Plato's terms and as Milton understood it. The matter of differentiating and defining truth, and thereby illuminating Milton's concept of rhetoric, turns on religion.

Truth for Milton was defined mainly by his religious beliefs, a fact so evident as to otherwise pass over were not its implications fundamental to his vision of rhetoric as a purposeful and valuable art. While Protestants and Catholics alike claimed privileged access to Christian truth, the Calvinist-Puritan overtones that imbued Milton's religious make-up placed him in a tradition that seized this claim with fanatical conviction. Instances abound of the extremity of religious belief in England; from their narratives emerges a portrait of the truth on which those beliefs were founded. As shown in the testimony of Henry Ramsey and his fellow martyrs in *The Acts and Monuments*, Christian truth is infallible and exclusive: 'we ... be of the true church, and ye be not.' Its epistemology conflates typically discrete states of apprehending the truth: opinion and knowledge. Opinion is an intermediary state, 'something darker than knowledge but brighter than ignorance,' which apprehends only the semblance of eternal, unchanging truth that is the province of knowledge;[13] in religion, however, 'opinions *be* the very truth,' their normative basis in probability and subjective belief having been swept away by the force of sectarian zeal. The martyr's love convinces him, far beyond the reach of any counter-argument, that the opinion of his doctrine is the absolute truth, the sublime knowledge formerly reserved for Plato's philosopher and now imagined to be possessed solely by members of 'the true church.' It was more to be wished for than dreaded that loving the sanctified truth might come at the price, gladly paid, of exchanging one's temporal life for life everlasting.

Socrates paid the same price for a similar love, but Plato's rhetorical truth is of a different, more practical order. One kind of dialectic, in the *Republic*, is used to approach the mystical Form of the Good, from which all subsequent knowledge is deduced. This method prepares the philosopher's ascent to universal truth. In the *Phaedrus*, another kind of dialectic defines a subject through collection or division in order to generate probable arguments about it. When Plato refers to an art of speaking whose practitioners grasp the truth, he means truth in this limited, provisional sense of understanding a subject just well enough to argue about it in a manner that will bring an audience around to the speaker's point of view. Rhetorical truth, then, so called, is merely the speaker's opinion that he would have his audience *accept* to be true. Although rhetorical truth ideally shares the qualities of its philosophical counterpart, manifesting a genuine knowledge of its subject, Plato states in the *Phaedrus* how matters really stand in public life, where 'probability is to be rated higher than truth' (267A). Plato and Aristotle define probability differently, the distinction being that while Plato the moralizer judges it, Aristotle the systematizer does not. Aristotle treats it as a neutral component within the art of rhetoric, defining probability as that which happens for the most part. Plato, on the other hand, holds it to moral account. He gives it a pejorative connotation, drawing attention to its potential abuse by defining it as a resemblance to truth – an opinion – that the public finds acceptable. Orators, he knew, do not love the truth; they don't even respect it, nor should they: 'Never mind the truth – pursue probability through thick and thin in every kind of speech; the whole secret of the art of speaking lies in consistent adherence to this principle' (272E–273A). There is no love in Plato's rhetoric, no philosophical knowledge or eternal truth on which to build a system of belief. There are only the ever-changing variables of situation and moment, of *kairos*, that the successful orator needs to control as tightly as possible in order to win hearts and minds.

Love is the key differentiating feature between this and the Christian concept of truth. Its presence or absence has clear implications for rhetoric. Subtract love, and rhetoric appears in Plato's terms as the calculated manipulation of probability and opinion in order to mislead an audience (a purpose we will examine in depth later). The addition of Christian love completely redefines probability and opinion and, along with them, the purpose of rhetoric. Probability now becomes certainty, causing opinion to be dichotomized: preferred opinion is truth, competing opinion is error. Rhetoric is an evangelical tool for bringing those in error to love the indisputable, univocal truth of God's Word, which by nature cannot mislead. Eve wanders from this truth, which presides over the rhetorical universe of *Paradise Lost*, in a collision of these two rhetorics. Led astray by Satan's eloquence, which assaults truth with opinion and probable argument exactly as Plato says it should, she is misdirected from loving the truth, embodied in the sole command and inculcated by Adam and Raphael.

Milton joins rhetoric to eternal truth. He sets it in the world of Christian absolutes, where love takes opinion and truth for the same thing: 'I claim no eloquence except that which lies in truth itself' (*YP*, 4i: 604). Claiming alliance with absolute truth argues correspondingly absolute rhetorical authority – a standard polemical tactic, yet nonetheless sincere in Milton's case. So it was for Oliver Cromwell, who appealed to truth in a similar way. Certain that his wishes reflected the will of God, who was enlisted on behalf of the army, the man for whom Milton wrote propaganda ruled on a platform of divine sanction, to which he appealed at every turn in order to justify political expediency. Scarcely a moment passes in his extant speeches without reference to God's inspiring, protecting, guiding, blessing, or seconding him in his actions. The Protector was so carried away by righteous fervour that he frequently wept during his parliamentary orations.[14] It was not an uncommon state for men who combined a certain religious temperament with gifts of rhetorical expression; the passion in themselves that they would arouse in others was one of those gifts. In speaking out against prelaty Milton felt himself inflamed, 'transported with the zeale of truth to a well heated fervencie' (*YP*, 1: 663). Much of his writing shows him fixed on pursuing a millennial vision rooted in truths, civil and religious, that he believed in beyond the shadow of a doubt. Of war he observes, 'Victory is based, not on Strength or Military Experience, but on whether he who begins the war has God on his side' (*YP*, 1: 498). In his polemical wars he, like Cromwell, believed that God was on his side, whether he started the conflict or was provoked, and that his arguments accordingly rang with absolute truth: 'I have written nothing of such a kind that I was not then and am not now convinced that it was right and true and pleasing to God ... I care little for victory, provided that truth be victorious' (*YP*, 4i: 587, 661). Milton was cut from martyrs' cloth. He loved God, and God repaid that love by kindling in him the fires of eloquence and sanctifying him as the golden-tongued instrument of Reformed truth.

Rhetoric's chief value was that it promulgated truth. As it had been for Valla and Erasmus, the truth that Milton's orator must possess is Christian wisdom – or, in light of rhetoric's strong ties with ethics, Christian moral philosophy grounded in the authority of the Word. Milton describes the Christian orator's responsibility when he distinguishes the lower wisdom of contemplating natural causes from the higher wisdom that occupies the person 'who hath obtain'd in more than the scantest measure to know anything distinctly of God and of his true worship ... the only high valuable wisdom indeed.' The orator must particularly direct his energies to 'how and in what manner he shall dispose and employ those summes of knowledge and illumination, which God hath sent him into this world to trade with' (YP, 1: 801). Knowing God and his true worship means distinguishing good from evil and applying that knowledge towards living by God's commands. Milton implies that for the eloquent Christian the burden of this divine wisdom is not so much acquiring it as transferring it to others, a communicative office, in the humanist tradition, that devolves to rhetoric. For clearly, the task to 'dispose' these 'summes of knowledge and illumination,' and to determine 'in what manner' to dispose them, implies three of the main offices of classical rhetoric: *dispositio, inventio*, and *elocutio*. Classical method and sacred wisdom formed an easy concord by the mid-seventeenth century, thanks to the authoritative influence of writers such as Augustine and Erasmus, who will be discussed in the next chapter. Milton's enthusiastic advocacy of studying profane writers suggests that, like Lorenzo Valla, he unreservedly adopted the classical system of rhetoric; he noted approvingly that it was among the arts that had advanced early Christianity (YP, 1: 377; 2: 510).

Rhetoric's primary claim to legitimacy in the Christian era was its origin, shared with all other arts: 'I am supposing that no one doubts that the primary efficient source of an art is God, the author of all wisdom. Even the ancient philosophers were aware of this' (YP, 8: 213). Rhetoric was a divine art, and it informed two other divine arts, poetry and preaching. From descriptions Milton gives of poetry and preaching, we see that rhetoric subsumes both: poetry is in one sense very much like preaching, and preaching is very much like rhetoric. All three are concerned with persuasion: 'These [poetic] abilities are the inspired guift of God rarely bestow'd ... and are of power beside the office of a pulpit, to imbreed and cherish in a great people the seeds of vertu, and publick civility' (YP, 1: 816). 'Certainly there is no imployement more honourable, more worthy to take up a great spirit, more requiring a generous and free nurture, then to be the messenger, and Herald of heavenly truth from God to man, and by the faithfull worke of holy doctrine, to procreate a number of faithfull men, making a kind of creation like to Gods, by infusing his spirit and likenesse into them, to their salvation, as God did into him' (*YP*, 1: 721). Milton's descriptions of the powers of these two types of speech correspond with the rhetorical-ethical assessment of them in the Renaissance. Both the poet and the preacher, having received their knowledge and abilities as a divine gift, have a rhetorical calling: the poet, to persuade to virtue; the preacher, to persuade to a love of holy doctrine, thereby assisting in salvation. We should note that while Milton's concept of poetry as a divinely inspired gift is conventional, he means it to be taken literally, not as a hyperbolic turn of phrase. The image of the inspired poet was already old by the Middle Ages: 'Whoever was once a poet, that man was a vessel of God,' wrote Albertino Mussato.[15] Milton firmly believed this of himself. Poetry flows from God, as in *Paradise Lost*: 'Hail holy Light, offspring of Heav'n first-born ... Bright effluence of bright essence increate' (III. 1, 6). And God speaks through poets, 'for the poet is sacred to the gods, he is their priest.'[16]

Milton's lover of truth now turns to the rhetorical task of expressing his thoughts: 'Those whose mind so ever is fully possest with a fervent desire to know good things, and with dearest charity to infuse the knowledge of them into others, when such a man would speak, his words (by what I can express) like so many nimble and airy servitors trip about him at command, and in well order'd files, as he would wish, fall aptly into their own place' (*YP*, 1: 949). Christian zeal and charity eventually supersede training and adherence to rules as the keys to eloquence. Religious virtues inspire. When Milton says that apt words for expressing the truth fall into place as a matter of course, however, he is emphasizing the Platonic imperative to grasp the truth, not diminishing the application of style in rhetoric any more than Valla would have done. The linguistic art of *elocutio* always concerned the orator. Given that it was the core of the classical and Renaissance concept of eloquence, it is unlikely that Milton judged style to follow content as automatically as he makes out here. At St Paul's, in fact, a student's first imitative exercises concentrated on acquiring a correct and eloquent style, more advanced exercises on finding something to say.[17] Milton had learned style and technique prior to tackling subject matter, the very reverse of the process he outlines above. An eloquent style, the product of seasoning and maturity, could come intuitively only to one who had been drilled intensively in its theory, imitation, and practice.

Ideas and their production were similarly founded on theory and art. Although Milton contended that they materialized before the zealous writer, who, in a state of inspired receptivity, 'desire[d] to know good things' and to communicate that knowledge, he understood that rhetorical invention and disposition, at any rate for those learning to write, required more mundane assistance: 'Logic therefore so much as is usefull, is to be referr'd to this due place withall her well coucht heads and Topics, until it be time to open her contracted palm into a gracefull and ornate Rhetorick' (*YP*, 2: 402). Milton's prescription rests on the northern continental tradition, originating with Agricola's *De inventione dialectica libri tres*, which instituted a system of rhetoricized dialectical *topoi* – topics, or places, or commonplaces – that inquired into the nature and parts of a particular matter and constructed probable arguments about it on both sides. Milton's student prepared for rhetoric by first studying logic, especially these topics or commonplaces where material for invention could be found out or hunted after, each topic providing a different heading that prompted discourse on any subject and opened it to expansion. A cause, for example, could be distributed into its effects or a whole into its parts, or comparisons could be drawn, definitions given, and so forth, a mode of searching that eventually furnished probable arguments on either side of a question. When Milton compiled the topics in *The Art of Logic*, he would have had in mind this kind of application to rhetorical invention.

Eloquence for Milton, as for Plato, was more a philosophical and moral attitude than a linguistic art, a keenness to be wise before anything else. Knowing and loving the truth was an orator's first obligation. Hence, the poet-orator ought to find his motive for composition not in the execution of stylistic hat tricks, but in the desire to promulgate wisdom and virtue, as Milton implies in his avowal 'not to make verbal curiosities the end, that were a toylsom vanity, but to be an interpreter & relater of the best and sagest things' (*YP*, 1: 811). Thoughts and words, *res* and *verba*, were equally important and commanded equal attention. Humanists captured their interdependence in the metaphor of mind and body: 'We wish to stand firm,' wrote Mario Nizolio, 'both by the authority of the ancients and the testimony of Cicero, that philosophy and oratory are not two separate capabilities but are one and the same, composed out of thoughts and words, just as a living man is composed out of body and mind.'[18] Milton used another familiar metaphor to make the same point. In a poem he wrote at Cambridge he tells his 'native Language':

> I have some naked thoughts that rove about
> And loudly knock to have their passage out;
> And weary of their place do only stay
> Till thou hast deck't them in thy best array.[19]

In the image of words as clothing that will dress a writer's thoughts, Milton is acknowledging that style is an office of rhetoric no less important than that of invention. In the first place, it is simply indispensable. Without it, thoughts remain locked up; the poet is mute: 'sans l'Élocution serait inutile et sans fruit tout notre invention et disposition, ainsi q'un couteau demeurant en sa gaine.'[20] Beyond this necessity of enabling speech, style must also dress thoughts in the 'best array,' in diction that is – according to the four classical virtues – lucid, correct, ornate, and appropriate. Thomas Wilson writes that 'elocution ... with such beauty commendeth the matter that reason seemeth to be clad in purple, walking afore both bare and naked.'[21] For Erasmus as well, 'style is to thought as clothes are to the body,' an analogy he uses to explain the importance of paying close attention to *elocutio*: 'Just as dress and outward appearance can enhance or disfigure the beauty and dignity of the body, so words can enhance or disfigure thought. Accordingly a great mistake is made by those who consider that it makes no difference how anything is expressed, provided it can be understood somehow or other.'[22] Erasmus agreed with Ascham that it was not enough simply to be understood. The humanist believed that discourse, while it must be clear, must also be beautiful, dignified, abundant, and appropriate to the ideas it expresses. These stylistic features were cultural insignia, constituents of the *logos* that defined civilization, that opened to men the twin paths of wisdom and eloquence, and that could persuade others to follow virtue and shun vice. The weight that style carried for humanists registered on Milton, whose metaphors of clothing and captivity looked towards traditional Renaissance ideas about the nature of style. The thoughts of the reformer and the spiritual adviser waited to be elegantly dressed, to be animated by beautiful, enticing words that would create images to seize the emotions and lead minds enchained to right reason and salvation. Due application to style, moreover, indicated that those who practised it understood the primacy of language, possessed the socially cohesive values and rhetorical skills of the *logos*. A technical necessity, aesthetically desirable, vital for affective persuasion, and a cultural cachet, rhetorical style occupied Milton as much as it did his humanist forerunners. It stood alongside, rather than behind, the responsibility of Milton's orator to know the truth about the subject that he dealt with and to love the higher truth of which he was the messenger and herald.

Milton's concept of rhetoric included several kinds of discourse, all derived from God. Yet whether the rhetorician was a poet, a preacher, or a state orator, his character had to embrace a criterion that naturally co-existed with a love of the truth. In a tradition that passed from Isocrates, Plato, and the Roman rhetoricians through to the Renaissance, the eloquent man must be a good man. Milton repeats the proposition, with a characteristic emphasis on right reason: 'For doubtlesse that indeed according to art is most eloquent, which returnes and approaches nearest to nature from whence it came; and they express nature best, who in their lives least wander from her safe leading, which may be call'd regenerate reason. So that how he should be truly eloquent who is not withall a good man, I see not' (*YP*, 1: 874). The good man's adherence to the safe path of reason means, as we have seen, that he is prudent, both rhetorically and ethically. Following reason, *logos*, lets him ascertain how to say the right thing, which makes him eloquent, and how to do the right thing, which makes him virtuous. *Logos* comprises reason, wisdom, eloquence, and moral inquiry into right and wrong. Milton's ethical stance, therefore, is rhetorical in this Isocratean sense, a matter of discerning the right thing to do in the difficult and contingent world of moral choice: 'Good and evill we know in the field of this World grow up together almost inseparably; and the knowledge of good is ... involv'd and interwoven with the knowledge of evill, and in ... many cunning resemblances hardly to be discern'd' (*YP*, 2: 514).

But how was one to sift good from evil in finding the noblest way to act? How was one to arrive at the most fitting way to speak? Both, Milton believed, came down to decorum, 'the grand master peece to observe' (*YP*, 2: 405). Classical rhetoricians furnished the precedent for a twofold decorum of speech and life. 'In an oration, as in life,' writes Cicero, 'nothing is harder to determine than what is appropriate. The Greeks call it πρέπον; let us call it *decorum* ... The universal rule, in oratory as in life, is to consider propriety.' Living up to it, in the fleeting moment of *kairos*, is a cardinal virtue: 'To know what is appropriate to a particular occasion is a matter of prudence.' Quintilian adds, 'there is nothing not merely in oratory, but in all the tasks of life that is more important than prudence ... Again this same quality [*virtus*] teaches us to adapt our speech to circumstances of time and place and to the person with whom we are concerned.'[23] Prudence is the operative principle of decorum. It considers a given rhetorical situation or ethical decision in order to determine what is appropriate. The precise manner in which decorum is achieved, however, resists the explication of method. Isocrates believed that dealing with contingencies, both in speech and in life, defied the standardization of rules. Because every situation is unique, including rhetorical situations, no system of knowledge can account for the proper way to handle each one, which must be left to the philosophically educated man's 'powers of conjecture to arrive generally at the best course.'[24] Vives recognized that decorum in rhetoric and prudence in life each contemplated the best means for handling their respective circumstances. Although he suggested guidelines for meeting the requirements of decorum – including how to order arguments effectively, what qualities of style were suitable for various speakers and audiences, as well as for philosophy and for achieving *gravitas sententiae*, to name a few – he conceded beforehand that neither decorum nor prudence could be taught or systematized by rules: 'we can help it along by passing on techniques, but not bring it to perfection; encourage it, but not completely fix it in place.'[25] 'Herein resteth the difficultie,' George Puttenham writes of decorum, 'to know what this good grace is, & wherein it consisteth, for peradventure it be easier to conceave then to expresse.'[26] Longinus states that an understanding of sublime writing can be acquired, mainly through learning rhetoric; but literary judgment, the intuitive grasp of sublimity, 'comes only as the final product of long experience.'[27] There is no theory for acquiring it. Augustine stresses decorum continually, but distances it from art with his belief that it is inspired by God and that 'the appropriateness of the words' is 'determined by the ardour of the heart rather than by careful choice.'[28] Gasparus Laurentius denies that any art or set of rules can teach in detail how to comprehend and execute the forcible style (*deinos*) that results from intuitively discerning the various elements of decorum.[29]

Milton is no exception in this regard, as he does not elaborate what decorum is, how to attain it, or what art treats it. Indeed, the concept apparently does not yield to such scrutiny.[30] If not the definition, the *source* of Miltonic rhetorical decorum may at least be surmised. The taste and sound aesthetic judgment necessary for its practice originate, like many other qualities of eloquence, in the virtue that a person cultivates by following right reason: the eloquent man must be a good man.[31] Being good, he will thereby have tactful artistic discretion, which guarantees literary propriety. Training hones technical skills; reason and upright character bestow the fine evaluative sensibilities that an orator requires if he is to be attuned to the promptings of decorum. But propriety wore another face in seventeenth-century polemic, and the sensibilities exercised in its name were not always fine. Thomas Kranidas observes that the zeal of truth dearly held could burst forth in 'the flaming rhetoric of personal inspiration, a language of demand and of dismissed boundaries.'[32] Zeal tolerates no lukewarm adherence, advocates extremity as a virtue, and shatters moderate boundaries of decorum in dismissing opposing arguments out of hand, often in flagrantly abusive terms. Milton writes that even Christ and God sharpened their tone as the rhetorical situation demanded (*YP*, 1: 899–902); he could, if he wished, cite examples of *argumentum ad hominem* from illustrious orators, and no rhetorical law prohibits that practice (*YP*, 4ii: 734). Milton was suspicious of conventional decorum in any walk of life, and his recourse to 'offensive' language establishes his own contrasting decorum of vituperation and contempt, entirely appropriate under circumstances as he saw them. If decorum is 'the grand master peece to observe,' its Miltonic observation admits of fluent reinterpretation from one situation to the next, from the classroom to the pamphlet wars, from prelacy to political leadership, from urbane irony to thunderous excoriation. Such adaptability accords with the Roman and sophistic traditions of oratory, and particularly with the philosophy of Isocrates.

Milton repeatedly states that good character is a prerequisite of proficient speech or writing; therefore, 'he who would not be frustrate of his hope to write well hereafter in laudable things, ought him selfe to bee a true Poem, that is, a composition of the best and honorablest things' (*YP*, 1: 890). Only 'th'upright heart and pure' (*PL* I. 18), preferred by the muse, can hope to obtain 'answerable style' (*PL* IX. 20) in relating epic subjects. Milton maintained an Isocratean faith in the importance of *ethos* as a principle of education, for moulding good citizens, and in its efficacy as a principle of rhetoric, for persuading an audience. As Augustine writes, 'the life of the speaker has greater weight in determining whether he is obediently heard than any grandness of eloquence ... let him so order his life that he not only prepares a reward for himself, but also so that he offers an example to others, and his way of living may be, as it were, an eloquent speech.'[33] Milton had this principle in mind when, as a means of reinforcing his *ethos*, he identified his own voice with truth and goodness, dichotomized against the lies and evil of his opponent's voice. He believed, along with writers such as Erasmus, Vives, and Bacon, that *ratio* nurtured, and expressed itself in, *oratio*. Words showed a writer's moral constitution. On the grounds of this association, a fluent style conveyed the impression of a man of virtue[34] – and, by extension, trustworthiness. There was a direct relationship between a man's moral character and his aptitude for language: a good man was eloquent, a bad man was not.[35] With this in mind, Milton assaulted his opponents' rhetoric along with their characters. In his dispute against his most illustrious opponent, Claude Saumaise, he calls 'on almighty God, giver of all gifts, to grant that just success and righteousness ... so [he] may now with good success and in very truth refute and bring to naught the ill-tempered lies of this barbarous rhetorician' (*YP*, 4i: 305–6). The upright heart of the lover of truth flowed forth in eloquence and wisdom, whereas base characters, enemies of truth, produced barbarous, clumsy rhetoric and lies. Although such scathing remarks are to be read within their polemical context as *ad hominem* attacks, taken more generally they also sort with Milton's programmatic view of rhetoric, properly employed, as connected to wisdom and reason.

In Milton's scheme of wisdom, rhetoric – like the prudent man who employed it, and like any other art – had to be useful: 'Everyone agrees that what is taught should be useful in a man's life ... and that whatever does not aim at some good or utility in a man's life which is at the same time morally commendable, does not deserve the name of art, since to such good or utility all precepts of an art are referred. Therefore it necessarily follows that the form of an art is the laying down of precepts for something useful' (*YP*, 8: 214). Rhetoric is practical, to be used in the world, and Milton emphasizes its practicality with Roman insistence. He passed over rhetorical rules in order to define eloquence as a love of truth. Just as significantly, he observes that these rules, as applied in school exercises, operate in a moral and political vacuum where eloquence lies inertly starved of the element that gives it life, civic duty:

We who as youths under so many masters are accustomed to toil at imaginary eloquence, and think that its rhetorical force lies in invective no less than in praise, do at the desk bravely strike down, to be sure, the names of ancient tyrants. If chance allows, we kill Mezentius over and over again in stale antitheta, or with the sad bellowing of enthymemes, we burn alive Phalaris of Agrigentum, as in his own bull. I mean in the debating room or in the school of rhetoric ... And yet it were proper either not to have spent our youth in such imaginary eloquence, or, when it is needful to our country, when the Commonwealth requires it, casting exercise-shafts aside, now to venture into the sun, and dust, and field of battle, now to exert real brawn, brandish real arms, seek a real enemy. (YP, 4i: 795)

As Erasmus had said, 'armour is useless if it is good only for display, and so is not even ready to hand when action calls.'[36] Instilling the desire for public service and the upright character necessary to perform it is the true task of education. In Milton's school, for example, students would be trained in philosophy and rhetoric, 'forming them to be able writers and composers in every excellent matter ... fraught with an universall insight into things. Or whether they be to speak in Parliament or counsell, honour and attention would be waiting on their lips. There would then also appear in Pulpits other visages, other gestures, and stuffe otherwise wrought then what we now sit under' (YP, 2: 406). The wisdom of 'an universall insight into things' – acquired through philosophy, expressed publicly through rhetoric – would enable men to bring eloquence to the fore when the Commonwealth had need of it.

Eloquence, wisdom speaking copiously, was a civic virtue. For the statesman or churchman to undertake 'the guidance of a civill state to worldly happinesse,' he needed to combine 'contemplation and practice, wit, prudence, fortitude, and eloquence' (YP, 1: 753). Earlier termed 'the daughter of vertue' (YP, 1: 746),[37] eloquence is listed here in company that shades its meaning for Milton. Contemplation and practice are the two phases of Miltonic wisdom. Wit is reason or understanding, but also the stylistic harmonization of 'Thoughts and Words, elegantly adapted to the Subject'[38] – reason as manifesting the taste and judgment of decorum. Prudence and fortitude are distinctly republican virtues, those 'capacities that enable us willingly to serve the common good.'[39] Milton would exercise them when called to serve the Republic in March 1649, having been motivated 'solely by considerations of duty, honor, and devotion to my country' (YP, 4i: 587), even at the sacrifice of his remaining eyesight and depleted health. Eloquence assumes a natural place in this assembly of intellectual, literary, and social virtues, where rhetoric justifies itself as a useful art by furnishing the argumentative weaponry needed to engage the enemies of truth, thereby allowing the wise man to serve his country no less valuably than the soldier in the field. Milton writes that his own background in the liberal arts prepared him to defend 'the counsels of my country and ... this excellent cause' with words professing 'such wisdom as I owned' far better than he could have done by martial exertions: 'Truth defended by arms be also defended by reason – the only defence truly appropriate to man' (*YP*, 4i: 553).

In a grand flourish of peroration Milton compares himself to the classical world's most renowned defender of republicanism and its greatest orator in that cause. Just as Cicero had maintained 'that by his efforts alone he had saved the state and the city, so I too ... may venture this assertion at least, calling on God and men as my witnesses' (*YP*, 4i: 536). In the hands of the right men, and supported by complementary virtues, eloquence rendered invaluable service to the state, defending its freedom and advancing its rise to national greatness. Individual liberty thrived as a result. Rhetoric could be put to no greater use and achieve no higher good. But how much power does eloquence actually wield in the political sphere? Milton spoke more truly than he knew in 1651 in comparing himself to Cicero: neither man's oratory was ultimately able to save the state as the republican citadels of Rome and England fell to autarchic forces. Milton experienced at first hand the failure of eloquence in a good cause. He would later dramatize a similar failure in *Paradise Lost*, where Raphael's political rhetoric cannot avert man's deception at the hands of another accomplished orator, Satan, though the angel's failure is part of the providential scheme in which rhetoric, along with mankind, is eventually redeemed. Only that Redeemer, not rhetoric, can save the state.

Whatever degree of influence eloquence may have on directing the course of history, it plays a critical role in relating it. Throughout history it has been the case that 'great deeds often do not lack great relaters; as by a certain Fate great Acts and great Eloquence have most commonly gon hand in hand, equalling and honouring each other in the same Ages' (*YP*, 5i: 39–40). To be a relater of great deeds, which is the job of the historian, itself amounts to a vocation of greatness: 'He alone is to be called great who performs great deeds, or teaches how they may be done, or writes about them in terms becoming their greatness' (*YP*, 4i: 774). Writing about great deeds in fitting terms poses the greatest challenge to the historian, 'because the style must be equal to the deeds' according to Sallust, Milton's favourite historian. How may the historian acquire such a style? 'I think thus,' Milton wrote to Henry de Brass; 'he who would write worthily of worthy deeds ought to write with no less largeness of spirit and experience of the world than he who did them, so that he can comprehend and judge as an equal even the greatest, and having comprehended, can narrate them gravely and clearly in plain and temperate language' (*YP*, 7: 501). As one of the *studia humanitatis*, history was a rhetorical discipline, so it was natural that Milton located the difficulty of its practice in handling the rhetorical elements, especially style and decorum. Humanist historiography gravitated to style largely on the authority of Cicero, for whom 'historians are essentially *exornatores rerum*' with an 'aesthetic commitment' to assign particular genres of history the correct artistic form and level of style.[40] Humanists believed that an eloquent style could bring history to life, as we read from Lapo da Castiglionchio: 'I consider this to be the most noble and distinguished function of eloquence, that it proclaims the most celebrated deeds of our ancestors with the chronicles and records due to them, by which mortal men seem to be made immortal, perishable things eternal, absent persons to be present, dead men to live, the mute to speak, and even the blind to see.'[41] When joined with eloquence, the exemplary actions of famous soldiers and statesmen would move the will of others to imitate them, since history's link with rhetoric included the use of epideixis to teach proper conduct.[42] Milton acknowledges the importance of teaching for all practitioners of rhetoric, including historians, who may 'relate well and orderly things worth the noting, so as may best instruct and benefit them that read' (*YP*, 5i: 4).

From religious and rhetorical truth we turn now to historical truth, the nature of which depends on the kind of history in question, namely, secular or universal. Secular or world history uses carefully selected primary sources to discover what likely happened in the past, whereas universal history, wholly Christian, situates events on the continuum of eternal time, beginning with the Creation and ending, through successive stages, in the timeless bliss of the Last Judgment.[43] Truth in world history is not absolute. As a historian, Milton may be seen comparing and contrasting sources and drawing conclusions from them based on probability, in order to determine the most likely version of past events.[44] With this basis in probability, world history is epistemologically aligned with rhetorical truth. Universal history, however, applies the fixed standard of religious truth because the events narrated, past and future, are claimed to be absolutely true on the authority of their source, the Bible. Although history moved away from the universalistic approach and gradually became secularized during the Renaissance,[45] Milton practised both types, blending a humanist conservatism in relying on primary sources with a providential view of history in which 'human events constituted a record of God's constant intervention in the affairs of the world.'[46] The two historical models readily co-exist: even when constructing a history of Britain from the chronicles of older writers and working to dispel myth and speculation, Milton imputes the course of the nation's past to divine judgment, especially the successive conquests that are part of history's lesson on the connection between virtue and liberty. His belief in universal history would eventually inform *Paradise Lost*, which recounts the traditional Christian chronology from start to anticipated finish, with the aftermath of the Fall as a vantage point for looking backward under Raphael's guidance and forward under Michael's. Later chapters of the present work will discuss Raphael's and Michael's rhetorical use of history in *Paradise Lost*, particularly as their different reasons for speaking to Adam – and very different rhetorical situations – determine their respective styles.

Milton returned consistently to the centrality of style, often with its attendant moral, cultural, and psychological accents. A forceful style, by moving the emotions and engaging the imagination, captivated hearers. Polished language argued sound reason in the individual, flourishing culture in the Commonwealth. Wisdom and eloquence intertwined in the necessity for noble thoughts to be expressed in beautiful words. Nothing better signifies the primacy of style than that the same canon that guided decisions in one's moral life, decorum, also governed the use of language. A well-crafted style brought praise both to a writer's discourse and to himself, not only as a deft manipulator of words, but also as a man. Yet although rhetoric's third office drew Milton's due attention, by itself it did not dominate his concept of rhetoric. He was not, in short, a Ramist, contrary to the argument that since 'Milton *bought* the Ramist division between thinking and speaking ... in [his] epistemology there could be *no* rhetorical thinking; for [Ramist] rhetoric is merely a process of selecting styles or conventional verbal forms for truth.'[47]

    In the first place, the Ramist division between thinking and speaking, between dialectic and rhetoric, fails in practice: 'the three dark powers of rhetoric [thought, discretion, embellishment] reveal themselves as the two parts of the dichotomized art of dialectic [invention, judgment] in not very convincing disguise.'[48] Ramist rhetoric actually included Ramist dialectic, thus reunifying the traditional rhetorical skills of invention, disposition, and style that Ramus himself had tried to separate. Even if the Ramist system had successfully dichotomized thinking and speaking, it would be difficult to imagine that Milton would have 'bought' it. This chapter has shown that his concept of rhetoric, far from dividing thinking and speaking, recognized in typically humanist fashion that thoughts and words share a mutual reliance, that *inventio* and *elocutio* cannot be studied or practised separately, since wisdom and eloquence are unified in the belief that every subject requires an appropriate level of style. More specifically, the closing lines of Milton's *Art of Logic*, a recension of Ramus's *Dialecticae*, amount to a repudiation of Ramus's dialectic in the province of the two arts Milton most valued, rhetoric and poetry. In the final chapter, 'On Method,' Ramus writes that orators and poets, 'whenever they propose to teach a listener, want to follow this way' – that is, dialectical method – 'although they do not always enter into or persist in it.' Milton glosses Ramus's remark: 'But to orators and poets should be left their own account of method, or at least those who teach the art of oratory and poetry' (*YP*, 8: 394, 395). Ramus's dialectic was too rigid to accommodate oratory and poetry. Milton realized that its artificial constructions applied in practice only to Ramist dialectic itself and that, consequently, rhetoricians and poets should rely instead on the methods of their respective disciplines.

As a body of rules, the unified system of technical rhetoric guided writers in the particulars of both invention and stylistics. Rhetoric informed all stages of literary production, figured prominently in a liberal education, and also revealed and defended the truth while pointing out the way to the good life. Milton consistently understood rhetoric as performing these invaluable functions, despite the claim of some critics that later in his career he developed an ambivalence or even a hostility towards it.[49] They allege these sentiments in lines such as Satan's corrupt but successful use of rhetoric in *Paradise Lost*, where Milton's comparison of Satan to the ancient orators (IX. 670–6) has been interpreted as a condemnation of the art itself, or the Son's rejection of Athenian learning in *Paradise Regained*, including the achievements of Greek political eloquence. These appear worthy,

But herein to our Prophets far beneath,
As men divinely taught, and better teaching
The solid rule of Civil Government

In thir majestic unaffected style
Than all the Oratory of *Greece* and *Rome*.   (IV. 356–60)[50]

Such passages, however, appear anti-rhetorical only when detached
from their thematic and narrative contexts and when their relationship
to Milton's theology is not duly considered. The Son dismisses not classical learning itself, but rather the terms in which Satan presents it, as a
substitute for the true wisdom that resides only in faith and revelation,
against which all forms of secular knowledge 'are false, or little else but
dreams, / Conjectures, fancies, built on nothing firm' (IV. 291–2). Even
so, Jesus acknowledges that it is rhetoric that communicates true wisdom – that it is

more heavenly, first
By winning words to conquer willing hearts,
And make persuasion do the work of fear,   (I. 221–3)

echoing an argument that Milton had made as far back as 1642: 'the
perswasive power in man to win others to goodnesse by instruction is
greater, and more divine then the compulsive power to restrain man
from being evill by terrour of the Law' (*YP*, 1: 722). Thirty years later, in
Paradise Regained, Milton is still affirming the value of rhetoric in the service of truth. It expresses wisdom, in particular the certain knowledge of
Christian revelation; it wins people over to virtue and salvation; and, by
declaring the truth, it exposes the lies and deceptions of false eloquence.
David Norbrook writes of republican sentiments in Satan's speech in
Paradise Lost 'that diabolic – or Cromwellian – language of public interest should not discredit the language itself, merely the context in which
it becomes a vehicle for tyrannical speech-acts.'[51] Rhetoric ought to be
approached with the same sensitivity to local context: it was the abuse
of rhetoric as a vehicle for lies, not rhetoric itself, that earned Milton's
disapproval. When employed according to the best classical standards,
the *ars dicendi* affirmed the oratorical and ethical ideals, the correct
choices for both words and actions, that were essential for the exercise of
prudence and faith.

5 The Voice of God: Rhetoric and Religion

A man died after being bitten by a rattlesnake he had brought to church because the Bible says believers 'shall take up serpents.' Dewey Bruce Hale, 40, of Enigma, Georgia, was bitten during a service at New River Free Holiness Church and died soon after, the sheriff's office said. The death was ruled accidental. Martha Hale, his cousin, said church members take the Bible literally, particularly a passage in the Gospel according to Mark saying that one sign of those who believe in Christ is that 'they shall take up serpents.'

International Herald Tribune

The principles of rhetoric, universally taught in early modern Europe, were both widely used in literary practice and often discussed in terms of the theories behind their use. What was rhetoric, and what did it mean for the understanding and performance of a given discipline? How was it, and how should it, be employed? One context that generated a significant body of discussion on these points was religion. In the homiletic and exegetical tracts that sprang from the polemical atmosphere of the Reformation, rhetoric was continually cited as a matter of theological import. Since late antiquity, when the Church Fathers reconciled Christian culture with the principles of classical rhetoric, religious discourse and rhetoric enjoyed a close relationship. Bound up with them, for virtually as long a period, was another application of language, one that in the seventeenth century is aptly assessed alongside Renaissance rhetoric: poetry. Religious themes continued to dominate English poetry well into the seventeenth century. The interpenetration of these three subjects – religion, rhetoric, and poetry – suggests the importance of formal rhetorical considerations for a poet wishing to undertake a Christian topic. Such considerations were especially important for John Milton, and they became crucial in fitting language to subject for the most singular passages of *Paradise Lost*, the speeches of God. This chapter examines the points of contact between rhetoric, seventeenth-century religious discourse, and poetry and attempts to see what linguistic norms lay behind the concept of a speaking, poetic God.

In many ways, the main characteristics of seventeenth-century religious rhetoric correspond to those of rhetoric in general during that time, which changed as part of a broader cultural movement. Having largely assimilated scholastic logic over the preceding two centuries, rhetoric had become complex and unwieldy. Calls were made for its simplification. Ramism had attempted to simplify rhetorical theory by reducing its purview to ornamentation and gesture. Bacon famously criticizes the infatuation with rhetoric during the Tudor reigns as a formalistic attitude to language that hindered 'the severe inquisition of truth and the deep progress into philosophy.' Thus, 'the more severe and laborious sort of inquirers into truth ... will despise those delicacies and affections, as indeed capable of no divineness.'[1] Although 'Bacon's injunctions appl[ied] only to the establishment of a body of scientific data, not to language as a whole,' it was the pursuit of truth, not the choice of words, that preoccupied many seventeenth-century thinkers and in whose name rhetoric was frequently devalued as meretricious: 'the correlation between a naked style and the naked truth recurs throughout the seventeenth century ... Truth required no other ornament than her own naked beauty. To deck her out in schemes and tropes was to make her indistinguishable from a harlot.'[2] Furthermore, the scope of rhetorical invention, which for humanists had included the discovery of new knowledge, was now restricted to retrieving what was already known: 'Invention is of two kinds, much differing; the one, of Arts and Sciences,' was creative and discovered new knowledge, 'the other, of Speech and Arguments,' was recollective, summoning forth previously known facts, and therefore was 'not properly an invention.'[3] Dialectical invention, on the other hand, contributed a method of finding arguments that could be adapted to investigation and research in philosophy and science.[4] Rhetoric remained an essentially linguistic art, a status open to attack given that language itself, undergoing close scrutiny on grounds both moral and scientific, yielded up none of the certitude sought by moral and natural philosophers. Bacon, Hobbes, Locke, and the scientific community at large expressed dissatisfaction at the imprecision generated out of figurative – that is, rhetorical – language. Hobbes, for example, claims that one 'cause of absurditie' is 'the use of Metaphors, Tropes, and other Rhetoricall figures, in stead of words proper'; though admirable in 'common speech' – like Bacon, he does not dismiss rhetoric out of hand – 'yet in reckoning, and seeking of truth, such speeches are not to be admitted ... The Light of humane minds is Perspicuous Words.'[5]

Such attitudes and statements, Brian Vickers points out, should not be construed as a repudiation of figurative language in the later seventeenth century. Bacon, a great influence on that period, had, in fact, prescribed plain language only in the arena of scientific method and the communication of experiments, recognizing that stylistic rhetoric and language aimed at the imagination were legitimate in other types of writing. Thomas Sprat's preface to his history of the Royal Society, conventionally misread as anti-rhetorical, attacked not rhetoric and imaginative appeals themselves but rather their misuse. Seventeenth-century attacks on rhetorical style, moreover, ought to be read against their contemporary polemical backdrop as extensions of political or religious controversies, intended to disparage an opponent's language along with his character, and to do so in particular instances of dispute; they were not presented as general theoretical pronouncements on how to write. The idea that Puritans or New Scientists held to a programmatically anti-rhetorical concept of language is mistaken.[6] Figurative language continued to be used by natural philosophers, who found it useful for describing observations in their writings. Rhetoric, it is true, was challenged in the seventeenth century, criticized in light of its complexity, unsuitability as a method of inquiry, unsteady relationship with truth, and the new requirements for language. Yet far from undergoing a decline, it remained woven into the fabric of European intellectual life as tightly as ever. Rhetoric was inescapable, and its traditional functions that had been revived by humanism – of appealing to the imagination, of persuading, of guiding style and composition – maintained widespread currency throughout the period in a range of disciplines from experimental science to religious poetry.

An ambivalence towards rhetoric similar to that found in seventeenth-century natural philosophy – theoretically rejecting it while employing it in practice – informed the outlook of the early Church. Open to the utility and elegance of classical learning on the one hand and sensitive, on the other, to the primacy of the Bible as the foundation of Christian teaching, Church Fathers, in defining the institution's intellectual base, debated over adopting the rhetorical strand of Greco-Roman culture. Jerome felt that studying pagan rhetoric, especially its style, was indispensable, whereas Augustine believed that Christianity could import from it what was useful, then jettison the rest. Tertullian rejected classical learning outright; Cyprian advocated simple expression in contrast to the florid eloquence of the Second Sophistic. Yet even when the rhetorically learned would give no public endorsement of the art, as in the case of Jerome, or when its validity in a Christian context was criticized, as it was by Gregory of Nazianzus, Basil the Great, and Gregory of Nyssa, a tacit acceptance of it shows in the rhetorical mastery of many early Christian writings.[7] Lorenzo Valla points to that mastery in defending the role of rhetoric in theology, citing numerous Fathers, Latin and Greek, 'who in every age have clothed those most precious gems of divine utterance in the gold and silver of eloquence; and they did not abandon one knowledge on account of the other.'[8]

The great synthesis of classical rhetorical theory and Christian doctrine was realized in the writings of St Augustine. In the third and fourth books of *On Christian Doctrine*, Augustine adapts much of the system of western classical rhetoric to Christian preaching and exegesis. He assigns to homiletics the three offices of ancient rhetoric, *docere, delectare, movere*, and, correspondingly, an approximation to Cicero's three levels of style: the subdued, for teaching; the temperate, for pleasing; and the majestic, for moving or swaying the mind.[9] Whatever style the preacher employs, his speech ought always to be clear, beautiful, and persuasive. Though these three virtues are interdependent, clarity is tacitly advanced as chief among them, for it is not only requisite to aesthetic pleasure and persuasion, but also essential for explicating the 'useful and healthful obscurity' of the prophetic mysteries. Thus, preachers 'should first of all speak so that they may be understood, speaking in so far as they are able with such clarity that ... the difficulty and subtlety lie not in the manner of speaking but in the things which we wish to explain and show,' things that are often shaded in allegory, parable, and enigma. Teaching is the primary goal, but the Christian orator's duty often entails rousing recalcitrant hearers to practise the truth he preached, appealing to the imagination as well as reason to get through to the will. It is mainly for this purpose that the use of rhetoric is sanctioned: 'It is necessary ... for the ecclesiastical orator, when he urges that something be done, not only to teach that he may instruct and to please that he may hold attention, but also to persuade that he may be victorious. For it now remains for that man, in whom the demonstration of truth, even when suavity of diction was added, did not move to consent, to be persuaded by the heights of eloquence.' Achieving the power of eloquence licenses the preacher to employ 'entreaties and reproofs, exhortations and rebukes, and whatever other devices are necessary to move minds,'[10] such as the tropes and figures. Rhetoric, with due attention to style, was central to Augustine's method of preaching.

Eloquence was justified as a means of teaching, moving, and persuading a Christian audience because the Bible, the core of doctrine and faith for every Christian and the source of every sermon, is a densely rhetorical text. One passage of *On Christian Doctrine*, which would later serve as a key hermeneutic principle during the Renaissance, acknowledges the rhetorical style of sacred scriptures, in particular its tropes: 'Lettered men should know, moreover, that all those modes of expression which the grammarians designate with the Greek word tropes were used by our authors, and more abundantly and copiously than those who do not know them and have learned about such expressions elsewhere are able to suppose or believe. Those who know these tropes, however, will recognize them in the sacred letters, and this knowledge will be of considerable assistance in understanding them.' Though he does not discuss them himself, he says that they should be learned elsewhere. Additionally, he notes that 'not only examples of all of these tropes are found in reading the sacred books, but also the names of some of them, like allegoria, aenigma, parabola,'[11] and that they occur in the speech even of those unschooled in tropal lore. For Augustine, the scriptures were the summit of eloquence.[12] Writing in part 'to reply to the ill-taught men who think our authors contemptible,' as he himself had thought in his youth, Augustine says that he would be able to show, had he the time, 'all the virtues and ornaments of eloquence on account of which those are puffed up ... in those very sacred books which divine providence provided.'[13] Jerome had made just such a demonstration: in his commentary on Jeremiah, he recognized the stylistic parallels between classical and sacred rhetoric by comparing the rhetorical figures of the prophets with those of Virgil.[14] Augustine himself touched on the metaphorical eloquence of the prophets and discussed the Epistles of Paul, who, he showed, was a masterful rhetorician. It was the chief virtue of Paul's eloquence that he seamlessly fused rhetorical techniques with the wisdom of Christian doctrine; his manner of writing, like that of the apostles and prophets, naturally accompanied the divine message: 'they have used our eloquence in such a way through another eloquence of their own that it seems neither lacking in them nor ostentatious in them. For it was not fitting for them either to condemn it or to make a display of it ... These words were not devised by human industry, but poured forth from the divine mind both wisely and eloquently, not in such a way that wisdom was directed toward eloquence, but in such a way that eloquence did not abandon wisdom ... Therefore let us say that our canonical authors and teachers were not only wise but eloquent in that kind of eloquence which is appropriate for such persons.'[15] Much as the classical rhetoricians had envisaged, wisdom and eloquence went hand in hand, the one finding its most efficacious expression in the other, an ideal illustrated for Augustine no more convincingly than by the divine mind expressed in the rhetoric of sacred scripture.

Augustine's legacy was the Christianized aspect that rhetoric wore through late antiquity and the Middle Ages in the writings of authors such as Isidore, Bede, Alcuin, John of Salisbury, and Notker Balbulus. Augustine's syncretism was later taken up by Erasmus, who consolidated sacred rhetoric in Renaissance theology. Like *On Christian Doctrine*, Erasmus's *Ecclesiastae, sive de ratione concionandi libri quator*, published in 1535, discusses the role of rhetoric in preaching and in interpreting the Bible. Following Augustine, as he often did, Erasmus notes that the preacher should teach, delight, and move (*flectat*) his audience, the last so that he might seize upon its affections, the most powerful means of persuasion and one that incited the will to virtue and piety. He emphasizes that, in this task, the duty of the Christian orator differs from that of the forensic and political orator discussed in the classical manuals: 'Now we will treat the several duties of the orator, but only on the condition that you should remember that we instruct not a legal advocate, but a herald of the word of God.'[16] And later, he says that it is necessary for a statesman to be able to persuade firmly concerning which political options are to be pursued or avoided (*de expetendis et fugiendis*), 'but much more so for the preacher, who is the true leader of men,'[17] who leads them, unlike the lawyer or politician, to salvation. At the level of style, he distinguishes the forensic orator's deceitful, sophistic amplification, which makes a thing appear greater or less than it truly is, from that of the ecclesiastical orator, which reveals things in their true light.[18] Erasmus took pains to Christianize rhetoric, to partition sacred applications of it from traditional worldly ones, underscoring its contemporary spiritual utility by excluding or diminishing its pagan offices.[19]

Like Augustine, Erasmus recognized that a knowledge of tropes and figures may be put to two purposes: to move the will of the sluggish auditor by means of the emotions, and to aid in the understanding of the Bible, a text composed of rhetorical devices. The early Church, he writes, regarded the study of tropes to be an unworthy theological pursuit, 'but Augustine assesses that they should be carefully attended to, and even held in the memory, because a knowledge of them is, as he says, especially necessary for dissolving the ambiguity of the scriptures.'[20] Erasmus cites a number of tropes in passages from the Bible, including, for example, a circumstantial discussion of various kinds of synecdoche found there, and notes that, of all the tropes, allegory is the most essential to know for revealing rhetorically hidden meaning in the Bible.[21] With respect to preaching, he suggests that rhetorical figures of words, images, and amplification be deployed to move an audience, for it is more effective to engage the mind with such devices than simply to present words in their literal meanings. Amplification is a particularly apposite rhetorical style for instructing and for capturing the attention of the multitude. Figures conveying vivid imagery, such as hypotyposis, are especially efficacious in stirring the emotions. Rhetorical *schemata*, of which he furnishes both classical and Christian examples, often from the Bible, 'produce sharpness and force of expression',[22] and are always discussed in terms of their affective dimension, often with cautions concerning usage. By assimilating them, Christian discourse equals the classics in *verba* while surpassing them in *res*, as Erasmus remarks elsewhere: 'As for style, insofar as it depends on the employment of tropes and figures, we are there even on a level with Cicero; in faith and grandeur of subject matter we are his superiors by far.'[23]

Erasmus lays out two special prescriptions for the preacher who would use rhetoric to raise emotions and persuade his hearers. The first, standard in early modern preaching manuals, observes that, 'in order to excite pious feelings, there is nothing more efficacious than having been piously affected yourself ... It has been neatly said that nothing kindles except a flame. A fiery mind makes for a fiery tongue ... No one effectively inflames others to piety except a person who is truly pious. No one checks others from vice more capably than one who himself hates vice from within his heart. For the very spirit of God speaks through this man, and he transfers his own gift to his hearers.'[24] A vehicle for the Word of God, the preacher himself must feel those emotions and divine sentiments that he wishes to instil in his audience; he must also be pious and of divine *ethos* – he 'must first bee godly effected himselfe,' as William Perkins later wrote. If transferring piety to others requires a virtuous character and affective sympathy, its success also depends on the preacher's concealing his rhetorical techniques: 'I fear that it may seem to anyone that it is foolish to mention here the rules of rhetoric, because the expression of the art lessens the credibility of the speaker to such a degree that the best orator judges that the chief precept of the art is to hide the art. For whoever believes that someone whom he hears is speaking artfully, since he supposes that a plot is being hatched against him by a cunning speaker, is on his guard against assenting and instead concentrates his mind on the speaker, so that he may observe how ingeniously or how skillfully he speaks, not how wholesomely.'[25] Erasmus criticizes ingenious pulpit eloquence, full of gaudy figures, as affected (*molesta*) and more elaborate than befits a preacher. The ideal rhetorical style, found in the Bible, is unobtrusively eloquent in the manner of the apostles, whom Augustine had praised: 'Sacred letters have their own elegance and beauty, though they are unacquainted with disguise and finery.'[26] They hide their art, a virtue on which the preacher should base his own art of speaking.

The comprehensive Augustinian assessment of hermeneutics and preaching in the *Ecclesiastes* set it apart from other sixteenth-century sacred rhetorics, which for the most part addressed preaching alone. While Erasmus's long work is the best-known example of this genre, some of the main principles presented there had already been handled by others, including Johannes Reuchlin, whose *Liber congestorum de arte praedicandi* appeared in 1504. Reuchlin made no mention of Augustine, nor did he explicitly delve into rhetoric as such – he considered it to be the a priori foundation of preaching. Both omissions probably occurred because the concept of Christian eloquence was so well established that the fusion of preaching and the classical rhetorical tradition, as well as Augustine's part in it, were taken for granted: 'The art of preaching is the faculty of enticing men to moral perfection and to divine contemplation by the public declaration of the sacred scriptures. The preacher is a devout man, skilled at speaking, an overseer in the church pulpit by decree from on high. Therefore, the person who discourses intelligently, using careful arrangement and an apt style, speaking from memory and with a certain majesty of delivery, about whatever matter arises that is necessary to men's spiritual health and that needs to be explained through oratory will be judged worthy to be called by the esteemed name of preacher.'[27] In this synopsis, preaching is seen as a type of persuasion, the five offices of rhetoric are presented as the instruments of effecting that persuasion, and the preacher, as *vir religiosus dicendi peritus*, is a Christianized incarnation of the ideal classical *vir bonus dicendi peritus*, the virtuous and wise orator. Another German humanist, Reuchlin's great-nephew Philipp Melanchthon, similarly embraced the classical tradition, maintaining its religious applications alongside secular ones: 'For what purpose is eloquence useful? In order to express all the greatest and most difficult matters in the entire range of civil life; to maintain and to elucidate the religion of God; to explicate and to protect the laws.' In this religious sphere, rhetoric naturally assumes the duties of preaching: 'You see that we have borrowed certain manners of stirring an audience (*concionum genera*) from rhetoric, since the method of preaching is either a certain part or a reflection of this art.'[28]

Melanchthon's borrowing also characterized the homiletics of Andreas Hyperius. *The Practis of Preaching*, translated into English in 1577, acknowledges that 'many things are common to the Preacher with the Orator.' Some writers unreservedly imported the classical paradigm directly into preaching. Hyperius is more selective, incorporating much of the classical system but, like Erasmus, carefully excluding some parts and elevating Christian rhetoric above its secular counterpart. On the authority of Augustine, the five parts of rhetoric 'may rightly be called also the partes of a Preacher,' whose tasks are 'to Teache, to Delight, to Turne,' according to three levels of style, 'Loftye, Base, Meane ... Moreover, the whole craft of varienge the Oration by Schemes and Tropes, pertaineth indifferently to the Preacher and Orator.'[29] Given these shared techniques, preaching is a species of rhetoric, so preachers might most conveniently learn their art from classical sources. Yet the Christian orator's method is distinctive, chiefly in terms of *inventio*. The demonstrative, deliberative, and judicial divisions of speech, unsuitable for Christian themes, are replaced by doctrine, redargution, correction, institution, and consolation, and by five types of sermon.[30] Additionally, the complex of emotions that a preacher must provoke, such as sorrow, indignation at sins, compassion for and love of one's neighbours, fear of God's judgment, 'is not altogether like unto that, that the Orators use in their Forum or Consistory.' These emotions are intended to bring about salvation, not mere conviction. The preacher's main superiority rests in the source of his invention, the Bible, which is natu-

rally more persuasive, to both reason and the imagination, than any secular proposition.[31]

Largely in light of Augustine's commentary, which was highly influential in later times, Renaissance theologians acknowledged the rhetorical nature of the Bible. Bartholomew Westheimer believed, like his
contemporary Erasmus, that 'not the least part of the comprehension of
sacred letters has been placed in those very tropes and formulas of
speaking familiar to each language.'[32] The Bible's style, and what that
style accomplished, drew the attention of Protestant exegetes such as
Matthias Flacius Illyricus and Salomon Glass, who remarked on its con-
densed brevity, full of tropes, which creates force and grandeur, and on
its *efficacia* and *evidentia* (power and vivid imagery), which evoke emotion in the reader. Such a style, transmitted less through verbal figures
than through figures of thought suggestive of lively imagery, achieved
magnitudo, or vivid description, which brought *praestantia*, an excellent
object, removed and unknown, within reach of the human mind.
Through the comparison of divine things, couched in figurative language, with things more nearly knowable to man, the divinely inspired
biblical authors could partially close the gulf between the incomprehensible mysteries of God and human understanding, the nature of
those further mysteries adumbrated or hinted at by the analogies of
metaphor and imagery. These rhetorical techniques, engaging not so
much reason as the imagination, created 'a nondiscursive apprehension
of spiritual reality.'[33]

The tropes and figures so abundant in scriptural style received special emphasis during the Reformation. Augustine, having said that the
knowledge of tropes would be of considerable assistance in understanding the scriptures, gives the reason: 'an awareness of [tropes] is
necessary to a solution of the ambiguities of the Scriptures, for when
the sense is absurd if it is taken verbally, it is to be inquired whether or
not what is said is expressed in this or that trope which we do not
know; and in this way many hidden things are discovered.'[34] Beyond
its literal or verbal signification, a given passage had an allegorical level
of interpretation as well, where God had hidden a spiritual meaning
and where a knowledge of tropes could be applied to discover that
meaning by stripping away the allegorical cortex. In the seventeenth
century this Augustinian mode of exegesis was the Protestant norm. It
was implemented in manuals such as John Smith's *The Mysterie of
Rhetorique Unvail'd*, which viewed a familiarity with *elocutio* as the key
to discovering scriptural meaning and cited more than 100 rhetorical

devices, providing scriptural examples for each. Smith hints at the mis-interpretations that had arisen out of 'the ignorance of Rhetorique,' which is 'one ground, yea, and a great one, of many dangerous Errors this day.'[35] William Perkins, author of the first Puritan *ars praedicandi* (art of preaching), invoked the Bible's figurative nature in disputing what he considered an error based on such ignorance: the doctrine, endlessly debated, of the Real Presence in the Eucharist. Perkins, following Calvin, interprets I Corinthians 11.24, 'This is my *body* which is broken for you,' not as a literal statement denoting transubstantiation, but rather as meaning, 'in this place the bread is a signe of my body; by a Metonymie of the subject for the adjunct ... therefore the bread is not properly the body, but symbolically or by way of signification.'[36] Perkins demonstrates here how rhetoric may be put to practical use in hermeneutics, confuting what he saw as a Catholic or Anglican failure to recognize figurative language, a literalism that led to errant superstition. Erasmus discerned a trope in this same passage, acknowledging an interpretation such as Perkins's, but preferring one that read the body as a metaphor for the Church.[37] Elsewhere he noted, in characteristically non-committal fashion, that a passage read by Augustine in terms of hypallage was taken literally by others, with no trope at all.[38] As these different interpretations of the same passage indicate, rhetoric either could be used to create a variety of figurative meanings, or could be ignored, thus leading to a literal interpretation. A powerful force in the Reformation, it helped to construct scriptural meaning and, consequently, Christian belief. How and to what degree one applied rhetoric in reading the Bible could be a matter of life and death – and so it is even today, though on bizarrely different terms, when the issue remains as alive as the poisonous snakes that certain Christian fundamentalists reportedly handle in literal adherence to Mark 16.18.

Perkins's method characterized the tropology of later Puritans, such as Richard Bernard,[39] John Owen, and Henry Lukin. Lukin's *Introduction to the Holy Scripture* discussed the Bible's tropes and figures in detail; but he remarked that repeated reading continually turned up previously unnoticed tropes and figures, 'the Scripture being too rich a Treasury to be exhausted all at once.' Owen, who provided a preface 'To the Christian Reader' for Lukin's treatise, commented that he, too, was always finding more tropes in his own reading.[40] These two personal remarks illuminate how the seventeenth-century rhetorical theologian read his Bible. A Puritan divine, educated in the Augustinian tradition of biblical eloquence, was always aware of and actively engaged with formal rhetoric, with the stylistic dimension of the text that he digested along with the spiritual content. As Augustine had noted, content and style, *res* and *verba*, were indivisible in the scriptures, for an appreciation of style enlightened a reader to the rhetorically encoded meaning of the divine message. True to that dictum, as Owen's and Lukin's sensitivity to tropes suggests, God's wisdom and God's eloquence flowed side by side for the seventeenth-century reader.

Renaissance theologians, engaged with the interpretive problems of biblical rhetoric, were also concerned with the preacher's application of rhetorical strategies to sermons. English Protestants based their homiletic precepts on the Bible. Since the Bible's style was rhetorical, composed largely of tropes and figures, preaching took on a similar cast. The results were not always happy. We can sympathize, for example, with the Sunday congregation forced to sit through Henry Smith's 'A Glasse for Drunkards.' A taste: 'It is said that drunken porters keep open gates, so when Noah was drunken, he set all open; as wine went in, so wit went out: as wit went out, so his clothes went off. Thus Adam which began the world at first, was made naked with sinne: and Noah which began the world againe is made naked with sinne, to shew that sinne is no shrowder but a stripper.'[41] Such examples – and the reader of seventeenth-century sermons encounters them often – give point to Milton's hope that one day there may 'appear in Pulpits other visages, other gestures, and stuffe otherwise wrought then what we now sit under, oft times to as great a triall of our patience as any other that they preach to us' (*YP*, 2: 406).

As in seventeenth-century natural and moral philosophy, criticism of rhetorical style for sermons, in the name of conveying the naked truth, did not entail the rejection of rhetoric. William Perkins, although he endorsed the hermeneutic application of rhetoric and recognized it as a branch of human learning that the preacher might legitimately (but moderately) employ when preparing a sermon, advocated simple, plain, unadorned speech in the pulpit itself.[42] The audience was still to be moved, but by the preacher's passion, derived from 'the Spirit of God in him and by him,' rather than by his rhetorical diction. Protestant opinion varied over how much rhetoric a preacher's style ought to employ.[43] In practice, however, stylistic rhetoric was a widely accepted homiletic convention. This was the case even for Puritans, from whom the call for plainness was most often heard, but who, like their Anglican counterparts, resorted to the tropes and figures. Richard Bernard recognized the importance of rhetorical figures both in understanding the Bible and in preaching.[44] The Anglican bishop Joseph Glanvill declared that while preaching style should be plain, the tropes and figures, as well as *actio*, necessarily complement it. He distinguishes those few to whose dispositions an intellectual appeal is suitable from the common people, whose 'affections are raised by figures, and earnest and passionate representations; by the circumstances of the voice, and gesture, and motion; so that ... these ... must be heeded, and suited to the capacity of your hearers.'[45]

Perkins's conjunction of the naked truth with a naked style and his belief in the primacy of teaching were repeated by the Puritan Richard Baxter: 'All our teaching must be as Plain and Evident as we can make it. For this doth most suite to a Teacher's end. He that would be understood, must speak to the capacity of his hearers, and make it his business to make himself understood.'[46] Yet Baxter's own pulpit oratory, while relatively plain, is by no means shorn of rhetorical devices. His 'A True Believer's Choice and Pleasure. Sermon for the Funeral of Mrs Cox,' dated 19 November 1669, exhibits more obviously the prized Puritan art, dialectic, rather than rhetoric. Despite Peter Ramus's attempt to partition the two arts, Renaissance rhetoric had largely subsumed dialectic, and the dialectical constructions of this sermon often function very much like rhetorical amplification. In one long passage, for example, Baxter enumerates twenty points to illustrate how Mrs Cox lived by God's covenants, a catalogue of virtues that constitutes a passage of demonstrative praise; later, he cites twenty instances of how living by God's testimonies has benefited him personally. Amplifying the desirability of the pious life, these logico-rhetorical figures are intended to move Baxter's audience to live likewise. Similarly, he uses the disjunctive proposition, followed by a question, to rhetorical effect: 'either God's word seconding the light of nature, must give you hopes of a better life, or you must live and die in mere despair. And shall that be your willful choice?' This sermon contains many similar passages, the rhetoric often urging the importance of virtuous choice, and it exhibits a variety of other standard rhetorical tropes and figures. Though Baxter's continual ramifications of logical structure often make his argument hard to follow, his art is unobtrusive, a good example of the decorous application of 'humane learning' to Puritan homiletics.

The sermons of other Puritan preachers followed a rhetorical program similar to Baxter's. Both classical and patristic learning lay behind the homiletic preparation of Thomas Adams, whose 'Plaine-

Dealing, or A Precedent of Honestie' used logically based constructions for amplification and frequently but judiciously incorporated other rhetorical devices into the speech. One point in the sermon, which dilates on Genesis 25.27, shows that Puritan preaching could utilize the more elaborate figures, such as antimetabole: 'All that can be said is this: *Esau* preferred his belly before his Birthright: *Jacob* his Birthright before his belly. The one sold spirituall things for temporall, the other with temporall things bought spirituall.' A later passage demonstrates how rhetorically laden Adams's style could become:

> The Church esteemes Heaven her home, this world but a *Tent ... Arise and depart, for this is not your rest* [Micah 2.10]. Though you depart with grief, from Orchards full of fruits, grounds full stocked, houses dightly furnished, purses richly stuffed; from musicke, wine, junkets, sports; yet goe; you must goe, every man to his own house. He that hath seene heaven with the eye of Faith, through the glasse of Scripture, slippes off his coate with *Joseph*, and springs away ... The world is full of troubles; winds of persecutions, stormes of menaces, cold of uncharitablenesse, heate of malice, exhalations of prodigious terrors, will annoy thee. *Love it not:* Who can effect his owne vexations?[47]

The particulars of the tropes and figures here may be passed over, for his rhetorical manner of amplifying the *contemptus mundi* theme is clear. John Brinsley employs hermeneutic rhetoric within the sermon itself in order to clarify Jeremiah's technique at 47.6–7: 'the Prophet here in the close of the Chapter, the verses I have now singled out, breaketh forth into a most emphaticall *Apostrophe*, turning his speech to the *Sword* itselfe, *parlaying with it* (as it were) *about a cessation.*'[48] Brinsley glosses Jeremiah's style with the appropriate rhetorical term, apostrophe, clearly expecting that his audience, at a 'Publick Fast' in Norfolk, would be familiar with the name and the principle behind it. 'The Sword, what properly and literally it is, I shall not need to tell you' – but of course he goes on to do so all the same, the sword undergoing something of a rhetorical metamorphosis. It starts out as a general metaphor ('Every notable, terrible judgement is a Sword'), becomes a metonymy ('In this sense understand the word in the text. *O thou Sword* ... the Sword of a forraigne Enemy, the Armie of the *Chaldeans* or *Babilonians*, that should come up against the *Philistins*'),[49] and is finally animated by prosopopoeia ('So impartiall an Officer will the Sword shew it selfe, when it commeth to doe execution').

Joseph Hall, a Calvinist who often preached to the court of James I, was a poet as well as a cleric with whom Milton crossed swords in the divorce controversy. Educated at Emmanuel College, he was a noted scholar and twice delivered public lectures on rhetoric while at Cambridge. Evidence of that rhetorical acumen is furnished in his sermons, where he confidently deployed a wide range of tropes and figures, and where he sometimes pointed out their occurrence in the words of the prophets. He was assured of being understood, and appreciated, on both counts, since his audience's educational background would usually have been similar to his own. In 'The Deceit of Appearance,' preached before James's court on 15 September 1622, Hall elaborated his topic verse from John 7.24, 'Judge not, therefore, according to the appearance,' in passages of cumulative, balanced amplification:

> If we should judge according to the appearance, we should think basely of the saviour of the world. Who, that had seen him sprawling and wringing in the cratch, flitting to Egypt, chopping of chips at Nazareth, famishing in the desert, transported by Satan, attended by fishermen, persecuted by his kindred, betrayed by one servant, forsaken of all, apprehended, arraigned, condemned, buffeted, spat upon, scourged to blood, sceptered with the reed, crowned with thorns, nailed to the Cross, hanging naked betwixt two thieves, scorned of the beholders, sealed up in a borrowed grave, could say other than, *He hath no form nor beauty; when we shall see him, there is nothing, that we should desire him?*[50]

Eight more aspects of Christ's lowly appearance follow – the rhetorical figure that piles up the details of a general fact or idea is called denumeratio. The passage continues with abundant – and noticeable – rhetoric, full of the same vivid imagery, which enforces the demonstration of Jesus' glory despite appearances. When the rhetorical strategies found in the Bible drew Hall's attention, he sometimes tagged them with their classical names. In 'Christ and Caesar,' delivered at Hampton Court, he cross-references his theme text, John 19.15, with Haggai 2.22, in a brief hermeneutic exercise with the figure antonomasia: 'This [kingdom] of the Romans [in John] is taken for that *Regnum Gentium, The kingdom of the Gentiles, Hag.ii.22.* by an antonomasy; which was therefore so much more hated, as it was more prevalent and imperious.'[51] Or he would name the rhetorical devices that he himself used: having personified a deceitful heart as 'The Great Imposter,' which he proposes to arraign at the bar before his Gray's Inn audience on 2 February 1623, Hall says, 'therefore, as an Epiphonema to this just complaint of deceitfulness, is added, *Who can know it?*'[52] Formal rhetoric was public knowledge, not clerical esotericism. The Puritan or Calvinist preacher could name his figures and assume that his entire sermon would be viewed through rhetorical eyes by the average educated man. Hall's own pulpit style sometimes vied for attention with his theological content, a rhetorical exuberance perhaps to be expected from an Elizabethan poet. Whether or not his human learning adhered to the principle of decorum, however, his theological learning often did not: biblical quotations often run so thick that his argument becomes difficult to follow.[53]

Like the natural philosophers who remained reliant on metaphor and analogy, 'the Puritans ... use[d] rhetoric, as everyone must.'[54] The tradition of the Bible as rhetorical in style determined, as it did with hermeneutics, that preaching would assume the techniques of classical rhetoric. Even among the stricter Protestant factions, rhetorical art maintained a noticeable presence and a considerable significance in the *ars praedicandi*. As the preceding examples illustrate, a practical knowledge of tropes and figures could be used to gloss a scriptural verse, to reinforce and complement logic, to elevate the register to the grand style and mainly, as had been the case since Augustine's day, to amplify points of doctrine for the sake of teaching and to move the emotions and the will to embrace that teaching. Rhetoric was not inimical to the Puritan ideal of plainness. As long as a preacher remembered the Augustinian prescription that 'in his speech itself he should prefer to please more with the things said than with the words used to speak them ... nor should the teacher serve the words, but the words the teacher,'[55] then stylistic rhetoric was acceptable, even necessary as 'the means of calling men to right conduct, of arousing them to a sense of sin and an abhorrence of evil.'[56] Rhetoric's hold on Protestant theology, however, went beyond its persuasive role in sermons or its presence in – and function of interpreting – the Bible. Rhetoric also demanded close attention because of its relationship with the Bible's true author.

'Rhetoric,' wrote John Smith, 'is a good gift of God, proceeding from the Father of lights.'[57] God created tropes and figures in order to speak to man, to bridge the gap between heaven and earth, through human language: 'The entire discourse of men,' stated Erasmus, 'has been scattered about with tropes. So it seemed proper to God's wisdom to stutter along with us, so to speak, using a very accessible style.'[58] Joseph Glanvill's justification for using tropes and figures in homiletic points to the same divine origin: 'God himself doth so condescend; he speaks in our language, and in such schemes of speech as are apt to excite the affections of the most vulgar and illiterate.'[59] In saying that God 'condescends' to man by means of rhetorical devices, Glanvill suggests a concept of God that itself is a trope. 'Anthropopathia,' wrote Salomon Glass, 'is a metaphor whereby what properly belongs to man is applied, through a certain analogy, to God and divine matters. And it is called 'stepping down to' [συγκατάβασις] or 'descending into our company' [condescencio], because Jehovah descends to our level, as it were, in sacred speech, and expresses his own heavenly mysteries in human words.'[60] Bartholomew Westheimer gives a similar definition. In attributing human actions and speech to God – 'so the prophet David represents God sitting, seeing, mocking scornfully, speaking in anger to his enemies' – anthropopathia 'can be termed the formation of a character, by means of which things said [by God] in a human manner might become thoroughly fixed in our senses. In truth we may regard such a figure as a kind of prosopopoeia.'[61] The shared nature of the two figures is evident in Susenbrotus's direction that 'it is prosopopoeia ... whenever we attribute to non-human things a character, speech, or action consistent with those of humankind,' of which, after several examples, 'finally we depict God himself and divine utterances. Thus the prophet Micah represents God earnestly remonstrating with his own people.'[62] God teaches by speaking to men in their own language, often in rhetorical devices, as Erasmus and Glanvill pointed out. His vehicle for doing so is, of course, the Bible. God cannot speak to man directly, writes Matthias Flacius, because 'the works and acts of God are incomprehensible, and we could not understand anything of these matters unless Sacred Scripture used formulas for speaking about God that are near to human affairs. So on account of the weakness of our understanding, it pleases the Holy Spirit, the author of the Scriptures, to speak with us in our stammering manner through signs and words, which is a style that is more ingratiating and more lowly than is appropriate for such grandeur.'[63] The formulas used in the Bible, those stammerings through which God must convey truths incomprehensible to the human intellect, are, again, figures and tropes, especially allegory: 'I have used similitudes' (Hosea 12.10). Having descended to man's understanding by speaking through the prophets and apostles – 'Certainly there is great power in these words, from which we understand not that the prophets themselves speak, but God by the tongue of the prophets'[64] –

God is *Scripturarum auctor*. Hugo Grotius's discussion of 'Sacrarum Literarum stylum' mentions the propriety of divine rhetoric: 'At one time He is distinguished by the boldest tropes of rhetoric, at another by the most humble, although He does not present Himself in a mean condition, which, if it were otherwise, could not be held divine.'[65] From God, rhetoric's source, the Bible derived its highly rhetorical character, noted by St Augustine and the Reformation theologians. They perceived God as a rhetorical speaker, a stylist of the highest skill.

'The Holy Spirit is the perfect rhetorician,'[66] an aspect of Christian divinity emphasized by John Donne, the dean of St Paul's Cathedral, in whom the identification of God and Holy Writ with stylistic rhetoric received its fullest expression. Donne locates the origin of the Bible's surpassing eloquence in the tropal and figural eloquence of God: 'The Holy Ghost in penning the Scriptures delights himself, not only with a propriety but with a delicacy, and harmony, and melody of language; with height of Metaphors, and other figures, which may work greater impressions upon the Readers, and not with barbarous, or triviall, or market, or homely language.'[67] God's tropes and figures, which stir readers' emotions as well as instruct them, constitute a majestic style neither homely nor fulsome: 'The Holy Ghost is an eloquent Author, a vehement, and an abundant Author, but yet not luxuriant; he is far from penurious, but as far from a superfluous style too.'[68] Donne here defends the divine biblical style as elevated and declares the appropriate degree and quantity of the rhetorical devices therein, suggesting that God has observed decorum, has treated elevated subjects with an elevated style. In doing so, Donne's God is less the condescending communicator of Erasmus, Flacius, and Glanvill than an artistically aware rhetorician who expresses the grandeur and complexity of His Word with a style that is correspondingly grand and complex. Henry Lukin judges God's style similarly: 'For Rhetorick the whole Scripture abounds with Tropes and Figures; and although there is nothing Pedantick in it, there is such a mixture of loftiness and gravity as becomes the Author and matter of it.'[69] 'Every Psalme,' George Wither claims, 'hath that same kinde of Rhetorick which the nature of the subject requires.'[70] This perception of God's craft squares with Augustine's remark on the seemliness of the prophetic and apostolic style: God's eloquence, the eloquence of the biblical writers through whom He speaks, complements the majesty of his wisdom.[71] His speech reconciles philosophy and rhetoric, perfectly counterpoises form and content. If the ideal Puritan preacher spoke plainly, Donne's God certainly does not – plainness would not befit the grandeur of the Word. The nature of divine eloquence is characterized in Donne's apostrophe to 'My *God*, my *God*, Thou art a *direct* God, may I not say, a *literall* God ... But thou art also ... a *figurative*, a *metaphoricall God* too: A God in whose words there is such a height of *figures*, such *voyages*, such *peregrinations* to fetch remote and precious *metaphors*, such *extentions*, such *spreadings*, such *Curtaines* of *Allegories*, such *third Heavens of Hyperboles*, so *harmonious eloquutions*, so *retired* and so *reserved expressions*, so *commanding perswasions*, so *perswading commandements* ... such *things* in thy *words*, as all *prophane Authors*, seeme of the seed of the *Serpent*, that creepes; thou art the *dove*, that flies.' While this God still teaches and communicates – 'what words but thine, can expresse the inexpressible texture, and composition of thy word' – His style delights, attracting attention for its literary merits from a minister famous in his own day for his splendid pulpit eloquence, but who much later would be better known as a poet. God uses the full range of tropes and figures, abundantly deployed, so that biblical style suits the dignity of *res divinae*. Donne presses home the central rhetorical idea implicit in the works of other seventeenth-century theologians, that the eloquence of God inheres in the dense, interlaced network of these rhetorical devices in both the Old and the New Testaments: 'Neither art thou thus a *figurative*, a *Metaphoricall God*, in thy *word* only, but in thy *workes* too. The *stile* of thy works, the *phrase* of thine *Actions*, is *Metaphoricall*. The *institution* of thy whole *worship* in the *old Law*, was a continuall *Alegory*; *types* and *figures* overspread all; and *figures* flowed into *figures*, and powred themselves out into *farther figures* ... Neither didst thou *speake*, and *worke* in this *language*, onely in the time of thy *Prophets*; but since thou spokest in thy *Son*, it is so too. How often, how much more often doth thy *Sonne* call himselfe a *way*, and a *light*, and a *gate*, and a *Vine*, and *bread*, than the *Sonne of God*, or of *Man*? How much oftner doth he exhibit a *Metaphoricall Christ*, than a *literall*?'[72] The types of divinely inspired human eloquence in the Old Testament – Moses, Aaron, Amos, Solomon, and David – culminate in the metaphorical wisdom of the Son of God, whose parables and various tropes underpin the restrained didacticism of his sermons.

Twenty-five years before he dramatized a rhetorical God in *Paradise Lost*, Milton addressed the subject in a brief exegetical passage concerning God's style, showing a clear familiarity with the tradition examined in this chapter. Like Donne, Milton emphasized the aptness of divine eloquence, uttered in accord with the matter it addressed; in his *Christian Doctrine*, he commends the plainness of God's language as 'fitting' [*æquum*] (*YP*, 6: 147). In defending the strident polemical tone of his final antiprelatical tract, *An Apology Against a Pamphlet*, Milton writes that God's having made 'tart rhetorick' available to Luther for the Protestant cause justifies his own rhetoric of a similar kind. But Milton, arguing both from authority and *a fortiori*, asserts that the precedent for such vehemence extends beyond Luther to the source of Luther's rhetoric, God: 'the Spirit of God who is purity it selfe, when he would reprove any fault severely, or but relate things done or said with indignation by others, abstains not from some words not civill at other times to be spok'n' (*YP*, 1: 901–2). 'Turne,' for instance, 'to the first of Kings [14.10] where God himselfe uses the phrase; *I will cut off from Iereboam him that pisseth against the wall*' (*YP*, 1: 902; he cites other scriptural examples as well). Milton upbraids those commentators who have blanched over the phrase by euphemistically emending it to '*I will cut off all who are at years of discretion,*' as though they 'were of cleaner language than he that made the tongue ... Fools would teach men to read more decently than God thought fit to write' (*YP*, 1: 902, 903). Milton identifies God as the origin of eloquence and asserts the decorum of divine speech in its matching of style to subject, eloquence to wisdom: 'God who is the author both of purity and eloquence, chose this phrase as fittest in that vehement character wherein he spake' (*YP*, 1: 902). The Holy Spirit is again, as for Donne and Augustine, the perfect rhetorician.

Having examined the emphasis on rhetoric in seventeenth-century exegesis and homiletic and their foundation in the eloquence of the Bible and of God as its author, I will now outline the place of poetry within this scheme. The relationship between poetry and Christian theology ran as deeply as the one between poetry and rhetoric. Petrarch believed that poetry was the medium best suited to presenting religious ideas (and that rhetoric's role was to bring Christians closer to God and to make them good).[73] In terms of poetic practice, most early Christian poets worked within classical literary genres, especially epic, in attempting to build up 'a literature of Christian content in antique form.'[74] In terms of theory, Boccaccio perceived the Bible's allegorical linguistic texture as poetic: 'Theology and poetry can be considered as almost identical when their subjects are identical. In fact, I will go even further and decree that theology is nothing less than the poetry of God. For what else is it if not poetic fiction when Christ is sometimes presented in the Scriptures as a lion and at other times as a lamb? ... He is also called by many other names which are too numerous to list. And what else do the words of the Savior in the Gospel, except to a teaching that is not dictated by the outward senses? We refer to this process by using a very common word, 'allegory.' And so it is clear that not only is poetry theology but also that theology is poetry.'[75]

Invoking Augustine at several points, Coluccio Salutati similarly related poetry to the Bible, which, with its double sense (*bilinguis*), was founded on poetic principles.[76] Having elected to pass over the content and ideas of the Bible, he asserted that its *verba simplicia* were composed of poetry and rhetoric, which he perceived, in typical Renaissance fashion, as tightly intermeshed: 'Metaphors and all improper usages of diction and shifts in normal word order, schemes, tropes or whatever else is placed under these headings, are applicable to the poetic art, because it comes forth in a great many figures and is commonly employed by all orators as well as by all poets. Therefore, it happens that whatever in divine Scripture departs from a characteristic and natural meaning, and whatever is asserted figuratively concerning another thing, is entirely poetic and so thoroughly so that it shows by indirection, not by the proper sense, what is intended.'[77] Salutati repeats Augustine's theory of sacred rhetoric, that tropes conceal scriptural meaning beneath a stylistic veil, and extends it by adding poetry as a sister art with the same function. Boccaccio in effect had done the same thing. Sidney, like Salutati an apologist for poetry in general, divided poetry, 'an art of imitation,' into three general kinds: 'the chief, both in antiquity and excellency, were that they did imitate the unconceivable excellencies of God. Such were David in his Psalms; Salomon in his Song of Songs, in his Ecclesiastes, and Proverbs; Moses and Debora in their hymns; and the writer of Job.'[78] The Bible, as theological poetry, achieves the chief aim of Sidney's critical system: it teaches, delights, and moves men to embrace virtue. By treating *docere* and *delectare* as mutually exclusive principles, Thomas Aquinas made a notable attempt to disclaim poetry's connection with the Bible. He noted that metaphor, which 'is proper to poetry,' is also used in the scriptures to convey spiritual matters in terms of material things. He attempted, however, to sever the metaphoric ligature between the style of poetry and that of Holy Writ on the grounds of utility: 'Poetry employs metaphors for the sake of representation, in which we are born to take delight. Holy teaching, on the other hand, adopts them for their indispensable usefulness' in bridging the gap between the spiritual and the material.[79]

Thomas ignored the shared characteristics of poetic metaphor and scriptural metaphor: that poetic representation not only may delight but also may be useful in the accommodative fashion he describes, and that biblical metaphors may delight as well as express spiritual meanings. Delight functions alongside teaching and moving for Augustine, who comments 'on the eloquence of the prophets, where many things are obscured by tropes. The more these things seem to be obscured by figurative words, the sweeter they become when they are explained.'[80] The reader of the Bible, according to the Horatian formula, is both instructed and delighted. In God's speech, then, metaphor and other rhetorical techniques function poetically both by delighting and by teaching divine truth.

God sets forth Christian truth in especially literary colours – that is, poetry and rhetoric are in high relief – in the Psalms and in the Book of Job. The Psalms, wrote John Diodati, were 'stirred and raised up by the holy Ghost, who with his power accompanied the stile, the numbers, and poeticall art of them, and the grave and holy concerts of music.'[81] This divine style was recognized early in Christian exegesis as rhetorical.[82] Interested in the didactic as well as the spiritual benefits to be gained from reading the Psalms, Cassiodorus annotated them with marginal notes that traced the occurrences of rhetorical concepts: $\overline{\text{RT}}$ for rhetoric, $\overline{\text{SCHE}}$ for schemata, $\overline{\text{TOP}}$ for topoi, and so on, found everywhere throughout his *Expositio Psalmorum*. Later commentators regarded these as valuable observations. The ninth-century exegete Notker Balbulus noted: 'Cassiodorus, although he has said many things, in this alone seems to be useful, that he has made clear that the wisdom of the ages, that is, the schemes and most pleasing variety of tropes, lies hidden in this book.'[83] During the English Renaissance, the Psalms as poetry drew the attention of critics such as Philip Sidney and George Wither. For Sidney, they epitomize the genre of theological poetry: 'the holy David's Psalms are a divine poem ... even the name 'Psalms' will speak for me, which, being interpreted, is nothing but songs; then that it is fully written in meter, as all learned Hebricians agree ... lastly and principally, his handling of prophecy, which is merely poetical. For what else is the awaking his musical instruments, the often and free changing of persons, his notable *prosopopeias*, when he maketh you, as it were, see God coming in his majesty, his telling the beasts' joyfulness, and hills' leaping, but a heavenly poesy.'[84] Sidney's appraisal reflects the conflation of poetry and rhetoric in English criticism (note his appropriation of prosopopoeia as 'poetical'), a critical perspective shared by Wither, who had Sidney's general poetic principles in mind at several points in his *Preparation to the Psalter*. The Psalms may have been written in verse, Wither speculated, because their metrical harmony pleases God by imitating the harmony of his creation. Of tropes and figures: 'I dare maintain that no volume of the same bignesse, hath so many as this. For there be scarce two verses together, but they have some or other ornament of speech; yea, in many Psalmes, almost every verse hath his flowres of Poesy.' If he wished, he claimed, he could cite occurrences in the Psalms of every rhetorical device found in Greek and Latin poetry, and, moreover, 'such flowers of Rhetoricke as among them could never yet be found.' Against the background of this long tradition, this concentration on the style of the Psalter, Jesus refers in *Paradise Regained* to 'our Psalms with artful terms inscrib'd' (IV. 335) – devices of poetry and rhetoric that conferred on the Psalms a stylistic majesty commensurate with the sublimity of the Word.[85] As Donne and Milton asserted, God observes decorum in translating His message by means of the human arts.

Joseph Caryl, one of Milton's opponents in the divorce controversy, observed the poetry of God's rhetoric in the most spectacular of the many passages in the scriptures where rhetoric and poetry conflate in divine speech. At the conclusion of the Book of Job, God, hidden in a storm, expounds a theodicy in answer to Job's lamentations and the superficial speculations of his friends. Caryl locates God within the familiar tradition of sacred rhetoric, describing divine speech with accents of Cicero's ideal orator and the ideal preacher of Augustine and Erasmus: 'in the latter part of this Book, we may well conceive God speaking, he speaks so like himself: For here the understanding Reader may perceive a wonderful copiousness of speech, and largness of discourse, strengthened with the exactest and weightiest reasons, set forth with such variety of matter, with such gravity of expressions, with such pressing queries and interrogations ... All this the Lord contracts into two Orations.' For rhetorical commentary Caryl's attention fixes mainly on the second of these orations, God's ekphrasis of Behemoth and Leviathan (40.15–41.32), cast 'in the liveliest colours, and highest expressions of divine eloquence, for [Job's] yet fuller conviction and humiliation.' 'The fourth part of this description,' on Leviathan, 'contains many particulars concerning his parts, power, and proportion, as also the wonderful effects of his power, all which are set down in the highest strains of divine rhetorick, from the 11th verse to the end of 32.'[86] Caryl is alive to the sublimity of the grand style in God's speech here and elsewhere in the Book of Job, where he points out such rhetorical elements as metaphor, arguing from the less to the greater, and the tendentious energy of the barrage of questions heaped on Job.

Caryl's first-person paraphrase of God's words at 41.12, 'I will not conceal his parts,' discloses the rhetorical intent of the Voice from the Whirlwind: 'I will fully, largely, and evidently declare the partes, the power, and the comely proportion of Leviathan ... I will do it exactly, not slightly ... but like an Oratour declare all his excellencies ... So that, when the Lord saith, I will not conceal, he intends much more than he expresseth ... his purpose was to speak copiously and largely.'[87] To intend much more than one expresses, Caryl well knew, is one form of litotes, or understatement. God is understatedly saying, as Caryl makes plain, that He is an orator, that He is about to use the rhetorical techniques of *copia* and amplification to depict Leviathan. He does precisely this in the lines that follow, spoken 'in the highest strains of divine rhetorick':

I will not conceal his parts, nor his power, nor his comely proportion.
Who can discover the face of his garment? or who can come to *him* with his double bridle?
Who can open the doors of his face? his teeth *are* terrible round about.
His scales *are his* pride, shut up together *as with* a close seal.
One is so near to another, that no air can come between them.
They are joined one to another, they stick together, that they cannot be sundered.
By his neesings a light doth shine, and his eyes *are* like the eyelids of the morning.
Out of his mouth go burning lamps, *and* sparks of fire leap out.
Out of his nostrils goeth smoke, as *out* of a seething pot or cauldron.
His breath kindleth coals, and a flame goeth out of his mouth.
In his neck remaineth strength, and sorrow is turned into joy before him.
The flakes of his flesh are joined together: they are firm in themselves; they cannot be moved.
His heart is as firm as a stone; yea, as hard as a piece of the nether *millstone.*
When he raiseth up himself, the mighty are afraid: by reason of breakings they purify themselves.
The sword of him that layeth at him cannot hold: the spear, the dart, nor the habergeon.
He esteemeth iron as straw, *and* brass as rotten wood.
The arrow cannot make him flee: slingstones are turned with him into stubble.
Darts are counted as stubble: he laugheth at the shaking of a spear.

Sharp stones *are* under him: he spreadeth sharp pointed things upon the
  mire.
He maketh the deep to boil like a pot: he maketh the sea like a pot of
  ointment.
He maketh a path to shine after him; one would think the deep *to be* hoary.
Upon the earth there is not his like, who is made without fear.
He beholdeth all high *things:* he is king over all the children of pride.

(Job 41.12–34)

In the Book of Job, where rhetoric, poetry, and the Word intersect at the
crossroads of Judeo-Christian eloquence, God is a consummate rhetorician in the manner noted by John Donne and others. And, as we will see
in chapter 6, He is able in this role to provide further answers about His
ways to mankind for readers of a longer, later biblical epic.

6 The Rhetoric of Heaven

When Milton approached the problem of putting words in the mouth of God, he turned to rhetoric as the formal basis of divine speech. Rhetoric was the universally accepted technical grid on which any written composition had to be mapped out, its interrelationship with poetry being a standard critical assumption during Milton's lifetime. For Milton, however, the affinity between rhetoric and poetry was uncommonly close, given 'what Religious, what glorious and magnificent use might be made of Poetry both in divine and humane things' (*YP*, 2: 405–6). When Milton writes of poetry as 'subsequent, or indeed rather precedent' (*YP*, 2: 403) to rhetoric and dialectic, it is the religious use of poetry that he means, whose power is 'beside the office of a pulpit, to imbreed and cherish in a great people the seeds of vertu, and publick civility' (*YP*, 1: 816). Milton's art of poetry amalgamates rhetoric, dialectic, poetry, theology, and moral philosophy. Poetry is both subsequent and precedent to rhetoric and dialectic: subsequent in that theological poetry derives from a knowledge of those two arts; precedent in that, because its province is the timeless realm of Christian history, it also contains rhetoric and dialectic, and indeed all things, within its eternalized perspective.[1] While poetry and rhetoric had always been united formally, Milton sees them united temporally – together they articulate a prophetic vision that spans the Creation and the sixth and final stage of history.

In *Paradise Lost*, Milton's definition of theological poetry made it inevitable that the divine author of providential history (and of the Bible that reveals it) should be a rhetorician, partly on the warrant of the exegetical traditions discussed in the preceding chapter. At the same time, Milton knew that rhetoric could undercut the true and the good; as the voice of satanic lies, it lay near the source of man's expulsion from Paradise. But he believed too strongly in the discipline's salutary influence on human speech and action to allow a pejorative impression of it to dominate *Paradise Lost*, and so he made rhetoric the voice of divine truth and a powerful force behind man's redemption. He could no more strongly affirm rhetoric's ultimate alignment with Christian ideals than to incorporate it into the speech of God. The rhetorical expression of divine speech elevates the art of rhetoric, keeping it unsullied by its competing association with temptation and the Devil. God's rhetorical speech also supplements Milton's own rhetoric: the *ethos* and eloquence of God increase the persuasive impact of the poem's Christian argument, provide the best example of rhetoric's best possible use, and throw corrupt eloquence into relief for Milton's readers to see, condemn, and shun. Divine rhetoric in *Paradise Lost* thus exemplified for Milton's audience the concept of the *ars dicendi* that the poet himself maintained throughout his career.

Milton greatly expanded the main narrative source for *Paradise Lost*, the record of the Creation and the Fall in the first three chapters of the Book of Genesis. Among his most remarkable feats of poetic augmentation is the speech of the Father, built up from the twenty-six verses of Genesis that contain the words of the Mosaic God, the terse gravity of those relatively few words spun into extended passages where rhetoric makes its characteristically essential contribution to poetics. God and the Son speak both in heaven and in Paradise, the difference in location and the difference in audience that accompanies changes in location bringing with them significant variations and adaptations in the rhetoric of the empyreal characters. God speaks first in heaven, where the nature of divine rhetoric and of the problems related to its dramatization manifest themselves in the 'conversation' between the Father and the Son:

Only begotten Son, seest thou what rage	80
Transports our adversary, whom no bounds	
Prescrib'd, no bars of Hell, nor all the chains	
Heapt on him there, nor yet the main Abyss	
Wide interrupt can hold; so bent he seems	
On desperate revenge, that shall redound	85
Upon his own rebellious head. And now	
Through all restraint broke loose he wings his way	
Not far off Heav'n, in the Precincts of light,	

> Directly towards the new created World,
> And Man there plac't, with purpose to assay   90
> If him by force he can destroy, or worse,
> By some false guile pervert; and shall pervert;
> For Man will heark'n to his glozing lies,
> And easily transgress the sole Command,
> Sole pledge of his obedience: So will fall   95
> Hee and his faithless progeny: whose fault?
> Whose but his own? ingrate, he had of mee
> All he could have; I made him just and right,
> Sufficient to have stood, though free to fall.
> Such I created all th' Ethereal Powers   100
> And Spirits, both them who stood and them who fail'd;
> Freely they stood who stood, and fell who fell.
> Not free, what proof could they have giv'n sincere
> Of true allegiance, constant Faith or Love,
> Where only what they needs must do, appear'd,   105
> Not what they would? what praise could they receive?
> What pleasure I from such obedience paid,
> When Will and Reason (Reason also is choice)
> Useless and vain, of freedom both despoil'd,
> Made passive both, had served necessity,   110
> Not mee.   (III. 80–111)

Stylistic elements merit attention here, for the rhetorical figures uttered by the Father are the product of anthropopathia, the trope by which God descends, through speech, to a level that human beings can understand. The term can also refer, in a theological sense, to God's possessing and displaying emotions. Milton rejected the latter construction of the term, however, urging theologians to discard an anthropopathetic image of God and claiming that although God did feel emotions such as grief and repentance, they were perfected in the divine character and therefore infinitely removed from equivalent human feelings (*YP*, 6: 134–6). Yet Milton's theory of accommodation corresponds with the *rhetorical* definition of anthropopathia as the term was encountered in the preceding chapter:[2] 'God is always described or outlined not as he really is, but in such a way as will make him conceivable to us.' In conveying emotions to mankind, God 'has brought himself down [*demisit*] to our level,' 'adjusted [*accommodat*] his word to our understanding,' and 'disclosed just such an idea of himself to our understanding as he wishes us to possess' (*YP*, 6: 133, 136). God's accommodation to human understanding, as other Renaissance writers had pointed out, involved adopting human forms of speech, in particular the tropes and figures,[3] which communicate the *logos* of Christian doctrine and the *pathos* of divine emotions. This verbal aspect of anthropopathia appealed to Renaissance theologians, but it was an obvious necessity for Milton in the poetic enterprise of dramatizing the speech of God and the Son.

Milton's God immediately establishes a rhetorical mode of speaking, not simply saying that the Adversary has escaped, which would satisfy the straightforward requirements of logic, but distributing the four circumstances that the former angel had to overcome in doing so (lines 81–4). Of the numerous other figures in these lines, those achieving the most notable effect are rhetorical questions, the interrogative mood being almost entirely absent in all the Father's subsequent speech in heaven.[4] *Interrogatio* deserves particular attention because it confirms the divine capacity for impassioned utterance. In it, contrary to the belief of some critics,[5] the passible deity emerges – much as he does near the close of the Book of Job, where God strings together questions as accessories to the grand style, expressive of fury and indignation, thrown down to chasten and humiliate (Job 41.1–11). In Milton's God a much more subdued indignation, a more moderate style, and a different intention are reflected in varieties of rhetorical question such as anthypophora, where a speaker asks a question and answers it himself. It occurs in 'whose fault? / Whose but his own?' (lines 96–7), where the second question, which answers the first, strongly implies its own answer. This type of 'self-answering' question, called erotesis, crops up again twice consecutively (lines 103–6). It presents its own answer with a simple directness which underlines the rhetorical gravity that it imparts to the argument of its user.

In order to understand the rhetorical intention behind this sequence of questions, we need to distinguish between two kinds of rhetoric in poetry: that of the characters within a dramatic or narrative poem, attempting to persuade each other, and, in any sort of poetry, that of the poet who seeks to influence the attitude of the reader.[6] The former, operating within the narrative, the rhetoric *in* the poem, may be called 'internal,' while its counterpart, directed outward at the poem's audience, is the rhetoric *of* the poem, which may be called 'external.' It is mainly the latter rhetoric – Milton speaking to his readership – which governs the Father's opening lines. God's figurative speech is a vehicle for Milton's theodicy, part of the rhetoric of accommodation by which

Milton makes the ways of God accessible to a human audience. This revelatory divine speech takes most of its rhetorical content from the office of teaching, *docere*, as God foretells the future, explains the aetiology of the Fall – that responsibility for it rests squarely on man – and illuminates the conditions of the doctrine of free will. God's rhetorical questions play a key role in this transfer of ideas from Milton to his audience because they elicit answers that induce readers to participate in their own instruction. For example, to the question 'what praise could they receive?' (line 106), the obvious answer, 'none,' sounds in the reader's mind as the correct response, which reinforces Milton's doctrinal lesson that loving God must be a free choice, actively demonstrated. The interplay of question and answer thereby establishes a sort of catechism between the character of God in the poem and the audience reading the poem. God's rhetorical questions invite no answer from the Son, for their implied answers are to be formulated by Milton's audience.

God's speech is the external rhetoric that the poet employs to influence an audience and that may be more readily attributed to Milton than to God himself. Its status as the rhetoric *in* the poem, however, by which characters persuade one another – or for that matter communicate with each other – is compromised. The reason stems from God's audience; ostensibly, it is His 'Only begotten Son.' Theological considerations concerning the nature of the Son, particularly with regard to the divine trait of omniscience, throw into question the viability of internal rhetoric in heaven. Milton asserts in *Christian Doctrine* that the Son, subordinate to the Father in every way, is not omniscient (*YP*, 6: 227, 265–6, 274). On the other hand, the Son of God in *Paradise Lost* is 'Equal to God, and equally enjoying / God-like fruition' (III. 306–7) and affirms himself 'Image of [the Father] in all things' (VI. 736), including, these descriptions suggest, a being who knows all things. The anti-trinitarianism of the *Christian Doctrine*, which denies omniscience to the Son, does not consistently determine the relationship of God and the Son in *Paradise Lost*. The two are distinguished as separate beings only during dramatic scenes in which they speak to one another, while at other times they act and are identified under a single godhead.[7] In fact, the Son is called God when he creates the universe and earth (VII. 232–504) and when he judges Adam and Eve (X. 97–208). United in power and in name, they share the same attributes. The Son demonstrates that he possesses foreknowledge by outlining the future consequences of his willingness to become the agent of Atonement, from his carnal death to his triumph at the Apocalypse and the beatitude the elect will enjoy after the Final Judgement (III. 241–65).

Having proleptically summarized Christian history in this way, the Son evidently knows everything the Father knows. Their shared foreknowledge is what challenges the internal rhetoric of heaven. As Boethius explained of divine *praescientia*, everything for God – and here, for the Son as well – appears as a continuous present. Just as time, according to divine perception, is no longer a linear progression, so speech loses its character as a linear presentation of ideas, unfolding in time, with the result that the whole of any spoken exchange stands immediately present within the view of both God and the Son. The high point of their discussion, the Son's offer to die for man, is as foreknown to both of them as every other act of speech, or episode of any sort, that will ever take place. Each knows beforehand what the other will say. Divine foreknowledge, then, impairs the contingency inherent in traditional rhetoric, the possibility that the outcome of a rhetorical situation, suspended in doubt and uncertainty, may be decided one way or another based on the effectiveness of a given argument. The statements, questions, and responses of God and the Son can follow only one course: the one both have seen and have always in sight. This restriction of contingency poses a unique problem that informs the divine colloquy in numerous ways.

To exemplify how the certainty generated by omniscience or foreknowledge affects the rhetoric of heaven, we may refer to the closing words of God's second speech, the open request for a redeemer:

> Say Heav'nly Powers, where shall we find such love,
> Which of ye will be mortal to redeem
> Man's mortal crime, and just th' unjust to save,
> Dwells in all Heaven charity so dear?   (III. 213–16)

'He ask'd, but all the Heav'nly Choir stood mute, / And silence was in Heav'n' (III. 217–18). That silence represents one of the most crucial moments in *Paradise Lost*: the fate of mankind hangs on each instant that passes; the primal sin, if not redressed, will mean the end of humanity. Yet, from the point of view of the Father and the Son, none of this uncertainty exists. The same power that has forecast the occurrence of the Fall, divine foreknowledge, likewise knows in advance that the Son will break the silence and that man will be saved: 'Father, thy word is past, man shall find grace' (III. 227). God's question appears to entreat an intercessor for man, whereas its true function is to prompt the Son's foreknown reply. When the Son similarly asks the Father a series of questions, the purpose is the same:

> For should Man finally be lost, should Man
> Thy creature late so lov'd, thy youngest Son
> Fall circumvented thus by fraud, though join'd
> With his own folly? ...
> Or shall the Adversary thus obtain
> His end, and frustrate thine, shall he fulfil
> His malice, and thy goodness bring to naught,
> Or proud return though to his heavier doom,
> Yet with revenge accomplish't and to Hell
> Draw after him the whole Race of mankind,
> By him corrupted? or wilt thou thyself
> Abolish thy Creation, and unmake,
> For him, what glory thou hast made?   (III. 150–3, 156–64)

He knows the answer to all these questions, whose true intention is to prepare the way for the Father to speak the next instalment of the theodicy. Their questions to each other, as well as their responses, are factitious, artificially staged for the instruction and persuasion of two different audiences, only one of which is important for the present analysis, that being the 'Heav'nly Choir.'[8] Angels do not share the omniscience of the godhead. For them, humanity's fate is a truly contingent affair, and the moments following God's question contain genuine uncertainty. The Father and the Son accordingly take full advantage of the opportunity to craft a forceful political message; they manage the *dispositio* of their dialogue, with its exaltation of mankind's future saviour, under the rhetorical motive of convincing the heavenly host of the Son's merit to rule. Like Machiavelli's princes or France's Louis XIV, who advocated such a strategy to the dauphin, the Father and the Son are absolute rulers who employ spectacle, a brilliant public display of imperial power, as a rhetorical tactic to confirm their subjects' hierarchical station and to overwhelm them with awe for their king(s), thereby affirming the *status quo*.[9] Although the power that the Son demonstrates here is that of charity, hardly the stuff of Machiavellian power politics, the absolutist undertones of the scene are apparent in the manipulation of persuasive spectacle, and they may even suggest an aspect of imperial rhetoric noted of Louis XIV in Molière's *Tartuffe*, that the rulers of Milton's heaven actually depend on rhetoric in order to hold and entrench their power.[10] After all, the rebellion that drew away one-third of heaven's citizenry is still a fresh event. A grand confirmation of regal greatness may deepen the loyalty of even the faithful.

The heavenly dialogue clearly exemplifies the kind of rhetoric that attempts to influence the attitude of Milton's reader. Its identity as the internal rhetoric that functions among the poem's characters is less stable, since divine foreknowledge undermines a contingent future in which arguments and decisions have free play. God and the Son do not – cannot – persuade one another. In the face of this the angels are vital to the rhetoric in the poem, since the heavenly dialogue and its climactic exaltation of the Son exert a genuinely rhetorical effect on them – they are finally moved, 'uttering joy' (III. 347), to sing the kerygma of praise for the Father and the Son. Their perception of the future as contingent and their susceptibility to rhetoric's power over the emotions foster an atmosphere where persuasion can occur, a condition that offsets the force opposed to traditional rhetoric, the omniscience of the Father and the Son. Divine foreknowledge puts rhetoric on the defensive, in need of compensatory assertions of its existence and efficacy in heaven. By providing the speech of God and the Son with an audience in the poem, an audience able to be moved by the rhetoric of imperial spectacle, the angels highlight the impression of divine speech as rhetoric, as public oratory directed at gaining zealous assent. They serve the same function later, when God tells them about the transgression and dispatches Michael (XI. 84–125). God manages the rhetorical stage in the same way, moving from His customary imperative mood to subjunctive constructions of purpose and conditional clauses: 'Lest therefore now his bolder hand / Reach also of the Tree of Life'; 'lest the Fiend ... some new trouble raise'; 'Yet lest they faint / At the sad Sentence rigorously urg'd'; 'If patiently thy bidding they obey'; 'Lest Paradise a receptácle prove / To Spirits foul, and all my Trees thir pray'. Of course none of these situations is the least bit uncertain, despite God's implications. These later speeches derive their rhetorical content from God's obvious manipulation of the speech moment, which holds the angels in the grip of dramatic irony – for all they know, the Fiend may raise some new trouble. The angels, unforeknowing, impart to God's words at least a semblance of future contingency that is otherwise entirely absent in dialogue between the Father and Son. While the angels support rhetoric in the face of divine omniscience, rhetoric in heaven receives additional fortification from other sources, concentrated especially in *elocutio*. Assessing the nature of rhetoric there requires a detailed examination of style, particularly of the tropes and figures traditionally associated with the speech of God.

The recurrence of one figure in the heavenly dialogue may be traced as a norm of stylistic usage in divine speech, which is characteristically unobtrusive, solemn, and harmonized with content. Conduplicatio, or reduplication, which repeats one or more words in successive clauses, appears at least sixteen times in the speech of God in Book III. It is prevalent in the first part of his opening speech, quoted above, and afterward: 'I form'd them free, and free they must remain' (line 124); 'the high Decree ... which ordain'd / Thir freedom: they themselves ordain'd thir fall' (lines 126–8); 'All hast thou spoken as my thoughts are, all / As my eternal purpose hath decree'd' (lines 171–2), and so forth. Closely related to this figure is polyptoton, which repeats a word in a different form ('And be thyself *man* among *men* on earth'). It occurs with conspicuous frequency, often in the lines of the Son, and contributes to the subtle effect of verbal doubling. These figures create an incantatory undercurrent of repetition that highlights the words involved for special consideration (fault/fault, man/men, death/death, etc.), that conveys emotion ('O thou in Heav'n and Earth the only peace / Found out for mankind under wrath, O thou / My sole complacence!'), and that even suggests a lexical parallel to the paired unity of the Father and the Son. Most notably, it formally echoes the culminating idea of the entire heavenly dialogue, which the Father sums up with three final instances of conduplicatio. When the Last Judgment has taken place,

> Then thou thy regal Sceptre shalt lay by,
> For regal Sceptre then no more shall need,
> God shall be All in All. But all ye Gods,
> Adore him, who to compass all this dies,
> Adore the Son, and honor him as mee.   (III. 339–43)

The reduplicated word patterns scattered throughout God's speech have been leading up to the fulfilment of Christian destiny that is contained in the climactic reduplication, echoing St Paul (I Corinthians 15.28), of God's being 'All in All.' As the entire sequence of doubled words ultimately resolves itself in this phrase, achieving the harmonization of form, so the divine will, now fully justified, arrives at the perfected state that the phrase contains, the final harmonization of all things: 'All in All.' The gradual completion of the figural pattern formally parallels the gradual realization of providence through the mediation of the Son; in other words, the stylistic expression of the idea is part and parcel of the idea itself. Conduplicatio, along with its cousin polyptoton, may be thought of as the master rhetorical scheme of heaven, since its rhythms anticipate and lay stylistic foundations for the state of God's completeness, and the completeness of all things in God.

Similar rhetorical figures occur in the speech of the Son, who integrates another kind of repetition into the Logos:

> Behold mee then, mee for him, life for life
> I offer, on mee let thine anger fall;
> Account mee man; I for his sake will leave
> Thy bosom, and his glory next to thee
> Freely put off, and for him lastly die
> Well pleas'd, on me let Death wreck all his rage;
> Under his gloomy power I shall not long
> Lie vanquish't.   (III. 236–43)

Conduplicatio (mee, mee; life, life) turns into ploce, the rhetorical figure of repeating a word several times, often with a new signification after the intervention of other words. Here, it is on 'mee,' which the Son repeats in calling divine justice down on himself. The pronoun refers to him initially as the divine Son, but shifts to signify a mortal man who, like all men, will die. This figure, combined with polyptoton (Thy, thee; die, Death), is part of the music of repetition leading to the climactic 'All in All,' and contributes to raising these lines to the grand style, which culminates in the prosopopoeia of Death. That the Son repeats this word in a similar manner at two other points in the poem reveals an important side of his oratorical persona. After the Fall, prevenient grace having at length enabled Adam and Eve to repent in prayer, the 'great Intercessor' entreats the Father,

> Now therefore bend thine ear
> To supplication, hear his sighs though mute;
> Unskilful with what words to pray, let mee
> Interpret for him, mee his Advocate
> And propitiation, all his works on mee
> Good or not good ingraft, my Merit those
> Shall perfet, and for these my Death shall pay.   (XI. 32–6)

'Me' and 'my' recur several more times in this speech. The result is the same figure that the Son had spoken in Book III, a stylistic echo that indicates the primacy of timing and occasion, the *kairos*, and the Son's responsiveness to it. Book XI sees the climactic moment of reconciliation, of mediation between God and the fallen human pair, a moment that asks that rhetoric meet the gravity of the situation by resummoning, through the same figure, the tone and the circumstances of the Son's sacrificial offer in Book III when he steps forward as Saviour. The ploce on 'me' in these lines from Book XI invokes that previous acceptance of the role of saviour and now expands it to include the role of mediator.

The figure's first usage in the chronological order of events occurs in a very different context, immediately before the rebel host is defeated, where it shifts the burden of hatred from the angels to the Son as later, in the instances cited above, it will transfer to him the burden of sin. He tells the angels,

> stand only and behold
> God's indignation on these Godless pour'd
> By mee; not you but mee they have despis'd,
> Yet envied; against mee is all thir rage,
> Because the Father, t'whom in Heav'n supreme
> Kingdom and Power and glory appertains,
> Hath honor'd me according to his will.
> Therefore to mee thir doom he hath assign'd;
> That they may have thir wish, to try with mee
> In Battle which the stronger proves, they all,
> Or I alone against them, since by strength
> They measure all, of other excellence
> Not emulous, nor care who them excels;
> Nor other strife with them do I voutsafe.   (VI. 810–23)

In the two instances already examined, the iterated 'me' casts the Son as a redeemer and a vehicle of mercy; here, as a destroyer and a vehicle of justice, and also as a hero, since by his emphasis on 'me' he accepts not only all the hatred of his foes but the full measure of glory in vanquishing them. The figure's capacity to voice these different roles of sonship depends on the timing of its utterance, conditioned by the orator's response to audience and situation. The Son's manner of responding to the *kairos* here, while he speaks to his army of angels, customizes the literary battle oration in line with the unique circumstances that exist in heaven. Whereas generals traditionally respond to the martial *kairos* by attempting to stir their troops to fury and bloody action – Henry V at the gates of Harfleur, Richard III at Bosworth – the Son does the opposite, a contrast of objectives meant to be recognized immediately and therefore highlighted in his opening words: 'Stand still in bright array ye Saints, here stand / Ye angels arm'd, this day from battle rest' (VI. 801–2). The epanalepsis (starting and finishing a line with the same word) on 'stand' accentuates the reversal of expectations for the battle speech – the troops are bid to stand and rest, not to fight. The Son's understanding of providence and of the power he wields within its framework liberates him from any need or impulse to urge them otherwise.

Assured of success in the foresight of 'Second Omnipotence' (VI. 684), moments ago he had heard the Father tell him,

> Two days are therefore past, the third is thine;
> For thee I have ordain'd it, and thus far
> Have suffer'd, that the Glory may be thine
> Of ending this great War, since none but Thou
> Can end it.   (VI. 699–703)

As to the war in heaven, God, having 'foreseen / This tumult, and permitted all' (VI. 673–4), has 'ordain'd' that the Son will end it. The Son's speech to the angels, robbed of anticipatory urgency in the face of God's decree, derives its rhetorical content from other sources: from its style, including the figures mentioned above, and from the opportunistic assessment of *kairos*, in particular the moment chosen for speaking. For the Son, having received the Father's directive, need not speak at all, but can simply act and go to war. Addressing the loyal angels, however, publicly affirms his leadership, much as he had demonstrated his merit in Book III by publicly sacrificing himself for humankind. The other angels, once again, are not privileged to know the outcome beforehand, and they react to words, spectacle, and actions in the same way as a human audience would. When the Son accepts the full burden of the war, their relief, and awe at his courage, may be inferred. Victory brings glory as the angels,

>   who silent stood
> Eye-witness of his Almighty Acts,
> ... him sung Victorious King ...
> Worthiest to Reign.   (VI. 882–3, 886, 888)

The Son's battle oration serves a more general purpose in the rhetoric of heaven. Its familiarity as a topos, as a recognizable application of rhetoric, supports the idea of rhetoric against the undermining influence of divine foreknowledge. The speech demonstrates rhetoric in use, purposefully directed, and the reactions of the angels, in Books III and VI, show it working on an audience. These events affirm the presence and efficacy of rhetoric in heaven despite the absence of contingency from the viewpoints of the two main speakers there, the Father and the Son.

Discourse in heaven exhibits other traditional elements and functions of rhetoric that militate against this restriction of contingency. One is epideixis, the rhetoric of praise or blame, which dominated humanist oratory and often characterizes the words of the Son. Although the Son's judgment of the serpent, Eve, and Adam assigns blame (X. 175–208), his epideictic attitude is usually one of praise, and his praise is mostly of the Father:

O Father, O Supreme of heav'nly Thrones,
First, Highest, Holiest, Best ...
                    in the end
Thou shalt be All in All, and I in thee
For ever, and in mee all whom thou lov'st.   (VI. 723–33)

The Son's praise reinforces the *ethos* of the Father. The other two forms of Aristotelian proof, *pathos* and especially *logos*, are evident in heaven, along with other characteristics of classical structure. The Father's own rhetoric, defending or justifying His ways to men, is often forensic (appropriately so, as theodicy is a form of defence). Projected at Milton's audience, this forensic presentation of theodicy is directed at teaching (*docere*), a major function of rhetoric in *Paradise Lost*. God's speech is theologically instructive to readers; the dialogue of God and the Son teaches the angels and, as their reaction proves, also moves (*movere*) and delights (*delectare*) them. In Book VIII God descends to Eden and teaches Adam, though in a less straightforward manner, as I will discuss in chapter 10. Heavenly rhetoric's translation to the Garden of Eden, in particular through Raphael and Michael, adds the deliberative mode to the epideictic and forensic, as the two angels advise Adam about the future both before and after the Fall.

Wherever the rhetoric of heaven is spoken, whether in Paradise or in heaven itself, style figures as one of its defining traits. Milton's attentiveness to style in all his works mirrored the aesthetic priorities of the literary culture he lived in, a culture in which the presumptive alliance of rhetorical *elocutio* and poetics entailed that the *ornatus* of tropes and figures was adopted as the core of stylistic method in Renaissance poetry. The preoccupation with *elocutio* that by and large marked Renaissance rhetoric also reached into seventeenth-century poetry, where tropes and figures were the clothing that attired the invention of poetic fancy. But because they were also native to the speech of God, Milton made them a special signature of divine eloquence and the basis for the most stylistically intricate passage in *Paradise Lost*:

> So Man, as is most just,
> Shall satisfy for Man, be judg'd and die,
> And dying rise, and rising with him raise
> His Brethren, ransom'd with his own dear life.
> So Heav'nly love shall outdo Hellish hate,
> Giving to death, and dying to redeem,
> So dearly to redeem what Hellish hate
> So easily destroy'd, and still destroys
> In those who, when they may, accept not grace.   (III. 294–302)[11]

Words, like all created things, fall under the dominion of the Father, who is the perfect rhetorician. Reminiscent of the baroque in its control of form and precise stylistic detailing, this passage shows another side of God's eloquence, amplified from its customarily muted rhythmic effects into a display of technical skill that operates at the furthest limit of rhetorical virtuosity. Wisdom could hardly speak more copiously while living up to the ideal of *ars est celare artem* (true art conceals its artificiality). As Longinus had said, 'a figure is generally thought to be best when the fact that it is a figure is concealed.'[12] The sequence of interlaced figures, although unrivalled in the poem for difficulty of execution, nearly escapes notice as ornament, merging fluidly with the sense of the passage. Milton hereby establishes that God sets the standard for eloquence – that is, the harmonizing of *res* and *verba* – and for the command of style in its own right, across its entire spectrum from the relatively spare, discussed earlier, to the most ornamental, seen here. This passage conforms to, even exaggerates, the long-standing idea that God's speech is rhetorical, although it consists exclusively of figures, with none of the tropes often seen in divine speech.

Both tropes and figures can provoke in readers a wide range of responses. These may be intellectual, emotional, or both, and may include an attendant appreciation of style. But figures, because they are spatial, working language into audible or visible patterns, point back more obviously than tropes to the process of stylistic creation and to the artist who uses them. In their most expert application, figures provoke wonder at the skill of this spotlighted artist, a reaction that the schemes here are meant to induce. Their abundance, tightly controlled and moulded to the sense, confirms God's mastery over language and rhetoric. The sure-handedness demonstrated in their arrangement, in their elegant configuration, is an important quality of divine rhetoric. Such a style is a creative force: 'Silence, ye troubl'd waves, and thou Deep, peace, / Said then th' Omnific Word, your discord end' (VII. 216–17). The first sentence of the Creation is a chiasmus,[13] a scheme managed by firm syntactic control which parallels the control that the Son exerts over Chaos. Its geometric pattern – starting at a point, moving outward, and returning to the start by a similar route – corresponds with his use of

> the golden Compasses ...
>   to circumscribe
> This Universe, and all created things:
> One foot he centred, and the other turn'd
> Round through the vast profundity obscure.   (VII. 225–8)

The Son's efficient power flows directly from his power over language. Milton stresses that the Son is the Word (VII. 163, 175, 217), the Logos, which includes *sermo* and *oratio*, which in turn often refer to issues of style or manner of expression. His nature, therefore, is intimately connected with rhetoric, with a command over language. The roles of the stylist and the creator are tightly knit; well-ordered words impose order on Chaos and initiate the creative act: 'speak thou,' the Father tells the Son, 'and be it done' (VII. 164). The creation invokes the full range of the word *kosmos*: order and arrangement, ornament and embellishment, ruler or regulator, and, metaphorically, the universe, viewed as a perfectly ordered collocation of parts. The rhetoric of Christian divinity transcends the Ciceronian duties of teaching, delighting, and moving. It also creates – a power immanent in its stylistic forms.

The rhetoric of heaven nevertheless undertakes the offices of the Ciceronian model, especially when Raphael and Michael bring their embassies to the Garden of Eden. Teaching is their primary objective: they instruct Adam on one level, Milton's readership on another. The angels share three rhetorical roles. Both are poets, Raphael's poetic activity more closely approximating that of Milton – the poet as *vates*, divinely inspired, charged with ensuring that events and ideas proper to heaven are 'told as earthly notion can receive' (VII. 179). As types of the poet-orator, Raphael and Michael share Milton's poetic resources of words and images. Both are preachers: the pre-eminently instructive and hortatory strains in both discourses find clear parallels in homiletic. And both are historians: Michael, the 'Seer blest' (XII. 553), presents and helps Adam to interpret 'the Visions of God' (XI. 377) that unfold the providential future, while Raphael, the 'Divine / Historian' (VIII. 6–7), must find language to accommodate the past events of cosmic history to the limited capacities of human understanding.

Despite these and other similarities, an important rhetorical distinction aligns Raphael's discourse with Eden, while Michael's, to be treated here, remains properly of heaven. The partition falls according to the status of contingency in the different rhetorical situations to which God assigns them. Contingency is a live rhetorical variable during Raphael's visit, when the obedience he exhorts is left to Adam and Eve's free will; but its relevance declines during Michael's visit, as the human pair, having chosen wrongly and submitted to the bondage of sin, forfeit the freedom to control their own destiny and must leave Eden. Diminished free will is not the only hindrance to rhetorical contingency, which is dealt a further blow when the province of history becomes the future in Books XI and XII. Constructing a history of the future is theoretically impossible under normal circumstances; the past, being necessary, is the only legitimate sphere of historical inquiry. The future lies beyond the reach of such inquiry for reasons whose importance to rhetoric has already been established: 'The future ... is the contingent, the indeterminate, that which can only be described by saying "if A happens, then x will follow; if B happens, then y will follow; but though it may be wise to assume that A will happen and B will not, we cannot give valid reasons for the assumption." Of course, the future will be what it will be; but that only means that when it happens it will be the present, and will have all the actuality of the present. It is not lying somewhere ready formed, waiting to happen.'[14] Raphael's narrative obeys these rules of 'earthbound' historiography, of world history. He relates the necessary past, not the contingent future, which remains open to causal deliberation and probabilistic speculation but cannot be reckoned with as history. Universal history, however, breaks these rules, for it is not only retrospective, summoned from Raphael's memory of the past, but also uniquely prospective, generated by Michael's 'forward memory' of the future. Thus, in

Michael's history the future is no longer the contingent and the indeterminate; rather, it is as certain and inevitable as the past, and no less
available than the past to historical excavation. His prophetic visions
show a future ready formed and waiting to happen – a condition naturally inimical to deliberative rhetoric, which relies on the tension of
future contingents in order to be fully viable. But deliberative rhetoric
is out of season after the Fall, and so Michael adopts a different kind of
rhetoric, one that seeks to regenerate Adam's reason by transforming
the future into a theatre of instruction rather than an arena of action.
In relation to this goal, the degree of future contingency is relatively in-
consequential.

Variation in contingency influences the intentions and procedures of
heavenly rhetoric spoken on earth, the respective attitudes with which
Raphael and Michael approach their rhetorical agendas. Raphael's
rhetoric is monitory. It presents the circumstances of the war in heaven
as an example of disobedience and its consequences, and warns of the
threat that Satan poses. Its deliberative stance, counselling circumspec-
tion and forbearance, presupposes the human couple's freedom to
choose when confronted with Satan's lies and deceit. Michael's rhetoric, on the other hand, is revelatory. It is an authoritative proclamation
of divine truth, which at first presents its argument as law and which,
in accord with the epistemology of religious rhetoric, is based on certainty, not probability. It too offers a morally instructive example, this
time one to be emulated, in the person of Jesus. But the *imitatio Christi* is
less Adam's choice than an obligation after the Fall, when he must
relearn obedience and love from their perfected display in the life and
death of the Saviour. Michael's rhetoric limits the alternative possibilities Adam may consider – he becomes wiser, but faces inevitable expulsion from the garden. The application of Michael's forward memory,
imparted to Adam, shifts the rhetorical foundation of Books XI and XII.
Michael's speech and imagery secure their rhetorical content not from
persuasion fused to the classical principle of contingency, as before the
Fall, but from evangelical instruction sourced in the absolute authority
of revealed Christian truth.

The formal structure of revelation includes logic, expressive of the
reason inherent in divine wisdom. Michael's rhetoric in Books XI and
XII, just as Renaissance rhetoric often did, assimilates logic and applies
it to rhetorical ends. Combining words and images, this rhetoric
instructs Adam in two matters. It gradually leads him to understand
the prophecy that, as the Son tells the serpent, '[woman's] seed shall

bruise thy head, thou bruise his heel' (X. 181). It also leads him, as part of that understanding,

> to learn
> True patience, and to temper joy with fear
> And pious sorrow, equally inur'd
> By moderation either state to bear,
> Prosperous or adverse: so shalt thou lead
> Safest thy life, and best prepar'd endure
> Thy mortal passage when it comes.   (XI. 360–6)

Adam must embrace a Stoic acceptance of his lot, an emotional equilibrium that will reassert the claim of reason, overthrown by the Fall. Its goal, as we shall see, is not the eradication of the emotions but their steady government, a state of mind achieved along the lines of a Christian response to Stoicism, which asserts the propriety of certain emotions, even strong ones, that are conducive to piety.[15] This ethical policy implicitly sanctions rhetoric's traditional function of arousing the passions, provided that, while it does so, it also teaches which emotional responses soundly express zeal and faith and which do not. Knowing the difference is a point of Christian wisdom, the ultimate state to which Michael's rhetoric seeks to lead Adam.

That rhetoric, from the outset, is deeply affective. Sent to Eden with a mandate to 'Dismiss them not disconsolate' (XI. 113), Michael delivers his post-lapsarian rhetoric in a manner that initially does not seem at all consolatory. Adam's first impression of Michael, that he is not 'sociably mild / As Raphael ... But solemn and sublime' (XI. 234–6), intuits qualities that are rendered in the angel's solemn and sublime speech, as in his opening lines:

> *Adam*, Heav'n's high behest no Preface needs:
> Sufficient that thy Prayers are heard, and Death,
> Then due by sentence when thou didst transgress,
> Defeated of his seizure many days
> Giv'n thee of Grace, wherein thou mayst repent,
> And one bad act with many deeds well done
> May'st cover: well may then thy Lord appeas'd
> Redeem thee quite from Death's rapacious claim;
> But longer in this place to dwell
> Permits not; to remove thee I am come,

> And send thee from the Garden forth to till
> The ground whence thou wast tak'n, fitter Soil.   (XI. 251–62)

Divine rhetoric heard in the garden after the Fall differs markedly from that heard before it, from God and Raphael. It is unceremonious and terse, giving only what is 'Sufficient': Michael uses 'no Preface' or exordium, Adam is accorded no titles, and the provisions of man's sentence – that Death has been forestalled, that repentance can bring salvation, that eviction from Eden is imminent – are retailed in fewer than 100 words. Michael's style is relatively plain; however, because his speech is a prime example of the Longinian sublime, its style is beside the point; for its effect, 'the combination of wonder and astonishment,' is of the kind that 'always proves superior to the merely persuasive ... Sublimity ... produced at the right moment, tears up everything like a whirlwind, and exhibits the orator's whole power at a single blow:'[16] 'Adam at the news / Heart-strook with chilling gripe of sorrow stood, / That all his senses bound,' and Eve, 'with audible lament,' reacts with a series of exclamations, rhetorical questions, and apostrophes (XI. 264–6, 268–85). Michael's sublime speech is plain in form yet grand in effect, even though he delivers it impassively, without any intention of augmenting the emotive power latent in the terms of God's sentence. In Eden, the expression of God's will does not need a fiery delivery or the stylistic devices of the *genus grande* in order to move deeply. Adam realizes why it does not call on such techniques of amplification: 'gently hast thou told / Thy message, which might else in telling wound' (XI. 298–9). For the message to have been 'else in telling,' that is, in a higher style, would have produced an unbearable emotional effect, 'And in performing end us' (XI. 300). As delivered, Michael's style condescends to the emotional as well as the intellectual limitations of a human audience. Mercy first and last shall brightest shine, and Michael's rhetoric reflects the fact. Justice reaches human ears through his plain style, a style intended, Adam sees, to lighten the weight of the decree.

Mercy also tempers justice as Michael proceeds from this first purpose of his mission, serving notice of banishment, to the second, prophetic revelation, which mitigates the punishment by showing, as Adam comes to realize, 'That all this good of evil shall produce, / And evil turn to good' (XII. 470–1). This last stage of understanding in Milton's theodicy, the paradox of the *felix culpa*, is gradually revealed to Adam through Michael's rhetoric, which, rooted in logic, opposes and corrects the fallacies of the preceding visitor to Eden, Satan. Michael states at the outset that he will be employing formal logic:

> *Adam*, now ope thine eyes, and first behold
> Th' effects which thy original crime hath wrought
> In some to spring from thee.   (XI. 423–5)

Michael is alluding to a mode of argument that Milton discusses in the *Art of Logic*: 'Distribution occurs when the whole is distributed into its parts' (*YP*, 8: 297); in this particular case, 'Distribution from effects occurs when the parts are effects' derived from the whole of a cause (*YP*, 8: 301), as is true at this point in the narrative where the cause, 'original crime,' is about to be distributed into its future effects, commencing Adam's lesson. To know the causes of things is demonstrative knowledge, the ideal of knowledge in Milton's day. '*Scire est cognoscere per causas* runs the familiar tag: true knowledge is of necessary connections, demonstrative arguments linking causes to effects with certainty.'[17] These necessary causal links and connections are what Michael teaches Adam. Superior to any of the conjectural probabilities related to rhetoric, demonstrative knowledge rebuilds the formal structures of knowledge and reason that satanic eloquence had toppled.

The first vision Adam sees, that of Cain murdering Abel, shows the primary effect of original sin: Death. Michael goes on to distribute it from causes,[18] 'the many shapes / Of Death, and many ... ways that lead / To his grim Cave,' in addition to murder:

> Some, as thou saw'st, by violent stroke shall die,
> By Fire, Flood, Famine, by Intemperance more
> In Meats and Drinks, which on the Earth shall bring
> Diseases dire, of which a monstrous crew
> Before thee shall appear, that thou may'st know
> What misery th' inabstinence of Eve
> Shall bring on men.   (XI. 471–7)

Death having been distributed from its causes – murder, flood, fire, famine – the last cause cited here, intemperance, is now distributed into *its* effects: diseases. Intemperance is given special emphasis. When the causal hierarchy is delved into further, the cause of original sin is declared to be Eve's 'inabstinence,' an intemperance that had allowed the passions to overmaster reason. It is substantially the same error that

Adam must correct through Stoic self-control. The effects that he will behold emanating from the mortal sin of gluttony amplify the importance of self-government in general, whether over the body or the mind (Michael's Christian version of Stoicism absorbs the Peripatetic doctrine of the mean in prescribing 'the rule of not too much, by temperance taught, / In what thou eat'st and drink'st': XI. 531–2). Michael's rhetoric of images reveals the horrors of disease, a genus, by distributing it into its species:

               all maladies
Of ghastly Spasm, or racking torture, qualms
Of heart-sick Agony, all feverous kinds,
Convulsions, Epilepsies, fierce Catarrhs,
Intestine Stone and Ulcer, Colic pangs,
Dæmonic Frenzy, moping Melancholy
And Moon-struck madness, pining Atrophy,
Marasmus, and wide-wasting Pestilence,
Dropsies, and Asthmas, and Joint-racking Rheums.   (XI. 480–8)

Michael's distributive genealogy of mortal sin, traced back as far as Eve's inabstinence,[19] charts the proliferation of original sin into death, intemperance, diseases, and kinds of disease, with various relationships of cause to effect and genus to species occurring among them. This mass of ideas, words, and images produces a rhetorical impact: 'Sight so deform what heart of Rock could long / Dry-ey'd behold? Adam could not, but wept' (XI. 494–5). The presentation employs logic, Michael's examples of distribution corresponding to Milton's treatment of this procedure in the *Art of Logic*. Adam responds, however, not as to a logical argument but as to a rhetorical one, aimed at the passions.

Adam's response shows how Milton, in typical humanist fashion, conflated logic and rhetoric. Logic he considered to be not only propaedeutic to rhetoric, but also a storehouse of 'well couch't heads and Topics' (*YP*, 2: 402) such as those discussed in his logic handbook, to be drawn on for rhetorical *inventio*. Logic and rhetoric shared a set of argumentative procedures whereby each attempted to influence different faculties. Distribution in Milton's logic, for example, which divides wholes into parts in order to appeal to reason, was in English Renaissance rhetoric a kind of amplification, performing the same function but in order to move the passions: 'Amplification is a certain affirmation very great & waighty, which by large and plentifull speech, moveth the minds of the hearers, & maketh them to believe that which is said.' Through it the orator, in terms familiar to Milton, 'may easily draw the mindes of his hearers whether he will ... he may move them ... to weepe, to pitty, to loth, to be ashamed, to repent,' and so on.[20] Under amplification, Peacham lists distribution as a main heading.[21] It subsumes, among other figures, partitio (whole divided into parts), enumeratio (cause into effects) and divisio (genus into species) – the same techniques explained in the *Art of Logic*, except that for Peacham their status shifts from topics of logic to figures of rhetoric. For Milton, they could serve either function: a particular argumentative and verbal construction, such as distribution, could be either a logical topic or a rhetorical figure, depending on the context of its application. In theory and practice, Milton endorsed the incorporation of logic into rhetoric – and naturally, at the same time, into poetry. Cicero notes that 'the topic of the effects of causes ... is wont to give a marvelous fullness of expression [*copia dicendi*] to orators and poets,'[22] precisely the reason that Milton looks to it in Books XI–XII. In poetry, the usefulness of logic for Milton resided in the topics' natural tendency to generate *copia*.

Michael's logical constructions, employed for the sake of rhetorical amplification, recall those of the Puritan sermon as practised by the likes of Richard Bernard and Thomas Adams. Through this coalition of logic and rhetoric, Michael appeals jointly to Adam's emotions and reason and teaches the proper management of both. The purpose of stirring Adam's emotions is mainly to teach him that they should be moderated. Adam is appalled at the sight of gluttony's consequences and is ready to quit life after Michael describes the attributes of yet another cause of death, old age. Another kind of distribution is that of a subject into its adjuncts, as 'when a subject receives its implanted or inhering attributes' (*YP*, 8: 243):

> This is old age; but then thou must outlive
> Thy youth, thy strength, thy beauty, which will change
> To wither'd weak and gray; thy Senses then
> Obtuse, all taste of pleasure must forgo,
> To what thou hast, and for the Air of youth
> Hopeful and cheerful, in thy blood will reign
> A melancholy damp of cold and dry
> To weigh thy Spirits down, and last consume
> The Balm of Life.   (XI. 538–46)

'Henceforth I fly not death, nor would prolong / Life much' (XI. 547–8), says Adam at hearing this grim account. 'Nor love thy life, nor hate; but what thou liv'st / Live well, how long or short permit to Heav'n' (XI. 553–4) is Michael's correction (to 'Live well' is to strive for the *summum bonum*, virtue, along with love, as we will see presently).[23] Although the angel exhorts Adam to moderation of every kind along this philosophical course, Stoicism as perceived in Christian terms recognizes the desirability of strong emotions that express faith, a provision demonstrated in Michael's approval of Adam's anger upon hearing of Nimrod's presumption. 'O execrable Son so to aspire / Above his Brethren ... Wretched man!' exclaims Adam, to which Michael responds,

> Justly thou abhorr'st
> That Son, who on the quiet state of men
> Such trouble brought.   (XII. 79–81)[24]

Michael is saying that Adam's abhorrence of Nimrod is righteous because it flows from zeal, the same emotion that shortly thereafter triggers a change in Michael's style:

> O that men
> (Canst thou believe?) should be so stupid grown,
> While yet the Patriarch liv'd, who scap'd the Flood,
> As to forsake the living God, and fall
> To worship thir own work in Wood and Stone
> For Gods!   (XII. 115–20)

The mention of idolatry moves Michael away, for the first time, from his customarily plain exegetical discourse and into the grand style, thereby seconding the righteous indignation that Adam had felt at Nimrod's pride. The pious emotional life, Adam is learning, includes feelings that issue from zeal.

Michael further assists Adam's progression towards wisdom by using tropes, especially when answering Adam's inquiry concerning the seed of woman, Jesus, and the serpent, Satan: 'say where and when / Thir fight, what stroke shall bruise the Victor's heel' (XII. 384–5). 'Dream not of their fight,' replies the angel, 'As of a Duel, or the local wounds / Of head or heel' (XII. 386–8). Think metaphorically, Michael is saying. Interpreting the prophecy is a hermeneutic exercise that, like interpreting scripture, demands rhetorical awareness:

> not therefore joins the Son
> Manhood to Godhead, with more strength to foil
> Thy enemy; nor so is overcome
> *Satan*, whose fall from heav'n, a deadlier bruise,
> Disabl'd not to give thee thy death's wound:
> Which hee who comes thy Saviour, shall recure,
> Not by destroying *Satan*, but his works
> In thee and in thy Seed.   (XII. 388–95)

The key to unlocking the prophecy is the trope of synecdoche: destroying Satan means destroying the *works* of Satan. The prophecy substitutes
the agent for the action, Satan for his works; the job of the rhetorical
interpreter is to discern this synecdochal relationship of convertibility
between the two terms. In pointing out the trope and explaining what
it means, an exercise familiar to virtually every seventeenth-century
reader of *Paradise Lost*, Michael clarifies a central theodical concept that
enables Adam to understand the remaining explanation of how Christ's
sacrifice will bruise the serpent's head. Satan's works will be destroyed,
Michael continues, by the obedience and love expressed through the
redemptive death of Jesus, 'nail'd to the Cross / By his own Nation,
slain for bringing Life';

> But to the Cross he nails thy Enemies,
> The Law that is against thee, and the sins
> Of all mankind, with him there crucifi'd,
> Never to hurt them more who rightly trust
> In this his satisfaction.   (XII. 413–19)

Literary rhetoric had had two functions since antiquity, composition
and criticism; Michael's knowledge of tropes is applied to both. The
metaphor he uses here raises the style of his speech by enumerating the
malign influences that are figuratively nailed to the cross along with
the Son, a patch of amplification that contributes to Adam's feeling
'Replete with joy and wonder' (XII. 468) when the oration concludes.
As an example of rhetorical criticism, Michael's gloss on the prophecy
of the serpent and the seed of woman, based on synecdoche, prepared
the way for Adam to understand the full significance of Christ's sacrifice by first telling him precisely how Satan will be destroyed. 'O goodness infinite, goodness immense!' exclaims Adam. 'That all this good
of evil shall produce, / And evil turn to good' (XII. 469–71). Michael's

rhetoric, consolatory after all, has taught Adam the workings of theodicy and moved him to joy, another emotion springing from zeal and in keeping with the life of the Christian Stoic.

Adam finally sums up what he has learned, principles that include a particular disposition of thought and speech:

> Henceforth I learn, that to obey is best,
> And love with fear the only God, to walk
> As in his presence, ever to observe
> His providence, and on him sole depend,
> Merciful over all his works, with good
> Still overcoming evil, and by small
> Accomplishing great things, by things deem'd weak
> Subverting worldly strong, and worldly wise
> By simply meek; that suffering for Truth's sake
> Is fortitude to highest victory,
> And to the faithful Death the Gate of Life;
> *Taught by his example* whom I now
> Acknowledge my Redeemer, ever blest.   (XII. 561–73, my italics)

Michael's two-book-long exercise in distribution from effects, culminating in the most crucial effect of all, Christ's birth, has taught Adam about the fortunate fault, ideal worship by the Son's example, and the ultimate triumph of mankind, through Christ, over the serpent. Adam not only encapsulates these ideas here but also disposes them as Michael would, by distribution, partitioning the whole – what he has learned – into its parts. Adam, in fact, has two examples to imitate: an ethical model in Christ, who teaches pious living, and an oratorical model in Michael, who teaches speaking, a rhetoric tied in with logic. Together they present a version of the classical ideal *bene vivendi et copiose dicendi*, of living well and speaking copiously. Adam implicitly acknowledges Michael's exemplary role by patterning his speech on the same logical format, which indicates that he has also learned two important principles connected with logic: reason and obedience. According to Renaissance convention, the contents of Adam's heart are reflected in his words: 'speech is the sign of one's character,' wrote Petrarch.[25] Michael tells Adam, 'thou hast attain'd the sum / Of wisdom,' which includes Adam's emergent oratorical skills, and he then recommends a combination of the Stoic cardinal virtues and the Christian virtues:

> only add
> Deeds to thy knowledge answerable, add Faith,
> Add Virtue, Patience, Temperance, add Love,
> By name to come call'd Charity, the soul
> Of all the rest.   (XII. 581–5)

Patience is Christian fortitude. Having learned the need to practise it, along with the other virtues embodied in Christ, the regenerate Adam is now equipped to leave the paradise of Eden and to cultivate, as Michael says, 'A paradise within thee, happier far' (XII. 587). His readiness to do so is testimony to the complete success of Michael's rhetoric.

We saw that when the omniscience of the Father and the Son virtually nullifies future contingency in heaven, certain conventions of language and oratory, especially stylistic ones, step into that empty space to assert and protect rhetoric. The situation is similar when the rhetoric of heaven is transferred to earth. Contingency here fares hardly better than it had in heaven, as the necessary future becomes the subject of history; yet rhetoric manifests a variety of conventional expressions that declare its thriving presence in Books XI and XII. Michael is a preacher, and his homiletic art, abundantly rhetorical, displays the affecting plain style that teaches Adam and the sublimity that moves him deeply in order to reinforce that teaching. These rhetorical ends draw on logic, Michael's distributive constructions both clearly laying out the lessons of providence and creating the amplification whose cumulative imagery works a powerful emotional effect. In the Renaissance, rhetoric gave voice to the literary arts of the *studia humanitatis*, and its relationship to history and moral philosophy here reflects on that traditional disciplinary connection. Michael's revelatory universal history and his Christian response to Stoicism depend on rhetoric in order to be effectively communicated. The latter, in particular, legitimizes the role of rhetoric after the Fall, since this variety of Stoicism invites the arousal of righteous anger, and rhetoric was recognized as the surest means of bringing about intense emotional states of every kind, including the anger that impiety ought to spark, and the preacher ought occasionally to kindle, in the Christian spirit. Michael uses rhetoric to interpret Christian doctrine as well as preach it. We see its hermeneutic application in the telling of the Protevangelium, the revelation of the meaning behind the trope that the seed of woman will bruise the serpent's head. As it does throughout *Paradise Lost*, style leaves an indelible rhetorical mark and defines speakers' characters as nothing else can. Michael modulates his style in perfect accord with its content and with the dictates of the moment, a quality that all empyreal speakers share, while the change in Adam's style, adapted to that of his teacher, signals the fundamental relationship between words and the mind from which they issue. Certainty rules Paradise in these closing books, the future is as necessary as the past, but rhetoric nevertheless overcomes these epistemological obstacles by calling on the themes and functions of its long tradition.

Rhetoric in heaven continues its ascent in the episode whose rhetorical situation most closely resembles that in which Adam and Eve are placed in the Garden of Eden. Envious at the exaltation of the Son of God, Satan tries to increase the discontent of the angels under his command and to stir them to rebellion against God. At this point Satan has already fallen within his own mind, and when he speaks to his legions, the rhetoric of hell, although spoken in heaven, makes its first public appearance. His oration resorts to numerous fallacies in tempting his audience to believe that obedience to the Son compromises their freedom. Among the hearers only Abdiel

> Stood up, and in a flame of zeal severe
> The current of his fury thus oppos'd.
> O argument blasphémous, false, and proud!
> Words which no ear ever to hear in Heav'n
> Expected, least of all from thee, ingrate,
> In place thyself so high above thy Peers.   (V. 807–12)

Whereas the angels' customary rhetorical voice is praise, Abdiel's fury shows the other side of the epideictic paradigm, blame or censure. The pathos of zeal, speaking out in the face of blasphemy, runs high throughout the course of Abdiel's rebuttal. He directs at Satan the type of rhetorical question whose tone reproaches, epiplexis:

> Canst thou with impious obloquy condemn
> The just Decree of God, pronounc't and sworn,
> That to his only Son by right endu'd
> With Regal Sceptre, every Soul in Heav'n
> Shall bend the knee, and in that honor due
> Confess him rightful King?   (V. 813–18)

Emotional fervor, Longinus noted, may cause irregularities in syntax,[26] a result evident in the figures of Abdiel's speech as he excitedly declares,

> unjust thou say'st
> Flatly unjust, to bind with Laws the free,
> And equal over equals to let Reign,
> One over all with unsucceeded power.   (V. 818–21)

More coherently, he means, 'unjust[ly] thou say'st [that it is] flatly unjust, to bind with laws the free.' For the adverb 'unjustly' Abdiel substitutes the adjective 'unjust,' a switching of grammatical forms called anthimeria. And in his zealous haste to assert the falsity of Satan's argument, he leaves out a few words – the figure ellipsis – that would clarify his statement.

Despite its emotional tone, Abdiel's speech nevertheless retains the classical structure of an oration. The lines cited above constitute the partitio, which sets forth what is to be proved: that Satan's charge of divine tyranny is unjust. The angel then proceeds to the amplificatio, which states the arguments for the case. He adduces two points: (1) that it is wrong for Satan to dispute the laws of the God who created and ordered all things; and (2) that prior experience shows God's beneficence, not oppressiveness, towards them. Next comes the refutatio, which refutes the opponent's arguments: Satan's claim that the Son rules over those who are 'by right / His equals' (V. 795–6) is false. The Son is not their equal but their ruler by right, set atop a chain of being that accords honour to those who serve within it. Abdiel's peroration becomes deliberative in urging that Satan

> Cease then this impious rage,
> And tempt not these; but hast'n to appease
> Th' incensed Father, and th' incensed Son,
> While Pardon may be found in time besought.   (V. 845–8)

Abdiel's *logos* and *pathos* should have moved the audience to repent, 'but his zeal / None seconded, as out of season judg'd' (V. 849–50). The *kairos* is unpropitious; Abdiel fails, and Satan's appeal to envy prevails over the wisdom of the good angel.

By no means a rhetorical misstep, however, Abdiel's speech is, in the most important ways, a triumph. For the true measure of success in this context is not, as it usually is, that the speaker wins over the audience to his side, but rather that he maintains this morally justified point of view, and argues for it, in the face of universal opposition. Abdiel scores a victory on the ethical side of rhetoric, deciding in virtue's favour by resisting the same temptation that perverts his fellows: 'Among the faithless faithful only hee ... His Loyalty he kept, his Love, his Zeal' (V. 897, 900). Angels, like men, possess free will – 'Such [God] created all th' Ethereal Powers / And spirits' (III. 100–1) – and choose obedience or the alternative. That Abdiel is portrayed as exercising free will charges the rhetorical dynamic of heaven by means of a contingent event; that he chooses correctly shows him to be an exemplar of Milton's most persistently dramatized lesson: how one ought to react to temptation. And Abdiel is an ideal model for speech as well as action. He fails to reach the rest of the assembly not for lack of eloquence but for a reason beyond his control, that God has denied the envious angels the grace that would soften their hearts and allow them to heed the loyal angel, 'in word mightier than they in Arms' (VI. 32). Abdiel's rhetoric is founded in 'the Cause / Of Truth' (VI. 31–2), not in opinion. Proclaiming it in such circumstances, and with such force, confirms his oratorical mettle. Wisdom and reason arm him for spiritual warfare, higher than the martial sort and the kind of battle in which Milton saw himself engaged. With these attributes, Abdiel sees through sophistry and turns away from its consequences. Millions of his fellow angels, not to mention Adam and Eve, are less perspicacious and fall prey to Satan's masterful rhetoric. The Devil's role as the father of mortal sin in Michael's distributive genealogy derives largely from that oratorical skill, the subject to which I now turn.

7 Satan and Rhetoric

They lay under the boardlike hide of a dead ox and listened to the judge calling to them. He called out points of jurisprudence, he cited cases. He expounded upon those laws pertaining to property rights in beasts mansuete and he quoted from cases of attainder insofar as he reckoned them germane to the corruption of blood in the prior and felonious owners of the horses now dead among the bones. Then he spoke of other things.

Cormac McCarthy,
Blood Meridian; or, the Evening Redness in the West

Writing in 1563, Johan Wier enumerated the formidable attributes of the Devil, whose expulsion from heaven had left his powers virtually undiminished: 'It is clear that he has abundant strength, extraordinary cunning, superhuman wisdom, the sharpest insight, supreme alertness, unmatched craft in contriving the most destructive tricks by means of highly plausible dissimulation, infinite malice, and a hatred towards mankind that is implacable and incurable.'[1] This was Satan as Renaissance theology inherited him from late antiquity and the Middle Ages. Wier's description emphasizes that Satan was conceived above all as the great Adversary who worked ceaselessly to destroy mankind, and that one of the most destructive forces involved in this enterprise was the Devil's craft or cunning (*calliditas, astus*). Craft enabled Satan to deceive people and lead them away from truth, a deception that he sometimes accomplished by speech: he was commonly perceived and depicted as an accomplished orator. Glossing the Devil's words at Genesis 3.4–5, Wier notes that Satan 'deluded Eve with a most smooth-tongued cunning, in which there seemed to be no deceit at hand,' and that he 'exhilarated Eve with false promises in expectation of far greater honors and superior power' and 'tried to attract her to the same inclination [to which he himself succumbed] by the enticements of charming persuasion.'[2] This idea that Satan was a glib dissembler, skilled at fallacy and lies, had long been popular, especially in literary portraits of him. Rhetorical facility constituted an important feature of his character. Rhetoric was the source of much of his deception; and, from a creative standpoint, it licensed writers to expand greatly the tantalizingly brief biblical accounts of his speech. Milton was one of many who dramatized Satan's rhetorical skill, but no other writer made speech such a centrally defining trait of the satanic character. The present chapter discusses the rhetorical heritage of Milton's Satan in *Paradise Lost*, mainly in light of some earlier and contemporary poetic representations. Included with them is an account of the tempter in *Paradise Regained*, whose rhetorical encounter with Jesus merits treatment independent of his speech in *Paradise Lost*, to be examined in the following two chapters.

Before we address these issues, the special nature of satanic rhetoric must be explored, particularly in terms of how it diverges from the classical-humanist rhetorical model discussed so far. Satan's evil rhetoric, like much of his other behaviour, inverts the principles of its morally good counterpart. What he inverts is the traditional definition of eloquence, specifically the belief that true eloquence, according to Cicero and Renaissance humanists alike, is wisdom speaking copiously. Satanic speech indisputably embodies one side of this equation: it exhibits *copia*, sweetness and fluency in all manner of adornment. As we shall see, the Devil found in literature is a masterful stylist. The question remains as to the other component of eloquence, wisdom. Satan's relationship to wisdom may be best understood if the concept's moral neutrality is accounted for. Although Renaissance wisdom was most fully realized as an intellectual or moral virtue rooted in the good, it had a moral obverse: a knowledge not only of logic and truth, but of fallacy and lies and how to use them, was considered a type of wisdom – a 'crooked wisdom.' 'We take cunning for a sinister or crooked wisdom,' wrote Bacon. Hobbes referred to 'that crooked wisdom, which is called craft.'[3] The ideas, speech, and conduct of Milton's Satan are 'wise,' yet in a qualified way that sees conventional wisdom transformed into its 'crooked' or inverted senses of cunning and craft. The *logos* is turned upside down, its constructive and harmonizing values mocked, by the fallen Lucifer's exchanging wisdom for craft, which turns the knowledge and skills of the wise man to evil account, to wickedness rather than virtue. Craft is the same capability as wisdom, changed only in its moral orientation, and none the less potent for that change: 'the Divells by creation were good Angels, as powerfull, wise, quick, speedie, invisible, immortal, &c. as any other Angels ... onely the qualities of his nature and properties [are] altered from good to evill ... as wise before to good, so subtill now to evill.'[4] Satan, subtly wise, as well as being a gifted stylist, fits the definition of subverted eloquence.

Given its importance in the paradigm of infernal eloquence, craft may be further defined in terms of ethics. Craft is a category of the Renaissance wisdom akin to prudence, which occupies itself with the sphere of practical affairs. 'Prudence,' writes Aristotle, 'is concerned with the affairs of men, and with things that can be the object of deliberation.'[5] So too is craft, prudence's evil twin (Cicero warns that 'careful attention must be given ... to save ourselves from being deceived by those vices which imitate virtue. For cunning masquerades as prudence').[6] Bacon illustrates the practical bent of cunning by discussing it in the context of policy at court, where it is implemented in the backstabbing jostle for preferment. The Adversary's telling God that he has arrived 'from going to and fro in the earth, and from walking up and down in it' (Job 1.7), indicates that he is always vigilant for opportunities to undermine good and inflict pain. Satan is a man of action. Just as wisdom degenerates into craft, so wisdom's adjunctive intellectual virtue, prudence (*phronesis*), has a pejorative analogue in cleverness or *deinotes* (a word that refers especially to an orator in Thucydides, Demosthenes, and Isocrates). By definition, Aristotle observes, prudence functions in tandem with moral virtue: 'virtue ensures the rightness of the end we aim at, prudence ensures the rightness of the means we adopt to gain that end.' When prudence and prudential deliberation are divorced from their proper application – the fulfilment of self-interest in light of moral virtue – the result is cleverness, which is the same capacity for figuring out what means we should adopt to gain an end, but without the touchstone of virtue. In the clever person, 'vice perverts the mind and causes it to hold false views about the first principles of conduct. Hence it is clear that we cannot be prudent without being good.' True prudence 'studies that which is just and noble and good for man.'[7] Cleverness, by inference, studies only what is expedient.

Both the good and the expedient are achieved through deliberation, which forms opinions regarding the surest means of achieving a desired end. The process of deliberating well, which 'is the most characteristic function of the prudent man,' is also characteristic of the clever or unscrupulous man. 'Deliberative excellence is a form of correctness in deliberation. However, "correctness" [ορθοτης] in this connexion is ambiguous, and plainly it is not every kind of correctness in deliberation that constitutes Deliberative Excellence. A man of deficient self-restraint or a bad man may as a result of calculation arrive at the object he proposes as the right thing to do, so that he will have deliberated correctly, although he will have gained something extremely evil; whereas to have deliberated well is felt to be a good thing. Therefore it is this kind of correctness in deliberation that is Deliberative Excellence, namely being correct in the sense of arriving at something good.'[8] Although a clever man cannot be prudent, cannot make choices conducive to the attainment of virtue, he can still exercise the calculative and investigative functions of deliberation that acquire for an individual what is in his own interest. The process of fulfilling this morally bad self-interest cannot exemplify deliberative excellence, but can nevertheless be 'correct' insofar as it accomplishes what it sets out to do. Thus, the prudence of Satan may be more accurately defined as cleverness, by which he is able to deliberate correctly – that is, to scheme effectively – in executing an evil design. If eloquence is wisdom speaking copiously, it is clear that satanic eloquence is predicated on what were recognized as ethically debased phases of the intellectual virtues: the crooked wisdom that is craft, the crooked prudence that is cleverness, the crooked deliberation that machinates evil ends.

Craft and cleverness are the executive powers that direct Satan's eloquence, that read situations before he speaks, that evaluate contingencies. Just like Isocratean or Erasmian rhetorical prudence, they tell him what to say, how, when, and to whom to say it. These abilities to bring the variables of speech under control manifest themselves in numerous ways. Before Satan speaks to those he would tempt, for example, he determines what features of their character may be targeted and speaks accordingly. It is notable that, in doing so, Satan is imitating an element of divine rhetoric. For John Donne, God's rhetorical identity displays itself partly in the tactic of speaking to particular qualities of men's characters: 'God will speak unto me, in that voice, and in that way, which I am most delighted with, and hearken most to. If I be *covetous*, God will tel me that heaven is a pearle, a treasure. If cheerful and affected with mirth, that heaven is all *Joy*. If ambitious, and hungry for preferment, that it is all *Glory*. If sociable, and conversable, that it is a *communion of Saints.'*[9] Robert Burton, for whom 'the cause of death and diseases ... was the sinne of our first parent *Adam* ... by the Divells instigation and allurement,' recognized that the Devil did the same thing, that he took into account his audience's disposition in order to persuade each listener most effectively:

> he hath severall engines, traps, devices, to batter and enthrall, omitting no opportunities, according to mens severall inclinations, abilities, to circumvent and humour them, to maintaine his superstition, sometimes to stupefie, besot them, sometimes againe by oppositions, factions, to set all at oddes, and in an uproare, sometimes hee infects one man, and makes him a principle agent ... If of meaner sort, by stupidity, Canonicall obedience, blinde zeale, &c. If of better note, by pride, ambition, popularity, vaineglory. If of the Cleargie and more eminent, of better parts than the rest, more learned, eloquent, he puffeth them up with a vaine conceit of their own worth, *scientia inflati.*

Burton grinds his axe to an amusingly keen edge on the stone of clerical pride, which he presents as the spiritual failing that Satan most easily discerns and exploits. 'So cunning, that he is able to deceive the very elect,' Satan appeals successfully to the vanity of the clergy, who, among numerous unhappy results, 'out of too much learning become mad.'[10]

It was commonly held of Satan that 'for diverse persons, divers conditions, and dispositions, hee hath diverse temptations,'[11] as William Gouge writes. William Spurstowe, noticing, in addition, the Devil's sensitivity to seasonable timing, writes that 'Satan ... fully understands when and how to apply himself to every age and constitution.'[12] In *Mundorum Explicatio,* a poem about the temptation and Fall published six years before *Paradise Lost,* Samuel Pordage warns that Satan will 'suit all Humours: By their humours try / To work for his advantage.' He tempts baser souls to 'grosse sins'; of the studious and temperate, however, he

> Their strength doth know; therefore with policy
> His shape he changes, and with subtle guile
> Corrupts their knowledge; and with errours vile
> Their Brains doth fill: if in Theology
> Their study be; their errours are more high.
> A prying mind finds he in men of Parts,

He subtlely draws them to his blacker Arts,
Where with most strange delusions them delude
And thus himself in every one intrude
He will; and suting to their inclination
With cunning art, unseen work their destruction.[13]

Although Pordage recognizes the verbal side of satanic temptation, dramatizing the seduction of Eve earlier in the poem, he acknowledges here that satanic art usually works 'unseen.' Most people undergo temptation from sinful ideas that the Devil plants in them or gradually draws them to. In such cases Satan does not 'speak' per se. The dynamic of temptation remains, however, rhetorical, since he is still persuading, and still sensible of the rhetorician's need to gauge his hearer's inclinations and to watch for opportunities and ripe occasions.

In responding quickly to these episodes of weakness or pride and by tempting people according to whatever sin most affects them, Satan expertly observes the *kairos*. Like Ulysses, another masterful dissembler, Satan excels at this opportunism;[14] he knows, in conjunction with the susceptibilities of his audience, the critical moment at which to take advantage of them: 'His long experience, as a Tempter, hath made him exact in descerning, and choosing the fittest seasons for it, the right timing of which hath a powerfull and effective influence into all kind of Enterprises whatever ... whose intreaties and perswasions doth with sweetness more allure, and with mildness overcome the harshness and severity of some Mens temper, then his, who observes *mollissima fandi tempora*, the softest and most calme seasons of speech?'[15] The Devil's rhetorical success derives largely from his knowing and seizing the right time at which to speak. In tempting women to embrace witchcraft, for example, 'the Devil bided his time until a suitable moment arrived, when bereavement or poverty would make his victim ready to welcome his advances.'[16] This skill, like other operations of deliberative correctness performed in relation to eloquence, is an offshoot of wisdom: 'Opportunity is the joynt of time,' Spurstowe continues, 'and he who wisely can hit it, is never disappointed in his aims.'[17] Bacon more explicitly identifies the *kairos* with wisdom: 'There is surely no greater wisdom than well to time the beginnings and onsets of things.'[18] Having chosen a propitious moment, Satan then speaks, intent on another kind of good timing, the sequence of arguments in his *dispositio*: 'hee well knoweth how to order his temptations: For first hee useth to make the on-set with light skirmashes, and to beginne with small temptations; and then by degrees to follow with greater and mightier forces. Thus came hee to Eve, first onely hee made a question whether God had forbidden them any of the trees: and then by degrees hee came directly to contradict the expresse word of God. So when hee tempted Christ, hee began with a doubt whether Christ were the sonne of God or no, and lastly tempted him to monstrous idolatrie.'[19]

Even more cunning than the arrangement of Satan's arguments is their substance, or lack of it. Perhaps the best commentator on diabolical *inventio*, especially as an unraveller of its snares, is Milton's contemporary Sir Thomas Browne. In the first book of *Pseudodoxia Epidemica*, Browne sets forth the deficiencies in human nature that have caused man to fall into error. The source of error, as it had been the source of disease for Burton, was the Fall of Adam and Eve: 'For first, They were deceived by Satan,' whom he calls 'the first contriver of Error, and professed opposer of Truth.' Satan's means of deceiving Eve are cited: 'Art and fallacy were used on her.' Fallacy was of particular interest to Browne, who believed that a proclivity to succumb to it, that is, a failure of the human intellect to adhere to logic, was one of the main causes of error. The 'art' Satan employs, which creates fallacy, is that which, misapplied, can give the appearance of logic: rhetoric. Common men are 'unable to wield the intellectual arms of reason,' much as Eve was unable to do: 'Thus unto them a piece of Rhetorick is a sufficient argument of Logick.' The consequences of accepting rhetorical arguments (intended to gain assent) in place of the tight reasoning of logic (aimed at attaining truth) are deception and error, pitfalls illustrated nowhere better than in Eve's credulous entrapment in the casuistry of the serpent. Browne promotes logic as necessary for discerning truth from falsehood. Part of his treatment of logic includes detailed descriptions of six fallacies, four of which he identifies as rhetorical tactics used by Satan. Browne shows how Satan's temptation of Eve involves equivocation, amphibology, and *petitio principii*; his analyses of these techniques will be taken up in chapter 9, in the context of the temptation in *Paradise Lost*. For the moment, Browne's account of another fallacy demonstrates clearly that the perversion of logic is the *modus operandi* of satanic rhetoric, as when the Devil attempted to ensnare a wiser interlocutor, Jesus:

A dicto secundum quid ad dictum simpliciter, when from that which is but true in a qualified sense, an inconditional and absolute verity is inferred; transferring the special consideration of things unto their general acceptions, or concluding from their strict acception unto that without all limitation. This fallacy men commit when they argue from a particular to a general; as when we conclude vices or qualities of a few upon a whole Nation. Or from a part unto the whole. Thus the Devil argues with our Saviour: and by this, he would perswade Him he might be secure, if he cast himself from the Pinnacle: For, said he, it is written, *He shall give his Angels charge concerning thee, and in their hands they shall bear thee up, lest at any time thou dash thy foot against a stone* [Luke 4.10–11]. But this illation was fallacious, leaving one part of the Text, *He shall keep thee in all thy wayes* [Psalm 91.11]; that is, in the wayes of righteousness, and not of rash attempts: so he urged a part for the whole, and inferred more in the conclusion, than was contained in the premises.[20]

Satanic rhetoric masquerades as logic by telling only half the truth. In this instance, the fallacy of accident appeals to a general statement from scripture, true in itself, but applies it to a particular case whose accidental circumstances render it inapplicable. A partial truth, superficially plausible, hides an underlying logical inconsistency. Browne's illuminating commentary exposes to view the precise mechanisms behind this basic principle of satanic rhetorical invention.

Fallacy was only one of the rhetorical instruments at Satan's disposal. He had a catholic range of invention that comprehended any subject or approach that might suit his present need. Browne elsewhere observed that, if circumstances demanded, Satan would appeal to reason, not try to undermine it by fallacy. Inasmuch as rational thought could be regarded as inimical to faith, because it submitted the tenets of faith to impious scrutiny and doubt, the Devil was a great exponent of reason, scientific knowledge, and empirical proof. In order to uphold faith the educated man had 'always to dispute with the Devill; the villany of that spirit takes a hint of infidelity from our Studies, and by demonstrating a naturality in one way, makes us mistrust a miracle in another.' Where the Bible presents a miracle, the Devil contradicts it with a rational explanation for the same occurrence. For example, Browne avers, 'I know that Manna is now plentifully gathered in *Calabria*, and Josephus tels me, in his dayes 'twas as plentiful in *Arabia*; the Devill therefore made the *quere*, Where was then the miracle in the dayes of Moses? the Israelites saw but that in his time, the natives of those Countries behold in ours. Thus the Devill playd at Chesse with mee, and yeelding a pawne, thought to gain a Queen of me, taking advantage of my honest endeavours; and whilst I labour'd to raise the structure of my reason, hee striv'd to undermine the edifice of my faith.' Within the struggling Christian mind, where Satan works 'unseen,' temptation happens rhetorically. Satan poses to Browne's imagination the blasphemous question and counter-argument, which engender rationalistic doubt concerning miracles, no less forcibly than if he had spoken them aloud. Satanic persuasion also lay behind another and more severe heresy, atheism, of which Browne remarked, "'tis the Rhetorick of Satan, and may pervert a loose or prejudicated beleefe.'[21] One had to beware of the Devil from every angle of argument, since he possessed a rhetorical flexibility that enabled him either to befuddle reason or to turn reason to his own benefit by advancing its claims where faith properly held sway. Spurstowe imagines a 'Satan, who like a cunning wrestler, or Fencer, is various, and uncertain in his Motions.' 'I find thou hast the art to sail with any wind,' as John Quarles wrote of him.[22] That manoeuvrability included resorting to scripture as well as reason, a tactic shown above in the account of Satan presented in Luke, where, for rhetorical purposes, he omits a verse in quoting the ninety-first Psalm. Somewhat giving away his game, Quarles's Satan tells the Soul, representative of all Christians, that

> 'tis I that can display
> The *Gospels* Colours ...
> There's nothing in that volume so obstruce,
> But I can winde and twist it to my use.[23]

Up to this point, *deinotes* has been shown to govern the decisions, actions, and resources involved in satanic eloquence. They include the stages preparatory to speech: determining the vulnerable traits of an audience and picking the right moment for tempting them; organizing arguments by increasing degree; and an opportunistically variable invention, which can be calibrated to use or abuse reason and truth as required. Having established the faculties and procedures behind satanic eloquence, we may now investigate the rhetoric generated by them. In the course of doing so, the style of Satan in literature will rise into view as a rhetorical technique complementary to those discussed so far. Detailed study, however, will not be undertaken here, but will be more intensively pursued in chapters 8 and 9 in the discussion of infernal rhetoric in *Paradise Lost*. For the time being, it may be remarked that Satan's dexterity in this rhetorical department becomes a vehicle of dissimulation in terms of both speech and speaker. On the one hand, his flowing style covers lies and deceit with an illusion of truth; on the other, it creates a false image of the character of Satan himself. As a rhetorical proof, *logos* becomes more forcible when augmented with a sage *ethos*, much of which Satan derives from his style. Renaissance humanists, we recall, likened words to clothing; they were the outward dress of ideas. Satan appropriates the cloak of the wise man, a proficient style, in order to make himself and the corruptive ideas he espouses appear truly wise on the strength of their expression.

The serpent's garb of wise-sounding words, which fooled Eve, intrigued the western poetic imagination from the first century AD on. There was an abiding interest in the speech of the Devil, the world's first political orator, whose rhetorical achievement in Eden precipitated the unfolding of Christian providence. St Paul influentially connected Adam and Eve's disobedience to the Redemption;[24] thereafter, the events surrounding the original sin, including Eve's deception, were transformed into subjects of the highest artistic calibre. Among early Latin verse adaptations of the Fall, Avitus's sixth-century *Poematum de Mosaicae historiae gestis libri quinque* stands out for the rhetorical representation of Satan's character partly because it is the first literary work in which the serpent, formerly a mysterious creature of uncertain identity, is directly associated with Satan. The view of Avitus, also adopted by Milton, that Satan entered the body of a serpent in order to approach Eve, fell within the exegetical tradition of patristic writers such as John Chrysostom: 'But it may be that someone reading this account may wonder whether the serpent was a partaker in rational nature. But it was not like this at all; far from it. The scriptures should always be understood in this way – that the words are the Devil's own ... He was using the beast as a convenient organ for his purpose, by means of which he might dangle the bait.'[25] In terms by now familiar, Avitus describes the attributes of the serpent that make him a particularly fit vessel for Satan: 'The jealous serpent, clever in his subtle heart, was perhaps more profound in craft than all other living beings.' As in heart, so in speech: 'O happy one, the most beautiful of women, whom the splendour of the world and shining beauty adorn with blushing modesty. You, future mother of the race, the great earth waits upon your motherhood. You, the first and only true joy and solace of your husband, without whom he himself could not live – although he is greater, he is yet justly subjected to your love, sweet wife, you who will bring forth his progeny.'[26] Satan immediately flatters Eve to conceal his motive and to gain her good will. He also inflates her pride by declaring Adam's de facto subjugation to her. This incitement to vanity continues as Satan proceeds to amplify Eve's supremacy, placing the world at her feet in polished figures that are sometimes difficult to reproduce in translation: 'A rightfully earned seat is given to you at the summit of paradise; the world's substance trembles at the sight of you, whom it serves submissively. Whatever the heavens and earth create, whatever the sea brings forth from its great whirlpool, is brought together for your use. Nature denies you nothing. Behold what power is given to you in all things!' Next, Satan ingeniously contrasts everything bestowed on Eve, which he has just enumerated, with the one thing that has been withheld: 'Indeed I am not envious – rather, I am surprised that permission to touch one sweet tree is nevertheless held back.' Finally, he again sets abundance alongside the prohibition, declaring, with feigned ignorance: 'I should like to know who commands these horrible things, who envies such gifts, and mingles deprivations with splendid wealth.'[27]

Enthralled by what she calls his 'sweet words' (*suaves dicta*), Eve accepts Satan's flattery. His copious, seemingly profound style has done its work, making Eve think him wise: 'most learned serpent' (*doctissime serpens*), she addresses him, as she asks to hear about death. 'Then the crafty serpent, now a willing expert on death, teaches about destruction and speaks thus to captive ears':

Woman, you fear but the empty name of terror. A sentence of sudden death will not come to you. But the unseen father has not assigned lots equally, nor has he permitted you to know those supreme matters which he has reserved for himself alone. What use is the apprehension of embellishment or the perception of the world, when blind minds are shut up in a wretched prison? ... Instead take my counsel: join your mind to those above, and stretch your aspiring thoughts up to the heavens. For this forbidden fruit which you fear to touch will give you knowledge of whatever secret the father stores away. Do not now restrain your touch, kept on tenterhooks for such a time, nor let pleasure, so long held captive, be restrained by law. For when you have tasted this divine delicacy in your mouth, purified light will make your vision equal to that of the gods, so that you know holy as well as sinful things and can distinguish right from wrong, false from true.[28]

Satan fulfils the oratorical duty that rhetoricians in all periods deemed the surest avenue to persuasion: *movere*, stirring the emotions of one's hearers. By inciting pride and envy, sparking curiosity, and playing on a deep longing for godhead, Satan's rhetoric evokes in Eve a complex of emotions that overwhelms reason. The affective surge he has induced in her proves too strong for her rational side, which struggles in vain. Herein features the main rhetorical strategy of satanic temptation – that it seeks to transfer reason's power over the will to the unreliable guidance of the emotions.

Reason itself can fall under the attack of lies. This is the dominating feature of the tempter's speech to Adam and Eve in 'Genesis B,' a poem of uncertain authorship written between the eighth and tenth centuries in Old English, a language that 'may well be wishful thinking' to ascribe to Milton.[29] In a notable departure from the biblical Genesis, the poet early removes Satan himself from the narrative action. Satan assembles an infernal council, proposes the plan to ruin Eden, and appeals to the loyalty of his retainers to undertake it. The unnamed demon who subsequently travels to Eden possesses rhetorical skill: 'Many a crafty speech he knew, many a crooked word.' Rhetoric also underpins his evil agenda: 'He would fain ensnare God's servants unto sin, seduce them and deceive them that they might be displeasing to God.'[30] In another modification of the Book of Genesis, the demon's first target is not Eve but Adam, to whom he lies that he is an angel and that God has sent him to command Adam to eat the forbidden fruit. The poet often repeats that the demon speaks 'with lies' (*mid ligenum*). Adam sees through them, holding faith in God's prohibition, and sends the serpent away. Having failed with Adam, the serpent approaches Eve and strings together numerous lies, capped with his assurance, 'I am not like a devil' (*ne eom ic deofle gelic*): 'So he urged with lies and luring wiles, tempting the woman unto sin, until the serpent's counsel worked within her – for God had wrought her soul the weaker – and her heart inclined according to his teaching.'[31] After she eats the fruit, the demon persuades her to make Adam eat it as well.

As 'Genesis B' shows, satanic eloquence in literature may belong not only to Satan but also to evil persuaders in general. The spirit of the Devil, as the embodiment of evil, is dispersed into the malevolent characters of European Renaissance literature. Edmund Spenser and Torquato Tasso locate satanic evil, terrestrial but associated with the underworld, in paired sets of male and female characters: Archimago and Duessa in *The Faerie Queene*, Hidraort and Armida in *Gerusaleme liberata*, which Edward Fairfax translated in 1600 as *Godfrey of Bulloigne; or The Recoverie of Jerusalem*. In Spenser's allegorical epic romance, one of

the most rhetorically inclined characters is the main antagonist of the
Red Crosse Knight and the princess Una, Archimago, whose name suggests his vocation as the master fabricator of images and dreams. He
can change his own appearance at will; his books of black magic contain spells and incantations for conjuring up demonic spirits to do his
bidding. His oratorical facility first manifests itself under the lulling
guise of the raconteur, as he entertains Una and St George in order to
gain their trust and good will (what rhetoricians call a *captatio benevo-
lentiae*):

> With faire discourse the evening so they pas
> For that old man of pleasing wordes had store,
> And well could file his tongue as smooth as glas.

Described variously as crafty, cunning, and subtle, Archimago dis-
charges his satanic mandate of deception rhetorically, by devising false-
hoods in both words and images. He focuses both types of rhetoric,
verbal and visual, on moving the passions of the Christian knights, hop-
ing to supplant the government of right reason, critical for their success,
with emotions such as wrath, jealousy, and lust. Like words, images are
able to incite strong emotions in an audience, and Archimago successfully avails himself of their potency. In one instance, the Red Crosse
Knight succumbs to jealousy and murderous rage when Archimago
shows him a replica of the princess Una and a young squire, moulded
from two shape-shifting demons, together.

> In wanton lust and lewd embracement:
> Which when he saw, he burnt with gealous fire,
> The eye of reason was with rage yblent,
> And would have slain them in his furious ire,
> But hardly was restreined of that aged sire.[32]

In this state of mind St George flees, deserting Una. Archimago's visual
rhetoric persuades him, in the most deeply affective manner, that the
real Una is unchaste, a falsehood of which he is disabused only much
later with the help of Prince Arthur.

Arthur, who represents the humanist ideal of wisdom conjoined with
and expressed in skilful speech, is Archimago's allegorical counterpoise with respect to eloquence. A comparison of the two characters
exemplifies how satanic rhetoric, like one of Archimago's phantasms,

itself amounts to a simulacrum of genuine eloquence based on wisdom. Having met Una, Arthur encourages her to relate her despair. His own rhetoric affirms reason's power to strengthen faith where the flesh weakens it and also wins over Una, thereby demonstrating that in him true wisdom and rhetorical prowess are harmonized:

> His goodly reason, and well guided speach
> So deepe did settle in her gratious thought,
> That her perswaded to disclose the breach,
> Which love and fortune in her heart had wrought.   (I. vii. 42. 1–4)

Arthur's sound reason and well-guided speech contrast with Archimago's perversion of the same principles in 'His practick wit, and his faire filed tong' (II. i. 3. 6).[33] 'Wit' is reason or understanding. The adjective 'practick' meant experienced, well versed, or skilled, but with sinister parallel significations of artful, crafty, or cunning. This line from the poem thus encapsulates Archimago's false similitude of Arthurian eloquence: his crafty reason expresses itself in a sophisticated style, a combination that creates 'subtile engines' and 'thousand other sleights' (II. i. 3. 5,7) directed at undercutting reason and destroying virtue. For Archimago, upsetting his enemies' good reason entails pitting against it his own crooked reason, assisted by all the tools of rhetoric to whose access the wise orator enjoys no privilege over the crafty one. Nevertheless, reason eventually defeats cunning rhetoric, discovering Archimago's evil designs with increasing ease as the poem continues. The wizard, 'with a faire countenance and flattring stile' (II. i. 8. 5), tells a rhetorically ornate lie about a violated maiden to Guyon, the Knight of Temperance, wishing to set him against St George. Archimago resorts to the grand style. His feigned distress and loss for words, his vivid portrayal of the indecencies committed against the maiden, and his climactic revelation about her assailant[34] arouse in Guyon 'fierce ire' (II. i. 13. 1). Yet Guyon's clash with George is averted when he recognizes his comrade in mid-charge and reins in his passions as he pulls up his horse, repenting his 'offence and heedlesse hardiment' (II. i. 27. 2). The two knights' exercise of reason and temperance quells the destructive passions engendered by Archimago's rhetoric and exposes that rhetoric for the false semblance it really is.

A close literary cousin of Archimago is Hidraort in Fairfax's *Godfrey of Builloigne*. The Syrian wizard's first-hand knowledge of the Devil, as he schemes to undermine Godfrey's crusaders, marks his close relationship to the values of satanic eloquence:

He, that was closely false and slilie wise,
Cast how he might annoy them most from far:
And as he gan upon this point devise,
(As counsellors in ill still neerest ar)
At hand was Sathan, readie, ere men in need,
If once they think to make them doe the deed.
He counselled him how best to hunt his game,
What dart to cast, what net, what toile to pitch.

'This enterprise thy cunning must pursew,' Hidraort tells his niece, Armida. Her character suits her for acts of rhetorical deception, her uncle commending her 'grave thoughts, ripe wit, and wisedome old' as he instructs her:

Goe to the Christians host, and there assay
All subtile sleights that women use in love ...
Take with the bait Lord Godfrey, if thou maste,
Frame snares, of looks; traines, of alluring speach.[35]

She appeals to the eye and the ear with 'her double charm of smiles and sugred words.' To Godfrey's brother Eustace, her flirting amounts to a 'dumbe eloquence, perswading more, than speach'; even before he falls in *Paradise Lost*, Adam describes himself as 'weak / Against the charm of Beauty's powerful glance' (VIII. 532–3). Armida disarms reason by a variety of rhetorical means as well, 'and with this craft a thousand soules welneare, / In snares of foolish ruth and love she hent.' Spenser describes Duessa's powers in similar terms, and he observes that a man must possess true wisdom and hold fast to right reason if he would roll back the veil of rhetorical deceit cast by false words and images:

What man so wise, what earthly wit so rare
As to descry the crafty cunning traine,
By which deceipt doth maske in visour faire,
And cast her colours dyed deepe in graine,
To seeme like Truth, whose shape she well can faine,
And fitting gestures to her purpose frame,
The guiltlesse man with guile to entertaine?
Great maistresse of her art was that false Dame,
The false Duessa, cloked with Fidessaes name.   (I. vii. 1)

Along with the literary transfigurations of Satan into characters such as those of Spenser and Tasso, Satan himself and the events of Genesis 1–3 remained popular subjects for Renaissance poets. Two seventeenth-century English poetic adaptations of Genesis stand out for their handling of the temptation and the role of the serpent's rhetoric in executing it. One is Samuel Pordage's *Mundorum Explicatio*, and the other is Joshua Sylvester's *Guillaume du Bartas, His Devine Weekes and Workes*, a translation of du Bartas's *La Sepmaine, ou Création* and *La Seconde Sepmaine*. Milton first encountered du Bartas through Sylvester's translation, parts of which are echoed in many passages of *Paradise Lost*. In a section of *The Second Weeke* entitled 'THE DECEIPT,' an exposition on Satan's entering the serpent reveals that the two beings are mutually compatible largely because they share a rhetorical aptitude. The lines addressing 'Why Hee hid him in a Body,' explain, 'The needfull helpe of language had he wanted, / Whereby Faiths ground-worke was to be supplanted.'[36] The serpent is amenable to rhetorical intrigue, since 'from his birth h'had / Hart-charming cunning smoothly to perswade' (304). When the Devil animates him, they become a perfect combination:

> So, while a learned Fiend with skilfull hand
> Doth the dull motions of [the serpent's] mouth command,
> This selfe-dumbe Creatures glozing Rhetorike
> With bashfull shame great Orators would strike.   (308)

The narrator further indicates Satan's rhetorical prowess in a bestiary of animals metaphorically linked to his evil offices. 'Thou play'st the foxe,' for example, 'when thou dooest faine-aright / The face and phrase of some deepe hypocrite':

> Thou play'st the Nightingale, or else the Swan,
> When any famous Rhetorician
> With captious wit and curious language, draws
> Seduced hearers, and subverts the law.   (309)

Behind this passage, which connects Satan with a concept of rhetoric as a socially divisive force of chaos, stands the ideal notion, originating in antiquity, that rhetoric had been a principle of order that had brought men together and civilized them.

'Sathans Oration,' as noted in the margin of 'THE DECEIPT,' begins with an exordium:

With th'air of th[o]se sweet words, the wily Snake
A poysoned air inspired (as it spake)
In *Eves* frail brest.

Claiming that God prohibits the fruit out of jealousy and that Eve will
have knowledge and godhead if she eats it, the serpent raises the style
of his peroration:

O Worlds rare glory! reach thy happy hand,
Reach, reach, I say: why dost thou stop or stand?
Begin thy Bliss, and do not fear the threat
Of an uncertain God-head, onely great
Through self-awed zeal: put on the glistring Pall
Of immortality: doe not fore-stall
(As envious stepdame) thy posteritie
The sovrain honour of Divinitie.   (312)

A later seventeenth-century English poet draped the serpent's arguments with still more rhetorical bunting. As much as his words do, the
character of the tempter in Eden receives fresh life from the pen of Samuel Pordage. Though Pordage's Satan speaks with a looseness and
profusion that cannot rival the economical compactness and supple
precision of Milton's tempter, the personality he projects through that
speech decorously complements his formal rhetoric. The tragic gravity
and close verbal calculation of Milton's Satan recalls a rhetor such as
Iago, while Pordage's serpent finds a parallel in Mercutio – brash, gre-
garious, effusive. He behaves in this manner throughout his oration,
and the force that such a personality lends his rhetoric, especially in his
peroration, is evident:

See how the glit'ring Fruit doth lade each bow:
Look how they're painted with Vermilion dye
Like golden starres set in a verdant Skye,
Or like the blushing Roses, which are seen
New peeping forth thorow a verdant Screen.
Look how the Apples blush, see how they stand,
See how the boughs, bow down to kiss thine hand;
All's at thy choyce: which on this fair-spread Tree,
(Come tell me Eve!) most liked is by thee?
See, here's a fine one, this? or this best likes

Thee? do but look what many pretty strikes
Of red, and yellow paint; here's one that skipps
Unto thy mouth: here thine own Cherry lips
Are answered; thy softer skin thou mayst
Here find; but there's a mellow one whose tast
So sweet-delicious that 'twil ravish quite
Thy looser sences with extream delight;
Thou hast such choyce thou knowst not which to choose:
Come take this on my word, try what accrews
By this: here take it, prethee eat, and try
If thou a Goddesse are not by, and by.[37]

Chapter 5 discussed the stylistic concept of *evidentia*, vivid presentation, as applied to biblical language that could bring an exalted object (*praestantia*) closer to its audience for their greater knowledge. Here, the serpent's powers of description bring a forbidden object closer to his audience. The remarkable variety and frequency of tropes and figures in these lines demonstrate how style *was* rhetoric for Renaissance writers like Pordage and Sylvester, as each assumes that the greater the number of figures, the greater the increase in the power of persuasion. Pordage's serpent, 'crafty in his hellish art' (55), hybridizes the decorative middle style (*genus floridum*) and the grand style in creating imagery that stirs Eve's emotions into rebellion against her reason. On the other hand, he invokes reason when reliance on it is improper, a satanic capability that Thomas Browne had noted: 'Pleasures are hardly left,' he entices her, 'when that our sence / Confirm'd by reason, and experience, / Find them both good, and just' (67).

The virtuoso rhetorical dexterity of the serpent in *Mundorum Explicatio* and other poems explains Eve's remark in Quarles's *God's Love and Man's Unworthiness*, set at the scene of divine judgment shortly after the Fall.

> *God*:   Unconstant *Woman!* Ah, why hast thou run
>   Beyond thy bounds? what's this that thou hast done?
> *Woman*:   The *Serpent's* flowing language swel'd too great
>   For my low banks: he tempted, and I eat.[38]

Although Satan's speech has not been dramatized, Eve's metaphor assures the reader that he had spoken in the grand style, her words recalling the traditional image of eloquence as a mighty stream.[39] God confirms that Satan is a formidable orator, rebuffing Adam's plea for clemency by saying that readmission to Eden would present to him all the previous circumstances,

> and thou mayst meet
> A Serpent too, whose oratorious skill
> May soon intreat thee to enact his will:
> He has a voyce to tempt, and thou an ear
> Will re-assume the priviledg to hear.[40]

To *God's Love and Man's Unworthiness*, Quarles appended 'A Dialogue Between the Soul and Satan.' The Soul's ripostes to Satan occasionally upbraid the tempter's rhetorical artfulness. 'Thy tongue fortels a storm,' says the Soul, referring elsewhere to Satan's 'strong Oratory,' which lacks 'the skill / To make me yield to your unsatiate will.'[41] Satan's tactics in this dialogue are clumsy and transparent compared with those he uses on Eve and Jesus in poems previously examined in this chapter. As a portrayal of the Devil's speech entirely outside the framework of Genesis, this work is of some interest. Yet the Soul's automatic rebuttals to the Devil's temptations carry out a didactic agenda – all good Christians should do the same – at the expense of any dramatic tension. Satanic eloquence, such as it is, makes no headway at all against the Soul's unshakeable piety. In the face of this, Satan is reduced to a straw man, the power of his rhetoric muted so that Christian ideals can reverberate the louder.

Satan's temptation meets the firmest possible resistance in Jesus during the Saviour's quarantine fast in the wilderness. In *Christs Victorie on Earth*, Giles Fletcher traces the Devil's speech and character in the barest outline, while the speech of Jesus is not dramatized at all, or is scarcely even narrated. The poem's eponymous event lies almost forgotten beneath long passages of allegorical description, heavily indebted to Spenser. From the allegory there emerges no character able to tempt with a rhetorical sophistication suitably matched to the *ethos* of the Son of God. Satan, although described initially as a formidable rhetorician,[42] is mainly a guide who leads Jesus to different allegorical tableaux where each of two of the resident *genii loci*, Presumption and Panglorie, proffers a temptation. Fletcher ends with Panglorie's delivering a pedestrian *carpe florem* to entice the Son to vain and carnal pleasures.[43] The Devil himself has no significant role in any of this, and does not speak again after urging Jesus to turn stones into bread (which, curiously, elicits no response of any kind).

In *Paradise Regained*, the Devil regains his primacy, as well as his full rhetorical array, in the trial of Jesus. Rhetoric supports and propels the narrative, for the central action of the poem revolves around a sustained deliberative oration, the arguments of which are alternately proposed by Satan and rejected by Jesus. As this exchange is played out, persuasion failing each time, Satan is gradually reduced from the oratorical *force majeure* of *Paradise Lost* to little more than a cheap trickster. His failure may be explained within the contexts of both theology and rhetoric. In terms of theology, divine providence ensures that satanic rhetoric will be ineffectual. The Adversary cannot successfully tempt the Son of God. But the dramatic irony that insulates Satan from this knowledge – he does not know precisely whom he is tempting – motivates him to avail himself of his oratorical resources in tempting Jesus, so that he will also fail on rhetorical grounds. In terms of rhetoric, why Satan fails is clear. The orator must be able to gauge the character and attributes of his audience – a talent that commentators had ascribed to Satan, but which, in this case, he lacks. Barbara Lewalski notes 'that Satan is too intelligent a rhetorician not to adapt his tactics to the very different circumstances which he here meets.'[44] Yet it is to this most important of circumstances that he fails to adapt, for he never sees it. He does not know about the kenosis, that the Son of God who drove him out of heaven has been incarnated in the man whom Satan saw John baptize in the Jordan and whom he has tracked into the Judean desert.[45] In his ignorance Satan underestimates Jesus, with the result that

> the persuasive Rhetoric
> That sleek't his tongue, and won so much with Eve,
> So little here, nay lost; but Eve was Eve,
> This far his over-match, who self-deceiv'd
> And rash, beforehand had no better weigh'd
> The strength he was to cope with, or his own.   (*PR*, IV. 4–9)

Satan's error is a lapse of rhetorical prudence. In weighing the character of Jesus, he does not reset the balance he had used for Eve and so mistakenly deploys the same kind of rhetoric.

From an early stage both the wisdom of Satan's new opponent and the inappropriately Edenic strain of Satan's rhetoric show themselves. Although Satan's speech in general is less florid in this poem, partly in imitation of the Son's own precise speech,[46] he often employs the style that had characterized his rhetoric in *Paradise Lost*. A couple of exam-

ples may be cited that typify the drift and style of this satanic eloquence. When Jesus turns aside the first temptation, to change stones
into bread, he immediately discerns and states the Devil's true identity.
No sooner has Satan given up his disguise and admitted who he is than
he begins to dissimulate afresh. The colours of his rhetorical style signal
their speaker's continued trust in flattery:

> Though I have lost
> Much luster of my native brightness, lost
> To be belov'd of God, I have not lost
> To love, at least contémplate and admire
> What I see excellent in good, or fair,
> Or virtuous; I should so have lost all sense.   (I. 377–82)

Feigned admiration builds on this type of repetition,[47] which Satan
turns to sophistic account during the temptation of the kingdoms:

> Think not so slight of glory: therein least
> Resembling thy great Father; he seeks glory,
> And for his glory all things made, all things
> Orders and governs, nor content in Heaven
> By all his Angels glorifi'd, requires
> Glory from men, from all men good or bad,
> Wise or unwise, no difference, no exemption;
> Above all sacrifice, or hallow'd gift
> Glory he requires, and glory he receives
> Promiscuous from all Nations, Jew, or Greek,
> Or Barbarous, nor exception hath declar'd;
> From us his foes pronounc't glory he exacts.   (III. 109–20)

A host of distributive figures amplifies the single phrase, 'he seeks
glory,' into a portrait of God as a megalomaniacal tyrant. It is a virtuoso
exercise in *copia*. The fallacy of equivocation makes 'glory' mean the
subjection of others, the kind of glory Satan has been urging Jesus to
accept. Jesus cuts through Satan's grandiloquence and wisely asserts
the true meaning of glory due to God from all created things, 'of whom
what could he less expect / Than glory and benediction, *that is thanks*'
(III. 126–7; my italics). Glory rightly signifies man's display of gratitude
and God's reception of it.

At certain points Satan reinforces such verbal pyrotechnics with images. He tempts Jesus to eat by setting before him 'A Table richly spread, in regal mode' (II. 340–65), a banquet intended to appeal to the full range of human senses. Satan underscores his more ambitious offer of heroic glory with sweeping views of the kingdoms of the world. In doing so, he persuades by synecdoche, that is, by showing Jesus Parthia and Rome, which effectively amount to the whole world:

> The rest are barbarous, and scarce worth the sight,
>
> ...
>
> These having shown thee, I have shown thee all
> The Kingdoms of the world, and all thir glory.   (IV. 86, 88–9)

Neither of these displays – the martial splendour of Parthia and the magnificence of Rome – can stir Jesus to any impulse that could prompt his acceptance. After each vision he is 'unmov'd' (III. 386; IV. 109), resistant in his patient wisdom to the affective force of Satan's rhetoric. When Satan presents the final temptation of Athens, with all its art and knowledge, he recommends wisdom not for its own sake but as another road to fame,[48] an offer the Messiah rejects in an Augustinian affirmation that divine inspiration is the most important source of knowledge:

> he who receives
> Light from above, from the fountain of light,
> No other doctrine needs, though granted true.   (IV. 288–90)

The Saviour's reliance on wisdom from above, including that of the prophets (IV. 356–64), foils the last of Satan's rhetorical sleights. Thereafter he can frame 'no new device, they all were spent' (IV. 443). The surging river of eloquence has run dry.

Satan's devices, tradition held, depended on rhetoric for their construction and on an orator's sense for gaining whatever advantages a rhetorical situation might present from moment to moment. Versatile and crafty, the Devil knew how to exploit vulnerable traits in his potential victims, how to introduce progressively bolder arguments, and how to time the onset of his temptation. As circumstances required, he could lie or tell the truth, undermine reason or uphold it, speaking to people's minds as 'an invisible Agent, and secret promoter without us, whose activity is undiscerned, and playes in the dark upon us.'[49] In literature, where the Devil leaves this realm of abstraction and materializes before those he would tempt, usually Eve or Jesus, the tactical manoeuvrability of the orator is second nature to him. Since temptation was an inherently rhetorical endeavour, poets could hardly avoid attributing to Satan the procedures of the orator. They dilated Satan's speech from a handful of biblical verses into orations in which an elaborate style spun plausible arguments out of insinuation, flattery, lies, and specious reasoning. From Avitus to Milton, the portrayal of satanic rhetoric suggested a corrupted form of eloquence in which wisdom was supplanted by craft or cunning, and in which the power of speech, indifferent to the moral status of its user and its application, could promote an evil cause as forcibly as a good one, or even promote an evil cause *as* a good one. In Milton's canon, the dissimulation created by satanic rhetoric is finally exposed in *Paradise Regained*. In Jesus, an example to Milton's readers as he had been to Adam, faith and reason combine to foil the rhetoric that had 'won so much with Eve.' The Son's act of obedience in the desert foreshadows his greatest act, that of dying in order to fulfil divine justice, which will finally destroy the works of the serpent and redress the damage – the propagation of sin and death – that satanic rhetoric had inflicted in *Paradise Lost*.

8 The Rhetoric of Hell

For whereas God almightie at the first, framed him a most excellent creature, furnished with most admirable gifts as the other angels, to the obedience of his will: now hee is become an enemy both to God, and man:
turning his wit and knowledge, into cunning, and deceit.

James Mason, *The Anatomie of Sorcerie*

The impact of Satan's rhetoric in *Paradise Lost* may be viewed in light of
the extraordinary power that classical and Renaissance rhetoricians,
including Milton, thought to be inherent in words. Rhetoric could
arouse the emotions in order to move the minds of listeners, who could
thereby be led – enchained, drawn along, enticed, incited, ruled over,
according to some of the common descriptions – to accept a particular
opinion or follow a suggested course of action. In *Paradise Regained*
Satan refers to the 'resistless eloquence' of the Athenian orators (IV. 28),
and although Milton believed that even the most forcible eloquence
could be resisted, he nevertheless acknowledged its strength, derived
largely from the affective channels of its operation. A 'rhetoric of affect'
is potentially harmful because it can bypass reason and put the emotions, by way of the imagination, in unmediated command of the will.
Another means by which 'the government of reason is assailed and disordered' is 'by juggleries of words [*per Praestigias Verborum*], which per-
tain to Rhetoric'; the purpose of rhetoric should rather be, writes Bacon,
'to second reason, and not to oppress it.'[1] Satan's rhetoric, intending
this oppression of reason, is a debased analogue of the classical-humanist ideal, corrupting wisdom into craft, prudence into cleverness, and,
finally, eloquence itself into sophistry.

Satan oppresses reason by making the weaker argument appear the stronger, an accusation that had been levelled against sophists such as Protagoras, Isocrates, and even Socrates, who was opposed to the sophists in Plato's dialogues but elsewhere – in the *Clouds* of Aristophanes, for example – was included among them. Socrates and Isocrates relate this charge to *deinotes*, or 'cleverness,' the ethical faculty linked in the preceding chapter to the speech and character of Satan. Socrates claims to have been misrepresented as 'a clever [δεινου] speaker' who 'can make the weaker argument defeat the stronger.'[2] Isocrates says his opponent has made him out to be 'clever' (δεινον) when 'he alleges that I am able to make the weaker cause appear the stronger.'[3] In Attic society *deinotes* came to mean cleverness particularly in speech or argument (*deinos legein* was a common expression), a facility attributed to certain sophists who, it was said, used it for the wrong purposes.[4] For the Greeks, misapplications of the *logos* went hand in hand with *deinotes*. Milton's Satan, with his 'juggleries of words' that assail the government of reason, clearly belongs to this depreciated part of the sophistic tradition. If envy, pride, and ambition motivate him, it is speech that enables him to act on those impulses and that establishes his identity as 'the Author of all ill' (*PL*, II. 381). As both the kind of clever sophist who makes the worse cause appear the better and the orator who captivates listeners by moving their passions, the Devil in *Paradise Lost* exhibits all of the characteristic traits and techniques of satanic rhetoric that we have just discussed. They make him a remarkably successful orator until his final appearance in the poem, an episode that reminds us that the power of infernal rhetoric is strictly limited, struggling for existence under the iron rod of divine justice.

Milton quickly establishes the limitations of that rhetoric in the first two books of *Paradise Lost*, where Satan and his fallen comrades demonstrate the Greek adage, popularized by Seneca and ingrained in Renaissance rhetorical theory, that 'as are men's lives, so is their speech' (*talis hominibus fuit oratio, qualis vita*). As Satan's speech uses fraud and guile to entrap others, so he and the other demons deceive themselves. A 'remarkable feature of the first two books is the skill with which Satan and his fellows seek to persuade themselves, and one another, that their very real degradation is a triumph and their humiliation an exaltation.'[5] This skill in self-delusion manifests especially in the rhetorical question, the distinctive signature of demonic speech. Suggestive of open-endedness and uncertainty, it expresses the fallen angels' desire to see an open-ended and uncertain future. In his first speech, for example,

Satan asks, 'what though the field be lost?' then asserts, 'All is not lost' (I. 105–6), as though the degradation of the rebels is not final and may even be reversed. Just as the past had entertained possibility, the war in heaven having been a 'dubious battle' (I. 104) that the rebels could have won, so does the future,

> Since through experience of this great event
> In Arms not worse, in foresight much advanc't,
> We may with more successful hope resolve
> To wage by force or guile eternal War.   (I. 118–21)

Satan's future, as he perceives it, is not fixed. Victory remains possible, or at any rate the overturning of God's plan for them:

>   If then his Providence
> Out of our evil seek to bring forth good,
> Our labor must be to pervert that end,
> And out of good still to find means of evil.   (I. 162–5)

Satan is self-deceived on every theological point. Rhetoric practised correctly entails a speaker's knowing the truth about whatever subject he is dealing with. Satan's ignorance is apparent in most of his rhetorical proceedings, including those internal ones that shape his perception of reality. At the close of his despairing soliloquy atop Mount Niphates, he reveals that he has, at best, a fragmentary knowledge of the truth:

> Evil be thou my Good; by thee at least
> Divided Empire with Heav'n's King I hold
> By thee, and more than half perhaps will reign;
> As Man ere long, and this new World shall know.   (IV. 110–13)

Satan correctly anticipates the extent of his future dominion in the temporal world but misconceives his relationship to God as that of a rival, too proud to recognize his actual station as a servant of God. The overarching structures of providence and theodicy, and the merely accessory function of evil within them, lie beyond his knowledge.

By his failure to comprehend these systems and their implications, Satan tricks himself into seeing a contingent future that no longer exists for the defeated angels. A true account of their destiny under God's rule is provided by another literary precursor of the Miltonic Satan, the soul-hunting 'feend' of 'The Friar's Tale':

> But, for thou axest why labouren we –
> For somtyme we been Goddes instrumentz,
> And meenes to doon his comandementz,
> Whan that hym list, upon his creatures,
> In divers art and in divers figures.
> Withouten hym we have no myght, certayn,
> If that hym list to stonden ther-agayn.[6]

The apostate angels in *Paradise Lost* are enslaved to providence on the same terms, acting within the limits of God's permissive will and destined, as 'Goddes instrumentz,' to abet the production of good out of evil. Milton underlines the subjugation of the fallen Lucifer:

> Chain'd on the burning Lake, nor ever thence
> Had ris'n or heav'd his head, but that the will
> And high permission of all-ruling Heaven
> Left him at large to his own dark designs   (I. 210–13)

– designs carried out under the provision that

> all his malice serv'd but to bring forth
> Infinite goodness, grace, and mercy shown
> On Man by him seduc't.   (I. 217–19)

Satan and his lieutenants, unlike Chaucer's enlightened fiend, are blind to these realities, imagining a cosmic order governed not by God's will but by fate and chance.[7] These pagan notions inform the devils' ignorance of providence and nurture their belief in what amounts to an illusory contingency, an imaginary freedom to determine their own future through words and deeds. These misconceptions have notable implications for an infernal rhetoric that is used solely for persuasion. Unlike the rhetoric of heaven, which, as Christian eloquence, may have purposes correlative to persuasion such as revelation, instruction, or admonition, the rhetoric of hell single-mindedly homes in on finding the available means of persuasion. Even Satan's private broodings eventually turn to persuading himself by steeling his own evil resolve. In order for persuasion to occur, however, in Milton's hell or anywhere else, an audience must be free to choose between alternative possible courses of action. Satan, as Milton emphasizes, is not free. His will, in bondage to the will of God, can choose only what God permits it to choose. Each decision he makes, or convinces others to make, initiates an action in step with the gradual fulfilment of theodicy. The divine *fatum* has rescinded contingency not only from infernal existence, but also from whatever rhetoric the devils may employ in an effort to order and influence that existence. Rhetoric in hell cannot operate at full capacity under the disadvantage of lost contingency; but it can, in order to assert some kind of identity as rhetoric, find ways of skirting around the problem, as the upcoming discussion of the pandemonic council in Book II will show.

Adam and Eve, in contrast to the reprobate angels, are left entirely free to determine their future, a point that is crucial to the status of infernal rhetoric in *Paradise Lost*. For it is only when the rhetoric of hell travels from its place of origin to the Garden of Eden, through Satan's journey, that it assumes rhetoric's traditional status as a vehicle of authentic persuasion, directed at beings whom God has left free to choose. I will examine the relationship of human free will to rhetoric in *Paradise Lost* more closely in the following chapter; for the time being, the point to be stressed is that setting or location significantly determines how closely Satan's speech approximates a genuine rhetoric of persuasion. In this context, setting is important not so much for its usual bearing on the rhetorical situation, that it functions as a variable of the *kairos*, to which the orator must react in deciding what and how to speak; rather, it is seen as determining the persuasive potential of Satan's rhetoric, a potential that fluctuates in line with the degree of contingency found in each setting. Eden, therefore, where future contingency is most present and active, confers a validity on Satan's rhetoric that had been lacking in hell: *where* he speaks is as important as *what* he speaks. That satanic eloquence overreaches Adam and Eve despite their possessing a type of foreknowledge, Raphael having warned them that they would be tempted, testifies to its effectiveness when deployed in Eden under contingent circumstances.

As Satan moves from one setting to another in *Paradise Lost*, there is little variation in the basic character of his speech, which remains consistently and consciously rhetorical, driven by a need to persuade. Satan relies on eloquence for the accomplishment of his deeds, and the urgency of this reliance hangs over nearly every situation in which he speaks. It is the urgency of the *vita activa*, of the man dedicated to solving problems and achieving his goals; it drives Satan as he exhorts others to action, rallies support, asserts his authority, threatens, propitiates, flatters or dissimulates. In this whirl of activity he is reacting continually to the shifting coordinates of the rhetorical moment – to the vagaries of occasion, to time, place, and the predispositions and inclinations of different audiences. God speaks, but Satan puts speech to work, using it tirelessly in the knowledge that its power to persuade is the surest means of furthering his aims and that against mankind it is his only means, brute force having been proscribed as an option.[8] In chapter 3 we noted sixteenth-century commentators urging the study of Hermogenes, Demetrius, and Longinus, since a copious and fitting style could give the orator an advantage in any situation, including courts and assemblies. Satan understands the utility of eloquence as a political instrument. In his dependence on speech he conforms much more closely than God to the humanists' image of the worldly orator, engaged in the cut and thrust of policy and intrigue, staking his lot on a quick wit and a glib tongue, prevailing on and – so he hopes – over those who would resist him. God, in contrast, is removed from the exigencies of argument and persuasion. He speaks for the most part with placid assurance, declaratively and instructively, certain that whatever happens will accord with the providence set in motion by His will.

Satan's adherence to typical patterns of oratorical conduct is evident almost as soon as he regains consciousness after the nine-day fall from heaven, during his first public address:

> Princes, Potentates,
> Warriors, the Flow'r of Heav'n, once yours, now lost,
> If such astonishment as this can seize
> Eternal spirits; or have ye chos'n this place
> After the toil of Battle to repose
> Your wearied virtue, for the ease you find
> To slumber here, as in the Vales of Heav'n?
> Or in this abject posture have ye sworn
> To adore the Conqueror? who now beholds
> Cherub and Seraph rolling in the Flood
> With scatter'd Arms and Ensigns, till anon
> His swift pursuers from Heav'n Gates discern
> Th' advantage, and descending tread us down
> Thus drooping, or with linked Thunderbolts
> Transfix us to the bottom of this gulf.
> Awake, arise, or be for ever fall'n.

> They heard, and were abash't, and up they sprung
> Upon the wing.   (I. 315–32)

This time, Satan's rhetorical questions are barbed with admonitory irony in order to induce action. In this he seeks the usual objective of the military commander, punctuated by the antithetically turned final line, 'Awake, arise, or be for ever fall'n.' The phrase and Satan's conventional oratorical posture contrast with the words and attitude of the Son, which had calmly presaged the onset of rebel defeat: 'Stand still in bright array ye Saints, here stand' (VI. 801). Satan speaks in the same vein and to the same stirring effect when he declares his Ulyssean resourcefulness at having invented the cannon and describes its potential to turn the war in their favour: 'He ended, and his words thir drooping cheer / Enlight'n'd, and thir languisht hope revived' (VI. 496–7). Like Achilles, Satan is a speaker of words and a doer of deeds. The forceful utterance of his words, backlit by the tradition of heroic martial exhortation, imparts to infernal speech a semblance of rhetorical efficacy that is really an illusion – one considerably less grand than the aspirations of its speakers.

The rhetorical question is a reliable and frequently employed resource of satanic eloquence. It is, in fact, the favourite rhetorical device of all the demons, a tendency that reflects on their rhetoric in general and on the way they think. John Steadman contends that during the pandemonic council 'one must not regard [the demons] as seduced by their own oratory. The arguments they exploit in the cause of their distinctive vices are essentially rhetorical in character and should not be taken for real motivation or sincere belief.'[9] I argue that the demons are, in fact, self-deceived; that the rhetoric of each speaker, while it may advocate his distinctive vice, also expresses sincere belief. Although God's providence controls their actions (I. 366), the aleatory world view of the fallen angels suggests to them a contingent future. It naturally follows that they engage in modes of thinking and speaking that assess and recommend alternative courses of future action, procedures that fall within the sphere of political or deliberative rhetoric. Satan convokes an assembly for this purpose in Book II, where speakers table prospective options concerning what to do next in their ongoing struggle against God. The persistence of the rhetorical question in demonic speech marks it as a deliberative signature, indicative of a predisposition to the activities and states of mind that are inherent in the form of the question itself:

doubt, uncertainty, speculation, forecasting. An apparently open future prompts questions as a matter of course. Apart from providing a measure of how the devils think, the rhetorical question also functions in its usual manner, as a persuasive tactic. No one is more eager to use it than Belial.

Belial turns in a masterful performance during the pandemonic consultation, and Milton takes care to give prior notice that he is the kind of orator who abuses the power of speech:

> he seem'd
> For dignity compos'd and high exploit:
> But all was false and hollow; though his Tongue
> Dropt Manna, and could make the worse appear
> The better reason, to perplex and dash
> Maturest Counsels: for his thoughts were low;
> To vice industrious, but to Nobler deeds
> Timorous and slothful: yet he pleas'd the ear,
> And with persuasive accent thus began.   (II. 110–18)

The description invokes, and identifies Belial with, both the denounced version of sophistry that paints unjust or immoral causes in a favourable light and the Platonic criticism that the art of speaking could be co-opted to this ignoble pursuit by pleasing an audience and enticing them to value that pleasure more highly than what is true or good.[10] Belial's love of pleasure naturally colours his speech. A reader's pleasure in his lines may seem a guilty pleasure, like that taken in any overproduced spectacle – perhaps that is why it is worth cultivating, as a break from high epic seriousness. We may experience this when Belial answers Moloch's rash bellicosity and his question, 'what can be worse / Than to dwell here' (II. 85–6), with a succession of his own questions, some contained in the following twenty-eight lines. Reading them is a good opportunity to think yourself back into a Renaissance frame of mind, a Renaissance appreciation for literary style in all its elaborate, filigreed glory. So let us forget the source and the context of the words, and the stern glare of Milton the teacher; instead, let us share in the pleasure of language, to be savoured in the rococo flights of Belial's sophistic aria:

> Say they who counsel War, we are decreed,   160
> Reserv'd and destin'd to Eternal woe;
> Whatever doing, what can we suffer more,

What can we suffer worse? is this then worst,
Thus sitting, thus consulting, thus in arms?
What when we fled amain, pursu'd and strook   165
With Heav'n's afflicting Thunder, and besought
The Deep to shelter us? this Hell then seem'd
A refuge from those wounds: or when we lay
Chain'd on the burning Lake? that sure was worse.
What if the breath that kindl'd those grim fires   170
Awak'd should blow them into sevenfold rage
And plunge us into flames? or from above
Should intermitted vengeance arm again
His red right hand to plague us? what if all
Her stores were op'n'd, and this Firmament   175
Of Hell should spout her Cataracts of Fire,
Impendent horrors, threat'ning hideous fall
One day upon our heads; while we perhaps
Designing or exhorting glorious war,
Caught in a fiery Tempest shall be hurl'd   180
Each on his rock transfixt, the sport and prey
Of racking whirlwinds, or for ever sunk
Under yon boiling Ocean, wrapt in Chains;
There to converse with everlasting groans,
Unrespited, unpitied, unrepriev'd,   185
Ages of hopeless end; this would be worse.
War therefore, open or conceal'd, alike
My voice dissuades.   (II. 160–88)

Belial combines a variety of elements in crafting this extraordinary oration. He proceeds by *argumentum ex concessis*, where a speaker reasons
from the premise(s) of an opponent – in this case Moloch's 'what could
be worse?' – and he resorts to a broad selection of figures. But the rhetorical heart of the speech consists in its questions, found thirteen times
in his 106 lines. Belial refutes Moloch's argument mainly by stringing
together rhetorical questions (lines 162–78), used as part of a sophistic
agenda to obscure his true motives, evoking a fear of worse punishment, but only in order to avoid having to take any action at all:

Thus Belial with words cloth'd in reason's garb
Counsell'd ignoble ease, and peaceful sloth,
Not peace.   (II. 226–8)

The epic narrator promptly raps us back to studious attention, lest we tarry in the garden of Belial's eloquence.

Rhetorical questions in Beelzebub's oration again stand out conspicuously. He understands, for example, at least part of the rebels' predicament, that they must 'remain / In strictest bondage' (II. 230–1) to a God more powerful than themselves:

> what peace will be giv'n
> To us enslav'd, but custody severe,
> And stripes, and arbitrary punishment
> Inflicted? and what peace can we return,
> But to our power hostility and hate,
> Untam'd reluctance, and revenge though slow,
> Yet ever plotting how the Conqueror least
> May reap his conquest, and may least rejoice
> In doing what we most in suffering feel?   (II. 332–40)

Belial had also seen their plight in similar terms, God being all-seeing and all-powerful:

> for what can force or guile
> With him, or who deceive his mind, whose eye
> Views all things at one view? he from Heav'n's highth
> All these our motions vain, sees and derides;
> Not more Almighty to resist our might
> Than wise to frustrate all our plots and wiles.   (II. 188–93)

God is a conqueror and the devils are in bondage, as Beelzebub says; but neither he nor Belial sees the other dimensions of God's nature or the purpose of their bondage. One stylistic symptom of their limited vision in these respects is the rhetorical question, a form of argument that reveals its speakers' state of mind.

Questions express ignorance and doubt, they seek answers. *Rhetorical* questions, although posed ironically and for argumentative effect, may occasionally contain reflections of the mentality and motives proper to the kind of question that is asked in earnest. Psychologically, then, the devils' continual use of questions is not merely a technique of public persuasion, but also an index of intellectual confusion, of an inability to declare truths – the consequences of their subjection, for example – which recede further out of reach with every new question. The pande-

monic debate's most cogent expression of the nature of God is contained
in a passage, spoken by Beelzebub, that, tellingly, leaves off questioning
and recalls a different kind of rhetoric:

> For [God], be sure,
> In highth or depth, still first and last will Reign
> Sole King, and of his Kingdom lose no part
> By our revolt, but over Hell extend
> His Empire, and with Iron Sceptre rule
> Us here, as with his Golden those in Heav'n.   (II. 323–8)

Two apriorisms of humanist rhetoric pervade these lines. The first, a
cultural one, is that style is the image of the speaker's character. The
second, for present purposes a major consideration of literary decorum,
is that style is the image of the thoughts it conveys – that it should have
an organic relationship to thought, as the body does to the mind. In
Beelzebub's lines, Milton arranges style to both speaker and thought.
The *res*, the moral content of the fallen angel's speech, declares the truth
of God's eternal glory and supremacy, ideas that take on the familiar
stamp of divine utterance. The style is that of heaven, of the kind to be
seen in the following books, spoken by God and the Son. As Beelzebub
speaks the wisdom of God's providence, his words manifest the elements of God's style, especially in the grave doubling patterns: 'highth
or depth,' 'first and last,' the polyptoton of 'King' and 'Kingdom,' the
antithesis of the iron sceptre and the golden one earlier invoked by
Abdiel (V. 886–8). He also drops interrogative bombast in favour of the
declarative plainness customary to divine speech; 'be sure' is even
imperative, the tense most particularly associated with God. For the
subjects of which Beelzebub speaks, the style borrowed from heaven is
clearly suitable. It is a style, moreover, that is also appropriate to its
speaker, despite the apparent incongruity of that speaker's evil character. While at a vast moral remove from his former state, Beelzebub is
nevertheless a fallen angel, with the same faculties and knowledge he
possessed in heaven – retained vestiges of angelic being that lend dramatic credibility to his momentary recollection of divine wisdom and
style.

  Beelzebub's grasp of providence is, however, necessarily imperfect.
Although he acknowledges the God who wields a golden sceptre, it is
the God of the iron sceptre who preoccupies him and his fellows. The
devils' pagan view of the world, revolving around fate and chance,

again deceives them, this time into perceiving God exclusively in terms of His strength. It hinders them from comprehending the order and harmony of providence: that the strength of God is channelled into justice; that justice, not chance, permanently checks and punishes their evil; and that their evil ultimately produces good within the scheme of trial, grace, and mercy that tempers justice. Precluded from understanding this providential system, the devils are necessarily precluded from understanding the God in whom the system originates. They see His strength – 'by strength / They measure all' (VI. 820) – but not the aspects of God that complement it and round out a fully realized providence: wisdom, justice, compassion, love, mercy. They see only one of the parts that constitute the whole of God.

The relationship of part to whole, we recall, figures centrally in the rhetoric of prophecy in Books XI and XII, where distribution from effects gradually reveals to Adam the paradox of theodicy. In hell, this relationship asserts itself in a different rhetorical manner, part related to whole this time through synecdoche, which governs the devils' parochial view of God. The trope of synecdoche works here not so much as a persuasive tactic (though this is partly the case) as a mode of perception. Quintilian's definition includes this function; it works, he writes, 'by making us realize [*intelligamus*] many things from one, the whole from a part, the genus from a species ... or on the other hand, the whole procedure may be reversed.'[11] That the demons see a whole in terms of a part, however, is not the same as realizing that whole, coming to know it, understanding it. When we realize a whole from a part, we are seeing it in terms of that part; but that part is also helping us to see *into* the whole, to sharpen our perception of it. The part that the devils imagine to represent God, His strength, does not bring them to realize God in His entirety, but rather hinders such a realization. Instead of enabling a fuller understanding of a whole, as it had done for Adam's comprehension of theodicy, synecdoche for the reprobate angels disables their understanding of God and therefore of providence and their place in it. God's nature defies their kind of halting synecdochal representation, numerous other parts being necessary in order to portray it more comprehensively. Synecdoche, like eloquence itself, is subject to debasement when appropriated by satanic rhetoric; ordinarily an instrument of illumination and clarification, its function is curtailed in hell, the part suggesting nothing other than or beyond itself, leaving the demons in ignorance. Synecdoche is the master trope of rhetoric in hell. Limiting the scope of understanding there, it raises the perceptual scaffolding for the devils' belief in pagan fate and a contingent future, and motivates infernal policy, to seek revenge against God the conqueror and to destroy His works.

In formulating demonic policy and ensuring that its implementation consolidates his leadership, Satan uses rhetoric flawlessly, exemplifying the political orator who can wring unqualified assent from his audience. At the close of the Stygian parliament, as his plan is taking shape, he demonstrates the reliance on eloquence, applied to the practical concerns of the *vita activa*, that characterizes all his public speech. In hell Satan holds complementary positions: the king of rhetoric and of the state. He is a master of controlling the situation and of all stylistic techniques, including, as ever, the rhetorical question. Like Belial, whose catalogue of horrors depicted potentially worse suffering, Satan amplifies his questions and the perils of the journey to Earth by imaging its prospective hazards:

> But first whom shall we send
> In search of this new world, whom shall we find
> Sufficient? who shall tempt with wand'ring feet
> The dark unbottom'd infinite Abyss
> And through the palpable obscure find out
> His uncouth way, or spread his aery flight
> Upborne with indefatigable wings
> Over the vast abrupt, ere he arrive
> The happy Isle; what strength, what art can then
> Suffice, or what evasion bear him safe
> Through the strict Senteries and Stations thick
> Of Angels watching round? Here he had need
> All circumspection, and wee now no less
> Choice in our suffrage; for on whom we send,
> The weight of all and our last hope relies. (II. 402–16)

Satan has used the figure peristasis, which amplifies by describing attendant circumstances. It brings about the first of two critical moments:

> This said, he sat; and expectation held
> His look suspense, awaiting who appear'd
> To second, or oppose, or undertake
> The perilous attempt. (II. 417–20)

He enlists the time-honoured tactic of deliberative oratory, as effective as it is crude, of painting a fearsome picture of the future in order to cow his audience and bring them to heel. The amplification provokes in his lieutenants the emotional response he had hoped for:

> but all sat mute,
> Pondering the danger with deep thoughts; and each
> In other's count'nance read his own dismay
> Astonisht. (II. 420–3)

'*Satan*, whom now transcendent glory rais'd / Above his fellows,' accepts the hardship of the voyage, but not before prefacing the acceptance with another peristasis, further describing the dangers of the task at hand: the fires and gates of hell, the void of Chaos, the unknown (II. 432–44). All of this rhetorical manoevring and amplification further raises his heroic stature and makes his actual acceptance, when it finally does arrive (II. 445–56), a deserved confirmation of his *virtù*. As he concludes his oration, the second *kairos* arrives, and he handles it with customary dispatch:

> Thus saying rose
> The Monarch, and prevented all reply,
> Prudent, lest from his resolution rais'd
> Others among the chief might offer now
> (Certain to be refus'd) what erst they fear'd. (II. 466–70)

The prudence thus exercised is, of course, *deinotes*. And in forestalling any attempt to dilute his glory, the Devil shows himself to be a model of the *deinos sophistes*, having spoken in perfect accord with the demands of timing and audience, having fortified that speech with *actio*, a rhetoric of physical gesture at least as commanding as verbal rhetoric,[12] and having guaranteed his success by virtue of an intimidating delivery: 'they / Dreaded not more th' adventure than his voice / Forbidding' (II. 473–5).[13] *Deinotes* should be understood here not only in its Aristotelian ethical sense, as cleverness, but also in its Hermogenean stylistic sense, as 'force': 'For if any speaker knows when he should use each particular style ... and where he should use it and for how long and against whom and how and why, and if he not only knows but also can apply his knowledge, he will be the most forceful of orators and will surpass all others, just as Demosthenes did' and as Satan does. Hermogenes further notes, 'the ancients used the word *deinos* in the sense of "feared"'[14] – yet a third signification of *deinotes* applicable to Satan, especially in the scene under discussion.

One of the debate's pivotal moments, in which Satan's crafty wondering aloud is met with silence, parallels an episode discussed in chapter 6. After God petitions for an intercessor for mankind, 'all the Heav'nly Choir stood mute, / And silence was in Heav'n' (III. 217–18). In much the same way as that scene is a point of departure for further comment on the nature of rhetoric in heaven, the mute consternation of Satan's audience leads to a similar line of inquiry, centred around the issue of contingency. In hell, rhetoric encounters obstacles comparable to those that confront it in heaven. The main one, however, is no longer divine foreknowledge, which imposes no necessity even in hell, but rather a provision of divine providence, that the fallen angels are now deprived of free will. Given that persuasion depends on an audience's being able to exercise free will, rhetoric in hell itself – unlike the crooked eloquence that Satan will use in Eden – appears to be virtually nullified. Decisions have no substance without free will and a choice between alternatives; the process of argument, without legitimate decisions to influence, becomes alienated from its purpose and emptied of its content. Yet, just as rhetoric in heaven manages to offset the stifling atmosphere of certainty by exhibiting various other elements of a rhetorical character, such as the presence of the angelic choir and the vigorous brushstrokes of Milton's *elocutio*, so too in hell the art of speaking finds its own outlets of preservation.

Rhetoric in hell derives its substance mainly from dramatic irony. The demons are unaware, as their references to fate and chance attest, that providence controls their future and that deliberative rhetoric can posit no genuine alternatives for them when their collective will has been reined in by the will of God. It thereby happens that, as an incidental consequence of divine justice, 'rhetorical' situations in hell are deprived of contingency, the absence of which defuses the power of infernal argument. For example, Satan, and no one else, will undertake the voyage to the newly created world. His going is not, in the providential scheme of things, an issue in question, coloured with doubt or uncertainty. But neither Satan nor the other reprobate angels know anything of this; so that when they sit in silence, Satan expectant, the others awed, the moment is a very real *kairos*, highly charged with rhetorical contingency, *if only among themselves*. It is this irony that lets internal rhetoric, the rhetoric *in* the poem among the characters, maintain a life of its own within the confines of hell. On these terms – and these terms alone – the devils really are deliberative orators, Satan really is persuading and manipulating others, his policy and forceful speech imposing his will upon the proceedings.

The life of this internal rhetoric is provisional, of course, ended as soon as the synecdochal perspective of hell, and the dramatic irony it produces, gives way to the panoptic viewpoint of heaven, which reminds us that the speakers at the infernal parliament are 'God's instruments.' The devils' belief in their own freedom creates, fittingly, a false image of persuasion, hollow at its core as their words are hollow, a falseness that mocks them, since they deludedly believe that their persuasive efforts constitute a rhetoric of substance and efficacy. The internal rhetoric of hell may be, after all, a rhetoric undermined by God's will, but it also stands in its own right as one that conforms to the thoughts of its speakers and that, in its ultimate futility, those speakers deserve. Its counterfeit contingency is a part of its decorum, the devils having forfeited a genuinely contingent rhetoric of choice as a consequence of their defeat.

That rhetoric in hell dissolves at the touch of providence is appropriate for its speakers and its setting. This very dissolution becomes integral to the success of rhetoric in hell from a critical perspective: being of a piece with decorum, it is one of the features that aligns infernal rhetoric with the principles and practices of the classical and Renaissance *ars dicendi*. The presence of these standard artistic components, of which decorum is one, consolidates the status of infernal discourse as rhetoric, providing a hedge against the absence of contingency. In many instances the speech of the devils maintains a general proximity to decorum that affirms its basis in rhetoric as Milton and his age conceived it. Decorum's foremost point of reference is style, as distinctive and appropriate to the speech of hell as it is to the words of the divine characters. The hidden art characteristic of empyreal rhetoric, such as the doubling patterns noted in the speech of God and the Son, the impassioned figures of Abdiel, or the tropes of Michael, contrasts with the hypertrophic style of the demons, composed of various kinds of amplification as well as the *figurae sententiarum*, such as the rhetorical question, which are intended to arouse strong emotion. It understates the matter to say that such rhetoric inclines, in Bacon's words, 'rather towards copie than weight.'[15] As opposed to heaven's relatively plain register of instruction, which balances *verba* and *res* and moves the passions only when appropriate, the demonic grand style is designed for coercion, its speakers papering over debased motives with elaborate figures and phrasing and continually playing on any emotion, particularly fear, that will sway their audience into agreement. Infernal speech is thus consciously and blatantly rhetorical, overly so, an excessiveness which – although a vice in itself and meant to be recognized as such – gives it a strong, unique rhetorical identity, at once differentiated from the rhetoric of heaven and tied to the Renaissance tradition of the *ornatus* and the affective orientation of persuasive speaking.

The grand style and the dominance of emotive proof are aspects of rhetoric that associate speech in hell with standard Renaissance concepts of the art. These familiar rhetorical elements, along with other techniques, references, and episodes scattered throughout the poem, partially offset the lack of contingency that undermines the deliberative efforts – and indeed the entire existence – of the fallen angels. Filling this same compensatory role is the setting of the parliamentary council, which, like the Son of God's battle oration, serves as a familiar topos of rhetoric, an instance where a speaker would be expected to use it. Satan's own rhetoric completely dominates that scene and continues thenceforward to gather momentum as a force to be reckoned with, bolstering the poem's internal rhetoric and sharpening the rhetorical outline of infernal speech in general. His success is due partly to a knowledge of his audience, which enables him to render an idea attractive 'according to mens severall inclinations,' in Burton's words.[16] He can appeal to self-interest: promising that Sin and Death will be fed (II. 840–4), he gets them to open the gates of hell; promising Chaos and Night that they will regain lost territory (II. 980–7), he receives directions that guide him through the void. He can also abuse nobler traits in a listener: in order to slip past Uriel on his earth-bound flight, Satan plays on the archangel's approval of zeal by hypocritically professing an

> Unspeakable desire to see, and know
> All these his wondrous works, but chiefly Man,
>
> ...
>
> That both in him and all things, as is meet,
> The Universal Maker we may praise.   (III. 662–3, 675–6)

Disguised as a cherub, Satan disguises his style in kind, imitating the plainer style of heaven, a place 'Where honor due and reverence none neglects' (III. 738); he therefore acknowledges Uriel's eminence (III. 654–61). The rest of his speech omits the majestic flourishes common to hell in favour of stating, in fervent yet simple terms, an adoration of God and a desire to see man. The ideas themselves, not the style, stand forth as Satan adapts his speech to the disposition of his audience.

When Satan's audience is an angel, the rhetoric of hell becomes invigorated, since the angels may deliberate and choose freely when confronted with what Satan is urging. Uriel's sinless oversight is not a case in point; the moral transgression of the future Beelzebub, on the other hand, entails a deliberate decision. Satan's career as a tempter begins with the seduction of this unnamed angel, when, on the same day as the Son's ordination, he poses the unforgettable rhetorical question:

> Sleep'st thou, Companion dear, what sleep can close
> Thy eye-lids? and rememb'rest what Decree
> Of yesterday, so late hath past the lips
> Of Heav'n's Almighty. Thou to me thy thoughts
> Wast wont, I mine to thee wast wont to impart;
> Both waking we were one; how then can now
> Thy sleep dissent? new Laws thou see'st impos'd;
> New Laws from him who reigns, new minds may raise
> In us who serve, new Counsels, to debate
> What doubtful may ensue; more in this place
> To utter is not safe.   (V. 673–83)

The first fruits of Satan's rhetoric, brought forth in heaven, are auspicious for its future success in hell and on earth:

> So spake the false Arch-Angel, and infus'd
> Bad influence into th' unwary breast
> Of his Associate.   (V. 694–6)

The words infusing that influence are persuasive in the fullest sense; for heaven, unlike hell, allows satanic rhetoric to function in an atmosphere of future contingency – the oration, though spoken in heaven, remains infernal rhetoric, since the angel that Satan once was is now infected with envy and pride (V. 662, 665). The speaker's character naturally informs the style, which is clearly that of hell. As we have seen, even in cases where contingency is absent from the workings of infernal rhetoric, style emerges, often spectacularly, to connect the rhetoric it expresses with the style-centred *ars dicendi* of the classical tradition. Of special note in the passage quoted above is the verbal trickery evident in the subtly transformed signification of the word 'new': through the course of its anaphora (lines 679–81), it changes from designating the new divine law of obedience to implying the new satanic law of apostasy. By this sleight of diction, Satan replaces the 'new Laws' of God with the 'new minds' and 'new Counsels' of rebellious discontent – the same replacement he wishes to encourage in the mind of his colleague. His stylistic facility makes the choice of disobedience seem as casual and easy as the smooth phrasing he uses to recommend it. And, once again, rhetorical questions augment the power of satanic persuasion. Satan's interrogatory tone prompts the other angel into a similarly questioning state of mind, receptive to 'new' ideas, and even insinuates a violation of the bonds of friendship and loyalty.

The Miltonic Satan exhibits oratorical skills as a seductive speaker in heaven and an opportunistic reader of character during his journey to Paradise. Once he arrives there, the rhetoric of hell continues to accrue traditional elements and dimensions, as when he explicitly says that inciting Adam and Eve to disobedience will be a rhetorical endeavour:

> Hence I will excite thir minds
> With more desire to know, and to reject
> Envious commands.   (IV. 522–4)

Behind Satan's plan lies the classical and Renaissance belief in the power of words to captivate men's minds and alter their opinions, a power corruptible to the service of immoral ends. The Devil's first attempt on the human pair finds him planting 'high conceits ingend'ring pride' (IV. 809) in Eve's mind as he speaks to her in a dream, a prelude to the temptation of Book IX. Eve's dream is significant as the second major instance, after the temptation of the unnamed angel in Book V, where satanic rhetoric operates on an audience in possession of free will, in an environment where decisions and events are entirely contingent. The farther Satan takes the rhetoric of hell out of hell's confines, the greater validity it assumes as rhetoric. Directed at Eve, who is free to choose, satanic eloquence carries the genuinely persuasive content that it had lacked in the company of the enslaved demons in hell, although its style in each of these cases remains the same.

Satan reverts from his angelic pose in Uriel's presence to his customary forms of speech. What had worked in heaven, on the unnamed angel, and in hell, on the fallen hosts, ought also to work in Eden: 'Why sleep'st thou *Eve*?' Satan begins (V. 38). The rhetorical question, Satan's favourite device, is the first thing Eve hears from him – appositely so, for he will unremittingly assail her with it, intent that the implication of doubt in his questions should contrast and undermine the declarative finality of the sole command ('Ye shall not eat thereof'), and prompt Eve to question her own relationship to knowledge, Adam, and God. Question everything, Satan's rhetoric implies:

> And O fair Plant, said he, with fruit surcharg'd,
> Deigns none to ease thy load and taste thy sweet,
> Nor God, nor Man; is Knowledge so despis'd?
> Or envy, or what reserve forbids to taste?
> Forbid who will, none shall from me withhold
> Longer thy offer'd good, why else set here?
> This said he paus'd not, but with vent'rous Arm
> He pluck't, he tasted; mee damp horror chill'd
> At such bold words voucht with a deed so bold. (V. 58–66)

As well as the familiar *interrogationes*, Satan imports from hell the kind of *actio*, or rhetoric of gesture, with which he had so authoritatively concluded the council scene. Here, he plucks and eats from the tree before Eve's eyes. The combination of words and witnessed action deeply moves her, a state enhanced by the sensuousness of the dream: Satan appears 'shap'd and wing'd like one of those from Heav'n' (V. 55); he describes the serenity of night-time in tactile, aural, and visual images (V. 38–43); 'his dewy locks distill'd / *Ambrosia*' (V. 56–7), and

> Even to my mouth of that same fruit held part
> Which he had pluckt; the pleasant savory smell
> So quick'n'ed appetite, that I, methought,
> Could not but taste. (V. 83–6)

The Devil tries to circumvent Eve's reason by arousing her carnal senses. Words and images, the whole fabric of the dream, allure her. Satan's language is as gorgeous as the ambient sights and scents. His prosopopoeia to the tree will recur as the rhetorical centrepiece of the temptation in Book IX; here, he uses this figure to flatter Eve ('Heav'n wakes with all his eyes' at V. 44–7), adding exotic touches such as polyptoton and climax: 'happy though thou art, / Happier thou may'st be, worthier can'st not be' (V. 75–6). The dream, in light of Eve's horrified reaction, serves notice of the formidable rhetorical arsenal that Satan has brought to Eden. It signals that infernal eloquence has arrived in Paradise as a complete rhetorical system in all parts and functions, having gained persuasive leverage through the future contingency attendant to human free will.

During Satan's next meeting with Eve, the rhetoric of hell fulfils the potential shown in the dream. The temptation's apparent success, however, in fact contains the germ of satanic rhetoric's ultimate failure along with the downfall of Satan himself, both of which receive divine confirmation during Satan's final appearance, in Book X. Up to this point, the rhetoric of hell has exerted considerable sway over the internal rhetoric of the poem, controlling, within the bounds of God's sufferance, the decisions and actions of angelic, demonic, and human characters. When permitted to influence genuinely contingent events, it initiated the war in heaven, abetted Satan's journey to Eden, and enabled him to precipitate the Fall of man. Now, overjoyed that the Son's judgment will not fall on him immediately, Satan returns to hell to boast of his most recent exploits (X. 460–503) but learns, among other lessons, that his rhetoric has no intrinsic power, having accomplished nothing beyond what God has allowed. He reveals, moreover, that his skill as a rhetorical speaker is not matched by his skill as an interpreter of divine rhetoric:

> True is, mee also he hath judg'd, or rather
> Mee not, but the brute Serpent in whose shape
> Man I deceiv'd: that which to mee belongs,
> Is enmity, which he will put between
> Mee and mankind; I am to bruise his heel;
> His Seed, when is not set, shall bruise my head:
> A World who would not purchase with a bruise,
> Or much more grievous pain?   (X. 494–501)

'Her Seed shall bruise thy head, thou bruise his heel' (X. 181): Satan picks up his knowledge of the Son's judgment second-hand, from eavesdropping on Adam and Eve (X. 342–5), *before* Michael teaches Adam the full implications of its meaning. Whatever account of the judgment Satan may have overheard, it could not at that point have revealed any of the metaphorical links vital for knowing in full what the prophecy ultimately intends: that the bruise to the heel of Jesus Christ, who is the woman's seed, is merely temporal death, a redemptive act that

> Shall bruise the head of *Satan*, crush his strength
> Defeating Sin and Death, his two main arms,
> And fix far deeper in his head thir stings
> Than temporal death shall bruise the Victor's heel,
> Or theirs whom he redeems, a death like sleep,
> A gentle wafting to immortal Life.   (XII. 430–5)

Set beside Michael's prophetic elucidation, Satan's dismissal of the bruise reveals his failure to comprehend that the world he thus purchases will be seized back, that the bruise he receives will be, at length, his final destruction. Satan understands theodicy – which justifies his existence – as he and the other demons understand God: in parts, without comprehending the whole. Whereas Michael's rhetoric of revelation nurtures in Adam hermeneutic skills – a figurative way of thinking, a critical application of rhetoric to discovering what mysteries biblical tropes conceal – Satan cannot construct an allegorical interpretation. Failing to apply rhetoric as a critical tool, he remains unaware of the anagogical meaning of the prophetic judgment.

Satan is taught that meaning in a far harsher manner than Adam, and taught at the same time a proper valuation of infernal rhetoric:

> So having said, a while he stood, expecting
> Thir universal shout and high applause
> To fill his ear, when contrary he hears
> On all sides, from innumerable tongues
> A dismal universal hiss, the sound
> Of public scorn; he wonder'd, but not long
> Had leisure, wond'ring at himself now more;
> His Visage drawn he felt to sharp and spare,
> His Arms clung to his Ribs, his Legs entwining
> Each other, till supplanted down he fell
> A monstrous Serpent on his belly prone,
> Reluctant, but in vain: a greater power
> Now rul'd him, punisht in the shape he sinn'd,
> According to his doom.   (X. 504–17)

It is no coincidence that the metamorphosis occurs as the coda to an oration, at a moment when the concept of rhetoric stands in the foreground. Hissing, not applause, rates the truth worth of infernal eloquence to the dictates of providence. God explicitly demonstrates His power over Satan in order to affirm that the king of hell lives always under the iron rod of justice and that the rhetoric of hell has no life of its own, no access to future contingency, without God's permission. To remind Satan and his counsellors that they possess and exercise their rhetoric as a provision of divine will, God deprives them of speech altogether:

> he would have spoke,
> But hiss for hiss return'd with forked tongue
> To forked tongue, for now were all transform'd
> Alike.   (X. 517–20)

The poem's closing image of hell shows the transformed demons presented with

> fair Fruit, like that
> Which grew in Paradise, the bait of *Eve*
> Us'd by the Tempter.   (X. 550–2)[17]

This fruit, symbolic of corrupted eloquence, is 'fair to sight' (X. 561) but composed of 'bitter Ashes' (X. 566), the same discrepancy between appearance and reality, fair form and bitter substance, that defines the rhetoric of the Tempter throughout *Paradise Lost*. That God deceives the fallen angels into eating this fruit and chewing its ashes not only serves 'to dash thir pride, and Joy for Man seduc't' (X. 577); it also punishes them in kind for the fair-seeming sophistry that had deceived humanity.

9 Temptation and the Rhetoric of Paradise

Only on Earth is there any talk of free will.

Kurt Vonnegut, *Slaughterhouse Five*

All roads lead to the Garden of Eden, the hub of Milton's rhetorical universe. Whenever Milton returns from his inspired depictions of heaven and hell to his 'Native Element' (*PL* VII. 16), the theological, dramatic, and discursive conditions exist for rhetoric to thrive on all levels. Paradise is the most completely rhetorical of the poem's three settings, for it is here, on account of human free will, that Aristotelian contingency is most fully realized, with salutary results for the art of persuasion. Eden's rhetorical energy is further intensified because it is the place where the three discourses of man, angel, and devil converge – an oratorical *palaestra* where good and evil vie for control over human fate, as speakers from both heaven and hell try to influence the decisions that Adam and Eve must make there. In the Garden of Eden the Judeo-Christian ideas of divine rhetoric and anthropopathia are taken to spectacular extremes, beyond their mediated forms in scripture, as God communicates directly through the revelation of angels and the voice of the Son, and in one remarkable scene even speaks *in propria persona* to Adam. And, of course, Milton's Satan arrives. His oratorical triumph over Eve, as spellbinding in its execution as it is fleeting in the grander scheme of things, crowns the literary tradition of the Devil as a past master of the arts of speech.

During these and other speeches that occur in Paradise, one aspect of rhetoric moves to the foreground in the course of Milton's adaptation of the Genesis myth: that speech exerts a power to influence, for better or worse, a person's behaviour. This influence extends to those decisions and actions that constitute the noblest phase of human existence, the life of the spirit, which, properly governed, can lead man up the Chain of Being towards God. Directly implicated in the efficacy of Christian moral philosophy, rhetoric transcends its function as a formal medium of composition for making a poem and becomes, in its own right, a theme of profound theological import and an integral part of Milton's doctrinal message in *Paradise Lost*. For the conflict at the heart of the Christian experience, the *psychomachia* of man's inner being during moments of trial, is, in essence, a rhetorical event.

The historical groundwork for this claim, which is founded on the procedural similarities between rhetoric and ethics, was established in chapters 2 and 3. Renaissance writers had adopted the classical idea, espoused in particular by Isocrates, that rhetoric as a method of speaking also implied a way of conducting one's life. The two activities are, in fact, the same process, each directed by the faculty of prudence, which consists in the ability to take the right decision as often as possible. In order to decide judiciously, one must respond correctly to the promptings of decorum – literary decorum in selecting a fitting style, moral decorum in determining the right thing to do. Isocrates had been the first to recognize this personal dimension of rhetoric[1] – much as Plato recognized of dialectic – that its motions could be internal and ratiocinative, that 'the same arguments which we use in persuading others when we speak in public, we employ also when we deliberate in our own thoughts.'[2] Bacon, too, distinguished rhetoric's private function from its public one, calling it 'this negotiation within ourselves.'[3] When Milton mentions 'the wily suttleties and refluxes of man's thoughts from within' (*YP*, 1: 817),[4] the phrase implies a similar understanding of private thought as the complementary obverse of public speech. Success in either activity depends on the wisdom and uprightness of character necessary for speaking eloquently or, internally, for governing the subtle and often conflicting ethical impulses of one's own thoughts, which all Christians, as well as Adam and Eve, must do.

As a point of departure for arguing rhetoric's pivotal function in the mechanism of Christian trial, another aspect of the kinship between rhetoric and moral philosophy may be reintroduced. Just as their means are the same, accomplished through prudential judgment, so too are their ends. Both rhetoric and ethics aim at persuasion – naturally enough in the realm of speaking, where the wise man judges how to secure the agreement of others, but also in day-to-day life, where ethical judgment comes down to persuasion of one's own will to accept the course of action most conducive to the good life. These two forms of persuasion combine to drive the narrative action of *Paradise Lost*, to propel it towards the Fall of mankind. Oratorical persuasion initiates this motion, as the characters representative of heavenly wisdom and demonic craft set their unique varieties of eloquence to arguing their respective policies; ethical persuasion continues it, as Adam and Eve then reflect inwardly to ponder what they have heard from both sides. This interaction of rhetoric's oratorical and ethical dimensions makes it the axis of original sin, responsible for influencing from without, and fashioning from within, Adam and Eve's behaviour leading up to and during the Fall. As the art by which speakers construct arguments, on the one hand, and by which an audience weighs them, on the other, rhetoric frames every speech of instruction, admonition, temptation, and redemption in *Paradise Lost* and every subsequent human response.

By reading God's parenthetical remark, '(Reason also is choice)' (III. 108), with a Renaissance awareness of the host of significations ascribable to *logos*, the fundamentally rhetorical nature of Christian moral philosophy in *Paradise Lost* becomes clear. When God says that reason, *logos*, is choice, we know that it is also wisdom and prudence, and that choice is an act of the will and of the rational deliberation (with an emphasis on *orthotēs*) that directs the will by discovering in action what is good. Michael includes virtue in the *logos* by equating it with reason (XII. 98). And, of course, *logos* signifies speech, which, in the case of these ethical faculties and objectives, is the inward speech attendant on reaching moral decisions. For Adam and Eve, who are 'Authors to themselves in all / Both what they judge and what they choose' (III. 122–3), the exercise of free will is a rhetorical activity, revolving around the *logos* as reason, wisdom, and speech. Miltonic wisdom means being able to distinguish good from evil and to translate that knowledge into living in accord with God's commands. Milton understood that consistently following such a policy was by no means straightforward, since good and evil could often appear, or be made to appear, very much alike.

One method of intentionally confusing good and evil was rhetoric, normally valued by Milton as an instrument for communicating divine wisdom, but which he acknowledged to have sinister uses as well. Satan employs the *logos* of public persuasion to confuse man's interior speech of reason and private deliberation. Through his oratorical craft in Book IX, a morally wrong alternative is elaborately disguised to seem good, thereby dissolving the unambiguous distinction between good and evil that God's interdiction of the Tree made so clear. In fact, Satan goes even further, challenging the idea that such a distinction, as Eve understands it, exists at all or, for that matter, that truth itself exists as an objective standard for lawful conduct. By creating this atmosphere of doubt and confusion, Satan is able to unsettle Eve's reason, play on her emotions, and make the worse choice appear the better one. It is, as we will see presently, a sophistical tactic, in whose implementation rhetoric and philosophy come together to reveal contrasting definitions of truth and to reveal precisely how Satan persuades Eve.

Rhetoric in *Paradise Lost* stages its grandest display, erected on the classical humanist framework of the art, at the point where drama reaches its greatest heights and the downward spiral of tragedy is initiated: 'Man's First Disobedience.' The epic invocation anticipates this momentous happening, pinning down its instigator as a cause of the Fall:

> say first what cause
> Mov'd our Grand Parents in that happy State,
> Favor'd of Heav'n so highly, to fall off
> From thir Creator, and transgress his Will
> For one restraint, Lords of the World besides?
> Who first seduc'd them to that foul revolt?
> Th' infernal serpent; hee it was, whose guile
> Stirr'd up with Envy and Revenge, deceiv'd
> The Mother of Mankind.   (I. 28–36)

Just as Eve's dream had foreboded in Book V, rhetoric is the instrument of guile by which the Devil would deceive 'The Mother of Mankind' in Book IX. Chapter 7 showed the same to be true in both earlier and contemporary treatments of Genesis 3; but no literary retelling of the temptation associated the serpent with the forms of classical oratory as obviously and persistently as Milton's. While Satan is the external cause of the Fall, rhetoric is its material cause, the resource utilized to bring it about. For Milton's Devil, however, rhetoric is more than crafty speech; it is *Dasein* his mode of being-in-the-world, the terms in which he perceives that world and that direct his approach to any set of circumstances, from preparation through to execution. Writers such as

Johan Wier noted Satan's alertness (*vigilantia*) as he waited to strike; Milton's Adam knows, too, that

> somewhere nigh at hand
> [He] Watches, no doubt, with greedy hope to find
> His wish and best advantage, us asunder.   (IX. 256–8)

> He sought them both, but wish'd his hap might find
> *Eve* separate, he wish'd, but not with hope
> Of what so seldom chanc'd, when to his wish,
> Beyond his hope, *Eve* separate he spies.   (IX. 42–4)

This is the *kairos*, the seasonable moment for proceeding, and Satan explicitly recognizes it as such:

> Then let me not pass
> Occasion which now smiles, behold alone
> The Woman, opportune to all attempts.   (IX. 479–81)

Shakespeare's Lucrece recognizes that Occasion smiles, more often than not, on evil-doers:

> O Opportunity, thy guilt is great!
> 'Tis thou that execut'st the traitor's treason;
> Thou sets the wolf where he the lamb may get;
> Whoever plots the sin, thou points the season.[5]

Quick to take advantage when Opportunity beckons, Satan, fantastic in appearance, approaches Eve and begins 'His fraudulent temptation' (IX. 531, 532–48) with the second type of proem, or exordium, described by Cicero, 'which by dissimulation and indirection unobtrusively steals into the mind of the auditor.'[6] It is blasphemous flattery of the sort usually put in the serpent's mouth (compare with Avitus, for example), which Milton's Eve has heard already in her dream (V. 38–47) and now starts to work immediately:

> So gloz'd the Tempter, and his Proem tun'd;
> Into the Heart of *Eve* his words made way,
> Though at the voice much marvelling; at length
> Not unamaz'd she thus in answer spake.   (IX. 549–52)

Eve's wonder, which compromises her reason, continues to grow at the notion that the serpent possesses *ratio* and *oratio*, that, so he claims, eating the fruit caused his birth as a rational, then as a rhetorical, being: 'Reason in my inward Powers, and Speech / Wanted not long' (IX. 600). His command of the *logos* becomes increasingly evident, and increasingly forceful, as he leads Eve before the Tree of Knowledge, whereof, she says, 'we may not taste nor touch; / God so commanded' (IX. 651–2):

> To whom the Tempter guilefully repli'd.
> Indeed? hath God then said that of the Fruit
> Of all these Garden trees ye shall not eat,
> Yet Lords declar'd of all in Earth or Air?   (IX. 655–8)

These are notable lines, as the first in Milton's expansion of Genesis 3.1–6 that correspond to the speech of the biblical model. As rhetoric they stand out both structurally and stylistically. First, in the overall structure of the temptation, they have been a long time coming. Although this sly query begins the biblical serpent's temptation, it arrives in *Paradise Lost* after a considerable lead-in, by design on Satan's part. If you want to create a likeness to the truth with deception in mind, Socrates tells Phaedrus, you need to proceed by degrees. 'Is a great or a slight difference between two things the more likely to be misleading?' 'A slight difference,' Phaedrus replies. 'So if you proceed by small degrees from one thing to its opposite then you are more likely to escape detection than if you take big steps' (261E–262A). Proceeding in this way is one of Satan's main strategies for tricking Eve into lowering her guard. On the serpent's opening words to Eve ('Yea, hath God said, Ye shall not eat of every tree of the garden?'), William Gouge comments, 'Thus came hee to Eve, first onely hee made a question whether God had forbidden them any of the trees: and then by degrees hee came directly to contradict the expresse word of God,' proof that 'hee well knoweth how to order his temptations.'[7] Milton draws out this gradual procession even further. Satan begins with flattery in his 'Proem' (IX. 532–48). He next tells Eve that he gained the power of speech from 'A goodly tree' (IX. 576), but not, of course, from *which* tree, a fallacious omission that allows him to praise the sight, smell, taste, and quickening power of the fruit without saying too much too soon. Only now, having put the question based on Genesis 3.1, does Satan pull out all the rhetorical stops and enjoin Eve to eat in a flurry of increasingly outrageous lies and fallacies (IX. 679–732).

The stylistic point to notice about these lines is their amplification of the biblical text, Genesis 3.1. Milton has followed the verse almost exactly – 'Yea, hath God said, Ye shall not eat of every tree of the garden?' – but appended this thought: 'Yet Lords declar'd of all in Earth or Air?' Here Satan's rhetoric employs comparison from the greater, where, if a greater thing is the case, a lesser thing must clearly be the case as well: if God has extended your rule over all things in earth or air, Satan implies, surely you therefore have licence to eat the fruit of all the trees? Milton has thus supplemented the scriptural *res* of Genesis 3.1 with a rhetorical topic of invention that we see again moments later: 'Shall that be shut to Man, which to the Beast / Is open?' (IX. 691–2). It is typical of the art he draws on to dilate the original myth (in which the serpent speaks only forty-six words) and typical as well of the material that Satan will incorporate into the astonishing oratorical performance which now commences.

Eve answers Satan by repeating, *for the second time in a dozen lines*, the provisions of the sole command:

> To whom thus *Eve* yet sinless. Of the Fruit
> Of each Tree in the Garden we may eat,
> But of the Fruit of this fair Tree amidst
> The Garden, God hath said, Ye shall not eat
> Thereof, nor shall ye touch it, lest ye die.   (IX. 659–63)

Preparing to undermine the immediacy and gravity of God's decree, the serpent 'New part puts on, and as to passion mov'd, / Fluctuates disturb'd' (IX. 667–8). The ability to play a part, a part that changes from one situation to the next, belongs to the man who lives and breathes rhetoric;[8] and it was a classical apriorism, accepted during the Renaissance, especially in homiletic theory, that one needed to feel passions while speaking in order to move an audience – or, as in Satan's case, pretend to feel them, 'with show of Zeal and Love / To Man, and indignation at his wrong' (IX. 665–6). An epic simile confirms the manner – and proleptically invokes the historical tradition – in which Satan is about to speak:

> As when of old some Orator renown'd
> In *Athens* or free *Rome*, where Eloquence
> Flourish'd, since mute, to some great cause addrest,
> Stood in himself collected, while each part,
> Motion, each act won audience ere the tongue,

> Sometimes in highth began, as no delay
> Of Preface brooking through his Zeal of Right.
> So standing, moving, or to highth upgrown
> The Tempter all impassion'd thus began.   (IX. 670–8) ·

Satan elects to begin 'in highth,' that is, in the grand style, with an apostrophe to the Tree (IX. 679–83), which sets the tone for the rest of his speech. Henry Peacham names the technique about to be employed: 'Protrope in Latine Adhortatio, is a forme of speech, by which the Orator exhorteth and perswadeth his hearers to do some thing.' Under 'The Caution,' a heading he added for each figure in the second edition of his *Garden of Eloquence*, Peacham describes the hazards that may attend its use: 'The greater power that this figure hath, the more mischiefe it may worke, if it be perverted and turned to abuse ... It is abused by moving and leading to unlawfull things, as by moving of sedition, tumults, or rebellion among the simple people, by leading ignorant persons into dangers and miserie, by seducing unstable mindes into false religion and vanities, and by many mo like effectes, which Sathan doth alwaies further to the uttermost of his power.'[9] Peacham's account of protrope's mischievous side, linked directly to Satan, displays a conventional Renaissance awareness of rhetoric's potential for abuse, and a similarly conventional equation of that abuse with threats to the political status quo – all of this is about to happen in the following episode. The only exception to Peacham's theoretical terms vis-à-vis the literary modelling of the temptation is that Milton's Eve, though ignorant in her innocence, is not a simple person, an idea I will return to later. From here, Milton fleshes out Satan's grandiloquent political oration from the skeleton of the serpent's remaining words in Genesis 3:

4 And the serpent said unto the woman, Ye shall not surely die:

5 For God doth know that in the day ye eat thereof, then your eyes shall be opened, and ye shall be as gods, knowing good and evil.

These verses remain the core of Eve's temptation in *Paradise Lost* (IX. 685, 705–9), exemplifying the art of satanic fallacy. In order to discover the mechanisms of that art, thereby showing how satanic rhetoric abuses logic, we turn again to the commentary of Sir Thomas Browne.

Browne writes that of the six types of verbal fallacy 'such as conclude from mistakes of the word,' two are especially notable: 'that is the fallacie of æquivocation and amphibologie, which conclude from the ambiguity of some one word, or the ambiguous sintaxis of many put together': 'This fallacy [i.e., both verbal types] in the first delusion Satan put upon Eve, and his whole tentation might be the same continued; so when he said, *Yee shall not die*, that was in his equivocation, ye shall not incurre a present death, or a destruction immediatly ensuing your transgression. *Your eyes shall be opened*, that is, not to the enlargement of your knowledge, but discovery of your shame and proper confusion. *You shall know good and evil*, that is you shall have knowledge of good by its privation, but cognisance of evill by sense and visible experience.'[10] Browne explains clearly how Satan deceives with half-truths, with statements that are true in a figurative, equivocal sense, a level of meaning deceitfully withheld, but that, if accepted literally, as Eve accepts them, are false. 'That hath been thy craft,' Jesus tells Satan in *Paradise Regained*, 'By mixing somewhat true to vent more lies' (I. 432–3).[11] The equivocation and amphiboly in the serpent's words combine with another logical fallacy to hoodwink Eve, that of '*petitio principii*, which fallacie is commited, when a question is made a medium, or we assume a medium as granted, whereof we remaine as unsatisfied as of the question. Briefly where that is assumed as a principle, to prove another thing, which is not conceaded as true it selfe. By this fallacie was Eve deceived, when shee took for granted, the false assertion of the devill; *Yee shall not surely die, for God doth know that in the day ye shall eat thereof, your eyes shall be opened, and you shall be as gods;* which was but a bare affirmation of Satan without any proofe or probable inducement, contrary to the command of God and former beliefe of herselfe.'[12] Milton's Satan, like his biblical forerunner, does not prove that the fruit will make Eve god-like in knowledge; but he avails himself of this fallacy even further, as Eve receives no proof of his initial, false claims: that he had eaten the fruit in the first place (IX. 595–8) and that, even if he had, it has given him the power of speech (IX. 598–601).

A close reading of Satan's temptation of Eve in *Paradise Lost* uncovers a succession of other types of fallacy: converting the consequent, false cause (both *non causa pro causa* and *post hoc ergo propter hoc*), *argumentum ad hominem*, fallacy of accident, and more examples of equivocation.[13] The rhetoric that conceals their illogic uses the techniques that have proved effective for Satan throughout the poem, most notably, as in Eve's dream, rhetorical questions and questions within questions – thirteen in this speech, twenty-six in total while disguised as the serpent. Indicating where and how all of these various devices function, however, still leaves unexplained the qualities that make Satan's oration as seemingly reasonable and as powerfully captivating as Eve finds it to be. How does Satan work his way into Eve's psyche, past the authoritative utterance of the prohibition, to lead her along a course that only moments before had appeared unthinkable? The answer may be traced to Satan's manipulation of probability, which Plato had called a likeness to the truth that the public finds acceptable. The terms of Plato's definition are especially apposite to the present discussion, since 'a likeness to the truth' (*homoiotēta tou alēthous*) exactly describes what Satan fabricates, and the emphasis on its acceptance by a particular audience rightly acknowledges the subjectivity of truth in a rhetorical situation, as the upcoming examination of Satan's sophistic method will show.

The more closely a fabricated likeness to truth resembles the real truth, the more successfully a dissembling speaker may pass it off as genuine. Satan emphasizes the probable likeness that pride bears to intellectual betterment, doing so on the principle that, as Richard Hooker observed, 'there is no particular evil which hath not some appearance of goodness whereby to insinuate itself. For evil as evil cannot be desired: if that be desired which is evil, the cause is the goodness which is or seemeth to be joined to it.'[14] Adam thus advises caution, 'Lest by some fair appearing good surpris'd / [Reason] dictate false' (IX. 354–5). Satan renders the proposed transgression attractive by assuring Eve that it will yield a good result:

> your Eyes that seem so clear,
> Yet are but dim, shall perfetly be then
> Op'n'd and clear'd, and ye shall be as Gods,
> Knowing both Good and Evil as they know.   (IX. 706–9)

Satan's false promise affects the appearance of goodness so convincingly because it resembles ideas that do, in fact, point to a genuine goodness and an elevation of man's spirit: 'that by proceeding in the knowledge of truth, and by growing in the exercise of virtue, man amongst the creatures of this inferior world aspireth to the greatest conformity with God ... With Plato what one thing more usual, than to excite men unto love of wisdom, by shewing how much wise men are thereby exalted above men; how knowledge doth raise them up into heaven; how it maketh them, though not gods, yet as gods, high, admirable, and divine? ... we are to search by what steps and degrees [the soul of man] riseth unto perfection of knowledge.'[15] Provided that we recognize the sinister figurative spin that equivocation may put on words such as 'knowledge,' 'truth,' and 'virtue,' this is precisely how the serpent encourages Eve to view eating the fruit: as a catalyst to the knowledge and higher perfection of godhead. These Neoplatonic strains of the ascendant soul, lifted higher by knowledge, reverberate in Satan's proposal, sharpening the likeness that it bears to real goodness. On Hooker's terms, such striving truly is good, pursuing an end that is 'high, admirable, and divine'; in the moral universe of *Paradise Lost*, however, it is blasphemy, recommended with typically unsound logic. Aristotle notes that 'in eristics [i.e., sophistic argument] not adding the circumstances and reference and manner makes for deception,'[16] and we see this tactic in play here. Satan has employed the fallacy of accident, applying a general rule – that one may worthily aspire to conformity with God by acquiring knowledge – to a particular case whose special or accidental circumstances render the rule inapplicable. And that special circumstance is none other than what 'our credulous Mother' herself had repeated only moments before: 'Ye shall not eat / Thereof, nor shall ye touch it, lest ye die.'

Paradise Lost maintains a conception of the dignity of pre-lapsarian man, not a humanistic one connected to seeking or acquiring knowledge of any kind:

> Heav'n is for thee too high
> To know what passes there; be lowly wise:
> Think only what concerns thee and thy being.   (VIII. 172–4)

The human soul may work its way heavenward on the Chain of Being, becoming 'as gods' in the righteous sense, but only by heeding the prohibition against eating the Fruit (V. 497–503; VII. 157–61), an act of the will that continually reaffirms devotion to the Creator and acknowledges His supremacy above all created things. For Eve to forget her station in this hierarchy, and to seek a shortcut to godhead in violation of the divine decree, is to commit the sin of pride, which was Lucifer's transgression in heaven and ever after: 'I will ascend above the heights of the clouds; I will be like the most High' (Isaiah 14.14). The Devil's planting such an aspiration in Eve requires that he unite rhetoric with a certain kind of philosophy, namely, sophism,[17] whose parameters are ideally suited to the task of reversing Eve's perception about what to expect from the Tree of Knowledge. Knowledge, in fact, is the issue that sophism addresses at a theoretical level. It posits a subjectivism that, when combined with satanic rhetoric, crosses into the practical sphere to become a mode of persuasion, one that questions the foundations of knowledge in order to undercut the authority of God's *ipse dixit* and to alter Eve's concept of her own standing in relation to God.

The Fall is a failure of reason, and sophism in its worst form creates and depends on such a failure in order to make its arguments appear convincing. Obedience is properly an act of faith, not of reason. Eve ought to have stood sufficient through faith alone, never permitting the sole command to have become an object of rational speculation in the first place, as Stanley Fish writes. He continues by saying that the reader is seduced to a similarly inappropriate application of 'carnal reason' if he tries to find a cause for the Fall, which, as a free act, has no cause. 'The Fall is no more an object of understanding than the prohibition it violates' and is 'not subject to examination.' Our first parents fell because they disobeyed, a non-explanation that 'has the advantage of preserving the autonomy of the Fall as an expression of free will, unlike other "explanations" which transfer the onus from Adam and Eve to an abstraction. The reader who finds a cause for the Fall denies it by denying its freedom, and succumbs to still another form of Milton's "good temptation"' in which 'the poet dangles before us the bait of justifying God's ways and the *ignis fatuus* of cause, designedly perplexing our reason with riddles it cannot possibly solve.'[18] Fish goes too far here, especially since Milton declares outright one cause of the Fall in a line that Fish talks around for several pages but that his thesis obliges him to pass over: 'th' infernal serpent; hee it was' (I. 34). 'This first Book,' Milton confirms, 'touches the prime cause of [man's] fall, the Serpent, or rather Satan in the Serpent' (*YP*, 8: 15). Far from making an *ignis fatuus* of cause or posing riddles, Milton hides nothing from us on this point: Satan caused the Fall. I agree with Fish that 'man disobeys by exercising, without constraint, the free will God gave him,' but I acknowledge here the cause Milton clearly indicates and think that rhetoric, which has many aspects other than the 'carnal eloquence' alone that Fish describes, helps us towards an understanding of how the Fall occurred.

'The historian,' writes E.H. Carr, 'believes that human actions have causes which are in principle ascertainable ... It is the special function of the historian to investigate these causes' and to reject 'the untenable hypothesis that voluntary actions have no cause'[19] – the hypothesis that

Fish maintains in the case of the Fall. If we treat the Fall as a historical event, as Milton and his original readers did, then we are led to search for its causes, since it was a voluntary action. Human free will, which Fish claims to be no cause, is the principal cause of original sin according to a theological tradition that Milton followed, as he also did in establishing that the procatarctic or external cause, that moving the principal cause from without, was Satan – more specifically in Eve's case, the speech of Satan.[20] An external cause acts on a principal cause to create an effect: 'Man falls deceiv'd / By th' other first' (III. 130–1). On Milton's warrant, therefore, critical attention proceeds to discovering how Satan caused human free will to commit the original sin, that is, how he caused Eve's reason to fail. The course of this inquiry starts naturally with rhetoric, from which the serpent weaves his deception and by which Eve's reason is suborned – 'Art and fallacy were used on her,' as Thomas Browne notes. The Fall is an object of understanding, with an assigned set of causes; that we would plumb its mystery through rhetorical examination is not a denial that it was an entirely free act. Because it is a rhetorical event does not mean that rhetoric transfers from Eve any of the responsibility for it. This is clear from what we know of both rhetoric and free will and from what Milton tells us. 'For Man will heark'n to his glozing lies,' satanic rhetoric will prevail in the short run, yet 'whose fault? / Whose but his own?' (III. 93, 96–7). Satan can externally cause man's first disobedience while leaving accountability for it squarely with man, for although eloquence may allure and entice, *it does not constrain*. Certainly, Milton knew the tradition attributing supreme power to eloquence, including the myth of Hercules Gallicus, who led men irresistibly by a golden chain from his tongue to their ears. But he also knew that persuasion was hardly so automatic a process as some theorists occasionally overstated it to be, for he believed that 'th' upright heart and pure' was sufficiently equipped to resist crafty eloquence, and he dramatized such patient and heroic resistance in Abdiel, as well as in Jesus, Samson, and (less heroically) the Lady of *Comus*. Rhetoric can lead Eve to the Tree of Knowledge and bid her to eat, but it cannot force her. The choice to obey or disobey rests solely with free agents, 'Authors to themselves in all / Both what they judge and what they choose' (III. 122–3). The transgression is thus a freely willed act, but it did not occur spontaneously. Some sequence of events shaped its unfolding, some external stimulus prompted Eve to commit it, something, in short, must have caused it: 'th' infernal serpent; hee it was,' the Father of Lies immemorially endowed with a forked yet golden tongue. And so I will delve further into the anatomy of the speech whose speaker caused the Fall, specifically by tracing its sophistic contours, for in doing so I see an explanation for the loss of Paradise that in no way denies its origins in human free will.

Satan's appeal to Eve's pride is, at bottom, sophistic, though beyond the seventeenth-century conception of sophistry as 'a show of reason to deceive withal.'[21] His speech reflects elements of sophism as it originated in ancient Greece, especially in the teachings of Protagoras and Gorgias, for whom (in contrast to Plato) truth was a construction of individual belief.[22] As Protagoras famously stated, 'Man is the measure of all things,' meaning that a person's own judgment is the sole criterion by which something is or is not 'true.' Truth is relative to each individual and is based on opinion (*doxa*),[23] not on any standard of objective or universal knowledge (*episteme*), for no such standard exists. The idea invests rhetoric with unrivalled sovereignty in human affairs, as Gorgias recognized, for truth effectively becomes whatever a person can be persuaded to believe. Here, we are in the realm of probability, where disputed matters can be argued on both sides with equal validity; and since opinions are neither true nor false, but only convincing or unconvincing, the acceptance of one over another as the subjective truth depends entirely on how skilfully its proponent advances it. Although Satan flouts the ethical stipulation of the Greek sophists, that persuasion ought to be used for advising the best course of action, he weaves together both threads of sophistic doctrine, the philosophical and the rhetorical: the equation of truth with belief, and the power of persuasion to create that belief in a speaker's audience.

Christianity views truth very differently. Lactantius writes that 'the first step to wisdom is to understand what is false; the second, to know what is true.'[24] The Lactantian path to wisdom implies a first principle of religious thinking, that truth and falsehood exist dichotomously, as real and discrete contraries to be categorically distinguished from one another – a positive conception of truth directly opposed to that of sophism. The difficulty of winnowing this sort of truth from the chaff of errant opinion is that, as Donne recognized along with Milton, 'truth and falshood bee / Neare twins.'[25] Their apparent similarity is produced (Milton's dramatic poetry shows this time and again) by the power of speech, by eloquence in the service of lies and deceit. It is this eloquence, in the Devil's incitement to godhead, that exacerbates the confusion of truth and falsehood in Eve's mind and portrays the evil of transgression as desirable by lending it the appearance of goodness. Fallacies inflict considerable damage in this respect, but their power to do so depends on putting Eve in a psychologically vulnerable state that will make her receptive to their operation. Enter the sophist, dressed for the occasion, approaching on

> Circular base of rising folds, that tow'r'd
> Fold above fold a surging Maze, his Head
> Crested aloft, and Carbuncle his Eyes.   (IX. 498–500)

Nothing is intrinsically wrong with opinion. One can hold an opinion that is true, and 'for practical purposes,' Socrates avers, 'right opinion is no less useful than knowledge, and the man who has it is no less useful than the one who knows.' But the man who has it is extremely rare, and the 'well-aimed conjecture' from which it derives, like virtue itself, 'cannot be taught and is not knowledge.'[26] Where philosophy encounters such obstacles, rhetoric finds the sphere of its (sometimes questionable) employment. Cicero's Antonius tells us that 'the activity of the orator has to do with opinion, not knowledge,' so that orators may 'speak of matters unknown to ourselves' and 'often take opposite sides.' The activity is amoral, since it may be expedient to 'maintain different opinions at different times on an identical issue,' even when 'one ... is dealing with a subject which is founded upon falsehood [and] ... sets its snares to entrap the fancies and often the delusions of mankind.'[27] In entrapping an audience to accept a falsified opinion as true, the primary weapon of the sophistic orator is the argument from probability, which Satan carries to its furthest limits in the Garden of Eden. Characters speaking in Eden employ probable argumentation for different purposes. God uses it to debate Adam on the subject of solitude (VIII. 357–451), Eve to justify separating from Adam on the fateful morning (IX. 205–384). Each is met, in standard rhetorical fashion, with Adam's probable arguments in the other direction: his request for fit companionship, his plea that Eve remain at his side. Satan departs from the usual terms of this exchange, for the target of his line of probable argumentation is not another probability, but rather an absolute certainty:

> of the Tree whose operation brings
> Knowledge of good and ill, which I have set
> The Pledge of thy Obedience and thy Faith,
> Amid the Garden by the Tree of Life,

Remember what I warn thee, shun to taste,
And shun the bitter consequence: for know,
The day thou eat'st thereof, my sole command
Transgrest, inevitably thou shalt die;
From that day mortal, and this happy State
Shalt lose, expell'd from hence in to a World
Of woe and sorrow.   (VIII. 323–33)

In its prescriptive finality, the interdiction embodies the authoritative certainty of religious rhetoric – not merely in the manner of Reformation polemic, of partisan opinion held up as the truth against some rival doctrine, but in the shape of the original Truth itself, the *sermo* of God issued both directly and through angelic mediation. It brooks no dispute; it transcends the terms of demonstrative proof; as the lapidary proclamation of God, it simply *is*.

This, at least, is how Milton would have it known (not believed), and how Eve might have known it. But the problem with authoritative testimony of any kind, even God's, was that it could not stand beyond the range of probabilistic assault because such testimony was, in fact, the very definition of probability during the Renaissance, when 'for many, probability itself simply meant backing by authority ... the Renaissance paradigm for explaining probability comes from rhetoric, and more directly from the "place" of "external" or "inartificial" proofs, that is, proofs which come from the testimony of more or less authoritative (and hence *probable*) witnesses.'[28] God is the most authoritative witness, whose testimony will therefore have the highest degree of probability and greatest weight as proof, as the Elizabethan logician Ralph Lever observes:

The witnesses upon whose authoritie proofes are grounded, are either heavenly, earthly, or infernall.

Gods word, his wonders, his miracles, and his message, sent to men by angels, and Prophetes, are alledged as heavenly witnesses:

Law, custom, othe, bargain, writings, sayings, and so forth, are accompted as humaine witnesses, and such as are taken of the credite of man:

Conjuring, witchcraft, appearing of ghosts, oracles and answeres of divels, are infernall and ungodlye witnesses, used onelye of the wicked, and suffered of God for a punishement to deceyve them, that will not beleeve the true meanes that god hath appointed.[29]

Milton similarly writes of testimony as inartificial proof, the force of which 'is the authority of the person giving testimony, on which the reliability of the testimony totally depends' (*YP*, 8: 318). '*Testimony is either divine or human*,' the divine comprising Lever's first and third categories:

> *Divine testimony is that which has God as its author.*
>
>   *Among divine testimonies are numbered not only the oracles of the gods, but also the responses of the seers and soothsayers.*
>
>   Whether these are true or fictitious, or from a true divine command or a false one, the logician does not consider, but only what force of arguing any given one has. And so also in civil and human affairs divine testimony has just as much probative force [*vim probationis*] as its author is a true or false god. (*YP*, 8: 319)

Like Lever, Milton attributes all divine testimony, true and false, to God (who suffers the juggleries of oracles and devils as part of the providential plan). Since divine testimony has just as much probative force – that is, probability – as its author is a true or false god, the God portrayed in *Paradise Lost* has supreme authority and the sole command has as much probability as any testimony could reasonably have. To put it another way, God is a reliable witness whose testimony ought to be believed. And this is only as far as Milton the logician is concerned; Milton the epic poet interpreted the divine commission as revelation unbounded by the rules of dialectical proof. Faith trumped logic, and Milton would have thought it wrong, if not blasphemous, to consider God as a witness whose testimony is merely probable. Yet if we accept the Renaissance concept of probability as testimony backed by authority and apply the logician's hierarchy of witnesses to Eve's temptation, this is the standing of God's word in Paradise. Eve, of course, does not know that the serpent's body houses, in Lever's words, an 'infernall and ungodlye' witness. Even so, the choice before her on the grounds of probability proceeding from authority is as follows: on the one side, the words of God, on the testimony of an angel and a man in direct communication with God; on the other side, a talking snake. Given that prima facie probability falls so lopsidedly towards God, Satan concentrates on finding a way to reverse this disadvantage.

The neutralization of divine authoritative testimony in Eve's mind relies on establishing central sophistic tenets. Relativism informs the invitation to pride, which leads Eve to understand that she is the measure of all things, that she herself can judge what is true and false, right and wrong, without referring to external authority. The same presumption surfaced earlier in Book IX, when she insisted, contrary to divine law because contrary to her husband's counsel, on separating from Adam for the morning's work. At this point Milton's Paradise evokes another Christian landscape, Dante's Purgatory, where pride is shown to be a sin of misdirected love. Eve exemplifies this. In chapter 4 we examined religious love, which holds its truth above scrutiny or contradiction, transfigures its own probabilities into certainty, and brands contradictory opinion as falsehood. Love properly directed at God through obedience would have guided Eve reliably, would have shown truth and falsehood in clear contrast to one another and made the right choice correspondingly clear. But the serpent misdirects Eve from loving the truth, embodied in the sole command, to loving herself; misdirects her from the straight path of religious truth and its dogmatically certain standard of conduct to the winding circuit of rhetorical truth and its relativistic injunction to disregard the testimony of heavenly authority. 'Shalt thou give Law to God?' (V. 822), Abdiel asked Satan, castigating the proposed disruption of hierarchical order. Satan, proposing just such a disruption in the hierarchy of witnesses, in effect inverts this question for Eve: 'Shalt God give law to thee?' Once satanic pride makes Eve a law unto herself, the queen of a sophistically ordered universe, the infernal and ungodly witness can assert his testimony over that of the heavenly witnesses – 'Look on me' (IX. 687) – as being more authoritative, and hence more probable, in the mind of its judge.

Satan knows that the more deeply self-centred Eve grows, the more readily she will forsake received wisdom for the promise of securing her better advantage. She will be readier still to abandon that wisdom if he can convince her that the order of knowledge on which it stands may be challenged, that the threat of death is not an incontrovertible truth, but only a probable opinion, liable to scrutiny and contradiction like any other. His strategy for doing so is to present the idea of eating the fruit as a *dissos logos*, a double argument of sophistic debate wherein the respective positions are God's command (obey or die) and the serpent's injunction (disobey and thrive). Satan's argument draws strength from a deeper source than words alone, from a philosophical foundation that permits the construction of dazzling rhetorical spires. The outright lie itself – 'do not believe / Those rigid threats of Death; ye shall not Die' – is not so powerful a force in Satan's favour, even with its myriad fallacies, as the general fact that God's word is being treated as *doxa* (opinion), not *episteme* (knowledge). By subjecting it to sophistic debate, in an attitude of casual ease rather than ceremonial awe, Satan desecrates the sole command and reduces it to the status of an opinion; as a result, God's law and the recommendation to break it now appear to stand on the same epistemological footing. Once Eve swallows that sophistic hook, she views tasting the fruit not in the absolute context of religion, as a mortal sin, but in the relative terms of sophism, as a choice between probable arguments – God's on the one side, the serpent's on the other – that compete for her belief. Who speaks the truth? For Eve the question can now mean only 'whose opinion should I believe?' Uncertainty of this order is a sophistically induced state of mind, and it puts her precisely where the serpent wants her. The perils of walking in the dark of opinion were proverbial among the sophists: 'on most subjects most people take opinion as counselor of the soul. But opinion, being slippery and insecure, casts those relying on it into slippery and insecure fortune,' vulnerable to being 'carried off by speech just as if constrained by force.'[30] Such is the misfortune of Eve, 'in wandr'ing mazes lost' (II. 561), having arrogated to herself the measure of all things, the serpent's rhetorical storm having extinguished the torch of religious truth, knowledge and opinion having been sophistically levelled – all of this exposes her to Satan's facility at making the worse argument appear the stronger. The Devil thrives in the realm of probability and subjectivism that his sophistry has created, circumstances under which the art of persuasion seems as formidable as the ancient sophists gave it credit for being: 'He ended, and his words replete with guile / Into her heart too easy entrance won' (IX. 733–4).

But we must remember one fact: Eve is not constrained after all, whatever influence sophistic speech may wield. She need only revert to faith – God told them not to eat – but that she does not, that she hearkens to the serpent's glozing lies, is entirely her own choice and testimony to the power of eloquence that could move her to make that choice. One thing might have prevented her from making it. Near the close of the poem, Michael approves Adam's account of reason and obedience and says, 'only add / Deeds to thy knowledge answerable, add Faith, / Add Virtue, Patience, Temperance, add Love' (XII. 581–3). He explicitly mentions two of the four cardinal virtues – temperance and patience, the latter of which is Christian fortitude – and leaves a third unstated as obvious, since justice has been Adam's lesson all along. The omitted virtue is prudence.

This might have been Eve's lesson: to faith add prudence, both in speech and deeds. Ethical decisions are complicated in the same way as rhetorical ones, and they make similar demands. Milton certainly makes this connection. We see, for example, that he invokes the *kairos* – relating it to speech as well as action – when he defines prudence: 'Prudence is that virtue by which we foresee what ought to be done with respect to the circumstances of time and place.'[31] Rhetorical and ethical prudence go hand in hand, but more than that, rhetorical prudence enables and fortifies its ethical counterpart. If one knows rhetoric and dialectic, an alarm sounds in the presence of their misuse: 'How great is the need for prudence' in rhetorical debate, Christoph Hegendorf reminds us, 'lest from too little caution we become trapped by the snares of our opponents!'[32] Understanding the use of syllogism and enthymeme offers a defence against fallacy and deceit, knowledge that Aristotle had included alongside arguing *in utramque partem*: 'one should be able to argue persuasively on either side of a question, just as in the use of syllogism ... in order that it may not escape our notice what the real state of the case is and that we ourselves may be able to refute if another person uses speech unjustly.'[33] Rhetoric and logic show us the real state of the case and give us the power to refute, thus making the morally right decision easier to reach. Great is the need for prudence. Like the other cardinal virtues, and like rhetoric itself, prudence is transvalued to fit the requirements of leading the good Christian life. Fish writes of 'slip[ping] into the error of believing that [Eve] might not have fallen, had she been a better logician.' I contend precisely this, adding better rhetorician as well, and hold it no 'overvaluing of the ... rational faculty,'[34] for logic and rhetoric are sacred arts when practised in their highest form: 'How often does Christ himself argue by syllogisms, and the prophets by enthymemes!'[35] Logic and rhetoric are the very opposite of, and offer protection against, a 'carnal eloquence' that would undermine faith; nor are they appurtenances of the fallen intellect, since they were perfectly manifested before the Fall, in Adam.

Adam, in conversing with God (VIII. 357–451), demonstrates prudence in his magnificent command of rhetoric and dialectic, gifts from the Creator, who gave man reason and speech in fashioning him after the divine image – gifts inequitably apportioned:

> for in thir looks Divine
> The image of thir glorious Maker shone,
> Truth, Wisdom, Sanctitude severe and pure ...
> ... though both

> Not equal, as thir sex not equal seem'd;
> For contemplation hee and valor form'd,
> For softness shee and sweet attractive Grace,
> Hee for God only, shee for God in him.   (IV. 291–3, 295–9)

Eve, for reasons beyond her control, is barred from some forms of rhetorical exercise. Quintilian, like Aristotle, advocates arguing on either side of a question because 'the nature of virtue is revealed by vice, its opposite, justice becomes yet more manifest from the contemplation of injustice, and there are many other things that are proved by their contraries.'[36] Eve cannot argue on these grounds, for her innocence precludes a knowledge of vice by which she may know virtue comparatively. Although Eve is innocent, we are mistaken if we think of her as simple or naïve, as C.S. Lewis notes.[37] Wise in her own right and able to share Adam's speculative interests, she possesses his intellectual nature to a high degree – but not his rhetorical prudence. This deficiency rests with Milton's God, who short-changed Eve in making 'both / Not equal,' leaving her prey to the clever sophist; that she does not face temptation as a better logician and rhetorician therefore is not her fault. If both Adam and Eve are sufficient to have stood, one of them, at least on these terms, was created more sufficient than the other. True, Eve needs only faith to withstand the serpent, and that lapse of faith is her fault; yet some grasp of rhetoric and dialectic, a natural prudence of the kind bestowed on her husband and fatally denied her, could only support faith in trying to beat back the tidal forces of corrupt eloquence. Giving the Devil his due, one is even left guessing about Adam, whether he, with his Achilles heel of uxorious devotion, would ultimately have fared any better than Eve had he stepped off the practice range with the jovial Father and met the wily serpent, a foe with an eye for finding weak spots and teeth for inflicting wounds that are long in healing.

As the serpent's words enter Eve's heart and begin to affect her will, Milton shifts attention from the oratorical rhetoric of the speaker to the internal rhetoric of the audience: '*kairos* immerses speakers in a moral-intellectual crisis when the choice to speak or act (and what and how one speaks or acts) determines an individual's "fate."'[38] How Eve speaks under crisis is telling, her style reflecting the transformation of her spirit that has already taken place. The rhetorical figures she employs fit a recognizable pattern, borrowed from the speech of the tempter, indicating that she has absorbed the substance of his lies along with their style – clearly, her actions to her words will soon accord. Satan's prosopopoeiae of the 'Fruit Divine' (V. 67) in her dream and of the 'Sacred, Wise, and Wisdom-giving Plant' (IX. 679) moments beforehand are echoed in the first line of her response to the temptation: 'Great are thy Virtues, doubtless, best of Fruits' (IX. 745), said later to be 'Of virtue to make wise' (IX. 778). Satan earlier referred equivocally to Eve's 'dauntless virtue' (IX. 694); her own usage of the word is now 'of true virtue void' (XI. 790), retaining only its signification of power and strength. In the most notable change, however, rhetorical questions enter Eve's speech with satanic frequency and purpose – 'In plain then, what forbids [God] but to know, / Forbids us good, forbids us to be wise?' (IX. 758–9) – her seventh question reasoning that

> Here grows the Cure of all, this Fruit Divine,
> Fair to the Eye, inviting to the Taste,
> Of virtue to make wise: what hinders then
> To reach, and feed at once both Body and Mind?   (IX. 776–9)

The answer already set in her own mind, 'she pluck'd, she eat' (IX. 781), a moment ushered in on the spectacular success of rhetoric as speech, and the failure of rhetoric as reason.

Eve, having fallen, confirms her new predilection for satanic rhetoric with another prosopopoeia and equivocation – 'O Sovran, virtuous, precious of all Trees / In Paradise, of operation blest / To Sapience' (IX. 795–7) – in preparing to take on the role of tempter. She equivocates again on virtue and also on 'Sapience,' wisdom, previously accorded her and Adam as an attribute of divinity (IV. 291–3) but now debased into the 'sinister or crooked wisdom' of cunning,[39] ready to complement her late-found style in the temptation of her husband. In this case, however, Eve's rhetoric derives a formidable supplementary power from sources beyond, though including, words. Adam tells Raphael that, for all the delights of Paradise, he is

> in all enjoyments else
> Superior and unmov'd, here only weak
> Against the charm of Beauty's powerful glance.   (VIII. 531–3)

It is a charm that is naturally persuasive. Shakespeare's Ferdinand recognizes that physical beauty and verbal eloquence form an irresistible combination:

> Full many a lady
> I have ey'd with best regard, and many a time
> Th' harmony of their tongues hath into bondage
> Brought my too diligent ear.[40]

Yet nothing, Adam claims, including even 'her out-side form'd so fair,'

> So much delights me, as those graceful acts,
> Those thousand decencies that daily flow
> From all her words and actions.   (VIII. 596, 600–2)

Adam is noticing a deeper quality in Eve, and a susceptibility in himself, that Claudio articulates when he observes that Isabella has a special gift,

> For in her youth
> There is a prone and speechless dialect
> Such as move men; beside, she hath prosperous art
> When she will play with reason and discourse,
> And well she can persuade.[41]

Beauty – both superficial (of appearance) and substantial (of character and spirit) – has an eloquence all its own. Eve's words accrue greater force from her actions and aspect; this hybrid rhetoric captivates Adam so completely that, as he had foretold (VIII. 551–4), he cannot assert his better nature against it. More so than her importunate sophistries, copied from Satan, Eve's 'prone and speechless dialect' pierces Adam's heart: 'with thee,' he tells himself, 'Certain my resolution is to die' (IX. 906–7). His fall stems from the passions' overthrow of reason, caused not, as in Eve's case, by fallacy and deceit, but rather 'Against his better knowledge, not deceiv'd, / But fondly overcome with Female charm' (IX. 998–9).

While Eve's charm impels Adam to disobedience, a different display, 'prone' in another sense, reconciles the pair after he subsequently scorns her. 'Out of my sight, thou Serpent' (X. 867), begins Adam's epideixis of blame, which reviles Eve and laments the creation of woman-kind:

> but *Eve*
> Not so repulst, with Tears that ceas'd not flowing,
> And tresses all disorder'd, at his feet
> Fell humble, and imbracing them, besought
> His peace, and thus proceeded in her plaint

by enacting Hecuba's advice to her doomed daughter, Polyxena, in supplication to Agamemnon: 'Stir him to pity. Fall and clasp his knees.'[42]

> Forsake me not thus, *Adam*, witness Heav'n
> What love sincere, and reverence in my heart
> I bear thee, and unweeting have offended,
> Unhappily deceiv'd; thy suppliant
> I beg, and clasp thy knees.   (X. 909–18)

'The human body is the best picture of the human soul,' including the body's rhetoric of gesture.[43] Eve's gesture expresses, with an impact beyond words, the soul's contrition; yet her words convey something more than remorse for what she has done, however keenly felt:

> On me exercise not
> Thy hatred for this misery befall'n,
> On me already lost, mee than thyself
> More miserable; both have sinn'd, but thou
> Against God only, I against God and thee,
> And to the place of judgment will return,
> There with my cries importune Heaven, that all
> The sentence from thy head remov'd may light
> On me, sole cause to thee of all this woe,
> Mee mee only just object of his ire.   (X. 927–36)

In chapter 6, we noticed that the Son repeated the same pronoun, 'me,' on three separate occasions, twice in order to transfer the burden of divine justice from mankind to himself – just as Eve now proposes to incur Adam's punishment in addition to her own, showing him how much she needs his mercy (the initial three occurrences of 'me') by her self-sacrificial willingness to bear God's justice (the final three). Partly through the stylistic ligature of this repeated word, Milton binds Eve's love and charity to that of the Son. The entire presentation of her eirenic overture, the gesture of repentance and the words of love

> 'in *Adam* wrought
> Commiseration; soon his heart relented
> Towards her ... his anger all he lost.   (X. 939–41, 945)

10 Descending from Heaven: Anthropopathia and the Rhetoric of Paradise

And He walks with me, and He talks with me.

C. Austin Miles, 'In the Garden'

Literature loves villains, and its most captivating ones are drawn from the original. Fiction holds up for our inspection the likes of Iago, Faustus, and Uriah Heep, who get their retributive comeuppance, as well as more recent representations of the satanic, who do not: *Blood Meridian* closes unforgettably on the scene of Judge Holden presiding over the timeless dance of human depravity. But Satan stands outside the company of his literary progeny in one important respect: he was not, in the period under discussion, a fictional character. Most devout Europeans in the Renaissance believed that the Devil was real, and that he intervened in human affairs in every way from general mischief to the possession of souls. Hamlet muses that

> The spirit that I have seen
> May be the devil, and the devil hath power
> T'assume a pleasing shape; yea, and perhaps
> Out of my weakness and my melancholy,
> As he is very potent with such spirits,
> Abuses me to damn me.[1]

The belief in Satan's power to materialize and to harm people in the present, his traditional role as the apostate and the destroyer of humanity's eternal bliss, his reputation for verbal showmanship, and the monstrous forms he assumed in pictorial art are some of the characteristics that made him an object of poetic fascination in a way that God, no less real than Satan but ineffably remote, was not and never could be. Representing divine speech in poetry would have been a less obviously inviting artistic proposition than embellishing the virtuoso eloquence of the tempter, yet Milton imparts to divine characters a dramatic immediacy and rhetorical verve comparable to Satan's, in part by having them visit the terrestrial realm that Satan was commonly thought to inhabit. Indeed, in terms of the present study, the sections of *Paradise Lost* 'where God or Angel Guest / With Man' (IX. 1–2) are the most intriguing of the whole poem for the problems they impose on rhetoric, as Raphael, God, and the Son visit Paradise: the first to instruct and warn Adam, the second to test his self-knowledge, the third to judge and sentence him.

The speeches and attitudes of these characters merge to compose a varied portrait of anthropopathia, the trope that puts the speech of divine beings in a separate artistic category and acknowledges the problematic discrepancy of such beings communicating with men. The final chapter of this book will revolve around the various manifestations of this exotic trope in *Paradise Lost*. I have assigned one of its chief instances in the poem, Michael's revelatory mission in Books XI and XII, to the rhetoric of heaven; the other characters from heaven, however, speak the rhetoric of Paradise. Michael stands apart because the future contingency corollary to free will, which animates rhetorical situations in Paradise, diminishes in the aftermath of the Fall when his discourse takes place. Michael arrives to teach, but with an imperative subtext: Adam and Eve must leave the garden, the time for rhetorical appeals to their reason and judgment having passed. The source of those earlier appeals, Raphael's rhetoric, belongs to Paradise because it influences, or attempts to influence, the operation of free will; God's rhetoric belongs here because He establishes in Eden a lively rhetorical persona, shaded with distinctive humanist overtones. Although the Son, like Michael, descends to earth after the Fall, at a similar ebb in future contingency, his terrestrial rhetoric so closely approximates a key feature of the Father's that it must be included here.

To begin, however, let us turn our attention to some of the circumstances that support rhetoric – an eloquent speaker, a pressing subject, an audience in need of counsel, an imminent choice between opposing arguments – and to a scene that provides a context for all of them, the visit of 'the sociable Spirit' (V. 221), Raphael, whose journey serves an important purpose.

According to divine justice, Adam must be reminded of the conditions of 'his happy state' and informed of Satan's identity and destructive intentions, 'Lest wilfully transgressing he pretend / Surprisal, unadmonisht, unforwarn'd' (V. 234, 244–5). Raphael draws the assignment. Like Michael, he brings knowledge from heaven to earth, but his task is more difficult than the prophetic angel's. Michael shows to Adam, a man, the future of the earth and of other men, a simpler exercise – especially with the aid of prophetic visions – than Raphael's obligation of relating to a man the past of heaven and the angels and hinting at the nature of the cosmos. Michael is a speaker. He needs primarily, and for the most part simply, to be clear. Raphael is a translator. He must convert, exclusively through 'procéss of speech' (VII. 178), things best apprehended by the intuitive reason of the angels into images that man's discursive reason can grasp; for, as Milton writes, 'God is always described or outlined not as he really is, but in such a way as will make him conceivable to us' (*YP*, 6: 133). God thus reveals himself, in the Bible and in *Paradise Lost*, through stylistic devices, especially tropes, a rhetoric of accommodation that bestows on a human audience a mediated knowledge of sacred matters. The use of this rhetoric now devolves to Raphael. Adam describes Raphael's accommodative procedure, grateful that the angel has 'voutsaf't / This friendly condescension to relate / Things else by me unsearchable' (VIII. 8–10), and telling him later, 'Gentle to me and affable hath been thy condescension' (VIII. 648–9). Adam's word invokes a familiar idea: 'condescension' was taken to be synonymous with anthropopathia.[2] Could Milton's Latinate term be referring to the rhetorical trope denoted by its Greek cousin? He is, at any rate, expressing in *Paradise Lost* the same idea as theorists of sacred rhetoric on the subject of anthropopathia: that divine beings descend, or 'condescend,' into human company, and that the attendant linguistic descent into the *verba* of humanity, in order to suit the relatively limited capacities of the speaker's audience, creates the problem of finding resources and formulas sufficient for making known the otherwise unfathomable *res* of heaven.

As a rhetorical problem, it naturally calls for a rhetorical solution. Raphael raises this problem, as well as a solution to it, when, having instructed Adam about free will and reminded him of the need for obedience (V. 519–43), he is asked to relate what happened when obedience was forgotten in heaven:

High matter thou injoin'st me, O prime of men,
Sad task and hard, for how shall I relate
To human sense th' invisible exploits
Of warring Spirits; how without remorse
The ruin of so many glorious once
And perfet while they stood; how last unfold
The secrets of another World, perhaps
Not lawful to reveal? yet for thy good
This is dispens't, and what surmounts the reach
Of human sense, I shall delineate so,
By lik'ning spiritual to corporal forms,
As may express them best.   (V. 563–74)

The solution to presenting invisible exploits to human sense is 'lik'ning spiritual to corporal forms,' a process described in a classical treatise that Milton probably read while at St Paul's,[3] the *Rhetorica ad Herennium*: 'Metonymy is the figure which draws from an object closely akin or associated an expression suggesting the object meant, but not called by its own name. This is accomplished by substituting the name of a greater thing for that of the lesser,'[4] or the name of a lesser thing for that of the greater – the corporeal for the spiritual, to meet Raphael's needs. Hyperius mentions in *The Practis of Preaching* that explaining the relation 'Of the Signe to the thinge signyfyed: Of a thinge spyrytuall to a thinge Corporall' is useful to 'hee that teacheth the people.'[5] Kenneth Burke, expanding the classical definition of metonymy, views the procedure in precisely the same sense – even the same terms – that Raphael uses in seeking a solution to his rhetorical problem: 'For *metonymy* we could substitute *reduction*, the *reduction* of some higher and more complex realm of being to the terms of a lower or less complex realm of being ... The basic "strategy" of metonymy is this: to convey some incorporeal or intangible state in terms of the corporeal or tangible ... [by a] "carrying over" from the spiritual back into the material ... as the poet translates the spiritual into an idiom of material equivalents.'[6] It is just such a materializing idiom that Raphael seeks, and he finds it, as these ancient and modern definitions indicate, in metonymy. Michael's rhetoric of prophecy is based on distribution, a figure of amplification; Raphael uses a rhetoric of accommodation, intended to diminish rather than amplify and informed by the reductive function of metonymy. As the trope that subtends the discourses of heaven and earth, that translates the spiritual, incorporeal, more complex vocabulary of the angels into the material, corporeal, less complex terms accessible to human understanding, metonymy accomplishes the work of anthropopathia in the middle books of *Paradise Lost*.

Metonymy of the sort that Raphael proposes will teach his audience, 'for it is frequently illuminating to compare great things with small.'[7] Metonymy establishes a discursive equivalent to the theological concept of providence 'by small / Accomplishing great things' (XII. 566–7). Great things are accomplished by an aggregate of small ones, which includes grand concepts being rendered comprehensible through representation by simpler ones. The most salient example of comparing great with small is the reduction of the war in heaven to a Homeric epic war. Although Raphael has already worked out his strategy for presenting it, he nevertheless finds the task daunting and adopts a rhetorical stance, common in Renaissance literature, that voices this misgiving. The professed impossibility of expressing oneself adequately to a situation takes its Greek name, adynaton; for example, Raphael's pause in his narrative, where Michael and Satan

> ended parle, and both address'd for fight
> Unspeakable; for who, though with the tongue
> Of Angels, can relate, or to what things
> Liken on Earth conspicuous, that may lift
> Human imagination to such highth
> Of Godlike Power.   (VI. 296–301)[8]

Raphael's adynaton emphasizes two things: the inherent obstacles of communication that anthropopathia recognizes as existing between a speaker from heaven and human hearers; and the potential of metonymy, as 'reduction,' to overcome these obstacles, to suggest the nature of greater objects, incomprehensible in themselves, by substituting the names or descriptions of lesser yet related ones: 'such as, to set forth / Great things,' the clash of the embattled angels,

> by small, if Nature's concord broke,
> Among the Constellations war were sprung,
> Two Planets rushing from aspect malign
> Of fiercest opposition in mid Sky,
> Should combat, and thir jarring Spheres confound.   (VI. 310–15)

The metonymical substitution of planets moves the single combat of Michael and Satan into the scope of Adam's comprehension. Raphael invokes astronomy because it is a human art, and its basis in visual observation suits it to the purpose of engaging the human imagination, but also because Adam has indicated an aptitude for it:

> And we have yet large day, for scarce the Sun
> Hath finisht half his journey, and scarce begins
> His other half in the great Zone of Heav'n.   (V. 558–60)

In order to use metonymy successfully, a speaker must know his audience, know which parallel subjects they will understand and will, moreover, appreciate, since heightened interest and enjoyment reinforce an oration and stamp it in the memory. In astronomy Raphael chooses exactly the right frame of metonymical reference to captivate Adam, who later inquires enthusiastically about the 'moving fires' (VII. 87) of the heavens and the disposal of the firmament (VIII. 15–38).

Raphael's rhetorical burden, that he must speak what is unspeakable, elicits the same posture of doubt at other times (VII. 112–14; VIII. 113– 14), partly from the knowledge that the revelatory capacity of his discourse is limited, that there are

> Things not reveal'd, which th' invisible King,
> Only Omniscient, hath supprest in Night,
> To none communicable in Earth or Heaven.   (VII. 122–4)

He is continually aware of the conceptual gulf between angels and men and of the need to bridge it with the rhetorician's psychological insight and stylistic resources; for his objective, too, is rhetorical, corresponding with the orator's most important social function, that of persuading men to live virtuously. His peroration to the war in heaven recapitulates what he has said and how he has said it, and underscores the rhetorical intention of his speech:

> Thus measuring things in Heav'n by things on Earth
> At thy request, and that thou mayst beware
> By what is past, to thee I have reveal'd
> What might have else to human Race been hid:
> The discord which befell, and War in Heav'n
> Among th' Angelic Powers, and the deep fall
> Of those too high aspiring, who rebell'd
> With Satan, hee who envies now thy state,
> Who now is plotting how he may seduce

Thee also from obedience ...
But list'n not to his Temptations, warn
Thy weaker; let it profit thee to have heard
By terrible Example the reward
Of disobedience; firm they might have stood,
Yet fell; remember, and fear to transgress.   (VI. 893–902, 908–12)

Raphael's accommodative technique – 'Thus measuring things in Heav'n by things on Earth' – functions as judicial or forensic oratory, which uses 'what is past' for leverage in defence or (as against Satan) accusation. This rhetoric, however, since it warns Adam to *'beware* / By what is past,' is ultimately aimed at influencing decisions to be made in the future and is, therefore, of the deliberative or political type – 'if there is narrative' in deliberative oratory, writes Aristotle, 'it is of events in the past, in order that by being reminded of those things the audience will take better counsel about what is to come.'[9] Raphael's exhortation to obedience derives its persuasive intensity from a staple of Renaissance poetry and rhetoric: the example.[10] Milton values poetry's utility for 'teaching ... sanctity and vertu through all the instances of example' (*YP*, 1: 816); for, as Spenser writes, 'so much more profitable and gratious is doctrine by ensample, then by rule.'[11] 'Example,' according to Rudolph Agricola, 'is a certain kind of comparison; for it is something greater, or equal, or less, which is taken up in order to be imitated or shunned.'[12] Each of Milton's angels furnishes Adam with an example of something greater: Michael's to be imitated, Raphael's to be shunned. Just as Michael later holds up the ideal example of the charity of Christ, so Raphael now presents the 'terrible Example' of 'the deep fall / Of those too high aspiring' – the tragedy caused by the sin of pride.

The tragic example of Satan alerts Adam to the consequences of disobedience. While it thoroughly instructs him, it also moves him:

He with his consorted *Eve*
The story heard attentive, and was fill'd
With admiration, and deep muse to hear
Of things so high and strange.   (VII. 50–3)

Raphael later seeks to arouse a similar emotional effect when, repeating God's words immediately prior to man's creation (VII. 519–23), he breaks in with an apostrophe:

This said, he form'd thee, *Adam*, thee O Man
Dust of the ground, and in thy nostrils breath'd
The breath of Life; in his own Image hee
Created thee, in the Image of God
Express, and thou becam'st a living Soul.   (VII. 524–8)

The angel's powers of speech are on full display: the arresting vocative, the antonomasia (Dust of the ground) and synecdoche (in thy nostrils), the empyreal repetitions of polyptoton (breath'd/breath) and conduplicatio (thee/thee, Image/Image), all of which form an auxesis to the last clause (and thou becam'st a living Soul). Preaching moves the affections to embrace virtue, but an important rider was attached to the use of the grand style, which could also be exploited to put those same affections in reckless command of the will. Raphael's closing words underscore the potential danger of such rhetorical appeals:

take heed lest Passion sway
Thy Judgment to do aught, which else free Will
Would not admit.   (VIII. 635–7)

Raphael moves and instructs Adam so that both reason and the passions support good judgment; he incorporates as well the third duty of the orator, to delight (*delectare*), which decorum excludes from Michael's rhetoric: 'sweeter thy discourse is to my ear,' says Adam, 'Than Fruits of Palm-tree pleasantest to thirst / And hunger both' (VIII. 211–13), a sentiment he expresses both early and late in the course of Raphael's visit (V. 544–8; VIII. 1–3). The aggregate of rhetorical skills and offices at Raphael's disposal justifies Adam's reference to the archangel's 'potent voice' (VII. 100): the interplay of teaching, delighting, and moving; the ingenuity of metonymical accommodation, which likens greater things to lesser ones that Adam can comprehend; a knowledge of his audience, which determines apt points of reductive comparison; the fabrication of a powerful didactic example from the tragedy of Lucifer's fall; and the application of judicial rhetoric to the political end of admonition and wise counsel. Furthermore, Raphael plies his art in earnest, believing in its potential to help mankind resist Satan. At the time of his journey to earth, he has no foreknowledge of the Fall.[13] Unaware that satanic guile will prevail in Eden, he speaks with genuine urgency and conviction, the authenticity of his rhetorical attitude undiluted by any pretence of ignorance that he would have to affect had he known beforehand that his mission would fail.

The basic circumstances of Raphael's visit to Paradise sustain rhetoric at every point of reference, particularly with respect to this curious modification of anthropopathia: that the divine being who has condescended to human company speaks without divine prescience and without knowing whether or not his arguments will help his audience to remain virtuous and obedient. If the case were otherwise – if, that is, Raphael foresaw the eventual failure of his political oration even while presenting it – the episode would be deprived of all rhetorical tension (besides making God's motive for sending him in the first place appear crassly self-vindicative). Omniscience in Paradise, as in heaven, unsettles the status of rhetoric. It is a singular achievement of Milton's poem, therefore, that when God arrives in Eden to speak to Adam, the imposing fact of divine foreknowledge, including anything that Adam will or could say, diminishes none of the rhetorical vitality of their encounter. Chapter 6 showed that, in heaven, God's foreknowledge detracts from rhetoric at several points by short-circuiting future contingency; yet an array of various rhetorical functions, styles, and themes, strongly assertive of the art from which they derive, compensates for lost contingency and allows a rhetoric composed of these elements, especially stylistic ones, to prosper. In Eden, however, no such initial problem arises. A deft adjustment of the rhetorical situation cancels out divine foreknowledge as an issue of serious impact or relevance, the adjustment consisting in the fact that God's motive for addressing Adam is entirely removed from persuasion. The Creator wishes instead to test the *logos* of His ultimate creation and to confirm him in wisdom. In this endeavour, the relevant consideration is the knowledge exhibited by and consolidated in Adam, not the foreknowledge possessed by God. The episode's concentration on the one relegates the other to the background, so that a strong rhetorical structure is built up around Adam's gradual expression of what he knows and around God's role, itself highly rhetorical, in prompting it. God, of course, knows how Adam will react and what he will say; but this foreknowledge, just as it 'had no influence on their fault' (III. 118), has no influence on Adam's reactions and speeches, which he alone controls. Both speakers in the dialogue project strong rhetorical personae that, along with various other rhetorical accents and constructions, reduce divine foreknowledge to an afterthought of little consequence in the larger picture of rhetoric that emerges.

The highlight of Adam's first meeting with God features the two divided on the subject of solitude. Their respective positions concerning it suggest the antithetical format of a commonplace book, God taking the *pro* side, Adam the *contra*. Their exchange, while apparently a debate, is truly so from only one perspective, Adam's, since God has agreed all along with Adam's opinion:

> I, ere thou spak'st,
> Knew it not good for Man to be alone,
> And no such company as then thou saw'st
> Intended thee, for trial only brought,
> To see how thou couldst judge of fit and meet.   (VIII. 444–8)

The nature of rhetoric in this scene stands fully revealed with God's admission that He has been playing a part, that He has endorsed solitude in order to draw forth Adam's soundly reasoned exposition of social decorum – of 'fit and meet' companionship. His tactic, defending whatever side of a question occasion or inclination calls for, exhibits an adaptability to different speaking situations that is characteristic of the rhetorical man, who also takes pleasure in his craft: God initiates their discussion, says Adam, 'As with a smile more bright'n'd' (VIII. 368). His motive, although ostensibly to test Adam's judgment, is unmistakably ludic as well. God is not above sport, a notion suggested in St Augustine's words to God, 'You are never in need yet glad to gain.'[14] God's playfully ironic façade – light-hearted, jocund, paternal in a more mundane sense – adds a more explicitly human face to anthropopathia, which here moves beyond the accommodation of human speech to the adoption of human personality. This persona shows Him, too, as less omniscient and foreknowing – less god-like – than simply wise, and desiring to impart that wisdom to His interlocutor.

The comparison with Plato's teacher is aptly drawn, for God's method is Socratic, a series of questions intended to lead an audience to knowledge. Extremely rare in God's discourse in heaven, rhetorical questions constitute most of His speech in addressing Adam, who asks, 'What happiness, who can enjoy alone, / Or all enjoying, what contentment find?' (VIII. 365–6). God responds:

> What call'st thou solitude? is not the Earth
> With various living creatures, and the Air
> Replenisht, and all these at thy command

To come and play before thee; know'st thou not
Thir language and thir ways?   (VIII. 369–73)

God's rhetorical questions, voicing apparent dissent, induce Adam to
work out for himself the justification for proportionate company, 'fit to
participate / All rational delight' (VIII. 390–1). The method of questioning, from God's standpoint, is heuristic, not eristic, that is, a rhetoric
geared not to argumentation, but to the discovery and expression of
truth. Isocrates acknowledged rhetoric's capacity to 'seek light for ourselves on things which are unknown,' as did Vives: 'Orations are substantial when they seem to say something not only by conveying the
appearance; but if someone investigates a subject, and lays it open, he
will discover much that lies hidden inside it.'[15] God engages Adam to
participate in a rhetorical investigation of solitude. Its purpose is not to
reveal any new truth on the subject, but rather one that is already
known,[16] that is 'hidden inside' and in need of Adam's formal recognition and explication. The Father's anthropopathetic image includes a
range of rhetorical identities and functions. He argues a contrary opinion, conceals His true motives, assumes the role of Socratic teacher,
establishes the heuristic format of the dialogue, asks rhetorical questions, and directs the course of inquiry. The actual process of discovery,
however, He leaves to Adam.

Adam naturally takes a different perspective on the purpose of the
dialogue. Dramatic irony, similar to that which prevents the fallen
angels from grasping their subjection to providence, withholds from
Adam the knowledge that God, in agreement with him all along, is putting up a polemical front for the sake of generating heuristic 'debate.'
And once again, as it did in hell, irony fortifies rhetoric, since in Adam's
eyes the situation is entirely contingent; he must argue with every
means at his disposal for the companionship that, as far as he knows, he
may or may not get. Adam, in contrast to God, has an eristic concept of
the dialogue, believing that his future happiness is at stake and that, if
he argues vigorously and persuasively enough, God will grant him
what he wants. Both Adam and the descended God are types of the rhetorical man; yet whereas God forgoes outright persuasion, Adam seizes
that objective enthusiastically, in the process taking a page from the classical textbooks. His persuasive efforts and his belief in their link to
future contingency considerably increase the rhetorical content of the
dialogue against the tacit presence of divine foreknowledge, itself virtually eclipsed by the Father's various and colourful rhetorical postures.

'We see,' wrote Hobbes, 'that all men are naturally able in some sort to *accuse* and *excuse*: some by chance; but some by method.'[17] Adam's natural abilities in this area are prodigious, though derived from neither chance nor method. Raphael explains their origin:

> Nor are thy lips ungraceful, Sire of men,
> Nor tongue ineloquent; for God on thee
> Abundantly his gifts hath also pour'd
> Inward and outward both, his image fair:
> Speaking or mute all comeliness and grace
> Attends thee, and each word, each motion forms.   (VIII. 218–23)

Eloquence is an attribute of God, a gift bestowed on Adam as part of the 'Inward' divine image and one that is inseparable from reason and wisdom under the *logos*: 'To man alone of all living creatures, as he is capable of reason and knowledge, God the father and author of all things has granted the gift of speech and eloquence.'[18] God has been testing Adam's verbal skills along with his rational ones and judges both worthy of praise in

> find[ing] thee knowing not of Beasts alone,
> Which thou hast rightly nam'd, but of thyself,
> Expressing well the spirit within thee free,
> My Image.   (VIII. 438–41)

Fittingly, the rhetoric by which Adam expresses the inspired image of God is technically sophisticated, making it 'a matter of just wonder,' as it is for another born orator, Sterne's Walter Shandy, 'that a man who knew not the names of his tools, should be able to work after that fashion with 'em':[19]

> Let not my words offend thee, Heavn'ly Power,
> My Maker, be propitious while I speak.
> Hast thou not made me here thy substitute,
> And these inferior beneath me set?
> Among unequals what society
> Can sort, what harmony or true delight?
> Which must be mutual, in proportion due
> Giv'n and receiv'd.   (VIII. 379–86)

One of Adam's tools, which God also uses frequently in this scene, is erotesis, the rhetorical question that strongly implies its own answer.

Adam here sets two in succession, striking a bold tone in light of whom he is addressing and indicative of the passion behind his words. With reference to 'harmony' and 'proportion,' he quickly grasps the importance of decorum, of 'fit and meet' (VIII. 448) as a standard that is both social, compelling him to object to the disparate society of the beasts, and rhetorical, allowing him to speak aptly and eloquently on that subject. On the rhetorical side of that equation, 'harmony' has further significance. 'For the Pythagoreans,' who predated Gorgias, 'sophia is nothing but harmony, which is equivalent, etymologically, to harmonia, the faculty employed by Pythagoras to determine the appropriate language (logous harmodious) and appropriate form for each person (prosarmottein hekaston hekasto).'[20] Harmony, then, is also the oratorical faculty that enables Adam to measure his words in speaking to God.

For the tools of investigative rhetoric, Adam turns to the topics of invention, 'by whose prompting,' writes Agricola, 'can be discovered that which is convincing in each thing.'[21] The topics were also employed to direct a course of inquiry;[22] therefore, their application could discover, along with convincing arguments about a particular subject, the nature of that subject as well – knowledge that, if initially hidden from view, might be brought to light through rhetorical excavation. In order to find support in favour of proportionately rational society, Adam visits the topic of comparison. The process yields the arguments he is looking for, and at the same time reveals a truth about the subject he has placed under topical scrutiny: himself.

'Comparison is made between things which are greater, or lesser, or equal,'[23] as when Adam compares himself with lesser things, the beasts. Two of the points considered in comparison, Cicero specifies, are quality and value: 'In comparing things with respect to their quality we prefer,' among other things, 'reasonable beings to those devoid of reason.'[24] Adam voices just this preference:

> Of fellowship I speak
> Such as I seek, fit to participate
> All rational delight, wherein the brute
> Cannot be human consort.   (VIII. 389–92)

He draws a comparison from the lesser: the beasts are unable to converse among themselves, so he, a rational being, is all the more unable to converse with any of them:

Much less can Bird with Beast, or Fish with Fowl
So well converse, nor with the Ox the Ape;
Worse then can Man with Beast, and least of all.   (VIII. 395–7)

At Adam's progress towards self-knowledge, God is 'not displeas'd'
(VIII. 398) yet continues to try Adam with further questions:

What think'st thou then of mee, and this my State,
Seem I to thee sufficiently possest
Of happiness, or not?   (VIII. 403–5)

I will shortly refer to these lines again, and their rhetorical significance,
when I discuss the final panel of the anthropopathetic tryptych of Eden,
the judgment imposed by the Son in Book X. For the moment, it need be
said only that God is using this implied claim of solitary happiness to
return Adam to the topic of comparison, though now from the greater,
as Adam compares himself with God, and with respect to value: 'In
regard to value, ... things which are sufficient in themselves [*ipsis con-
tenta*] are better than those that require help from others.'[25] God, unlike
man, is sufficient in himself, a superiority that Adam acknowledges
through sygkrisis,[26] the rhetorical device of systematic comparison:

Thou in thyself art perfet, and in thee
Is no deficience found; not so is Man.   (VIII. 415–16)

[God is] through all numbers absolute, though One;
But Man by number is to manifest
His single imperfection.   (VIII. 421–3)

Thou ... Canst raise thy Creature to what highth thou wilt
Of Union or Communion, deifi'd;
I by conversing cannot these erect
From prone, nor in thir ways complacence find.   (VIII. 427, 430–3)

It is notable that Adam's thus comparing himself with God is not comparison in the strict sense imposed by Agricola: 'We call it comparison
when two or more things are brought together in some third thing,
which is common to them. As it was lawful for Cato to pursue civil war,
consequently it will be lawful for Cicero to pursue it. This is common to
both of them, to pursue civil war.'[27] Adam's earlier comparison of himself with the animals fits this definition, since common to both is an

inability to converse. Nothing common, however, unites God and Adam in the present context, and this is precisely Adam's point: that God is incomparable, and so much surpasses Adam as a self-sufficient being as to exclude the possibility that any common feature links their natures in this respect.

It is clear from such passages that topical invention is doubly useful: to Adam, for bringing to light aspects of his relationship to God and the beasts, and to Milton, for its ability to generate *copia* and convey the wondrous oratorical facility of the original man. Guided by the Father's rhetorical questions, Adam has done more than simply advocate companionship over solitude. The process of rhetorical invention, of producing and presenting arguments, has also been a process of discovering knowledge, gradually unfolded both to himself and to Milton's audience. Topics find the material of invention; Adam's speech demonstrates that they can also lead the orator to wisdom by explicating the subjects that are drawn through them. A case in point is comparison, through which a thing may be better understood by measuring it against other things – whether it is greater or less than, like or unlike them, in terms of quality, value, intellect or completeness, to name only the criteria considered in this particular case. By visiting the place of comparison twice, once to express his superiority to the beasts and then to express his inferiority to God, Adam locates himself on the Great Chain of Being, seeing at once the lesser beings below him and the greater Being above him. Following this rhetorical line of invention leads Adam to truth, to the wisdom of self-knowledge, elaborated in a copious style that shows that he is, after the pattern of his maker, truly eloquent.

The rhetorical idea of discovering new knowledge leads naturally to the ethical idea that knowledge is useful insofar as it leads to right action, the determination of which is another fruit of the kind of debate dramatized here. For 'without debate in which both sides of the question are expressed,' Artabanus tells Xerxes, 'it is impossible to choose the better course. All one can do is accept whatever it is that has been proposed. But grant a debate, and there is a fair choice to be made. We cannot assess the purity of gold merely by looking at it: we test it by rubbing it on other gold – then we can tell which is the purer.'[28] It is one thing to discover knowledge through rhetorical debate, another to put one's knowledge towards proper action. This humanist lesson plays out in the contrast between the successful test of Adam's rhetorical prudence and the later test of Eve's ethical prudence, with her tragic choice of the false coin, counterfeited by the false moneyer, in place of the pure one. The transaction leads swiftly to a reckoning.

The Son, created by the same maker as man, establishes in Paradise an oratorical presence reflective of his lineage. In Book X, standing in as God's 'Vicegerent,' the Son descends to judge and sentence man; the near interchangeability of Father and Son further declares itself in their virtually identical rhetorical personae. For the scene of judgment Milton returns to Genesis 3, which he follows closely in framing the speech of the Son, filled out with amplifications of the biblical text that heighten the perception of God as an orator. The Son's opening words quote the God of Genesis 3.9, 'Where *art* thou?' then take up again the idea of solitude:

> Where art thou *Adam*, wont with joy to meet
> My coming seen far off? I miss thee here,
> Not pleas'd, thus entertain'd with solitude,
> Where obvious duty erewhile appear'd unsought:
> Or come I less conspicuous, or what change
> Absents thee, or what chance detains? Come forth.   (X. 103–8)

Speaking, behaving, and (in the histrionic sense) acting much as the Father did in Book VIII, the Son conceals his omniscience for the sake of prompting Adam to speak, once again, as the Father had done, through a series of questions. This time, however, Adam is being forced into confessing his mortal sin, not coaxed into Socratic dialogue; and what had been the gentle irony of the Father now gives way to the pointed irony of the Son: 'Where art thou *Adam*?' As a rhetorical question, its purpose, in both the Bible and *Paradise Lost*, has nothing to do with actual inquiry, as Salomon Glassius observes. 'Ignorance,' as an aspect of biblical anthropopathia, 'is attributable to God':

> To this end questions may be referred that are initiated by God, as though He does not know the answer, although properly speaking nothing escapes God's notice, nor does He have any need to ask questions. Genesis 3.9: 'And the Lord God called to the man, and said to him, where art thou?' This is a not question where the answer is unknown, but rather it invites an appearance and reminds Adam how much he has changed from that blessed state of immortality, now after he had fallen. Ambrose, *De paradiso*, chapter 14: 'Where is that bold self-confidence of yours, well

aware of itself? That fear acknowledges the fault, and concealment admits collusion. And so, where is it? I ask not in what place, but in what condition? Where have your sins led you, that you flee your God, whom before you used to seek? This is not, therefore, a question, but a reproach: from what good things, what blessedness, what grace, into what misery have you fallen!'[29]

The Son's opening question, along with the three at lines 107–8, reproaches Adam, calling him forward in order to call him to account. Susenbrotus discusses the straightforward question (*simplex*) alongside this kind of figurative question, 'which in the asking is used not to get information, but rather serves for expressing various strong emotions.'[30] The Son's angry, sarcastic questions demand that Adam consider the enormity of disobedience in all its repercussions of loss, shame, misery, and betrayal. Irony is notably present in divine rhetoric, among the heavenly host as well as on earth, as in the Father's address:

> O Sons, like one of us Man is become
> To know both Good and Evil, since his taste
> Of that defended Fruit.   (XI. 84–6)

Thomas Hall rhetorically glosses the relevant biblical verse, Genesis 3.22, much as Glassius did with Genesis 3.9: '*Ironia*, Ironicall, taunting speeches may lawfully be used, as occasion serves. 1. God himself used them. Gen. 3.22. the man is become one of us (i.[e.]) as one of the Trinity, whereby God declares his great disdaine of their affectation of an impossible preheminence in being like to God. q.d. by his sin he is become most unlike to us.'[31]

In light of the Son's performance, irony declares itself as the master rhetorical device of heavenly rhetoric in Eden, a designation accorded to conduplicatio ('All in All') when that rhetoric is spoken in its native environment. The transition from the figure, conduplicatio, to the trope, irony, is fitting as the rhetoric of heaven changes location via anthropopathia. Figures, as discussed in chapter 6, manifest order in language and the cosmos and express the divine creative force. Their symmetry reflects the perfection of the Creator and the order inherent in the created things that proceed from him. Tropes function differently; they bring rhetoric down to earth, enabling humanity to understand what God condescends to tell us. They signify something ineffable by way of a concept accessible to human interpretation, as we saw in biblical hermeneutics and in Michael's rhetoric. Irony masks the incomprehensible omniscience of God in order to convey reproach in Book X and in order to play with and test Adam in Book VIII. In both it is a catalyst for rhetoric; without it, divine omniscience would stifle rhetorical potential just as it occasionally does in heaven. Attributing ignorance to God is an essential technique of rhetorical preservation in *Paradise Lost*. But that attribution achieves more than mere preservation. God's readiness to assume an ironic façade, and to engineer rhetorical situations from behind it, boldly asserts the identity of this species of rhetoric made in the moment, a rhetoric purposefully created, like everything else, at the pleasure of the divine will. His omniscience negates rhetorical opportunity, so the Son feigns ignorance in Book X; certainty cancels out rhetorical play, so God in Book VIII creates the illusion of contingency in Adam's mind. The trope of irony eases God's descent into human company and inspires rhetoric whenever He uses it.

Having asked where the human couple is, the Son is relentless. Three more questions at lines 119–23 continue to pierce Adam's conscience, inducing his confession of guilt (X. 125–43). At this point the Son's questions shed their buffer of irony and raise the emotional pitch to outright scorn:

Was shee thy God, that her thou didst obey
Before his voice, or was shee made thy guide,
Superior, or but equal, that to her
Thou didst resign thy Manhood, and the Place
Wherein God set thee above her made of thee,
And for thee, whose perfection far excell'd
Hers in all real dignity.   (X. 145–51)

These lines support Erasmus's claim that 'the rhetorical question, when seasonably deployed, adds great force and sting to a speech.'[32] Other Renaissance commentators recognized the same qualities that Glassius and Erasmus note – that the rhetorical question was unrelated to sincere inquiry, its purpose being tendentious and eristic, and that its forcefulness derived from the vehement emotions that a skilled speaker could invest it with.[33]

With this barrage of questions, the Son, 'mild Judge and Intercessor both' (X. 96), is also the Inquisitor, as ready as the Father to vary his speech and persona from one rhetorical situation to the next. In order to exemplify the degree of flexibility that God exhibits according to these changing circumstances, we may compare two sets of lines, both addressed to Adam, that are found two books apart:

> What think'st thou then of mee, and this my State,
> Seem I to thee sufficiently possest
> Of happiness, or not?   (VIII. 403–5)

>   I miss thee here,
> Not pleas'd, thus entertain'd with solitude,
> Where obvious duty erewhile appear'd unsought.   (X. 104–6)

At one time, as in Book VIII, God may imply that solitude pleases Him; at another, during the prologue to man's judgment, He may say outright that it does not. The contrast points to yet another rhetorical attribute of divinity in *Paradise Lost*: that God's speech may take the form of opinions, which, in their stance on a particular issue, are no more consistent than the changing *kairos* in which they are voiced. Milton's descended God adopts the humanist attitude of arguing *in utramque partem*, thereby introducing into divine discourse the notion of probability, since God's contrasting remarks on solitude are the ad hoc responses of the orator. They contain none of the truth imbued with absolute certainty that is normally associated with divine utterances; they are merely *convincing*, true only to the extent that a particular audience believes them at a particular time. God alters His discourse in line with the specific circumstances of different situations – 'rhetoric seems to be able to persuade about "the given", so to speak,'[34] as Aristotle notes. Earlier, in discussing Eve's temptation, we saw how religious truth opposes sophistic truth. It is the *episteme* of revealed wisdom, its divine origin the seal of its unquestioned authority. The lines above, however, portray a God whose speech, unconfined to the normative certainty of religious truth, roams the wide latitude of sophistic opinion and honours only the rhetorical marks of time, place, subject, and audience. This one strand of the humanist approach to argumentation – its advancement of multiple lines of probable argument on a given question – merges with the sophistic conception of persuasion to form yet another aspect of God's protean rhetorical identity. The role of God as ironic sophist rounds out a diversified model of anthropopathia that ranges over four characters – God Himself, the Son, Raphael, Michael – and the various stylistic answers they apply to the hard task of speaking in the world of man.

Conclusion

Paradise Lost is the Grand Tour of English literature, a sweeping survey of *res cunctas*, all things, as Milton's friend Samuel Barrow wrote in one of the verse commendations prefacing the second edition of 1674. Despite all that the poem has to say about politics, religious controversy, gender, history, and any number of other subjects, every idea within its encyclopedic scope is both subordinate to an overarching poetic agenda and constitutive of an aesthetic achievement. Thus, like any other subject, rhetoric in *Paradise Lost* is properly studied not for its own sake but as an idea-in-poetry, related to the form that expresses it and to what Milton's poem is intended to do. Rhetoric's inherent association with form – it is arguably the primary source of artistic form in literature – makes it the ultimate idea-in-poetry. For poetry is rhetorical through and through: it both takes its form from the technical apparatus of rhetoric and expresses rhetorical intention by engaging its audience persuasively. As such, rhetoric is particularly valuable for writing a history of literary forms, the kind of history that this book has attempted to practice.

Rhetoric prevails in *Paradise Lost* as a convention that governs the poem thematically and formally, and the critical application of rhetoric elucidates both what Milton is saying and the thing which he makes. Assessing the poem from both standpoints, with special emphasis on the latter, has entailed a Grand Tour in its own right. We have travelled from the classical world to the end of the Renaissance, around the humanistic disciplines dependent on rhetoric for their voice, and between the worlds of the Miltonic universe, differentiated from one another by the qualities of their unique rhetorical environments. The art of eloquence informs *Paradise Lost* at every level. By analysing the history of its forms, we open to critical view some of the traditions underpinning the poem's construction: the classical rhetorical tradition, as instituted in Milton's list of authors; the biblical one, connecting rhetoric with exegesis and preaching, that relates to the speech of heaven-dwelling characters; the patristic and literary one that underlies satanic speech; a complex of humanist ones, tied to the *studia humanitatis*, that involves rhetoric structurally and thematically throughout the poem; and finally, what we may term an epistemological tradition, which foregrounds the concepts of probability, future contingency, and free will in my rhetorical reading of the poem. These traditions, examined historically, suggest the pervasiveness of rhetoric as a major idea-in-poetry, its conventions overseeing many of the more notable features of *Paradise Lost*, including the tripartite rhetoric that I hold to be the dominant formal motif of Milton's aesthetic achievement.

Just as rhetoric offers advantages to analysing poetry, poetry offers reciprocal advantages to the analysis of rhetoric. This is because, as Wayne Rebhorn writes, 'literature does ... what rhetoric treatises and handbooks are prevented from doing, except intermittently, by their form: it presents a direct modeling of rhetorical situations ... Renaissance literature subjects the issues presented in the discourse [of rhetoric] to a process of examination, clarification, and evaluation, a process which, if nothing else, exposes its many contradictions, evasions, and mystifications for all to see.' Through that process, authors 'are able not only to dramatize the ideas and perspectives of the rhetoricians but also to elaborate them in ways that clarify what sometimes remains obscure and expose to the light of contemplation what is often submerged or repressed within the discourse of rhetoric.'[1] *Paradise Lost* performs this kind of examination and evaluation of rhetorical discourse, often of its submerged elements, such as the issues involving future contingency, and often by portraying how rhetoric is used in, and conditioned by, the discursive circumstances characteristic of the three worlds of the poem. By modelling rhetorical situations, *Paradise Lost* extends and elaborates conventional ideas concerning the power of rhetoric, the moral terms of its proper use, and the techniques prescribed for eloquent, persuasive expression, while also illuminating unexplored reaches of rhetorical discourse, touched on only parenthetically in Renaissance theory, that are complicated by divine omniscience and irony, dialogue between human and supernatural beings, and the role of rhetorical probability within the superstructure of providential certainty. Literature provides what Rebhorn calls 'a liminal space, a site adjacent to but separate from the real world' where these obscure features of rhetorical discourse can be discovered and analysed.

Much as I have approached *Paradise Lost* in critical terms of both what the poet says and the thing which he makes, leaning towards the latter, so I have examined rhetoric from two historical perspectives: that of Milton's concept of rhetoric and that, as nearly as I can approximate, of the poem's original reader. Again, the second approach proved more serviceable than the first, though the first offered certain relevant insights, most notably Milton's definition of eloquence as a love of truth. For the purposes of discussing rhetoric in *Paradise Lost*, I have defined 'truth' in mainly religious terms. Emanating from God, proclaimed with the certainty of revealed knowledge, religious doctrine assumes the mantle of inviolable truth, exclusive of competing opinions. When Milton declares eloquence to be a love of the truth, this is the truth he means. When Satan enjoins Eve to love herself more than she loves God, this is the truth he undermines. Milton imagined that the Christian orator's love of the truth would deliver him the prompt eloquence required in truth's defence. Love fired the orator with zeal to expound the truth, whether in the role of preacher, poet, or historian. The Roman definition of eloquence, as wisdom speaking copiously, also fit into Milton's vision for these offices of Christian oratory, along with other basic conventions: the indivisibility of thought and expression, *res* and *verba*; the observance of decorum that found 'answerable style' for one's thoughts and the attendant concept of language as a token of refinement and humanity; and the necessity of weighing the contingencies of time, audience, and place. The cultural conviction in the *logos* was also an ethical conviction for humanists such as Milton. Wisdom dictated that the orator, having acquired divine knowledge by contemplation and virtuous conduct in his own life, should assume the responsibility of disseminating that knowledge within the community. Equipped by both training and character to apply rhetoric in the sphere of public instruction, the orator used the colours of eloquence to move his audience to a like-minded understanding and acceptance of what he himself knew. The poet, who combined the attributes of preacher and historian, was a special case. Divinely inspired, he nevertheless required the complementary benefits of a liberal education in order to practise his art in its highest form – Milton's theological poetry comprised logic, rhetoric, poetics, Christian moral philosophy, and history.

To what extent did Milton's humanist education in rhetoric shape him as a poet? It is reasonable to posit a connection between the rhetorical skills he acquired as a student and the formal structure of the greatest long poem in the English language, even though the value of such an education has been questioned. In contrast to Brian Vickers's concept of rhetoric's reintegration into a purposive whole in the Renaissance, John Ward agrees with other historians that Renaissance pedagogy 'actually continues the incomprehensible mindlessness of medieval education and prepares the Renaissance student for that brand of fluent docility applauded in the proliferating and increasingly tentacular courts of the Renaissance period.'[2] In Ward's account, much as Dickens's Mr Gradgrind wants children taught nothing but Facts, the Renaissance schoolmaster taught nothing but the manufacture of neatly wrapped *clausulae* in the interest of instilling empty eloquence and turning out legions of letter-writing automata. Given Milton's remarks on 'forcing the empty wits of children to compose Theams, verses, and Orations' that require far more mature judgment and 'mispending our prime youth at the Schools and Universities as we do ... in learning meere words' (*YP*, 2: 372, 376), this seems a depressingly accurate picture of the environment in which Milton went to school and learned rhetoric. But Milton's education was conducted more outside the classroom than within it, in his own time and on his own terms, and if St Paul's and Cambridge really did teach little more than insubstantial verbal fluency, they nevertheless thereby handed Milton the base materials for later acts of startling creative transmutation. He read the classics, polished his Latin through imitative themes and declamations, learned methods for generating *copia* of words and ideas, and kept a commonplace book to organize and store the miscellaneous thoughts and phrases that proliferated from his studies. And he combined all of this academic knowledge with 'ripest judgement,' tireless reading, and especially the artistic temperament – the Platonic inspiration contrasted with adherence to Horatian rules – that classroom instruction could not provide. Rhetoric is there, underneath it all, as the formal literary infrastructure, as part of Milton's creative mind. I think its presence partly explains, for example, the use in *Paradise Lost* of anthropopathia, which Milton understood in terms inherited from the Renaissance educational system. A pastiche of associations, reflective of other similar cases, may be reasonably inferred: learning in grammar school about the related figure of prosopopoeia, if not anthropopathia itself; identifying it first under guidance and soon independently in any number of classical texts; recognizing its occurrence in the divine machinery of epic poetry and in the Bible; and eventually adopting it as a suitable feature of the rhetorical universe of

Paradise Lost. Milton's rhetorical education undoubtedly contributed to his poetic technique, though the degree of intention behind his deployment of rhetoric is impossible to surmise. Because of the uncertainties involved in penetrating the inner workings of the creative process, trying to stand where Milton himself stood in composing yields limited results.

By standing on the other side of the text, however, as the hypothetical original reader who shared Milton's education and technical background in the linguistic arts, the formal history of *Paradise Lost* may be examined and described with greater precision. The reason is that the historically immersed critic is better positioned to understand a text, especially its technical intricacies, than the author who wrote it. When, for example, I call future contingency the central rhetorical problem of *Paradise Lost*, the designation refers to a critical problem, not one of composition. Far from thinking of it in terms of a problem when he wrote the poem, as a complicating factor of rhetoric in different cosmic settings, Milton almost certainly knew nothing about it. Although much of the creative process is shut to critical inspection, many qualities of the literary artefact are unknown to the author who made it yet amenable to rhetorical inquiry. This is rhetoric's chief value as a critical tool: applied with due historical consciousness, in synchrony with the original reader of a text, it reveals formal patterns and layers that are outside the perception of the author. Discerning those patterns and describing their arrangement and interrelationships have formed the purpose of this book; being able to do so has required thinking ourselves back into a Renaissance state of mind, achieved by understanding the rhetorical conventions that governed a work of literature produced in seventeenth-century England. A number of these conventions came to light in the interest of historically situating the literary forms of *Paradise Lost*, some of the most characteristic of Milton's age being those associated with style.

Perhaps the most distinctive element of *Paradise Lost*, famously demanding of the modern reader's perseverance, is its style. Milton's classicized vocabulary and syntax contribute to an overall departure from common usage beyond anything seen in English poetry up to that time, to a degree rivalled in any genre perhaps only by James Joyce's *Ulysses*. The language undergoes a singular transformation, often through techniques related to Milton's search for metrical harmony in 'the sense variously drawn out from one Verse into another' rather than the rhyming that was becoming increasingly fashionable in his day (*YP*,

8: 14). Words cleave tightly to their Latin roots; clauses pile atop one another in varying and sometimes vertiginous degrees of subordination; inversions part nouns from modifiers, subjects from verbs, in arrangements that appear alien and occasionally perplexing. Milton builds perplexity into the poem, whose readers are meant to struggle with it and to pay full attention on different levels, including that of acclimation to an outlandish stylistic idiom. Such unsettling effects may be linked to departures from common usage, but what is considered common or familiar usage changes over time (an idea at the centre of the Renaissance debate over *consuetudo* and the contemporary utility of post-classical Latin). In this temporal gap lies the disadvantage of the modern reader's perspective against that of the original reader who lived in Milton's time and who therefore more or less shared his standard of common usage, his set of literary and rhetorical conventions as well as social, religious, and political ones. Although the ascent of Milton's 11,000-line edifice would have been difficult even in the seventeenth century, the original reader's fuller sense of what Milton was doing with language would have aided an understanding of the poem across the board. While we are left guessing by the scarcity of printed allusions to *Paradise Lost* around the time of its publication in 1667 and 1674 – 'Discriminating and disinterested public praise of the epic had yet to come'[3] – we may infer that Milton's stylistic innovations would have surprised many of his contemporaries, but not shocked them, given a notion of common usage stabilized by the familiar art at the core of literary style: rhetoric. We cannot understand Milton's style without understanding rhetoric, and we cannot aspire to the preferred vantage point of the original reader without acknowledging the centrality of rhetoric and trying to revive the Renaissance appreciation for style.

Regarded as the definitive quality of eloquence by rhetoricians in all periods; singled out of the art for reasons aesthetic, philosophical, and spiritual; expressive of character as well as thought; critical to informed reading and elegant writing; and attentively cultivated by Milton himself, style (*elocutio*) demands close scrutiny in examining the literary forms of *Paradise Lost*. Milton's educational prescriptions concerning it (half the syllabus for rhetoric in *Of Education* is devoted to classical treatises that focus predominantly on style) reflect the influence of tradition and the priorities of a literary culture that retained strong ties to the humanistic conception of eloquence, which favoured the ability to find the right words for every thought or occasion. Style intersects with many other rhetorical themes in *Paradise Lost*. True to the Renaissance norm, it faithfully portrays the interior life of its speaker – speak that I may see thee. All characters are known by their stylistic signatures, defined largely by the tropes and schemes that made style an art in itself and that abound in *Paradise Lost* as integral parts of the rhetorico-poetic machinery. Their presence is ornamental, not so much in the decorative sense (festive blossoms in a garden of eloquence) as in the Renaissance sense, appropriate for epic grandeur, that looked to the primary Latin meaning of *ornamentum* as equipment or accoutrements.[4] Tropes and figures perform rhetorical work for their users. Artistically, they help Milton convey the terms of his 'great Argument'; in the narrative, they enable characters to define their roles within the framework of that argument; for example, the figures of verbal doubling in the empyreal speech of the Father and the Son, the solemn music of conduplicatio and polyptoton, which foreshadows the apocalyptic future when 'God shall be All in All.' Thought and style, *res* and *verba*, merge so completely here that the style *is* the idea: it is the Word. We see this again in the Son's chiasmus – 'Silence, ye troubl'd waves, and thou Deep, peace' – in which the figure and its making are emblematic of the formal work that *elocutio* does: it imparts order to things created by words. Figures ornament (equip) the Son of God, whether here as creator or elsewhere as destroyer, when he routs the rebel armies; or inquisitor, when he interrogates Adam and Eve; or judge, when he sentences them; or messiah, when he accepts the burden of their sin. His style defines his various functions within the providential scheme that the poem argues and that his use of rhetoric makes possible.

Stylistic devices do other important work as well, inflecting rhetorical themes that are fundamental to understanding what the poem says and how it is made. We observe this of metonymy, sygkrisis, distribution, and synecdoche, which elaborate the rhetorical topos of comparison. Comparison, as a mode of both reasoning and discoursing, pervades the formal structure of *Paradise Lost*, especially in the recurrent thematic pattern of great things in relation to lesser ones. Raphael's metonymical comparison of the greater to the lesser instructs Adam in 'what surmounts the reach / Of human sense,' while Adam's own systematic comparison (sygkrisis) of greater and lesser, which sees and interprets their mutual relations, exemplifies a Platonic 'ideal of ... perfect connexion and perfect explanation'[5] brought to full statement by the aid of the Father's line of Socratic questioning in Book VIII. *Paradise Lost* moves constantly towards a state of perfect connection and perfect explanation, a hermeneutic understanding of smaller parts by reference to other parts and to the larger whole, as we also see in Michael's distributive rhetoric that explains relationships of cause and effect, genus and species, subject and adjunct, and in his synecdochal explanation of the Protevangelium. All such logical connections, from those Adam draws in talking with God to Raphael's 'lik'ning spiritual to corporal forms' and Michael's distributions, resolve themselves in Adam's final recognition of divine providence 'by small / Accomplishing great things' (XII. 566–7). Here, the scale of forms, of greater and lesser, stands fully revealed, the providential and theodical mysteries perfectly explained as the many are collected into the one, suggesting the eventual unified completeness of all things. The rhetorical topic of comparison, elaborated by various tropes and figures, plays a major role in articulating this complex of ideas.

The overarching formal idea in my interpretation of *Paradise Lost* is that of future contingency and its effect on rhetoric in the poem, particularly on deliberative rhetoric, which urges what ought to be done in the future. Contingency and the associated idea of probability are the essential epistemological components of rhetoric. For we deliberate over contingent events, which may turn out other than they do, drawing our decisions from probable arguments, which may guide us appropriately, though we can never know with any certainty. Contingency's potential fluctuates in heaven, hell, and Eden; the nature and potential of rhetoric fluctuate correspondingly in all three settings, to the extent that a discrete rhetoric may be said to exist in each one. Contingency varies for different reasons. In heaven, it comes under challenge from divine foreknowledge; in hell, it falls under the shadow of providence; only in Eden does it operate unhindered. In heaven, divine foreknowledge attenuates future contingency in dialogue involving the Father and the Son, whose apprehension of the whole of time as a continuous present anticipates the outcome of any rhetorical situation, particularly those in which they themselves are speaking. Yet rhetoric still holds a persuasive edge in heaven, the only place where speakers can argue from certainty rather than probability. The drama of the Father's open call for a redeemer and the Son's acceptance, even when both know he will accept, exemplifies an imperial rhetoric of spectacle that sets the king above his subjects, confirming to the heavenly host the Son's pre-eminence and fitness to rule; the Son's battle oration achieves a similar effect. Contingency, and therefore rhetoric, gains back much of what it loses to the Father and the Son in that the angels are not omniscient and act freely, obeying the word of God by their own individual acts of will. For those angels who chose to disobey, and suffered for it, circumstances are much different. The constraints placed on rhetoric in hell are far more binding, for its inhabitants, having forfeited the privilege of free will, can now act only within the limited scope afforded by God's will. The predicament of Milton's demons, compelled to participate within the providential scheme of Christian theodicy, annihilates contingency in their future actions and in the rhetoric that would attempt to direct them. But rhetoric again holds its own, if more tenuously than in heaven. The synecdochal perspective of the demons, blinding them to the true nature of God and to the fact of their enslavement, lets them plan future actions under a false likeness of political rhetoric during the chthonic parliament. Satan's oratorical mastery gives the rhetoric of hell its most forceful injection of life, as he completely dominates proceedings there. His crooked eloquence is formidable enough to influence the outcome of a single contingent event, the Fall, but only after it travels to Earth and only to work the ultimate destruction of its speaker far in the apocalyptic future.

Transplanted into Paradise, satanic eloquence finds new life; Satan's earthward journey is a journey to rhetorical fruition. Human beings, like the angels, possess free will, which supports future contingency in the face of divine foreknowledge. I established the theological tenet, endorsed by Milton, that God's prescience of an event, including the Fall, imputes to Him no intervention in its occurrence. Eve, therefore, judges and acts independently, her error generated from the choice between alternative possibilities that is central to rhetoric as 'this negotiation within ourselves.' This is another presiding rhetorical convention of *Paradise Lost*, sitting alongside future contingency: that rhetoric has an internal function, that it is a method of reasoning as well as speaking, not merely an instrument of artistic composition and public persuasion. The *logos* as speech and a command of language coexists with the related concepts of reason, wisdom, and choice, which lifts rhetoric into the spheres of ethics and theology and thus places it at the heart of human experience. As Milton shows, our ethical natures amount to how wisely we are able to choose a course of action – choices presented, one way or another, as arguments, designed to appeal to our reason, passions, self-interest, and so on. Evaluating arguments in order to make sound moral decisions is difficult, as there is no science for doing so infallibly; those powers of conjecture that would help us find the best course of action *are* fallible and can lead us into error. Milton develops the idea that choice, in particular the acceptance of one argument over another, is a rhetorical process, both in one party's presentation of arguments and in another's deliberation over them. The same sense of decorum that availed a speaker to discourse aptly and copiously is also needed to conduct oneself as a virtuous Christian, a lover of wisdom and truth. In this rhetoricized ethics, free will becomes much more than a theological tenet; I devoted the better part of a chapter to establishing its theological validity because it is a key *formal* idea as well. For if necessity of any kind were to impair free will, future contingency and probability would wither away and, with them, rhetoric itself. Free will sustains rhetoric in *Paradise Lost* as a process of probable argument, voluntary decision, and moral action. The Garden of Eden gives rhetoric room to display its functional range from persuasion to decision, from the amoral art of speaking eloquently to the responsibility of sifting opposing arguments in order to live correctly.

In a world free from necessity, probability rules. Rhetoric for Milton was, in part, a concession to the imperfect intellect of fallen man, fated to perceive the world, which it had formerly known intuitively and directly, through the obscuring glass of probability and opinion. Probable arguments generate tentative conclusions, qualified by sceptical doubt, as a basis for decision and action – the best that can be hoped for in the absence of an objective standard of truth. Before the Fall, however, such a standard did exist, in the form of the sole command. Part of the corrupt model of eloquence that Satan imports to Eden is the argument from probability that would dispute the certainty of the sole command, sowing doubt in Eve, and would supplant the testimony of divine authority, proudly elevating her to godhead in her own mind. Although Satan obviously mocks Plato's provision that 'oratory is to be employed only in the service of right,' he nevertheless embodies the Platonic orator in his use of probability to establish a likeness of truth, intended to mislead gradually by imperceptible degrees of departure from actual truth. How could aspiring to knowledge, after all, be anything but praiseworthy? The effect of this brash rhetorical act, a patiently disposed fabric of equivocations and omitted premises, is galvanizing. If Satan owes much to the Garden of Eden for the legitimacy of his speech as rhetoric, the exchange works both ways: he contributes at least as much to the rhetorical vitality of that place in return. Eden provides the future contingency and the audience possessed of free will that permit satanic rhetoric to cast off the providential chains heaped on it in hell and to be transformed into a force to be reckoned with, a voice of real persuasion that influences freely contingent events. Satan must come to Eden; his rhetorical life depends on it. Yet nothing does more to invigorate rhetoric in *Paradise Lost*, in Eden especially, than the presence of Satan. As the embodiment of oratorical purpose, constantly using speech to achieve his political goals, he charges the rhetorical atmosphere wherever he goes, and he goes everywhere, being the only character to appear and speak in all settings of the poem where dialogue occurs (heaven, hell, Chaos, the sun, Paradise). The probable arguments he introduces are everything that the sole command is not, and they crackle with rhetorical energy. They are subjective, grounded in the speaker's opinion, and local, tied to a particular audience and occasion; the determination of probability, that this or that is more likely, falls squarely on the audience. These are radical notions, compared with the simpler terms of obedience in Paradise before Satan's arrival, and are a boon to rhetoric there. They violate the cloister of Edenic virtue, forcing her to sally out and see her Adversary.

Heaven fully extended its rhetorical powers to help Adam and Eve see their way clear of the crisis. Paradise confers on the rhetoric of heaven a greater potential than it had in its native element, as Raphael's oration, despite divine foreknowledge that it will fail, also works upon the faculties of man in an attempt to steer the course of a contingent future. Earth gives the other empyreal orators similar advantages: God finds in Adam an interlocutor ready to argue and advocate; Michael finds in him a student in need of instruction and consolation; and the Son plays the shame of the original sinners for maximum oratorical effect. The speech of these characters in these scenes exemplifies another remarkable formal feature of *Paradise Lost*, that divine travelling between worlds, anthropopathia, which confirms Paradise as the rhetorical hub of the poem. Raphael recounts his urgent retrospective history of heaven and Michael his solemn prospective history of mankind, each with the stylistic tools suited to their agendas: metonymy and example to warn Adam before the temptation, distribution and synecdoche to teach and comfort him in its ruinous aftermath. Both work from the familiar materials of sacred rhetoric, from vivid imagery, rational and emotive proofs, and, above all, the appeal to divine authority on which all preaching rests. Rhetoric is a divine illumination, a gift of God, and the strangest and most rhetorically significant instances of anthropopathia are reserved for the Father and the Son.

Traditionally, anthropopathia referred specially to God. The connection between the art of rhetoric and the speech of God was long-standing. Milton could turn to the exegetical tradition, created out of the fusion of classical rhetoric and early Christian learning, which understood the Bible in rhetorical terms. According to this hermeneutic approach, biblical teaching expressed itself through (but lay partially hidden in) allegories and other tropes, so that understanding the figurative language of the Bible and penetrating its meaning amounted to virtually the same process. Rhetoric, which explained the nature and practice of figurative language, supplied the key to reading and interpreting the scriptures whereby God 'descends into our company.' As the author of this rhetorical Bible, the God who speaks in the Old Testament became the origin and perfect exponent of rhetoric. Readers from Augustine and Cassiodorus to Hugo Grotius and Joseph Caryl drew attention to the rhetorical elements of the Bible, a linguistic perception of divinity that would reach its creative acme in the eloquence of the Father and the Son in *Paradise Lost*. Within this set of conventions, the Psalms and the Book of Job stand out as literary analogues to Milton's epic, since they added poetry to the representation of divine speech. Commentators praised these books for having combined rhetoric and poetics in a manner that equalled the classics in artistry and, with the addition of sacred content, excelled them in overall value. The combination of divine speech, rhetoric, and poetry, formally contained by anthropopathia, is the most striking filiation of the biblical rhetorical tradition that we find in *Paradise Lost*.

One rhetorical quality of the anthropopathetic God, notable in the Book of Job, enjoys heightened formal significance in *Paradise Lost*. That quality is irony, significant in that it challenges the conception of Christian doctrine as consistent, univocal, unambiguous truth. Refracted through irony, truth bends with the intention of its speaker and becomes the truth of the rhetorical moment – something closer to sophistic opinion. That the godhead assumes ironic personae, and sophistically alters the terms of the truth while doing so, greatly enriches divine rhetoric in *Paradise Lost*. The Father and the Son, not unlike Satan, demonstrate themselves men for all oratorical seasons, adaptable in speech and manner to any situation and audience. But they take the notion of managing the *kairos* to even greater lengths than Satan because they must not only adapt to rhetorical situations, they must also create them. In doing so, irony is their primary ornament. They use it to efface their omniscience and foreknowledge from their speech acts, both in heaven, during the Father's public call for a redeemer – even 'talking' to the angels constitutes a descent for them – and especially in Paradise, during the Father's conversation with Adam and the Son's judgment. Their postures of ironic questioning and feigned ignorance create dramatic irony in these scenes, as their audiences are left in suspense or awe, forced to think and argue, and exposed to shame in ways that generate rhetorical tension. In the changing faces of irony, the pathos of anthropopathia occasionally supersedes the logos characteristic of divinity, whether the emotion is mirth, 'As with a smile more bright'n'd' (VIII. 368), or scorn and sarcasm emanating 'from wrath more cool' (X. 95). At such points, what is truth, when the God that is the source of truth alters its terms to suit His rhetorical mood? When He starts asking questions instead of issuing commands?

When divine discourse leans away from eternal knowledge and towards ironic opinion, towards probable arguments that persuade an audience to accept such opinion as truth – rhetorical truth, manufactured for that place and moment – its purpose is to lead the audience to a fuller understanding of the absolute, unalterable truths that God manifests and always essentially speaks: the Son's love and strength surpass all others'; man needs proportionate companionship; the sole command is just; sin invites condign punishment. This is how God, in condescending to lower beings, uses rhetoric. He makes other characters negotiate their way around subjectivities and probabilities, divinely introduced into the rhetorical moment, in order that they may come by degrees to apprehend truths that are fixed, immutable, transcendent, beyond even the realm of demonstrative proof. Truth of such clarity is unavailable in post-lapsarian life, the circumstances of which offer no better assurance for a given course of action than probability. For even longer than rhetoric had been a formal art, it had been considered a practical means of dealing with the uncertainties of human existence. Sophists, Peripatetics, Academic sceptics, and the humanists versed in those philosophies all believed in rhetoric's heuristic properties. Rhetoric reasons and argues on opposite sides of a question to discover the nearest possible approximation to truth, and Milton's God wants humanity to employ it for exactly this purpose, as His ad hoc creation and finessing of rhetorical situations implies. The rhetorical work that God thereby sets for the angels and our first parents is the work that the poem's readers are meant to perform – always finding out the truth for ourselves, employing rhetoric as reason, testing contingencies, and discriminating between competing opinions so that we may see and walk the straighter path in the absence of any means of knowing for certain in which direction it lies. The life well argued is the life well lived.

Paradise Lost conveys the centrality of speech for all rational beings, dramatized in a manner that has, in the best tradition of Renaissance poetics, all the advantages of example over precept. It relates the conflict played out in the Christian soul, waged between the poem's two models of eloquence: the one, rooted in holy wisdom, which would teach and move mankind to faith and obedience, versus the other, driven by satanic craft, which would overthrow reason's proper government and undermine virtue. The portrayal of this struggle expresses, with a resonance no formal treatise could have managed, Milton's estimation of rhetoric's amplitude and capabilities, its potential for benefit or harm, and, above all, its profound relevance to Christian ethics. The nature of rhetoric is a theme Milton often revisits. The scope of this book has permitted only incidental discussion of *Paradise Regained* – the tones of its rhetoric muted yet darkly powerful, a Rembrandt next to the Rubenesque splendour of *Paradise Lost* – and none of the rest of a body of poetry that shows many rhetorical forms and strategies in play. *Paradise Regained*, in particular, offers many opportunities for analysis similar to that undertaken here, from questions concerning future contingency (which recedes to the eschatological vanishing point prefigured in Jesus's every word and action) to those concerning style, biblically modelled divine speech, and the balance between sacred and humanistic learning. Milton's twin epics together contain everything of importance that their author thought about rhetoric and cover many of the uses, sacred and secular, to which this most versatile of linguistic arts had been put from its Greek origins to the third quarter of the seventeenth century. There they stand as a grandly vaulted terminus to the Age of Eloquence.

Notes

Introduction

1 Bush, *The Renaissance and English Humanism*, 101.
2 George Kennedy prefers the terms *technical*, *prescriptive*, or *standard* classical rhetoric over *Ciceronian*, because the same body of precepts was also known and practised in the East, not through Cicero. *Classical Rhetoric*, 89–90.
3 Vickers, *Defence of Rhetoric*, chaps 4 and 5.
4 Kristeller, *Renaissance Thought*, 25, 28–9, 243.
5 Rhetoric in Latin is typically referred to as the *ratio* or *ars dicendi* (the theory or art of speaking), words that reflect its grounding in a set of rules (*praeceptio*) by which one could acquire it. 'Speaking' is conceived broadly to include authors and their writings as well as orators and the spoken word.
6 Kermode, introduction to Shakespeare, *Tempest*, lxxxviii.
7 Fish, 'Why Milton Matters,' 8, 10.
8 Lewis, *Preface to 'Paradise Lost*,' 1–3.
9 Skinner, 'Motives, Intentions and Interpretation,' 101–2.
10 Hale, 'Classical Literary Tradition,' 36.

1. Contingency, Probability, and Free Will

1 Marsh, 'Translation of *Rhetorica ad Alexandrum*,' 349.
2 See Green, 'Reception of Aristotle's *Rhetoric*,' 333n39.
3 Aristotle, *On Rhetoric*, I. ii. 1357a.14.
4 Ibid., i. 1355a.12.
5 Cicero, *Academica*, II. iii. 7–8.
6 Cicero, *De fato*, I. i. 1.
7 Cicero, *Academica*, I. xii. 46.

8 See Schmitt, *Cicero Scepticus*, 149–50.
9 Petrarch's letter to Francesco Bruni, in *Opera*, II, 824; trans. H. Nachod in *Renaissance Philosophy*, 34–5.
10 Poggio Bracciolini, *Lettere*, II, 412: 'Disceptando enim in utranque partem veritas elici consuevit.'
11 See Marsh, *Quattrocento Dialogue*; Cox, *Renaissance Dialogue*, chap. 5.
12 Agricola, *De inventione dialectica*, I. i, 2; trans. J. McNally, in 'Rudolph Agricola's *De inventione dialectica libri tres*,' 396.
13 Erasmus, *De libero arbitrio*, 38.
14 George Kennedy discusses this and other characteristics of 'a distinctive rhetoric of religion.' *New Testament Interpretation*, 6–7. The certitude of religious rhetoric, confirmed in ardent sectarian love, is discussed below in chapter 4.
15 Popkin, *History of Skepticism*, 13–14.
16 See Shapin and Schaffer, *Leviathan and the Air-Pump*; Shapiro, *Probability and Certainty*, especially chap. 2.
17 Montaigne, 'Apologie of Raymond Sebond,' 337.
18 Valla, *De voluptate*, III. iv. 29–30.
19 See Skinner, 'Moral Ambiguity,' 279–82.
20 Milton, *Areopagitica*, in *Complete Prose Works*, 2:514. Subsequent references to Milton's prose will cite this collection in the body of the text as *YP*, followed by volume and page numbers.
21 Agricola, *De inventione dialectica*, II. vi, 207; trans. M. Cogan, in 'Rodolphus Agricola,' 189.
22 Gaonkar, 'Contingency and Probability,' 154.
23 Aristotle, *On Rhetoric*, I. iv. 1359a.1–3.
24 Cicero, *De oratore*, II. lxxxii. 336.
25 Quintilian, *Institutio oratoria*, III. viii. 25–6.
26 Burke, *Rhetoric of Motives*, 50.
27 Kahn, *Rhetoric, Prudence, and Skepticism*, 35, 66
28 Charleton, *Darknes of Atheism Dispelled*, 241.
29 See Poppi, 'Fate, Fortune, Providence,' 641–2; Pine, 'Pietro Pomponazzi,' 101.
30 Augustine, *City of God*, V. ix; x: 'illud ut bene credamus, hoc ut bene vivamus.'
31 Boethius, *Consolation of Philosophy*, V. vi, 152–3.
32 For a fuller account of them see Normore, 'Future Contingents.'
33 William of Ockham, *Tractatus de praedestinatione et de praescientia Dei respectu futurorum contingentem*, Q. 1, 277–9, trans. Adams and Kretzmann, *Predestination, God's Foreknowledge*, 51.

34 Copleston, *A History of Philosophy*, 3:93.
35 Thomas Aquinas, *Summa theologiae*, 1a. q. 14, a. 13. All translations of this work are taken from the English version on the pages facing the Latin.
36 Valla, *Dialogue on Free Will*, 170–4, 180.
37 Although Valla disparages Boethius's use of philosophy, his discussion of foreknowledge draws on the same epistemological arguments made by Boethius.
38 Pomponazzi, *Immortality of the Soul*, 281, 302, 377.
39 Pomponazzi, *Libri quinque de fato, de libero arbitrio et de praedestinatione*, 326: 'Quoniam si Deus nunc scit omnia quae ventura sunt et iam in millennium scivit, cum igitur ad scientiam rei sequatur rem esse, quoniam non est scire quod non est ... sequitur igitur: si Deus scivit omnia quae erunt, illa erunt ... Ideo necessarium est ut omnia quae erunt, erunt quia non poterunt non esse. Cum itaque actus humani erunt, et de necessitate, aufertur liberum arbitrium; nam necessitas et talis libertas se excludunt.'
40 Erasmus, *De libero arbitrio*, trans. E. Rupp, 66.
41 Luther, *De servo arbitrio*, trans. P. Watson, 118.
42 Maurice Kelley, introduction to Milton, *Christian Doctrine*, YP, 6:83.
43 Perkins, *Christian and Plaine Treatise*, 619, col. 2.
44 Owen, *Display of Arminianisme*, 2–3.
45 Pierce, *Notes Concerning God's Decrees*, 48; see also 61: most human actions 'being not the effect, but the object only of God's Omniscience.'
46 Pierce, *Self-Condemnation*, 122, 126.
47 Hammond, *Pacifick Discourse of God's Grace*, 690, §1; my italics.
48 See Danielson, *Milton's Good God*, for a comprehensive survey.
49 Pierce, *Self-Condemnation*, 122.
50 Charleton, *Darknes of Atheism Dispelled*, 242.
51 Pemble, *Treatise of the Providence of God*, 275.
52 Goodwin, *Redemption Redeemed*, 26, §20.
53 Hammond, *Pacifick Discourse of God's Grace*, 692, §13.
54 Pierce, *Self-Condemnation*, 128.
55 Thomas Aquinas, *Summa theologiae*, 1a. q. 83, a. 1.
56 Perkins, *Golden Chaine*, 9.
57 Milton, *Art of Logic* (YP, 8:225): 'But these divisions of causes are not to be observed too rigorously in logic, since the whole force of an argument is contained in the proximate cause; and only to this cause does the general definition of cause apply.' It is notable that this concession undercuts his doctrine of compulsory necessity as stated in *Christian Doctrine* (YP, 6:159–60); moreover, it implies that Thomas Aquinas is, or could well be, correct in maintaining human free will as a contingent proximate cause subsumed

by the first cause of God's foreknowledge.
58 Erasmus, *De libero arbitrio*, trans. E. Rupp, 56.
59 Kahn, *Rhetoric, Prudence, and Skepticism*, 81.
60 Aristotle, *On Rhetoric*, I. ii. 1357a.12
61 Aristotle, *Poetics*, ix. 1451a.35.
62 Milton, *Paradise Lost*, III, 115–19, in *Complete Poems and Major Prose*. All quotations of Milton's poetry are from this edition. Subsequent references to *PL* are given in the body of the text, with book and line numbers.

2. Milton's Classical Rhetoricians

1 See Grafton, 'New Science'; Loewenstein, 'Humanism.'
2 Skinner, *Reason and Rhetoric*, 31; Mack, *Elizabethan Rhetoric*, 54.
3 See Skinner, *Reason and Rhetoric*, 32–5; Mack, *Elizabethan Rhetoric*, 12–14. John Colet, who founded Milton's Alma Mater, St Paul's, additionally recommended 'Cristyn auctours that wrote theyre wysdom with clene and chast laten other in verse or in prose' ('Statutes of St Paul's School,' 279). Erasmus hesitated, on stylistic grounds, to second Colet's recommendation; see Thomson, 'Latinity of Erasmus,' 121.
4 So called in Milton's tenth sonnet, 'To the Lady Margaret Ley,' 8.
5 DuRocher, *Milton Among the Romans*, 18.
6 Aristotle, *Nicomachean Ethics*, VI. iv. 1140a.3, cit. Aristotle, *On Rhetoric*, appendix IB, 289. See also Grimaldi, *Aristotle*, *'Rhetoric'*, 1:4.
7 Plato, *Phaedrus*, 277B–C (I have chosen George Kennedy's translation of this passage in *Cambridge History of Literary Criticism*, 1:189).
8 Grube, *Greek and Roman Critics*, 61.
9 See Gualdo Rosa, *La fede nella 'Paideia'*; Monfasani, 'Byzantine Rhetorical Tradition'; Nelson, '"True Liberty."'
10 Hunt, 'Plato and Aristotle,' 54.
11 Isocrates, *Panegyricus*, s. 49, in *Orations*, 1:149.
12 Isocrates, *On the Peace*, s. 8, in *Orations*, 2:11.
13 Isocrates, *Against the Sophists*, ss. 2–3, in *Orations*, 2:163–5.
14 Jaeger, *Paideia*, 3:61. The same is true in action as well as speech; on *kairos* and the rhetorical *paideia* of Isocrates see Sipiora, 'Introduction: The Ancient Concept of *Kairos*,' 1, 5, 7–15, esp. 9.
15 The primary meanings of *kairos* – 'fitness,' 'proportion,' and 'due measure' – align it with the concept of decorum. Decorum's lack of foundation in artistic principles is discussed on pages 87–9, below.
16 This expediency characterizes 'the Gorgian attitude to truth and *kairos*' (Guthrie, *Sophists*, 273n3). Gorgias, the renowned and well-travelled soph-

ist born in Sicily, was one of Isocrates' teachers.

17 Isocrates, *Panathenaicus*, ss. 30, 9, in *Orations*, 2:391–3, 379. See also *Panegyricus*, s. 9, in *Orations*, 1:125. As seen here, Isocratean *doxa* is not opinion, as in Plato, but a working theory for meeting the contingent circumstances of any human situation.

18 Isocrates, *Against the Sophists*, s. 12, in *Orations*, 2:171.

19 Isocrates, *Helen*, ss. 5, 6–7, in *Orations*, 3:63.

20 Isocrates, 'To Alexander,' s. 4, in *Orations*, 3:429.

21 Isocrates, 'To the Children of Jason,' ss. 8–9, in *Orations*, 3:439.

22 Isocrates, *On the Peace*, s. 39, in *Orations*, 2:33. *Areopagiticus*, s. 26, in *Orations*, 2:119–21.

23 Isocrates, *Nicocles*, ss. 7–9, in *Orations*, 1:81.

24 To get an idea of the word's scope, it may be noted that Erasmus cited six Latin equivalents of *logos: sermo, verbum, oratio, ratio, sapientia,* and *computatus*. He was justifying his own translation of *logos* in John 1.1 as *sermo*. See Boyle, *Erasmus on Language*, 8–9.

25 Isocrates, *Against the Sophists*, s. 21, in *Orations*, 2:177.

26 Isocrates, *To Philip*, s. 82, in *Orations*, 1:295.

27 Plato, *Gorgias*, 465A, 501A.

28 Aristotle, *On Rhetoric*, I. i. 1354a.2.

29 See Hunt, 'Plato and Aristotle,' 60–2.

30 See Kennedy, *New History of Classical Rhetoric*, 60.

31 Aristotle, *On Rhetoric*, I. i. 1355a.13.

32 Ibid., III. ii. 1404b.1–6; xii. 1414a.6.

33 Theophrastus probably treated more than four, and the idea probably did not originate with him. Attribution of the formula to him rests on the authority of Cicero, *Orator*, lxxix. See Grube, *Greek and Roman Critics*, 106–7.

34 Aristotle, *On Rhetoric*, III. ii. 1404b.1; vii. 1408a.1–b.11; III. ii. 1404b.4–5.

35 Cicero, *De oratore*, I. xiii. 55.

36 That is, created by the speaker's words, as opposed to inartificial proofs, already present at the outset – witnesses, evidence given under torture, contracts, and so forth – 'All that today would be called "evidence"' (Lanham, *Handlist of Rhetorical Terms*, 106–7). Aristotle discusses the artificial proofs at *On Rhetoric*, I. ii. 1355b.37–1356a.4; see also Grimaldi, *Aristotle, 'Rhetoric,'* 1:349–56.

37 Cicero, *De oratore*, I. xii. 53–5; II. xlii. 178; I. xi. 48, xii. 50, xiv. 63; III. v. 19, vi. 24; *Orator*, xiv. 44, xvi. 51, xix. 61.

38 Cicero, *De oratore*, III. x. 37, xiv. 53; I. viii. 32; II. xxii. 94.

39 Cicero, *De oratore*, I. viii. 33. See also *De inventione*, I. ii. 3.

40 Cicero, *De oratore*, II. xx. 85.

41 Quintilian, *Institutio oratoria*, XII. i. 1. He attributes the definition to Marcus Cato. See also I. Pr. 9.
42 Cicero, *De oratore*, II. xxxvi. 153.
43 Cicero, *De oratore*, III. xv. 57.
44 Cicero, *De partitione oratoria*, xxiii. 79.
45 Cicero, *De oratore*, III. xvi. 60, also II. xxxvi. 153. See also *Orator*, iv. 17.
46 Cicero, *De oratore*, I. xi. 48–9; xiv. 63; II. xxxv. 151; III. xxv. 143; *Orator*, iv. 14–18; xvi. 51; xxix. 62–5, xxxiii. 118; *De officiis*, I.i. 3–4.
47 Cicero, *De oratore*, II. ix. 35. Cf. Aristotle's implication that rhetoric, as a species of political science, 'lays down what we should do and from what we should refrain ... and [its] end must be the good for man.' (*Nicomachean Ethics*, I. ii. 1094b.7–8)
48 Cicero, *De oratore*, II. xvi. 68.
49 Cicero himself typified the *vita activa* during his long public career as a lawyer and, ultimately, as consul. Kennedy examines Cicero's rhetorical practice in some of his most famous orations (*New History of Classical Rhetoric*, 129–40).
50 Cicero, *De oratore*, II. lxxxi. 333.
51 Cicero, *Orator*, xxiv. 79–80.
52 Cicero, *De oratore*, III. liii. 202–6. (Quintilian quotes this passage verbatim, in *Institutio oratoria*, IX. i. 26–36.)
53 See Demetrius, *On Style*, 76 for the application of this figure in the grand style; 94–5 in the elegant; 121 in the forceful, where he notes that it is combined with two other figures.
54 Ibid., 90, 76.
55 See Kennedy, *Art of Persuasion in Greece*, 273–8.
56 Hermogenes, *Types of Style*, 1.
57 Ibid., 1.
58 See Patterson, *Hermogenes and the Renaissance*, 15–21.
59 Longinus, *On Sublimity*, i. 3–4.
60 See Grube, *Greek and Roman Critics*, 353; Russell, *Ancient Literary Criticism*, 146.
61 Longinus, *On Sublimity*, ii. 2.
62 Longinus, *On Sublimity*, xvi. 1.
63 Faber, *Dionysii Longini philosophi et rhetoris* ΠΕΡΙ ΥΨΟΥΣ, 'Notæ Minores,' 332–3: 'Ubi de figura aliqua, aut virtute orationis agit, illam exprimit, dum loquitur.' Renaissance esteem for *On Sublimity* is reflected in Faber's prefatory reference (sig. e^v) to 'Longinus in hoc AUREOLO libello (sic enim ... [Marc-Antoine] Muretus et [Isaac] Casaubonus vocarunt, non pessimi Veterum aestimatores).'

64 Longinus, *On Sublimity,* xxii. 1; xvii. 1–2; xvi. 3.
65 Longinus, *On Sublimity,* ix. 3.

3. Milton's Forerunners: Renaissance Rhetoric

1 Vickers, *Defence of Rhetoric,* 283.
2 Cicero, *Orator,* xiv. 44; xix. 61.
3 Moss, 'Humanist Education,' 147–9.
4 Vives, *De ratione dicendi,* in *Opera omnia,* 2:95: 'ita non disseret praesens
    institutio quid dicendum sit, sed quemadmodum. Quia vero, ut Julius dice-
    bat Caesar, verborum delectus origo est eloquentiae, de verbis erit primo
    agendum tamquam elementis huius propositi.'
5 Richard Lanham ascribes this linguistic virtuosity to *homo rhetoricus,* whom
    he discusses in relation to representative works from Renaissance literature
    (see *Motives of Eloquence*). On Shakespeare see Cunningham, '"With That
    Facility,"' 326.
6 Sturm's edition of Hermogenes, *De dicendi generibus,* sig. bii^v: 'Nam et sine
    rebus, verborum volubilitas est inepta atque ridicula; et rerum natura, qua-
    lis sit, intellegi non potest, nisi oratione explicetur, quae non solum elec-
    tione, sed etiam constructione verborum est conformanda.'
7 See Grafton, 'Renaissance Readers.'
8 Agricola, *De formando studio* in *Lucubrationes,* 196–7: 'In lectione id conan-
    dum in primis est, ut id quod legimus, quam maxime fieri poterit, intelliga-
    mus, et penitus habeamus perspectum nec rem tantum quae traditur, sed et
    verborum in disertis autoribus vim, proprietatem, structuram, ornatumque
    perspiciamus, quis decor, quod pondus sententiarum, quae vis explicandi,
    et res reconditas proferendi verbis, et velut in lucem conspectumque pro-
    trahendi.'
9 Kristeller, *Renaissance Thought,* 249–50.
10 Valla, *In quartum librum elegantiarum praefatio,* 620: 'nemo est qui nolit ele-
    ganter, et facunde dicere.'
11 Mosellanus, *Tabulae de schematibus et tropis,* sig. Ai^v: 'Omneis latini sermonis
    delicias, in figuris et tropis potissimum sitas esse, nemo est vel mediocriter
    eruditiorum, qui nesciat.'
12 Mack, *Elizabethan Rhetoric,* 84, 76–7.
13 Susenbrotus, *Epitome troporum ac schematum,* 83: 'Prosopopoeia, est cum rei
    sensu carenti ac mutae personam eidem idoneam fingimus. Cuiusmodi sunt
    Stultitiae apud Erasmum, Virtutis ac voluptatis, quas Prodicus sophista
    apud Herculem inter sese decertantes facit, ut autor est Xenophon.'
14 Not that this is the only way he read. See Festa, 'Repairing the Ruins,'

which discusses Milton's emendatory reading practices in relation to his teaching practice and, more broadly, identifies that manner of reading as expressive of right reason and judicious choice in the pursuit of truth.

15 Erasmus, 'To Johann von Botzheim,' trans. R.A.B. Mynors, in *CWE*, 9: 354.

16 Kristeller, *Renaissance Thought*, 251.

17 Vickers, 'Rhetoric and Poetics,' 736.

18 Peacham, *Garden of Eloquence* (1577), sig. Aiii[r].

19 Cicero, *Orator*, xxviii. 97; Erasmus, *De copia* in *Opera* I.6, 26, trans. B. Knott, in *CWE*, 24:297.

20 Kennedy, *Classical Rhetoric*, 116–19, 173.

21 Erasmus, *De ratione studii*, in *Opera* I.2, 117, trans. B. McGregor, in *CWE*, 24:670.

22 Bolgar, *Classical Heritage*, 269, 300. See also Vickers, 'Rhetorical and Anti-Rhetorical Tropes,' 106–7, 121.

23 Susenbrotus, *Epitome troporum ac schematum*, 1–2: 'ad autores et prophanos et sacros rite intelligendos, haud mediocriter faciunt ... quo ... simulque haberetis scribendi dicendique formulas, quas assiduo usu imitari liceret.'

24 See Grafton, 'Teacher, Text and Pupil,' 42–3; Blair, 'Ovidius Methodizatus,' 87–8.

25 See Moss, *Latin Commentaries*, 31, 134–5; Mack, 'Renaissance Habits of Reading,' 9, and 'Ramus Reading,' 118; Ward, *Ciceronian Rhetoric*, 205–9.

26 Sherry, *Treatise of Schemes and Tropes*, sig. Avii[v].

27 Keckermann, *Rhetorica ecclesiastica*, 122: 'quae mirifice faciunt ad amplificandum et movendos animos ... Id quidem verum est, magnum decus esse in *Schematibus*, quae vocant Rhetores, *Sententiarum*.'

28 Burton, 'Democritus Junior to the Reader,' preface to *Anatomy of Melancholy*, 1:13; Jonson, *Timber*, 8:625, cit. Martindale, *English Humanism*, 206. For the passage Jonson is translating see Vives, *De ratione dicendi*, in *Opera omnia*, 2: 130. Seneca's Letter 114 provides an influential classical analogue for this idea; for example, Caussin, *De eloquentia sacra et humana*, 78, incorporates part of it verbatim, beginning with the famous 'Talis hominibus fuit oratio, qualis vita,' into his discussion 'De optimo charactere eloquentiae.' Vives, cited above, also alludes to this letter.

29 See Vickers, 'Power of Persuasion.'

30 Edward Gibbon's most recent editor observes in his introduction that 'it is difficult to separate considerations of style and thought in *Decline and Fall*, and the reason for this lies in Gibbon's maxim that "style is the image of character." Not only might style express a pre-existing personality: one might equally fashion, through writing, a character to assume' (xiv).

31 See Rebhorn, *Emperor of Men's Minds*, 13.

32 Sidney, *Defense of Poesy*, 616.

33 Gadamer, *Truth and Method*, 337.

34 Colet, 'Statutes of St Paul's School,' 279.

35 Elyot, *Boke named the Governour*, 60. For his reference to Cicero see *De oratore*, I. xii. 51.

36 Ascham, *Scholemaster*, 265. Cf. Cicero, *De oratore*, III. xvi. 60–1; xix. 72–3; *Orator*, v. 17; also Erasmus, page 66 and n66 below. Arguments shading the other way are those of Pico, above, Bacon's famous caution against humanistic over-attention to style in *Advancement of Learning*, in *Works*, 3: 282–4, Caussin's very similar caution in *De eloquentia sacra et humana*, 359–60, and Keckermann's warnings, drawing on Aristotle and Augustine, that the 'gravitas' of homiletic subjects will be diminished by inappropriately splendid eloquence (*Rhetorica ecclesiastica*, 118–19). These writers, however, do not oppose Ascham's humanist position. The spirit of their advice is rather that equal attention should be paid to content and style, a unity 'betwixt the tong and the hart' consonant with the view of Ascham and Erasmus.

37 Peacham, *Garden of Eloquence* (1577), sigs. Aii^r–Aiii^r; Wilson, *Art of Rhetoric*, 187.

38 Monfasani, *George of Trebizond*, 266, 283.

39 Ibid., 331. See also Cantimori, 'Rhetoric and Politics,' on the tension between idealized and practical rhetoric in Italian politics.

40 Skinner, *Reason and Rhetoric*, 67–87.

41 See Gilbert, *Renaissance Concepts of Method*, 13, for the continuing influence of this idea in the Renaissance and 58 on its adoption by humanists. See also 69, 78, 111, 221.

42 Susenbrotus, *Epitome troporum ac schematum*, 3: 'Hanc obviis, ut aiunt, manibus excipite, legite, relegite, ac animo inscribite, tum in scribendi ac loquendi usum redigite, cum alioqui (ut saepenumero vobis inculcavi) citra meditationem ac usum ars omnis omni omnino utilitate vacet. Quod si feceritis Musarum ianuae proculdubio vobis aperientur.'

43 Erasmus, *Ciceronianus*, in *Opera* I.2, 626, trans. B. Knott, in *CWE*, 28:369.

44 Langbaine, *Liber de grandi loquentia sive sublimi dicendi genere*, 3: 'Pace vestra, Theologi, non majori compendio ad sacras literas itur quam per profanas; nec in acie Christiana fortius militaverit, quam qui in Gentilium castris tyrocinium egit.'

45 Vettori, *Commentarii in librum Demetrii Phalerei De elocutione*, sig. biv^v: 'De utilitate huius operis, et quantos fructus ferre possit illis qui diligenter ipsum legerint, nihil attinet disputare ... Hanc [eloquentiam] igitur, quae

tantam vim habet, in primis ipsum tenere et validam undique, omnique ratione auctam exornatamque possidere oportet.'

46 Laurentius, *In Hermogenis tractatum De ideis*, 594: 'Quanta sit autem vis, et praestantia in his duobus libris Hermongenis perspicient illi ... qui orationes habent in foro, in Curia, in Comitiis, in Conciliis, in Senatu: imo et in ipsa Dei Ecclesia. Illi denique, qui in munere oratorio occupati, pro diversarum rerum tractandarum ratione, coguntur uti variis dicendi generibus.'

47 Pagano, *De sublimi genere dicendi* (unsigned leaves): 'eis tu quoque omnibus gravissime, ac sapientissime respondes, quique tanta dicendi granditate, tantoque artificio in rebus belli, pacisque tractandis uteris, ut non mirum sit, si ita tuorum senatorum animi permoveantur, ut facere non possint, quin tibi omnibus in rebus assentiantur.'

48 da Petra, *De grandi, sive sublimi genere orationis*, 7–8.

49 Rebhorn, *Emperor of Men's Minds*, chap. 1, esp. 46–55. Norbrook, *Writing the English Republic*, 137–9, 215; on the English republicans' revival of classical rhetoric and humanist political eloquence see 36, 135, 209, 282, 331, 359.

50 Cicero, *De oratore*, II. ix. 35.

51 Vives, *De ratione dicendi*, in *Opera omnia*, 2:164, 183–4.

52 Bacon, *De augmentis scientiarum*, in *Works*, 1:672; trans. F. Headlam, in Bacon, *Works*, 4:455–6.

53 See Briggs, *Francis Bacon*, 17, 157–69.

54 Bacon, *De augmentis scientiarum*, 4:456.

55 Wilson, *Art of Rhetoric*, 42; Rainolde, *Foundacion of Rhetoric*, fols i^r, ii^v; Erasmus, *De copia* in *Opera* I.6, 232, 236, 258, trans. B. Knott, in *CWE*, 24:607, 611–12, 635.

56 See Gray, 'Renaissance Humanism,' 208.

57 Peacham, *Compleat Gentleman*, 1:121.

58 Pender, 'Open Use of Living,' 385.

59 George of Trebizond, *Rhetoricorum libri quinque*, 350: 'Haec quum maxima pars prudentiae sit ... tum vel maxime singularum circumstantiarum acri existimatione conficitur. Qua in re, si quis non parum profecerit, intelliget se multum et in providendo, et in dicendo, consecutum esse.'

60 Monfasani, *George of Trebizond*, 294; see also 267–8 on the amorality of this power.

61 Baumlin, 'Ciceronian Decorum,' 140, 143, 156.

62 Milton, *De doctrina Christiana*, in *Works*, 17:36: 'Prudentia est virtus qua prospicimus quo quidque tempore et loco sit agendum. Prov. xxix. 11. *totum spiritum suum profert stolidus; at sapiens reprimit eum.*' I abandon the Yale translation in this instance.

63 Burchard, 'Epistola Hermolai nova ac subditicia,' in Melanchthon, *Opera*,

IX, col. 694: 'Requirit [eloquentia] summam prudentiam in rebus investigandis, atque collocandis, copiam verborum amplissimam, iudicium acerrimum in delectu.'

64 More, 'Letter to Oxford,' trans. D. Kinney, *Complete Works*, 15:138–9.

65 Melanchthon, *De utilitate studiorum eloquentiae*, in *Opera*, XI, cols 368–9: 'Etsi enim non est exigua utilitas, instructum esse copia sermonis, tamen exercitatio dicendi etiam de multis rebus format iudicia ... Hae cogitationes aliquid ad prudentiam conducunt, ac de multis magnis rebus nos admonent, de moribus, de iure, de actionum ac iudiciorum varietate, de natura rerum.'

66 Hoffman, *Rhetoric and Theology*, 222. For Erasmus a polished style was 'important an expression of both the clarity of thought and the purity of ethical and religious disposition' (77). Boyle, *Erasmus on Language*, 40, compares Erasmus and Isocrates on language as a reflection of character; see also 41–2, 68.

67 Sturm's edition of Hermogenes, *De dicendi generibus*, 20: 'oportet ... ut eadem [oratio] habeat suum quasi animum, suam mentem, indolem, suum ingenium, et quosdam peculiares mores: ergo debent in oratione esse significationes morum, sapientiae, prudentiae, fortitudinis, religionis, pietatis, studii erga Rempublicam, oportet ut sit morata oratio, habeat ἦθος, quod genus dicendi comparatum est ad conciliandum.'

68 Curtius, *European Literature and the Latin Middle Ages*, 70 (cited hereafter as *ELLMA*).

69 Weinberg, *History of Literary Criticism*, 1:109. See also Plett, 'Place and Function of Style.'

70 Descartes, *Discours de la méthode*, 7; Vettori, *Commentarii in librum Demetrii Phalerei De elocutione*, 59: 'artificiumque poetae in caelum tollit.'

71 Tuve, *Elizabethan and Metaphysical Imagery*, 184.

72 Scaliger, *Poetices libri septem*, 2:310: 'Cum prisci oratores id agerent modo, ut moverent (incondite namque suadebant), poetae vero, ut oblectarent tantum (cantiunculis enim solis otium transigebant), utrique ab alteris postea id quo carebant mutuati sunt.'

73 Thomas Sébillet, 'Art Poétique français (1548),' cit. Plett, *Rhetoric and Renaissance Culture*, 89.

74 Sidney, *Defense of Poesy*, 608, 612.

75 Spenser, 'Letter to Raleigh,' 15, preface to *Faerie Queene*.

76 Jonson, *Timber: or Discoveries*, in *Works*, 8:595.

77 See Aguzzi-Barbagli, 'Humanism and Poetics.'

78 Valla, *Repastinatio dialecticie et philosophie*, 176; trans. Mack, in *Renaissance Argument*, 110–11.

79 Valla, *De voluptate*, III. proem, 1. Subsequent citations are incorporated into the text.
80 Cf. Quintilian, *Institutio oratoria*, VI. ii. 26–9; Cicero, *De oratore*, II. xlv. 189–90; chap. 5n24, below, on Erasmus and others.
81 Valla, *Encomium sancti Thomae Aquinatis*, in *Opera omnia*, 2:350; trans. as *In Praise of St Thomas Aquinas*, 24.
82 Vickers, 'Valla's Ambivalent Praise of Pleasure,' 293.
83 Lucretius, *De rerum natura*, I. 143–5.
84 Valla, *In quartum librum elegantiarum praefatio*, 616: 'Et si ex his qui bene canunt, bene pingunt, bene fingunt, caeterisque artibus multum usus atque ornamenti divinis accedit rebus, ut prope ad hanc rem natae esse videantur: profecto multo plus accedet ex eloquentibus.'
85 See Curtius, *ELLMA*, 159–62.
86 Boyle, *Erasmus on Language*, 70–1, 119. Most of the points in this paragraph draw on her book and on Hoffman, *Rhetoric and Theology*. See also Rice, *Renaissance Idea of Wisdom*, 156–63, on the construction of Erasmian wisdom out of both piety and human learning, scripture and the classics.
87 Erasmus, *Apologia contra Latomi dialogum*, cit. Hoffman, *Rhetoric and Theology*, 91.
88 Erasmus, *Ratio verae theologiae*, cit. Boyle, *Erasmus on Language*, 73.
89 Erasmus, *Ecclesiastes*, 126: 'Nunc per oratoris singula officia decurremus, sed ita ut memineris nos non patronum forensem, sed divini verbi praeconem instruere.'
90 Erasmus, *Ciceronianus*, in *Opera*, I.2, 650, trans. B. Knott, in *CWE*, 28:400.
91 Hoffman, *Rhetoric and Theology*, 191–200, gives a full discussion of prudence as a rhetorical virtue for Erasmus.

4. Milton's Concept of Rhetoric

1 Foxe, *Acts and Monuments*, 8:313–15.
2 Clark, *John Milton at St Paul's*, 158. Milton mentions analysis and genesis as the two types of artistic practice in *Art of Logic* (*YP*, 8:215). On Milton's rhetorical education at Cambridge see Fletcher, *Intellectual Development of John Milton*, 2:215–18.
3 Clark, *John Milton at St Paul's*, 176.
4 Agricola, *De inventione dialectica*, I. i, 1: 'docere quidem rem facilem esse, et quam quisque tantum non inertissimae mentis praestare possit: concutere vero affectibus audientem, et in quemcumque velis, animi habitum transformare, allicere item, audiendique voluptate tenere suspensum, non nisi summis et maiori quodam Musarum afflatu instinctis contingere ingeniis.'

5 Caussin, *De eloquentia sacra et humana*, 459: 'Atque eius quidem eloquentiae, quae in affectibus dominatur, summum est imperium: nam coetus hominum tenet, mentes allicit, voluntates impellit quo vult, et unde vult deducit, opem fert supplicibus, excitat afflictos, reis dat salutem, liberat periculis, ad summum, mitem quandem tyrannidem in pectoribus hominum constituit.'

6 Wilson, *Art of Rhetoric*, 42.

7 Vossius, *Rhetorices contractae*, 116–17. 'verum homines non ratione solum sed etiam affectu, imo magna pars hoc pene solo ducuntur. Quapropter accedemus nunc ad πάθη sive affectus ... quatenus conducunt ad persuadendum: atque ut tum moveantur, tum sedentur.'

8 See Conley, *Rhetoric in the European Tradition*, 157.

9 Vossius, *Rhetorices contractae*, 117, 118: 'apud viros sapientes, et cordatos, haud opus sit eos [affectus] ciere ... tamen apud rudem populum, qui rationum pondus parum perpendit, omnino movere animos opus est, quo ad honestas actiones melius perducatur ... Quod recte fieri, etiam Jesaiae, Pauli, et aliorum coelestium vatum exemplo docetur, qui non contenti docere, affectus quoque cient.'

10 Mosellanus, *Tabulae de schematibus et tropis*, sig. Ai^v: 'oratio non undique sui similis, verum suis interspersa figuris, suis variata tropis, auditorum aures capit, mereturque applausam.'

11 Colet, 'Statutes of St Paul's School,' 292.

12 Plato, *Phaedrus*, 260E.

13 Plato, *Republic*, 477A-480A, in *Collected Dialogues*.

14 Abbott, *Writings and Speeches of Oliver Cromwell*, 3:51.

15 Mussato, Epistle 7: 'Quisquis erat vates, vas erat ille dei,' cit. Curtius, *ELLMA*, 216.

16 Milton, 'Elegy 6,' 77: 'Diis etinem sacer est vates, divumque sacerdos.'

17 Clark, *John Milton at St Paul's*, 185.

18 Nizolio, *De veris principiis*, 2:33: 'Nunc tamen illud et veterum authoritate, et Ciceronis testimonio constare volumus, Philosophiam et Oratoriam non duas esse facultates separatas, sed unam eandemque ex rebus et verbis tanquam animantem quandam ex corpore et anima compositam.' Cf. Caussin, *De eloquentia sacra et humana*, 357; Sturm's edition of Hermogenes, *De dicendi generibus*, sig. bii^v; Vives, *De ratione dicendi*, 94, 130–5, 143–6.

19 Milton, 'At a Vacation Exercise,' 23–6.

20 Jacques Peletier, 'Art Poétique (1555),' cit. Plett, *Rhetoric and Renaissance Culture*, 113.

21 Wilson, *Art of Rhetoric*, 187. See also Puttenham, *Arte of English Poesie*, 138.

22 Erasmus, *De copia*, in *Opera* I.6, 36, trans. B. Knott, in *CWE*, 24:306; see also *Opera* I.6, 37n225.

23 Cicero, *Orator*, xxi. 70, 71; *De oratore*, III. lv. 212; Quintilian, *Institutio oratoria*, VI. v. 11.

24 Isocrates, *Antidosis*, s. 271, in *Orations*, 2:335. See also *Against the Sophists*, ss. 12–14, in *Orations*, 2:171–3.

25 Vives, *De ratione dicendi*, 183–4; *De conscribendis epistolis*, in *Opera omnia*, 2:265: 'a nobis vero tradendis artibus adjuvatur, non perficitur: admonetur, non omnino instituitur.'

26 Puttenham, *Arte of English Poesie*, 261.

27 Longinus, *On Sublimity*, vi. 1.

28 Augustine, *On Christian Doctrine*, IV. xx, trans. D.W. Robertson. All subsequent quotations of this text are from Robertson's translation.

29 Laurentius, *In Hermogenis tractatum De ideis*, 637: 'δεινός denique oratoris est quam Cicero Eloquentem appellat, oratoris munus complectens atque explens ea quae nulla arte, nullis praeceptis possunt nominatim tradi. Huius igitur munus est, dignoscere quid causa, quid res tractanda postulet, quid personis conveniat, locis, temporibus.'

30 The fullest explanation of what decorum consists in can perhaps be reached through Gadamer's discussion of the aesthetic consciousness, in particular of 'taste' and 'judgement' as two of the guiding concepts of humanism: 'Both taste and judgement evaluate the object in relation to the whole to see whether it fits in with everything else – that is, whether it is "fitting". One must have a "sense" for it. It cannot be demonstrated.' There is, then, no method or art involved in determining what is appropriate – doing so is a matter of 'tact,' resting on a priori principles. In literature, what is fitting, the correct choice of style for subject, emerges intuitively from an author's 'feeling for style' (*Stilgefühl*), with no rational account behind the choice that can be taught or even hinted at. How decorum works, in short, cannot really be explained. See *Truth and Method*, 9–42, 493–7. It is also noteworthy that Gadamer emphasizes the dual application of taste and judgment in aesthetics *and* ethics – making the right decisions both in evaluating art and in evaluating courses of action.

31 Kranidas, *Fierce Equation*, 91–102, discusses Milton's insistence on decorum of character.

32 Kranidas, *Milton's Rhetoric of Zeal*, 45.

33 Augustine, *On Christian Doctrine*, IV. xxvii, xxix. The earliest classical statement on the persuasive efficacy of the orator's character appears to be Isocrates, *Antidosis*, s. 278, in *Orations*, 2:339.

34 See Cicero, *De oratore*, II. xlii. 184.

35 Milton advanced this simple equation as a polemical convention and, of course, had a more complex and realistic view about the bad but eloquent speaker, which will be treated later in chapters 8–10.

36 Erasmus, *Ciceronianus*, in *Opera* I.2, 655, trans. B. Knott, in *CWE*, 24:407.

37 Cicero, *De oratore*, III. xiv. 55, designates eloquence one of the supreme virtues; cf. Quintilian, *Institutio oratoria*, II. xx. 8–9.

38 Dryden, 'The Author's Apology for Heroique Poetry; and Poetique License,' preface to *State of Innocence*, in *Works*, 12:97.

39 Skinner, 'Republican Ideal of Political Liberty,' 303.

40 Struever, *Language of History*, 31. On history and style see also von Maltzahn, *Milton's 'History of Britain,'* 50–2, 62; Mack, *Elizabethan Rhetoric*, 150–2.

41 'Lapi Casteliunculi oratio Bononiae habita in suo legendi initio ad scolares et alios tunc ibi praesentes,' in Müllner, *Reden und Briefe Italienischer Humanisten*, 135: 'illud praeterea pulcherrimum atque amplissimum munus ego eloquentiae esse arbitror, quod maiorum praeclarissimas res gestas monumentis suis et litteris prodat, quo uno mortales res immortales fieri, caducae aeternae, absentes adesse, mortui vivere, loqui muti, caeci denique videre videantur.'

42 See Kelley, 'Theory of History,' 747; Struever, *Language of History*, 61, 77.

43 See Patrides, *Phoenix and the Ladder*. He compares the classical view of history, cyclical in nature, in which everything that has been will be again, with the linear Christian view that begins in the Book of Genesis and ends in Revelation.

44 See Firth, 'Milton as an Historian,' 81–2.

45 Patrides, *Phoenix and the Ladder*, 36–8.

46 Patrides, *Milton and the Christian Tradition*, 257.

47 Sloane, *Donne, Milton*, 233.

48 Ong, *Ramus, Method*, 272.

49 See Major, 'Milton's View of Rhetoric'; Hardison, 'Orator and the Poet,' 40–1; Patterson, *Hermogenes and the Renaissance*, 212; Fish, *Surprised by Sin*, 127. For more accurate interpretations of Milton's views see Samuel, 'Milton on the Province of Rhetoric' and 'Milton on Style'; Steadman, *Hill and the Labyrinth*, esp. 57–8; Wittreich, 'Milton's Idea of the Orator,' and '"Crown of Eloquence."'

50 Jameela Lares writes that in this episode of *PR*, 'Milton's Christ participates in contemporary discussions about Scriptural style ... Christ's response about the "majestic unaffected style" of the Scriptures is by no means a retreat from rhetoric and humanism but a statement identifying Milton

with the progressive side in these discussions' (*Milton and the Preaching Arts*, 197–8).
51 Norbrook, *Writing the English Republic*, 454–5.

5. The Voice of God: Rhetoric and Religion

1 Bacon, *Advancement of Learning*, in *Works*, 3:283–5.
2 Vickers, *English Science*, 9; Steadman, *Hill and the Labyrinth*, 35, 54.
3 Bacon, *Advancement of Learning*, in *Works*, 3:384, 389.
4 Gilbert, *Renaissance Concepts of Method*, 120, discusses the gradual extension of dialectical methodology into 'a more empirically-minded tradition' of objective research. Bacon assigned topical invention a role in the production of new knowledge, since the topics could direct the course of inquiry; see *De augmentis scientiarum*, in *Works*, 1:635–6; Briggs, *Francis Bacon*, 199–201. For Agricola, 'dialectic ... is designed to exploit and improve the results of inquiry,' though it is not itself a method of inquiry or of discovering new knowledge; see Cogan, 'Rodolphus Agricola,' 182–9.
5 Hobbes, *Leviathan*, 35–6.
6 See Vickers, 'Royal Society,' and introduction, in *English Science*.
7 Kennedy, *Classical Rhetoric*, 143.
8 Valla, *In quartum librum elegantiarum praefatio*, 620: Jerome borrowed eloquence from his 'lectio gentilium' and carefully sifted their words, 'quod ceteri omnes Latini Graecique fecerunt, Hilarius, Ambrosius, Augustinus, Lactantius, Basilius, Gregorius, Chrysostomus aliique plurimi, qui in omni aetate praetiosas illas divini eloquii gemmas auro argentoque eloquentiae vestierunt, neque alteram propter alteram scientiam reliquerunt.'
9 Augustine, *On Christian Doctrine*, IV. xii, xvii–xxv. For cross-references to the relevant passages from Cicero's rhetorical treatises see the notes in *De doctrina christiana*.
10 Ibid., IV. xxvi, viii, xiii, iv.
11 Ibid., III. xxix.
12 Cassiodorus believed that they were in fact the original source of rhetoric, as well as of the other six liberal arts, and that the seeds of all secular disciplines, derived thence by the ancients, had been hidden there by God; see O'Donnell, *Cassiodorus*, 158–9. Ambrose thought similarly; see Murphy, *Rhetoric in the Middle Ages*, 52.
13 Augustine, *On Christian Doctrine*, IV. vi.
14 See Curtius, *ELLMA*, 40.
15 Augustine, *On Christian Doctrine*, IV. vi, vii.
16 Erasmus, *Ecclesiastes*, 126: 'Nunc per oratoris singula officia decurremus,

sed ita ut memineris nos non patronum forensem, sed divini verbi praeconem instruere.' Melanchthon, *De officiis concionatoris*, f. 55ᵛ, contrasts the
primacy of biblical testimony with 'coniecturae aut strophae, quae saepe
plurimum oratori in civilibus causis prosunt,' but that carry no weight (*nec
valent*) in the Christian arena.

17 Erasmus, *Ecclesiastes*, 185: 'Sed multo magis Ecclesiasten, qui verus est
Demagogus.'

18 Ibid., 269: 'Hoc tantum interest, quod forensis orator amplificando conatur
efficere, ut res maior appareat quam est: elevando, ut minor quam est.
Utrunque praestigii et imposturae genus est. Ecclesiastae satis est efficere,
ut res tanta videatur quanta est, maior aut minor, quam multis videtur.
Nam vulgi de rebus fere praeposterum est iudicium.' Cf. Hyperius, *Practis
of Preaching*, f. 36ᵛ.

19 Vickers, 'Recovery of Rhetoric,' 36, incorrectly says that 'Erasmus ...
refus[ed] any dichotomy between pagan rhetoric and Christian values.'

20 Erasmus, *Ecclesiastes*, 332: 'At Augustinus, vir tantus, censet vigilanter [tro-
pos esse] attendendos, atque etiam memoria tenendos, quod horum cognitio
Scripturarum ambiguitatibus dissolvendis sit, ut ait, praecipue necessaria.'
The passage of Augustine to which he refers is quoted below on page 106.

21 Erasmus, *Ecclesiastes*, 335: 'Constat igitur Scripturam canonicam, typis,
schematibus ac tropis opertam esse. Nullus tamen tropus, nec ullum
schema plus exhibet Ecclesiastis negotii, quam allegoria.' At 332–3 he cites
a number of biblical tropes, especially as interpreted by Augustine, and discusses synecdoche. See Hoffman, *Rhetoric and Theology*, 113, and Boyle, *Erasmus on Language*, 118–20, 125–6, on the centrality of allegory in Erasmian
hermeneutics.

22 Erasmus, *Ecclesiastes*, 294: 'Faciunt ad orationis acrimonium ac vehemen-
tiam'; for example, three varieties of repetitio are shown in biblical
instances where 'faciunt ... ad obiurgandum, exhortandum et exproban-
dum.' Amplification is discussed on 266–85 and the emotive appeal of figures of thought or imagery, 288.

23 Erasmus, *Ciceronianus* in *Opera* I.2, 646, trans. B. Knott, *CWE*, 28:395.

24 Erasmus, *Ecclesiastes*, 294: 'nihil esse efficacius ad concitandos pios affectus,
quam si ipse fueris pie adfectus ... Scite dictum est, nihil incendere nisi
ignem. Mens ignea linguam facit igneam ... Nemo efficaciter inflammat ad
pietam, nisi qui vere pius est. Nemo potentius revocat a vitiis, quam qui
ipse ex animo odit vitia. Per hunc enim spiritus ipse loquitur, suumque
donum transfundit in auditores.' Cf. Hyperius, *Practis of Preaching*, f. 43ʳ;
Perkins, *Arte of Prophecying*, 671; Glanvill, *Essay concerning Preaching*, 54. See
also Cicero, *De oratore*, II. xlv. 189–90.

25 Erasmus, *Ecclesiastes*, 109–10: 'Proinde vereor ne cui videatur ineptum hic de rhetorum praeceptis meminisse, quod artis significatio fidem dicentis elevet in tantum, ut summus ille orator existimet caput artis esse, artem dissimulare. Quisquis enim credit eum ex arte dicere quem audit, quoniam sibi putat strui insidias ab artifice, cavet ab assentiendo, et huc potius intendit animum, ut observet, quam ingeniose aut quam callide dicat, non quam salubriter.' Cf. Reuchlin, *Liber congestorum*, sig. Aiii^v; Hyperius, *Practis of Preaching*, f. 16^r; Perkins, *Arte of Prophecying*, 670; T. Hall, *Vindiciae Literarum*, 55.

26 Erasmus, *Ecclesiastes*, 127: 'Habent sacrae literae decorem ac speciem suam, licet fucum et lenocinia nesciant.'

27 Reuchlin, *Liber congestorum*, sig. Aiii^r: 'Ars praedicandi est facultas hominem alliciendi ad virtutes, et contemplationem divinam, ex sanctarum scriptuarum promulgatione. Praedicator est vir religiosus, dicendi peritus, autoritate superioris ecclesiastico pulpito praefectus. Quaecumque igitur res inciderit, hominum saluti necessaria, quae sit dictione explicanda, eam qui prudenter, et composite, et ornate, et memoriter dicet cum quadam actionis etiam dignitate, is tanto nomine dignus censebitur.'

28 Melanchthon, *Elementorum rhetorices libri duo*, 29–30: 'Ad quid Eloquentia conducit? Ad maximas ac difficillimas causas omnes in hac tota civili vitae consuetudine explicandas: ad retinendam Religionem, et illustrandam, Dei: ad interpretandas ac defendendas leges'; *De officiis concionatoris*, f. 54^v: 'Vides autem nos ex rhetorica, quoniam ratio concionandi illius artis, quaedam vel pars, vel imago est, quaedam concionum genera mutuatos esse.'

29 Hyperius, *Practis of Preaching*, f. 9^v. Tropes and figures, which he supposes to be already well known and to which the Christian orator has full licence, amplify and move the affections (ff. 36^v, 38^r, 48^r). Their abuse, however, impairs graceful speaking; therefore, decorum must moderate their use (f. 177^r).

30 Ibid., ff. 17^v, 18^r, 19^v. Cf. Reuchlin's discussion of the topics, based on Cicero, with biblical examples provided for many of them (*Liber congestorum*, sigs Avii^v-Biii^v).

31 Hyperius, *Practis of Preaching*, ff. 41^{r-v}, 49^v.

32 Westheimer, *Collectanea troporum*, sig. ii^r: 'sacrarum literarum haud postremam intelligentiae partem, positam esse in ipsis Tropis et formulis loquendi cuique linguae familiaribus.'

33 Shuger, *Sacred Rhetoric*, 93; see also 74, 92, 194–204.

34 Augustine, *On Christian Doctrine*, III. xxix. The passage influenced exegetes such as Erasmus (see n. 20, above) and Westheimer, who quotes it in *Collectanea troporum*, sig. Iiii^{r-v}.

35 J. Smith, *Mystery of Rhetorique Unvail'd*, preface, without signatures. He drew
    the idea from another advocate of tropological hermeneutics, Thomas Hall;
    see his *Rhetorica Sacra*, sig. L3^v: 'the ignorance of Rhetorick is one ground of
    many errors amongst us, as will appear in the opening of the Tropes, where
    you have not onely bare instances, but many Texts cleared and expounded.'
36 Perkins, *Arte of Prophecying*, 654–5.
37 Erasmus, *Ecclesiastes*, 335: 'Accipte, hoc est corpus meum, quod pro vobis
    traditur: si per tropum, *est*, interpreteris *significat*, aut *corpus* interpreteris
    signum corpus, non sunt defuturi qui tuae reclament interpretationi. At
    si hunc in modum interpreteris, hoc symbolum quod vobis exhibeo,
    significat indissolubilem unitatem meam, qui sum caput, et corporis mei
    mystici, quod est Ecclesia, quoniam tropus subservit recto sensui, non est
    rejiciendus.'
38 Ibid., 332: 'Tametsi non me fugit, esse qui locum hunc expediant absque
    tropo.'
39 Among a wide variety of human arts, even military discipline, 'Rhetoricke
    is also necessarie, because everywhere a Divine shall meet with figurative
    speeches in holy Scripture, which without Rhetoricke he cannot explain'
    (Bernard, *Faithfull Shepherd*, 47). Bernard gives a standard overview.
    Another defence of human learning, including rhetoric, as necessary for
    understanding the Bible is T. Hall, *Vindiciae Literarum*. Hall cites Solomon,
    Isaiah, and Paul as great orators. See also his *Rhetorica Sacra* and *Centuria
    Sacra*. John Prideaux, *Sacred Eloquence*, also gives detailed analysis of tropes
    and figures in a Christian context, often with biblical examples.
40 Lukin, *Introduction to the Holy Scripture*. His remark is at sig. A3^r and
    Owens's is at sig. A8^r.
41 H. Smith, 'A Glasse for Drunkards,' in *Sermons*, 281.
42 Perkins, *Arte of Prophecying*, 670.
43 See Lewalski, *Protestant Poetics*, 219–26.
44 Bernard, *Faithfull Shepherd*, 48.
45 Glanvill, *Essay concerning Preaching*, 20–3 (no leaf 21–2), 55–6.
46 Baxter, *Gildas Salvianus*, 123.
47 Adams, 'Plaine-Dealing,' 126, 130.
48 Brinsley, 'Parlie with the Sword,' 2.
49 See T. Hall, *Rhetorica Sacra*, 174, on one type of metonymy of the adjunct:
    'the signe is oft put for the thing signified, as ... the sworde for authority [or
    for an army], it being a signe of it,' like the sword in Jeremiah.
50 J. Hall, 'The Deceit of Appearance,' in *Works*, 5:130–1.
51 J. Hall, 'Christ and Caesar,' in *Works*, 5:282.
52 J. Hall, 'The Great Imposter' in *Works*, 5:137.

53 Mitchell, *English Pulpit Oratory,* 203, cites the 'honeycomb of biblical texts of which the sermons of the extreme Puritans consisted' as an abuse in preaching.

54 Ong, *Ramus, Method,* 284.

55 Augustine, *On Christian Doctrine,* IV. xxviii.

56 P. Miller, *New England Mind,* 347.

57 J. Smith, *Mysterie of Rhetorique Unvail'd,* preface (without signatures).

58 Erasmus, *Ecclesiastes,* 332: 'Totus enim hominum sermo tropis dissertus est. Sic autem visum est divinae sapientiae nobiscum vulgatissimo more quodammodo balbutire.'

59 Glanvill, *Essay concerning Preaching,* 56.

60 Glass, *Philologiae sacrae,* 1116: 'Ἀνθρωποπάθεια est metaphora, qua quod ... homini, proprie competit, ad Deum et res divinas per quandem ρimili-tudinem transfertur. Vocatur et συγκατάβασις, *condescencio,* quia in sermone sacrosancto Jehova quasi descendit ad nos, et verbis humanis mysteria sua coelestia exprimit.' On the origins of this term see Rex, *Reformation Rhetoric,* 176n1; he traces its substantive coinage for hermeneutic purposes to Martin Bucer (1529). Later, John Smith lists 'this metaphorical form of speech' anthropopathia, or 'condescencio,' in *Mysterie of Rhetorique Unvail'd* (1656), 204–5, discussing it in words that indicate virtually a direct translation of Flacius or Glass as his source.

61 Westheimer, *Collectanea troporum,* ff. 21^v–22^r: 'Sic propheta David, Deum sedentem, videntem, animam subsannantem, in ira hostibus loquentem facit: quae fictio personae dici potest, quo humaniter dicta poenitus sensi-bus insiderent. Talis vero prosopopoeiae habetur.'

62 Susenbrotus, *Epitome troporum ac schematum,* 66: 'Prosopopoeia (προσωποποιΐα Confirmatio, Personae fictio) est quum rebus inanimatis per-sonam, sermonem aut actionem homini congruam tribuimus ... Deum denique ipsum ac divos loquentes facimus. Ita Micheas propheta, deum introducit cum populo suo expostulantem.'

63 Flacius, *Clavis scripturae,* II. iv. col. 339: 'Incomprehensibila sunt Dei opera et actiones: neque nos assequi aliquid de iis possemus, nisi Sacra Scriptura iis uteretur loquendi de Deo formulis, quae rebus humanis propinquae sunt. Itaque Spiritui sancto Scripturarum autori placet propter captus nostri imbecillitatem nostro more balbutire, et blandius, humiliusque, quam majestati tantae, convenit, nobiscum per signa et verba agere.'

64 Beza, *Novum Testamentum,* 8: 'Certe magna vis est horum verborum, ex qui-bus intelligimus, non ipsos Prophetas, sed Dominum ore Prophetarum loqui.' See also sig. *iiii on the rhetorical expressions of 'loquens Spiritus

sanctus' in the New Testament and Beza's philological method of comparing them with examples 'ex profanis authoribus petita.'

65 Grotius, *Annotationes*, sig. A4ʳ: 'Nunc audacissimis Rhetorum tropis insignitur, nunc humillimo, licet non abjecto, se prodit statu; qui, si aliter esset, non Divinus haberetur.'

66 Lewalski, *Protestant Poetics*, 221.

67 Donne, 'Sermon LV, Preached upon the Penitentiall Psalms,' in *LXXX Sermons*, 556. See also Stanwood and Ross-Asals, *John Donne*, chap. 1, 'The Speech of the Trinity,' 11–43.

68 Donne, 'Sermon LXXIX, Preached at S. Pauls,' in *LXXX Sermons*, 812.

69 Lukiñ, *Introduction to the Holy Scripture*, 9.

70 Wither, *Preparation to the Psalter*, 75.

71 Augustine, *On Christian Doctrine*, IV. xxviii, advanced decorum as the key to speaking both wisely and eloquently: 'Quid est ergo non solum eloquenter, verum etiam sapienter dicere, nisi verba in summisso genere sufficientia, in temperato splendentia, in grandi vehementia, veris tamen rebus quas audiri oporteat, adhibere?'

72 Donne, *Devotions upon Emergent Occasions*, 99, 100.

73 See Trinkaus, *Poet as Philosopher*, 96–113.

74 Curtius, *ELLMA*, 459.

75 Boccaccio, *Life of Dante*, 41.

76 See Salutati, *Epistolario*, 4:239 (*Ep.* XXIV), where he states that those who have read Augustine 'videbunt ... totam divinam Scripturam mysticiis scatere sensibus et undique sacramentis variis abundare, quod est peculiare atque precipuum poetarum. Nam cum ... poesis pene semper intrinsecum occulat intellectum, quid facit aliud poetica quam divina Scriptura?' On Augustine see also 224, 238.

77 Ibid., 236 (*Ep.* XXIV): 'pertinent ad poeticam ... metaphore et omnis sermonum improprietas et metaplasmi, schemata, tropi, quiquidve sub istis reponitur, quod in plurimas figuras egreditur et ab omnibus tam oratoribus quam poetis communiter usurpatur. Quo fit ut quicquid in divina Scriptura a propria naturalique significatione discedit quicquidque figuraliter de alio predicatur, totum sit poeticum et prorsus tale quod oblique, non propria, quod intenditur representet.'

78 Sidney, *Defense of Poesy*, 608.

79 Thomas Aquinas, *Summa theologiae*, 1a. q. 1, a. 9.

80 Augustine, *On Christian Doctrine*, IV. vii.

81 Diodati, *Pious Annotations*, 95. On the divine authorship of the Psalms see also Cassiodorus, *Expositio Psalmorum*, Praefatio, I, 24: 'Quo dicto recog-

noscimus evidenter per Spiritum sanctum psalmos fuisse prophetatos';
Wither, *Preparation to the Psalter*, 33, 122.

82 See Conley, 'Byzantine Teaching,' 362–6, on rhetorical interpreters of the
Psalms in the East, and on the place in Byzantine exegesis of grammar, an
art that included, at the higher level, the study of schemes and tropes.

83 Notker Balbulus, *De interpretationibus divinarum Scripturarum*, II, cit. Cassiodorus, *Expositio Psalmorum*, Praefatio, vii: '... Cassiodorus Senator, cum
multa disseruerit, in hoc tantum videtur nobis utilis, quod omnem saecula-
rem sapientiam, id est schemata et troporum dulcissimam varietatem in eo
latere manifestat.'

84 Sidney, *Defense of Poesy*, 607.

85 Wither, *Preparation to the Psalter*, 63, 71, 75, 63–4.

86 Caryl, *Exposition*, 3, 661 (mispaginated 659), 659.

87 Ibid., 714–15.

6. The Rhetoric of Heaven

1 Grossman, 'Milton and the Rhetoric of Prophecy,' 174–5.

2 Patrides, *Milton and the Christian Tradition*, 9–10n2, cites a range of English
theological treatises in establishing Milton's theory of accommodation in
PL within the rhetorical tradition of an anthropopathetic God; see also his
'*Paradise Lost*,' 161–2n8. Lieb, 'Reading God,' coins the word 'theopathia' as
better suited to describe the emotional expression of Milton's God; but
since it is still the case that 'God ... accommodates himself to man's understanding' (227), theopathia becomes virtually interchangeable with anthropopathia.

3 G. Miller, 'Stylistic Rhetoric,' remarks on the profusion of rhetorical devices
in God's speech, indicating and analysing more of them than my present
purposes require. He notes modern critics who have failed to see God as a
stylist and rhetorician (112). See also Broadbent, 'Milton's Rhetoric'; Cope,
Metaphoric Structure, 167–76.

4 The most notable exception is the Father's appointment of the Son as judge
at X. 55–6: 'But whom send I to judge them? whom but thee, / Vicegerent
Son.'

5 Hughes, 'Filiations of the Celestial Dialogue,' 126, and Fish, *Surprised by Sin*
(esp. 62–5, on the lines quoted above) maintain God's impassibility. Murrin,
'Language of Milton's Heaven,' 360, contends that in Milton's portrayal
'the Father argues a perfectly rational logic.'

6 Kennedy, *Art of Rhetoric*, 386.

7 Patrides, *Milton and the Christian Tradition*, 22–5, and 'The Godhead in *Paradise Lost*.'

8 Milton has also orchestrated the 'dialogue' of the Father and the Son for the soteriological instruction of his readership, having the divine characters cue one another into speeches that, taken together, gloss Christian doctrine on the topics of free will, reason, love, obedience, mercy, and justice.

9 Rebhorn, *Emperor of Men's Minds*, 51, 53–4.

10 Ibid., 257–8.

11 The schemes here may be diagrammed as follows; the characteristic instances of verbal doubling – and in one case tripling – are particularly evident:

So [Man], as is most just,	[conduplicatio]
Shall satisfy for [Man], be judg'd and <{die},	{polyptoton}
And {dying} rise, and rising with him raise	polyptoton <auxesis>
His Brethren>, ransom'd with his own dear	
life.	
So *Heav'nly love* shall outdo [*Hellish	
hate*],	*antithesis*
Giving to death, and dying to [redeem],	[conduplicatio] polyptoton
(So dearly) to [redeem] what [Hellish hate]	
(So easily) destroy'd, and still destroys	polyptoton (paromoiosis)
In those who, when they may, accept not	
grace.	

12 Longinus, *On Sublimity*, xvii. 1.

13   x   y   y   x
    {Silence}, {ye troubl'd waves}, and {thou deep}, {peace}

14 Collingwood, *Idea of History*, 413.

15 See Kraye, 'Moral Philosophy,' 360–74; see also her 'Conceptions of Moral Philosophy,' 1286–90. Uriel remarks that the adoration of God 'leads to no excess / That reaches blame, but rather merits praise / The more it seems excess' (III. 696–8).

16 Longinus, *On Sublimity*, i. 4

17 Patey, *Probability and Literary Form*, 9.

18 Milton, *YP*, 8:299: 'A distribution by means of causes occurs when the parts are causes of the whole.'

19 Although it reaches further back: 'From Man's effeminate slackness it begins' (XI. 634). Michael relates the sons of Seth, whose uxoriousness will bring on the Flood, to Adam, whose acquiescence to Eve's wish to part (IX. 370–5) made possible 'th' inabstinence of Eve' and the Fall. As Eve tells

Adam, 'Hadst thou been firm and fixt in thy dissent, / Neither had I transgress'd, nor thou with me' (IX. 1160–1). The Son judges him on this ground: 'Thou didst resign thy Manhood' (X. 148). See also Milton, *Samson Agonistes*, 410–11.

20 Peacham, *Garden of Eloquence* (1577), sig. Nii[r-v].
21 See the expanded edition of the *Garden* (1593), 123–6. Like Peacham, Milton classes partitio and divisio under the main heading of distribution: 'Some, following Cicero [*Topica*, vi. 30 – vii. 30], call distribution of an integral whole into members *partition*, and that of genus into species *division*' (*YP*, 8:301). One method largely covered the classification and arrangement of materials in both logic and rhetoric.
22 Cicero, *Topica*, xviii. 67.
23 Augustine, *City of God*, XIX. iv, writes that the *summum bonum* for Christians is eternal life. Renaissance philosophers shared this view; see Kraye, 'Moral Philosophy,' 317–18. Within the framework of this belief, Christianity incorporated Stoic ethical doctrine; for example, Augustine, in *City of God*, claims that the cardinal virtues help one both to attain eternal life and to bear patiently the miseries of earthly existence. A similar syncretism informs the teaching of Milton's Adam, for whom the *summum bonum* remains the Stoic good of virtue, though a virtue leavened with a set of corresponding Christian spiritual attributes, including the Christianized fortitude that is patience.
24 In Dante, *Inferno*, viii, the shade of Virgil similarly approves the vehement anger of the Pilgrim at recognizing Filippo Argenti rising out of the Styx; in canto xix, the Pilgrim's more self-possessed anger in reaction to the sins of Pope Nicholas III elicits further praise from Virgil. Seventeenth-century commentators on Stoicism considered anger to be a valid emotion, based partly on the example of Christ; see Kraye, 'Conceptions of Moral Philosophy,' 1289.
25 Petrarch, *Familiarum rerum libri*, 1:9.2: 'index animi sermo est.'
26 Longinus, *On Sublimity*, xxii. 1.

7. Satan and Rhetoric

1 Wier, *De praestigiis daemonum*, 65: 'magnae illum esse constat virtutis, calliditatis incredibilis, sapientiae plus quam humanae, perspicacitatis acutissimae, vigilantiae summae, artificii technas struendi perniciosissimas fuco speciosissimo incomparabilis, maliciae infinitae, odii erga genus hominum ἄσπονδου καὶ ἀνήκεστου.'
2 Ibid., 34–5: 'hi spiritus [i.e., the fallen angels, a synecdoche for Satan] ...

deludunt ... [Evam] astu quam blandissimo, ubi nullus videbatur subesse fucus ... Evam erigunt falsis pollicitantionibus in spem longe maiorum ornamentorum, excellentiorisque potentiae ... in idem studium Evam pertrahere conatus est gratae persuasionis illecebris.'

3 Bacon, 'Of Cunning,' in *Essays*, 126; Hobbes, *Leviathan*, 53.

4 Gouge, *Whole Armor of God*, 40.

5 Aristotle, *Nicomachean Ethics*, VI. vii. 1141b.6.

6 Cicero, *De partitione oratoria*, xxiii. 81.

7 Aristotle, *Nicomachean Ethics*, VI. xii. 1144a.6; 1144a.10; 1143b.7.

8 Ibid., VI. vii. 1141b.6; ix. 1142b.4.

'9 Donne, 'Sermon 4, Preached at St Pauls,' in *LXXX Sermons*, cit. Stanwood and Ross-Asals, *John Donne*, 20.

10 Burton, *Anatomy of Melancholy*, 1:1.1.1.1, 122; 3:3.4.1.2, 358, 343.

11 Gouge, *Whole Armor of God*, 42.

12 Spurstowe, *Wiles of Satan*, 22.

13 Pordage, *Mundorum Explicatio*, 94.

14 See Steadman, *Milton and the Renaissance Hero*, 50.

15 Spurstowe, *Wiles of Satan*, 21.

16 Thomas, *Religion and the Decline of Magic*, 621–2.

17 Spurstowe, *Wiles of Satan*, 21.

18 Bacon, 'Of Delays,' in *Essays*, 125. The emblem of *Kairos*, familiar to Bacon, depicted a goddess with a long forelock, but bald at the back of her head. She represents the idea of literally grasping an opportunity during a fleeting critical moment – once missed, it is gone and will not present itself again. *Occasion* herself explains this in Geoffrey Whitney's *Choice of Emblemes*: 'What meanes long lockes before? *that such as meete, / Maye houlde at firste, when they occasion finde. /* Thy head behinde all balde, what telles it more? / *That none shoulde houlde, that let me slippe before'* (181).

19 Gouge, *Whole Armor of God*, 43.

20 Browne, *Pseudodoxia Epidemica*, 1:5, 58, 6, 16, 25–6.

21 Browne, *Religio Medici*, 30, 30, 31.

22 Spurstowe, *Wiles of Satan*, 5; Quarles, 'Dialogue Between the Soul and Satan,' in *God's Love and Man's Unworthiness*, 89.

23 Quarles, 'Dialogue Between the Soul and Satan,' 70. Literary villains quote scripture with the same motive as Shakespeare's Duke of Gloucester, *Richard III*, I. iii. 334–6: 'I clothe my naked villainy / With odd old ends, stol'n forth of Holy Writ, / [To] seem a saint when most I play the devil.'

24 See Evans, *'Paradise Lost,'* 60.

25 Chrysostom, *Homilies on Genesis*, xvi. 2, cit. ibid., 88.

26 Avitus, *Poematum de Mosaicae historiae gestis*, cols 332C, 333A. The Latin text

for this and the following quotations is found in Avitus, *Patrologiae Latina*, 59. Watson Kirkconnell offers an English verse translation of the lines discussed here, tending rather engagingly towards Elizabethan extravagance, in *Celestial Cycle*, 11–12.

27 Avitus, *Poematum de Mosaicae historiae gestis*, cols 333A–B.

28 Ibid, cols 333C–334A.

29 Hale, *Milton's Languages*, 7, 209n13.

30 'Genesis B,' 445–6, 450–2 in *Junius Manuscript*, 17, in *Caedmon Poems*, 21–2.

31 Ibid., lines 588–92 in ibid., 21, in ibid., 26. The rhetorical nature of Eve's deception is restated in similar terms at lines 647–52.

32 Spenser, *Faerie Queene*, I. i. 35. 5–7; ii. 5. 5–9. The 'aged sire' is Archimago, disguised as a holy hermit. Milton describes Satan as 'the first / That practis'd falsehood under saintly show' (*PL* IV. 121–2). Subsequent citations of *The Faerie Queene* appear in the body of the text.

33 On 'file(d)' as referring to artful and polished speech – as well as conduct – that practises dissimulation see Wyatt, 'Sonnet XVI,' in *Collected Poems*, 14. Chaucer's Pardoner knows that 'He moste preche and wel affile his tongue / To wynne silver, as he ful wel koude' (*Canterbury Tales*, I (A) 712–13).

34 At *Faerie Queene* II. i. 12. 2–5 Guyon questions Archimago, disguised as a humble miser: 'And lives he yet (said he) that wrought this act, / And doen the heavens afford him vitall food? / He lives (quoth he) and boasteth of the fact, / Ne yet hath any knight his courage crackt.' Archimago's amplification – that the alleged offender not only lives, but boasts of his heinous act – is a variety of 'argument from the greater' discussed in Milton's *Art of Logic*, *YP*, 8:76–8; see esp. 277 on its use in poetry.

35 Fairfax, *Godfrey of Bulloigne*, IV. xxii, xxv.

36 Sylvester, *Devine Weekes*, 304. Subsequent citations are in the body of the text.

37 Pordage, *Mundorum Explicatio*, 69. Subsequent citations are in the body of the text.

38 Quarles, *God's Love*, 17.

39 See page 56, above.

40 Quarles, *God's Love*, 29.

41 Quarles, 'Dialogue Between the Soul and Satan,' 72, 86.

42 Fletcher, *Christs Victorie*, xviii: 'well that aged Syre could tip his tongue / With golden foyle of eloqence, and lime, / And licke his rugged speech with phrases prime.' Satan first appears in the disguise of a holy hermit, like Archimago.

43 Ibid., lix. Another character related to Satan is the 'wily spright' in *The Locusts, or Apollynists* by Giles Fletcher's brother, Phineas: 'Proteus, now

Equivocus he hight, / Father of cheaters, spring of cunning lies, / Of slie deceite, and refin'd perjuries, / That hardly hell itselfe can trust his forgeries ... His matter fram'd of slight equivocations, / His very forme was form'd of mentall reservations' (46–7).

44 Lewalski, *Milton's Brief Epic*, 333.

45 Satan reckons that there are two sons of God: 'His first-begot [whom] we know, and sore have felt' and the man from Nazareth. See *PR* I. 89–93.

46 See Lewalski, *Milton's Brief Epic*, 333, 345, 350.

47 See Peacham, *Garden of Eloquence* (1577), sigs Fiii^v-iiii^r, for definition and examples of 'traductio, when one word is sundry tymes repeated in one sentence, to make the Oration more trimme.'

48 See McCaffrey, 'Style of Satan's Athens,' 9. See also Samuel, *Plato and Milton*, 125–9, on the superiority of faith to secular knowledge expressed in the Son's rejection of Athens.

49 Browne, *Pseudodoxia Epidemica*, 1:58.

8. The Rhetoric of Hell

1 Bacon, *De augmentis scientiarum*, in *Works*, 1:671–2; trans. F. Headlam in *Works*, 4.i:455–6.

2 Plato, *Apology*, 18B, 19B–C in *Collected Dialogues*.

3 Isocrates, *Antidosis*, s. 15, in *Orations*, 2:193.

4 See Guthrie, *Sophists*, 28, 32–3.

5 Steadman, 'Milton's Rhetoric,' 74.

6 Chaucer, *Canterbury Tales*, III (D) 1482–8. Experience at length teaches the Miltonic Satan that 'what [God] bids I do' (*PR* I. 377; see also I. 126–8, 421, 444–53, 495–6). Patrides, *Milton and the Christian Tradition*, 96–7n2, cites numerous Christian apologists who maintain God's complete control over the actions of Satan.

7 See their remarks at *PL* I. 116, 133; II. 197–8, 222, 232–3, 393. God dismisses chance and defines 'fate' as the enactment of the divine will (VII. 170–4). See also Milton, *YP*, 6:131: 'fate or *fatum* is only what is *fatum*, spoken, by some almighty power.' Justus Lipsius, *De constantia*, I. 19, puts forward a similar view of fate and divine providence.

8 God says that Satan will endanger Adam 'By violence, no, for that shall be withstood, / But by deceit and lies' (V. 242–3).

9 Steadman, '"Semblance of Worth,"' 256–7.

10 Belial presumes that others are as susceptible to pleasure as he is, and that Satan may tempt Jesus successfully if he will 'Set women in his eye and in his walk' (*PR* II. 153). Satan corrects his associate's rhetorical error of mis-

understanding the audience they wish to persuade – '*Belial*, in much uneven scale thou weigh'st / All others by thyself' (II. 173–4) – though, as noted in chapter 7, he falls into the same error during his futile temptation of the Son.

11 Quintilian, *Institutio oratoria*, VIII. vi. 19.

12 See also *PL* X. 458–9, where the Devil raises his hand to command silence before speaking.

13 See also *PL* I. 274, 78–9 on the affecting power of his voice: 'If once they hear that voice ... they will soon resume / New courage and revive.'

14 Hermogenes, *On Types of Style*, 101, 102.

15 Bacon, *Advancement of Learning*, in *Works*, 3:284.

16 Burton, *Anatomy of Melancholy*, 1:1.1.1.1, 122.

17 Milton equates the Apples of Sodom with false eloquence in *Eikonoklastes* (*YP*, 3:552), where they represent the empty substance of set forms of prayer.

9. Temptation and the Rhetoric of Paradise

1 Cogan, in O'Rourke et al., 'Most Significant Passage' (38–9) mistakenly claims this of Bacon.

2 Isocrates, *Nicocles*, 8, in *Orations* 1:81; Plato, *Sophist*, 263E, in *Collected Dialogues*.

3 Bacon, *Advancement of Learning*, in *Works*, 3:409; 'this means that in some sense the first and most important field of operation for rhetoric is internal and personal, rather than public' (Cogan, 'Rhetoric and Action in Francis Bacon,' 223).

4 Michael more specifically defines the nature of this inner struggle as 'supernal Grace contending / With sinfulness of Men' (*PL* XI. 359–60). On internal rhetoric see also the 'inward perswasion' that helps one to interpret the gospel (*YP*, 7:259).

5 Shakespeare, *Rape of Lucrece*, 876–9.

6 Cicero, *De inventione*, I. xv. 20.

7 Gouge, *Whole Armor of God*, 43.

8 Lanham, *Motives of Eloquence*, 4: 'Rhetorical man is an actor; his reality public, dramatic ... he assumes a natural agility in changing orientations.'

9 Peacham, *Garden of Eloquence* (1593), 77–8.

10 Browne, *Pseudodoxia Epidemica*, 22, 24. Cf. *PL* IX. 1053–4, 57–8: 'Soon found thir Eyes how op'n'd, and thir minds / How dark'n'd ... naked left / To guilty shame'; and Adam at IX. 1070–3: 'our Eyes / Op'n'd we find indeed, and find we know / Both Good and Evil, Good lost, and Evil got, / Bad Fruit of Knowledge, if this be to know.'

11 A realization Macbeth reaches too late: 'I pull in resolution, and begin / To doubt th' equivocation of the fiend / That lies like truth' (Shakespeare, *Macbeth*, V. v. 42–4).

12 Browne, *Pseudodoxia Epidemica*, 25.

13 Wurtele, '"Perswasive Rhetoric"' 26–30, discusses most of these fallacies in an excellent technical analysis of the temptation.

14 Hooker, *Laws of Ecclesiastical Polity*, I. vii. 6.

15 Ibid., v. 3–vi. 1.

16 Aristotle, *On Rhetoric*, II. xxiv. 1402a.10.

17 Although not a school of philosophy per se, sophism undeniably possesses philosophical dimensions, particularly subjectivism and relativism, as the following discussion explains.

18 Fish, *Surprised by Sin*, 256, 259–60.

19 Carr, *What Is History?* 95–6.

20 See Steadman, '"Man's First Disobedience,"' 190–1.

21 Hobbes, *Art of Rhetoric*, 529.

22 For the aspects of sophism summarized in this paragraph see Guthrie, *Sophists*.

23 Isocrates defined *doxa* differently; see page 38 and 2n17, above.

24 Lactantius, *Divinae institutiones*, I. xxiii: 'Primus autem sapientiae gradus est, falsa intellegere; secundus, vera cognoscere.'

25 Donne, 'Satyre III,' 72–3, in *Complete English Poems*, 224–9. Milton describes their relationship with the same metaphor; see pages 19, 87, above.

26 Plato, *Meno*, 98C–99C, in *Collected Dialogues*.

27 Cicero, *De oratore*, II. vii. 30.

28 Patey, *Probability and Literary Form*, 5.

29 Lever, *Arte of Reason*, 197.

30 Gorgias, *Encomium of Helen*, 11–12.

31 Milton, *De doctrina Christiana*, in *Works*, 17:36; see also page 66, above.

32 Hegendorf, *Defensio eloquentiae*, 203: 'Quanto denique prudentia opus est, ne parum circumspecti ab adversariis illaqueati capiamur!'

33 Aristotle, *On Rhetoric*, I.i. 1355a.12.

34 Fish, *Surprised by Sin*, 255, 241.

35 Hegendorf, *Defensio eloquentiae*, 203: 'Quoties Christus ipse syllogismis, quoties enthymematis Iudaeos concludit!'

36 Quintilian, *Institutio oratoria*, XII. i. 35.

37 Lewis, *Preface to 'Paradise Lost,'* 118–21.

38 Baumlin, 'Ciceronian Decorum,' 156. Satan parodies a 'moral-intellectual crisis' by feeling 'Stupidly good' (*PL* IX. 465) at the sight of Eve but quickly remembering 'What hither brought us, hate, not love' (IX. 475).

39 As Bacon and Hobbes define it; see page 000, above. Adam later refers to Eve as 'a Rib / Crooked by nature, bent, as now appears, / More to the part siníster from me drawn' (*PL* X. 884–6).

40 Shakespeare, *Tempest*, III. i. 39–42.

41 Shakespeare, *Measure for Measure*, I. ii. 172–6.

42 Euripides, *Hecabe*, 339 (I have chosen Philip Vellacott's translation).

43 Wittgenstein, *Philosophical Investigations*, II. iv, 178.

10. Descending from Heaven: Anthropopathia and the Rhetoric of Paradise

1 Shakespeare, *Hamlet*, II.ii. 587–92.

2 See page 113, above, especially Salomon Glass; see also Matthias Flacius and Joseph Glanvill.

3 Clark, *Milton at St Paul's School*, 197.

4 *Rhetorica ad Herennium*, IV. xxxii. 43.

5 Hyperius, *Practis of Preaching*, f. 38ᵛ.

6 Burke, *Grammar of Motives*, 503, 505, 507.

7 Cicero, *Orator*, iv. 14. Recent criticism has discussed the comparison of greater to lesser in Milton's poetry but does not identify it as metonymy; see Excursus 2.921, 'To Compare Great Things,' 435–8.

8 Cf. Shakespeare, *Antony and Cleopatra*, II. ii. 198–9, and *Winter's Tale*, V. ii. 41–2, 55–6, where characters resort to adynaton when narrating to others, as Raphael does, a remarkable sight or past event, and then proceeding to give a remarkable description of it. Adynaton also saw heavy service in panegyric; see, for example, Donne, 'The Relique,' 31–3, in *Complete English Poems*, 112–13. Shakespeare rings the changes on the inexpressibility topos in the course of his sonnets; see especially nos 78–86, 103, 106. For further examples in Milton's prose works see Steadman, *Hill and the Labyrinth*, 76n6.

9 Aristotle, *On Rhetoric*, III. xvi. 1417b.11.

10 Aristotle's remarks at *On Rhetoric* II. xx. 1393a.2–3, 1394a.8, and III. xvii. 1418a.5 further clarify Raphael's use of example in a deliberative context.

11 Spenser, 'Letter to Raleigh,' preface to *Faerie Queene*, 16. Chaucer's Monk locates a natural source of such *exempla* in the fall of tragic characters, including Lucifer; see *Canterbury Tales*, VII 1991–8.

12 Agricola, *De inventione dialectica*, I. xxiv, 133: 'Exemplum, est species quaedam comparationis. Est enim vel aliquid maius, vel par, vel minus, quod ad imitandum, vitandumque sumitur.'

13 On the 'double presence' of Raphael, who at one time (Book III) foreknows the Fall but at another (Books V–VIII) does not, see Reeves, '"Lest Wilfully Transgressing,"' esp. 91–2.

14 Augustine, *Confessions*, I. 4.

15 Vives, *De ratione dicendi*, 149: 'Solidae orationes sunt, quum non in speciem tantum aliquid videntur dicere, sed si quis excutiat, et enucleet, multum deprehendet intus latere.' For Isocrates see page 40, above.

16 See Plato, *Phaedo* 72E, *Meno* 81C–D in *Collected Dialogues*.

17 Hobbes, *Whole Art of Rhetoric*, 423.

18 Agricola, *De inventione dialectica*, I. i, 1: 'soli omnium animantium homini, ut rationis doctrinaeque capaci, parens ille et autor rerum Deus, loquendi atque orationis indulserit munus.'

19 Sterne, *Tristram Shandy*, 79.

20 Rostagni, 'History of Rhetoric and Sophistry,' 30.

21 Agricola, *De inventione dialectica*, I. ii, 9: 'cuius admonitu, quid in quaque re probabile sit, potest inveniri.'

22 See Altman, *Tudor Play of Mind*, 50–3.

23 Cicero, *Topica*, xviii. 68. See also Cicero, *De oratore*, II. xl. 172; Aristotle, *On Rhetoric*, II. xxiii. 1397b.4–5; Agricola, *De inventione dialectica*, I. xxiv, 133–4 and Alardus's commentary on this chapter.

24 Cicero, *Topica*, xviii. 69.

25 Ibid., 70.

26 On σύγκρισις see Grafton, 'Availability of Ancient Works,' 773.

27 Agricola, *De inventione dialectica*, I. xxiv, 133: 'Comparationem vocamus, cum duo, aut plura, in tertio aliquo conferuntur, quod commune sit eis. Ut Catoni licuit sequi bellum civile, ergo et Ciceroni licebit sequi. Commune est hic ambobus, sequi bellum civile.'

28 Herodotus, *Histories*, VII. 10 (I have chosen Aubrey de Sélincourt's translation).

29 Glassius, *Philologiae sacrae*, 1133–4: 'IGNORANTIA, cognitione contraria, Deo tribuitur ... Huc referantur interrogationes, a DEO institutae, tanquam ignorante, cum proprie loquendo DEUM nihil lateat, nec ulla opus habeat interrogatione. Genes. 3 vers. 9. *Et vocavit Dominus Deus hominem, et dixit ei, ubi es?* Non est interrogatio haec ignorantis, sed ad comparendum invitantis, et in memoriam reducentis Adamo, quantum mutatus ab illo immortalitatis beato statu nunc post lapsum esset: Ambrosius de parad. cap. 14. *Ubi est illa tua bene sibi conscia confidentia? timor iste culpam fatetur, latebra praevaricationem: Ubi ergo est? non in quo loco quaero, sed in quo statu? quo te perduxerunt peccata tua, ut fugias Deum tuum, quem ante quaerebas? Non ergo interrogatio est, sed increpatio: de quibus bonis, de qua beatitudine, de qua gratia, in quam miseriam recidisti!*'

30 Susenbrotus, *Epitome troporum ac schematum*, 56: 'quae sciscitandi gratia non assumitur, sed percontando variis servit affectibus.'

31 T. Hall, *Rhetorica Sacra*, 167.

32 Erasmus, *Ecclesiastes*, 294: 'interrogatio tempestive adhibita multum vigoris et aculeorum addit orationi,' a remark that Susenbrotus quotes in his discussion of the figure at *Epitome troporum ac schematum*, 57.

33 George of Trebizond observes that the rhetorical question 'non ... spiritu quodam interrogantis profertur, quamvis, et ipsa non longe ab acrimonia sit' (*Rhetoricorum libri quinque*, 548). For Keckermann, the rhetorical question 'habet ... acrimoniam et vim non tantum ad movendos affectus; sed etiam ad orationis varietatam, et ad connexionem partium plurimum valet' (*Rhetorica ecclesiastica*, 123). It was one of the eight most powerful predicatory techniques for Richard Bernard; see *Faithfull Shepherd*, 303. See also Flacius, *Clavis scripturae*, II. iv, cols 362–4; T. Hall, *Centuria Sacra*, 108; Perkins, *Arte of Prophecying*, 659.

34 Aristotle, *On Rhetoric*, I. ii. 1355b.1.

Conclusion

1 Rebhorn, *Emperor of Men's Minds*, 18, 22.
2 Ward, *Ciceronian Rhetoric*, 168.
3 Parker, *Milton: A Biography,* 1:609; see also his *Milton's Contemporary Reputation*, 48, 51–2.
4 See Ong, *Ramus, Method*, 277.
5 Nettleship, '*Republic*' of Plato, 253.

Bibliography

Primary Sources

Adams, Thomas. 'Plaine Dealing, or A Precedent of Honestie.' In *The Workes, Being a Summe of His Sermons, Meditations, and other Divine and Moral Discourses*. London, 1629.

Agricola, Rudolph. *De formando studio*. In *Lucubrationes*. Cologne, 1539. Repr. Nieuwkoop, 1967.

– *De inventione dialectica* [1479]. Edited by Alardus Amstelredamus. Cologne, 1539. Repr. Nieuwkoop, 1967.

Aquinas, St Thomas. *Summa theologiae*. 60 vols. London, 1963–76.

Aristotle, *Aristotle on Rhetoric: A Theory of Civic Discourse*. Translated and edited by George Kennedy. Oxford, 1991.

– *Nichomachean Ethics*. Translated by H. Rackham. Cambridge, Mass., 1968.

– *Poetics*. Translated by Stephen Halliwell. Cambridge, Mass., 1995.

Ascham, Roger. *The Scholemaster* [1570]. In *English Works*. Edited by William A. Wright. Cambridge, 1904. Repr. 1970.

Augustine, St. *De doctrina christiana*. Edited by William M. Green. *Opera*. Vienna, 1963. 6:6.

– *On Christian Doctrine*. Translated by D.W. Robertson, Jr. New York, 1958.

– *The City of God Against the Pagans*. Translated by William M. Green. 7 vols, Cambridge, Mass., 1963.

– *Confessions*. Translated by R.S. Pine-Coffin. New York, 1961.

Avitus, Alcimus Edicius. *Poematum de Mosaicae historiae gestis libri quinque*. In *Patrologiae cursus completus: series Latina*. Edited by Jacques-Paul Migne. 221 vols. Paris, 1844–64. Vol. 59, cols 323–82.

Bacon, Francis. *The Essays*. Edited by John Pitcher. New York, 1985.

– *Works*. Edited by James Spedding et al. 14 vols. London, 1857–74.

Baxter, Richard. *Gildas Salvianus: The Reformed Pastor*. London, 1656.
– 'A True Believer's Choice and Pleasure. Sermon for the Funeral of Mrs Cox.' In *The Practical Works*. 23 vols. London, 1830. 18:91–118.
Bernard, Richard. *The Faithfull Shepherd*. London, 1621.
Beza, Theodore. *Jesu Christi Domini Nostri Novum Testamentum, sive Novum Foedus*. 1565.
Boccaccio, Giovanni. *The Life of Dante (Trattatello in laude di Dante)*. Translated by Vincenzo Bollettino. New York, 1990.
Boethius. *The Consolation of Philosophy*. In *Cicero: On Fate (De Fato) & Boethius: The Consolation of Philosophy IV. 5–7, V (Philosophiae Consolationis)*. Translated and edited by Robert Sharples. Warminster, 1991.
Brinsley, John. 'A Parlie with the Sword about a Cessation.' 28 December 1642. London, 1643.
Browne, Thomas. *Pseudodoxia Epidemica; or, Enquiries into Very Many Received Tenents, and Commonly Presumed Truths* [1646]. 2 vols. Edited by Robin Robbins. Oxford, 1981.
– *Religio Medici*. In *Works*. 4 vols. Edited by Geoffrey Keynes. London, 1928. Vol. 4.
Burchard, Franz. 'Epistola Hermolai nova ac subditicia' [1558]. In Philipp Melanchthon, *Opera omnia*, ed. Karl G. Bretschneider and Heinrich E. Bindseil. 28 vols. Halle Braunschweig, 1834–60. Vol. 9, cols 687–703.
Burton, Robert. *The Anatomy of Melancholy*. Edited by Thomas C. Faulkner, Nicholas K. Kiessling, and Rhonda L. Blair. 4 vols. Oxford, 1989–98.
The Caedmon Poems. Translated by Charles W. Kennedy. London, 1916.
Caryl, Joseph. *An Exposition with Practical Observations continued upon the Thirty Eighth, Thirty-Ninth, Fortieth, Forty-First and Forty-Second Chapters of the Book of Job*. London, 1666.
Cassiodorus, Aurelius. *Expositio Psalmorum, I–LXX*. Edited by Marcus Adriaen, Turnhout, 1958.
Caussin, Nicholas. S.J. *De eloquentia sacra et humana libri XVI*. Paris, 1630.
Charleton, Walter. *The Darknes of Atheism Dispelled by the Light of Nature*. London, 1652.
Chaucer, Geoffrey. *The Canterbury Tales*. In *Works*. Edited by F.N. Robinson. Cambridge, Mass., 1957.
Cicero. *Academica*. Translated by H. Rackham. London, 1956.
– *De fato*. Translated by H. Rackham. London, 1942.
– *De inventione*. Translated by H.M. Hubbell. London, 1949.
– *De officiis*. Translated by Walter Miller. Cambridge, Mass., 1913. Repr. 2005.
– *De oratore*. Translated by E.W. Sutton and H. Rackham. 2 vols. London, 1942.
– *De partitione oratoria*. Translated by H. Rackham. London, 1942.

– *Orator*. Translated by H.M. Hubbell. London, 1939.

– *Topica*. Translated by H.M. Hubbell. London, 1949.

Colet, John. 'The Statutes of St Paul's School.' In J.H. Lupton, *The Life of John Colet*. London, 1887. Repr. Hamden, 1961.

Cox, Leonard. *The Arte or Crafte of Rhetoryke* [1532]. Edited by Frederic Carpenter. Chicago, 1899. Repr. Norwood, 1975.

Dante Alighieri. *The Divine Comedy*. Translated by Laurence Binyon. In *The Portable Dante*, ed. Mark Musa. New York, 1995.

Demetrius. *A Greek Critic: Demetrius on Style*. Edited by G.M.A. Grube. Toronto, 1961.

Descartes, René. *Discours de la méthode* [1637]. In *Oeuvres*, ed. Charles Adam and Paul Tannery. 12 vols. Paris, 1897–1913. Vol. 6.

Diodati, John. *Pious Annotations upon the Holy Bible Expounding the difficult places thereof Learnedly & Plainly*. London, 1643.

Donne, John. *The Complete English Poems of John Donne*. Edited by C.A. Patrides. London, 1985.

– *Devotions upon Emergent Occasions*. Edited by Anthony Raspa. Montreal and London, 1975.

– *LXXX Sermons Preached by that Learned Divine, John Donne*. London, 1640.

Dryden, John. *Works*. Gen. eds Edward Hooker and H.T. Swedenberg. 20 vols. Berkeley, 1956–94.

Elyot, Thomas. *The Boke named the Governour* [1531]. Edited by Donald Rude. London, 1992.

Erasmus, Desiderius. *The Collected Works of Erasmus*. Toronto, 1974–.

– *Ecclesiastae, sive de ratione concionandi libri quator*. Basel, 1535.

– *De libero arbitrio. Luther and Erasmus: Free Will and Salvation*. Translated and edited by E. Gordon Rupp, Philip S. Watson, et al. London, 1969.

– *Opera omnia*. Amsterdam, 1969–.

Euripides. *Hecabe*. In *Medea and Other Plays*. Translated by Philip Vellacott. Harmondsworth, 1963. Repr. 1985.

Faber, Tanaquillus. *Dionysii Longini philosophi et rhetoris ΠΕΡΙ ΥΨΟΥΣ*. Saumur, 1663.

Fairfax, Edward. *Godfrey of Bulloigne, or The Recoverie of Jerusalem*. London, 1660.

Flacius Illyricus, Matthias. *Clavis scripturae, seu de sermone sacrarum literarum*. Basel, 1617.

Fletcher, Giles. *Christs Victorie, and Triumph in Heaven, and Earth, over and after death*. Cambridge, 1610.

Fletcher, Phineas. *The Locusts, or Apollynists*. Cambridge, 1627.

Foxe, John. *The Acts and Monuments of John Foxe* [1576]. 8 vols. 3rd ed. London, 1837.

George of Trebizond. *Rhetoricorum libri quinque* [1433–4]. Paris, 1538.

Gibbon, Edward. *The History of the Decline and Fall of the Roman Empire*. Edited by David Womersley. 3 vols. London, 1994.

Glanvill, Joseph. *An Essay Concerning Preaching: Written for the Direction of a Young Divine and Useful also for the People, in order to profitable Hearing*. London, 1678.

Glass, Salomon. *Philologiae sacrae liber quintus, qua rhetorica sacra comprensa*. Frankfurt, 1653.

Goodwin, John. *Redemption Redeemed*. London, 1651.

Gorgias. *Encomium of Helen*, in *Aristotle on Rhetoric: A Theory of Civic Discourse*. Translated and edited by George Kennedy. Oxford, 1991. 283–8.

Gouge, William. *The Whole Armour of God; or, the Spirituall Furniture which God hath provided to keep safe every Christian Soldier from all the assaults of Satan*. London, 1616.

Grotius, Hugo. *Annotationes in Vetus et Novum Testamentum*. Basel, 1679.

Hall, Joseph. *The Works of Joseph Hall*. 12 vols. Oxford, 1837–9.

Hall, Thomas. *Centuria Sacra. About One Hundred Rules for the Expounding, and Clearer Understanding of the Holy Scriptures*. London, 1654.

– *Rhetorica Sacra; or, A Synopsis of the Most Materiall Tropes and Figures contained in the Sacred Scriptures*. London, 1654.

– *Vindiciae Literarum, The Schools Guarded; or, The Excellency and Usefulnesse of Arts, Sciences, Languages, History and all Sorts of Humane Learning, in Subordination to Divinity, & Preparation for the Ministry*. London, 1654.

Hammond, Henry. *A Pacifick Discourse of God's Grace and Decrees* [1660]. Repr. in *Works*. 2nd ed. London, 1684.

Hegendorf, Christoph. *Defensio eloquentiae*. Appendice alla traduzione del *Contra sophistas* [1528]. In Lucia Gualdo Rosa, *La fede nella 'Paideia': aspetti della fortuna Europea di Isocrate nei secoli XV e XVI*. Rome, 1984. 202–8.

Hermogenes. *On Types of Style*. Translated by Cecil W. Wooton. Chapel Hill, 1987.

Herodotus. *The Histories*. Translated by Aubrey de Sélincourt. Rev. ed. Edited by A.R. Burn. Harmondsworth, 1972. Repr. 1984.

Hobbes, Thomas. *The Art of Rhetoric, Plainly Set Forth. With Pertinent Examples for the More Easy Understanding and Practice of the Same*. In *English Works*. Edited by William Molesworth. 10 vols. London, 1839–45. 6:513–36.

– *Leviathan* [1651]. Edited by Richard Tuck. Cambridge, 1991.

– *The Whole Art of Rhetoric*. In *English Works*. Edited by William Molesworth. 10 vols. London, 1839–45. 6:423–510.

Hooker, Richard. *Of the Laws of Ecclesiastical Polity* [1593]. London, 1907. Repr. 1965.

Hyperius, Andreas. *The Practis of Preaching, otherwise called The Pathway to the Pulpet* [1552]. Translated by John Ludham. London, 1557.

Isocrates. *Orations.* Translated by George Norlin and LaRue Van Hook. 3 vols. Cambridge, Mass., 1928–45.

Jonson, Ben. *Works.* Edited by C. Herford and Percy Simpson. 12 vols. Oxford, 1925–52.

The Junius Manuscript. Edited by George Krapp. London, 1931.

Keckermann, Bartholomew. *Rhetoricae ecclesiasticae, sive artis formandi et habendi conciones sacras, libri duo.* Hanover, 1614.

Lactantius. *Divinae institutiones.* In *Patrologiae cursus completus: series Latina.* Edited by Jacques-Paul Migne. 221 vols. Paris, 1844–64. Vol. 6.

Langbaine, Gerard, ed. *Liber de grandi loquentia sive sublimi dicendi genere.* Oxford, 1630. Repr. of Gabriel da Petra's 1612 text with the editor's introduction and notes.

Laurentius, Gasparus. *In Hermogenis tractatum De ideis, sive De formis eloquentiae.* In *Operum Graecorum, Latinorum, et Italorum rhetorum.* 8 vols. Venice, 1644. 3:593–858.

Lever, Ralph. *The Arte of Reason* [1573]. Facsimile ed. Menston, 1972.

Lipsius, Justus. *De constantia libri duo.* London, 1586.

Longinus. *On Sublimity.* Translated by D.A. Russell. In *Ancient Literary Criticism: The Principal Texts in New Translations*, ed. D.A. Russell and Michael Winterbottom. 462–503. Oxford, 1972.

Lucan. *Civil War.* Translated by S.H. Braund. Oxford, 1992.

Lucretius. *De rerum natura.* Translated by W.H.D. Rouse. Cambridge, Mass., 1937.

Lukin, Henry. *An Introduction to the Holy Scripture, containing the Several Tropes, Figures, Proprieties of Speech used therein.* Introduction, 'To the Christian Reader,' by John Owen. London, 1669.

Luther, Martin. *De servo arbitrio. Luther and Erasmus: Free Will and Salvation.* Translated and edited by E. Gordon Rupp, Philip S. Watson, et al. London, 1969.

Melanchthon, Philipp. *De officiis concionatoris* [1529]. In *De arte concionandi formulae, ut breves, ita doctae et piae.* London, 1570.

– *De utilitate studiorum eloquentiae* [1538]. In *Opera omnia.* Ed. Karl G. Bretschneider and Heinrich E. Bindseil. 28 vols. Halle-Braunschweig, 1834–60. Vol. 9, cols 364–73.

– *Elementorum rhetorices libri duo.* Basel, 1519.

Milton, John. *Complete Poems and Major Prose.* Edited by Merritt Y. Hughes. New York, 1957.

– *Complete Prose Works of John Milton.* Edited by Don M. Wolfe et al. 8 vols. New Haven, 1953–82.

– *The Works of John Milton*. Gen. ed. Frank Allen Patterson. 18 vols. New York, 1931–40.

Montaigne, Michel de. 'An Apologie of Raymond Sebond.' In *The Essayes; or Morall, Politike, and Millitarie Discourses*. Translated by John Florio. 252–351. London, 1603. Facsimile ed. Menston, 1969.

More, Thomas. *The Complete Works of St Thomas More*. 15 vols. New Haven, 1963–86.

Mosellanus, Peter. *Tabulae de schematibus et tropis* [1519]. Cologne, 1529.

Müllner, Karl, ed., *Reden und Briefe Italienischer Humanisten*. Vienna, 1899. Ed. Hanna-Barbara Gerl. Repr. Munich, 1970.

Nizolio, Mario. *De veris principiis et vera ratione philosophandi contra pseudo-philosophos libri IV* [1553]. Edited by Quirinus Breen. Fratelli Bocca Edizione Nazionale dei Classici del Pensiero Italiano. Vols 3 and 4. Rome, 1956.

Owen, John. *A Display of Arminianisme: Being a Discovery of the Old Pelagian Idol Free Will*. In *Certain Treatises*. London, 1649.

Pagano, Pietro, ed. *De sublimi genere dicendi*. Venice, 1572.

Peacham, Henry. *The Garden of Eloquence* [1577]. Facsimile ed. Menston, 1971.

– *The Garden of Eloquence* [1593]. Facsimile ed. Gainsville, 1954.

Peacham, Henry, the Younger. *The Compleat Gentleman*. In *Seventeenth-Century Critical Essays*, ed. Joel Spingarn. 3 vols. Oxford, 1908. Vol. 1.

Pemble. *A Treatise of the Providence of God*. In *Works*. London, 1635.

Perkins, William. *The Arte of Prophecying; or, A Treatise Concerning the Sacred and Onely True Manner and Methode of Preaching*. In *Works*. 2 vols. London, 1631. Vol. 2.

– *A Christian and Plaine Treatise*. In *Works*. 2 vols. London, 1631. Vol. 2.

Petra, Gabriel da, ed. *De grandi, sive sublimi genere orationis*. Geneva, 1612.

Petrarch, Francesco. *Le familiari*. Edited by Vittorio Rossi and Umberto Bosco. 4 vols. Florence, 1933–42.

– *The Golden Chaine: or, the Description of Theology*. Cambridge, 1600.

– *Opera quae extant omnia*. 3 vols. Basel, 1554. Repr. Ridgewood, 1965.

– 'A Self-Portrait.' Translated by Hans Nachod. In *The Renaissance Philosophy of Man*, ed. Ernst Cassirer, Paul O. Kristeller, and John H. Randall, Jr. 34–5. Chicago, 1948.

Peyton, Thomas. *The Glasse of Time, in the First Age*. London, 1620.

Pico della Mirandola, Giovanni. *Oration on the Dignity of Man*. Translated by Elizabeth Forbes. In *The Renaissance Philosophy of Man*, ed. Ernst Cassirer, Paul O. Kristeller, and John H. Randall, Jr. 223–54. Chicago, 1948.

Pierce, Thomas. *A Correct Copy of Some Notes Concerning God's Decrees*. London, 1655.

– *Self-Condemnation*. London, 1658.

Plato. *The Collected Dialogues of Plato*. Edited by Edith Hamilton and Huntington Cairns. Princeton, 1961.

– *Gorgias*. Translated by Walter Hamilton. London and New York, 1960.

– *Phaedrus*. In *Phaedrus and Letters VII and VIII*. Translated by Walter Hamilton. London and New York, 1973.

Poggio Bracciolini. *Lettere*. Vol. 2, *Epistolarum familiarum libri*. Edited by Helene Harth. 3 vols. Florence, 1984.

Pomponazzi, Pietro. *Libri quinque de fato, de libero arbitrio et de praedestinatione*. Edited by Richard Lemay. Lugano, 1957.

– *On the Immortality of the Soul*. Translated by William H. Hay and John H. Randall, Jr. In *The Renaissance Philosophy of Man*, ed. Ernst Cassirer, Paul O. Kristeller, and John H. Randall, Jr. 280–381. Chicago, 1948.

Pordage, Samuel. *Mundorum Explicatio*. London, 1661.

Prideaux, John. *Sacred Eloquence; or, The Art of Rhetorick, as it is laid down in Scripture*. London, 1659.

Puttenham, George. *The Arte of English Poesie* [1589]. Edited by Gladys D. Willcock and Alice Walker. Cambridge, 1936.

Quarles, John. *God's Love and Man's Unworthiness: Whereto is annexed a discourse between the Soul & Satan*. London, 1651.

Quintilian. *Institutio oratoria*. Translated by H.E. Butler. 4 vols. London, 1921–2.

Rainolde, Richard. *The Foundacion of Rhetoric* [1563]. Facsimile ed. Menston, 1972.

Reuchlin, Johannis. *Liber congestorum de arte praedicandi* [1504]. In *De arte concionandi formulae, ut brevis, ita doctae et piae*. London, 1570.

Rhetorica ad Herennium. Translated by Harry Caplan. London, 1954.

Salutati, Coluccio. *Epistolario*. Edited by Francesco Novati Rome. 4 vols. 1891–1911.

Scaliger, Julius Caesar. *Poetices libri septem* [1561]. Edited by Luc Deitz. 3 vols. Stuttgart-Bad Cannstatt, 1994.

Shakespeare, William. *The Complete Works*. Gen. ed. Alfred Harbage. New York, 1969.

– *The Tempest*. Edited by Frank Kermode. London, 1954. Repr. 1988.

Sherry, Richard. *A Treatise of Schemes and Tropes* [1550]. Facsimile ed. Gainesville, 1961.

Sidney, Philip. *A Defense of Poesy* [1583]. In *The Renaissance in England: Non-Dramatic Prose and Verse of the Sixteenth Century*. ed. Hyder Rollins and Herschel Baker. 605–24. Lexington, 1954.

Smith, Henry. *The Sermons of Master Henry Smith, Gathered into one volume*. London, 1601.

Smith, John. *The Mysterie of Rhetorique Unvail'd*. London, 1656.

Spenser, Edmund. *The Faerie Queene*. Edited by Thomas P. Roche, Jr. New Haven, 1981.

Spurstowe, William. *ΣATANA NOHMATA: or, The Wiles of Satan*. London, 1666.

Sterne, Laurence. *The Life and Opinions of Tristram Shandy, Gentleman*. Edited by Graham Petrie. New York, 1967. Repr. 1985.

Sturm, Jean. *Hermogenis Tarsensis rhetoris acutissimi, De dicendi generibus sive formis orationum*. Strassburg, 1571.

Susenbrotus, Joannes. *Epitome troporum ac schematum et grammaticorum & rhetorum, ad autores tum prophanos tum sacros intelligendos non minus utilis quam necessaria*. Zurich, 1541.

Sylvester, Joshua, trans. *Guillaume du Bartas, His Devine Weekes and Workes*. London, 1605.

Valla, Lorenzo. *De voluptate. On Pleasure*. Edited and translated by A. Kent Hieatt and Maristella Lorch. New Haven, 1977.

– *Dialogue on Free Will*. Translated by Charles Trinkaus, Jr. In *The Renaissance Philosophy of Man*, ed. Ernst Cassirer, Paul O. Kristeller, and John H. Randall, Jr. 155–82. Chicago, 1948.

– *In Praise of St Thomas Aquinas*. Translated by M. Hanley. In *Renaissance Philosophy*, ed. L.A. Kennedy. 17–27. The Hague, 1973.

– *In quartum librum elegantiarum praefatio* in *Prosatori Latini del Quattrocento*. Edited by Eugenio Garin. 612–23. Milan, 1952.

– *Opera omnia*. Edited by J. Vahlen. 2 vols. 1886 repr. of Basle 1540 ed., plus other texts. Repr. Turin, 1962.

– *Repastinatio dialectice et philosophie* [1439]. Edited by Gianni Zippel. 2 vols. Padua, 1982.

Vettori, Pier. *Commentarii in librum Demetrii Phalerei De elocutione*. Florence, 1594.

Vives, Juan Luis. *Opera omnia*. Edited by Gregorio Mayans. 8 vols. Valencia, 1782–90. Repr. 1964.

Vossius, Gerard. *Rhetorices contractae, sive partitiorum oratoriarum libri V* [1621]. Oxford, 1631.

Westheimer, Bartholomew. *Collectanea troporum, sacrae scripturae candidatis utilissima, ex primariis tam Hebraeorum, quam ecclesiasticorum commentariis congesta*. Strassburg, 1535.

Whitney, Geoffrey. *A Choice of Emblemes, and other Devises, For the most parte gathered out of sundrie writers, Englished and Moralized*. Leiden, 1586.

Wier, Johan. *De praestigiis daemonum, et incantationibus ac venesiciis, Libri V* [1563]. 3rd ed. Basel, 1566.

William of Ockham. *Predestination, God's Foreknowledge, and Future Contingents*. Translated by Marilyn Adams and Norman Kretzmann. Indianapolis, 1983.

Wilson, Thomas. *The Art of Rhetoric* [1560]. Edited by Peter E. Medine. University Park, 1994.

Wither, George. *A Preparation to the Psalter.* London, 1619.

Wyatt, Thomas. *Collected Poems of Sir Thomas Wyatt.* Edited by Kenneth Muir and Patricia Thomson. Liverpool, 1969.

Secondary Sources

Abbott, Wilbur C., ed. *The Writings and Speeches of Oliver Cromwell.* 4 vols. New York, 1970.

Aguzzi-Barbagli, Danilo. 'Humanism and Poetics.' In *Renaissance Humanism: Foundations, Form, and Legacy.* Vol. 3, *Humanism and the Disciplines,* ed. Alfred Rabil. 85–169. 3 vols. Philadelphia, 1989.

Altman, Joel. *The Tudor Play of Mind: Rhetorical Inquiry and the Development of Elizabethan Drama.* Berkeley, 1978.

Baumlin, James S. 'Ciceronian Decorum and the Temporalities of Renaissance Rhetoric.' In *Rhetoric and Kairos: Essays in History, Theory, and Praxis,* ed. Phillip Sipiora and James S. Baumlin. 138–64. Albany, 2002.

Blair, Ann. '*Ovidius Methodizatus:* the *Metamorphoses* of Ovid in a Sixteenth-Century Parisian College.' *History of Universities* 9 (1990): 73–118.

Bolgar, Robert. *The Classical Heritage and Its Beneficiaries.* Cambridge, 1954.

Boyle, Marjorie O'Rourke. *Erasmus on Language and Method in Theology.* Toronto, 1977.

Briggs, John C. *Francis Bacon and the Rhetoric of Nature.* Cambridge, Mass., 1989.

Broadbent, J.B., 'Milton's Rhetoric.' *Modern Philology* 56 (1959): 224–42.

Burke, Kenneth. *A Grammar of Motives.* Berkeley, 1945.

– *A Rhetoric of Motives.* Berkeley, 1950.

Bush, Douglas. *The Renaissance and English Humanism.* Toronto, 1939.

Cantimori, Delio. 'Rhetoric and Politics in Italian Humanism.' *Journal of the Warburg and Courtald Institutes* 1 (1937): 83–102.

Carr, E.H. *What Is History?* 2nd ed. Edited by R.W. Davies. Harmondsworth, 1987.

Clark, Donald Leman. *John Milton at St Paul's School: A Study of Ancient Rhetoric in English Renaissance Education.* New York, 1948.

Cogan, Mark. Pp. 33–40 in O'Rourke et al., 'The Most Significant Passage on Rhetoric in the Works of Francis Bacon.' *Rhetoric Society Quarterly* 26 (1996): 31–55.

– 'Rhetoric and Action in Francis Bacon.' *Philosophy and Rhetoric* 14 (1981): 212–33.

– 'Rodolphus Agricola and the Semantic Revolutions of the History of Invention.' *Rhetorica* 2 (1984): 163–94.

Collingwood, R.G. *The Idea of History.* Rev. ed. Edited by Jan van der Dussen. Oxford, 1994.

Conley, Thomas. 'Byzantine Teaching on the Figures and Tropes: An Introduction.' *Rhetorica* 4 (1986): 335–73.

– *Rhetoric and the European Tradition.* Chicago, 1990.

Cope, Jackson. *The Metaphoric Structure of 'Paradise Lost.'* Baltimore, 1962.

Copleston, Frederick J., S.J. *A History of Philosophy.* 8 vols. London, 1953.

Cox, Virginia. *The Renaissance Dialogue: Literary Dialogue and Its Social and Political Contexts, Castiglione to Galileo.* Cambridge, 1992.

Cunningham, J.V. '"With That Facility": False Starts and Revisions in *Love's Labour's Lost.'* In *The Collected Essays of J.V. Cunningham.* 325–41. Chicago, 1976.

Curtius, Ernst Robert. *European Literature and the Latin Middle Ages.* Translated by Willard R. Trask. Princeton, 1953. Repr. 1990.

Danielson, Dennis. *Milton's Good God: A Study in Literary Theodicy.* Cambridge, 1982.

DuRocher, Richard J. *Milton Among the Romans: The Pedagogy and Influence of Milton's Latin Curriculum.* Pittsburgh, 2001.

Evans, J. Martin. *'Paradise Lost' and the Genesis Tradition.* Oxford, 1968.

Excursus 2.921. 'To Compare Great Things.' In *'Paradise Lost,' 1668–1968: Three Centuries of Commentary.* Edited by Earl Miner, Willam Moeck, and Steven Jablonski. 435–8. Lewisburg, 2004.

Festa, Thomas. 'Repairing the Ruins: Milton as Reader and Educator.' *Milton Studies* 43 (2004): 35–63.

Firth, Charles. 'Milton as an Historian.' In *Essays Historical and Literary.* 61–102. Oxford, 1938.

Fish, Stanley E. *Surprised by Sin: The Reader in 'Paradise Lost.'* 2nd ed. London, 1997.

– 'Why Milton Matters; or, Against Historicism.' *Milton Studies* 44 (2005): 1–12.

Fletcher, Harris F. *The Intellectual Development of John Milton.* 2 vols. Urbana, 1956–61.

Gadamer, Hans-Georg. *Truth and Method.* 2nd rev. ed. Translated by Joel Weinsheimer and Donald G. Marshall. New York, 1993.

Gaonkar, Dilip P. 'Contingency and Probability.' In *Encyclopedia of Rhetoric,* ed. Thomas Sloane et al. 151–66. Oxford, 2001.

Gilbert, Neal W. *Renaissance Concepts of Method.* New York, 1960.

Grafton, Anthony. 'The Availability of Ancient Works.' In *The Cambridge History of Renaissance Philosophy*, ed. Charles B. Schmitt et al. 767–91. Cambridge, 1988.

– 'The New Science and the Traditions of Humanism.' In *The Cambridge Companion to Renaissance Humanism*, ed. Jill Kraye. 203–23. Cambridge, 1996.

– 'Renaissance Readers and Ancient Texts: Comments on Some Commentaries.' *Renaissance Quarterly* 38 (1983): 615–49.

– 'Teacher, Text and Pupil in the Renaissance Classroom: A Case Study from a Parisian College.' *History of Universities* 1 (1981): 37–70.

Gray, Hannah H. 'Renaissance Humanism: The Pursuit of Eloquence.' In *Renaissance Essays. From the 'Journal of the History of Ideas,'* ed. Paul O. Kristeller and Philip P. Wiener. 199–216. New York, 1968.

Green, Lawrence D. 'The Reception of Aristotle's *Rhetoric* in the Renaissance.' In *Peripatetic Rhetoric After Aristotle*, ed. William W. Fortenbaugh and David C. Mirhady. 320–48. New Brunswick, N.J., 1994.

Grimaldi, William M.A. *Aristotle, 'Rhetoric': A Commentary*. 2 vols. New York, 1980–8.

Grossman, Marshall. 'Milton and the Rhetoric of Prophecy.' In *The Cambridge Companion to Milton*, ed. Dennis Danielson. 167–81. Cambridge, 1989.

Grube, G.M.A. *The Greek and Roman Critics*. Toronto, 1965.

Gualdo Rosa, Lucia. *La fede nella 'Paideia': aspetti della fortuna Europea di Isocrate nei secoli XV e XVI*. Rome, 1984.

Guthrie, W.K.C. *The Sophists*. Cambridge, 1971.

Hale, John K., 'The Classical Literary Tradition.' In *A Companion to Milton*, ed. Thomas N. Corns. 22–36. Oxford, 2001.

– *Milton's Languages: The Impact of Multilingualism on Style*. Cambridge, 1997.

Hardison, O.B. 'The Orator and the Poet: The Dilemma of Humanist Literature.' *Journal of Medieval and Renaissance Studies* 1 (1971): 33–44.

Hoffman, Manfred. *Rhetoric and Theology: The Hermeneutics of Erasmus*. Toronto, 1995.

Hughes, Merritt Y. 'Filiations of the Celestial Dialogue.' In *Ten Perspectives on Milton*. 104–35. New Haven, 1965.

Hunt, Everett Lee. 'Plato and Aristotle on Rhetoric and Rhetoricians.' In *Historical Studies of Rhetoric and Rhetoricians*, ed. Raymond F. Howes. 19–70. Ithaca, 19–70. 1961.

Jaeger, Werner. *Paideia: The Ideals of Greek Culture*. Translated by Gilbert Highet. 3 vols. Oxford, 1945. Repr. 1965.

Kahn, Victoria. *Rhetoric, Prudence, and Skepticism in the Renaissance*. London, 1985.

Kelley, Donald. 'The Theory of History.' In *The Cambridge History of Renaissance Philosophy*, ed. Charles B. Schmitt et al. 746–61. Cambridge, 1988.

Kennedy, George. *The Art of Persuasion in Greece.* London, 1963.
– *The Art of Rhetoric in the Roman World.* Princeton, 1972.
– *Classical Rhetoric and Its Christian and Secular Tradition from Ancient to Modern Times.* London, 1980.
– *A New History of Classical Rhetoric.* Princeton, 1994.
– *New Testament Interpretation through Rhetorical Criticism.* Chapel Hill, 1984.
– ed., *The Cambridge History of Literary Criticism.* Vol. 1, *Classical Criticism.* Cambridge, 1989.
Kirkconnell, Watson. *The Celestial Cycle: The Theme of 'Paradise Lost' in World Literature with Translations of the Major Analogues.* Toronto, 1952.
Kranidas, Thomas. *The Fierce Equation: A Study in Milton's Decorum.* London, 1965.
– *Milton's Rhetoric of Zeal.* Pittsburgh, 2005.
Kraye, Jill. 'Moral Philosophy.' In *The Cambridge History of Renaissance Philosophy,* ed. Charles B. Schmitt et al. 303–86. Cambridge, 1988.
– 'Conceptions of Moral Philosophy.' In *The Cambridge History of Seventeenth-Century Philosophy.* 2 vols. Ed. Daniel Garber and Michael Ayers. Cambridge, 1997, 2:1279–1316.
Kristeller, Paul Oskar. *Renaissance Thought and Its Sources.* Edited by Michael Mooney. New York, 1979.
Lanham, Richard. *A Handlist of Rhetorical Terms: A Guide for Students of English Literature.* Berkeley, 1968.
– *The Motives of Eloquence: Literary Rhetoric in the Renaissance.* New Haven, 1976.
Lares, Jameela. *Milton and the Preaching Arts.* Pittsburgh, 2001.
Lewalksi, Barbara K. *Milton's Brief Epic.* Providence, 1966.
– *Protestant Poetics and the Seventeenth-Century Religious Lyric.* Princeton, 1979.
Lewis, C.S. *A Preface to 'Paradise Lost.'* Oxford, 1942. Repr. 1961.
Lieb, Michael. 'Reading God: Milton and the Anthropopathetic Tradition.' *Milton Studies* 25 (1989): 213–43.
Loewenstein, Joseph. 'Humanism and Seventeenth-Century English Literature.' In *The Cambridge Companion to Renaissance Humanism,* ed. Jill Kraye. 269–93. Cambridge, 1996.
Mack, Peter. *Elizabethan Rhetoric: Theory and Practice.* Cambridge, 2002.
– 'Ramus Reading: the Commentaries on Cicero's *Consular Orations* and Vergil's *Eclogues* and *Georgics.' Journal of the Warburg and Courtald Institutes* 61 (1998): 111–41.
– *Renaissance Argument: Valla and Agricola in the Traditions of Rhetoric and Dialectic.* Leiden, 1993.
– 'Renaissance Habits of Reading.' In *Renaissance Essays for Kitty Scoular Datta,* ed. Sukanta Chaudhuri. 1–25. Calcutta, 1995.

Major, John. 'Milton's View of Rhetoric.' *Studies in Philology* 64 (1967): 685–711.

Maltzahn, Nicholas von. *Milton's 'History of Britain': Republican Historiography in the English Renaissance*. Oxford, 1991.

Marsh, David. 'Francisco Filelfo's Translation of the *Rhetorica ad Alexandrum*.' In *Peripatetic Rhetoric After Aristotle*, ed. William W. Fortenbaugh and David C. Mirhady. 349–64. New Brunswick, N.J., 1994.

– *The Quattrocento Dialogue: Classical Tradition and Renaissance Innovation*. Cambridge, Mass., 1980.

Martindale, Joanna, ed. *English Humanism, Wyatt to Cowley*. London, 1985.

McCaffrey, Phillip. 'Paradise Regained: The Style of Satan's Athens.' *Milton Quarterly* 5 (1971): 7–14.

McNally, James. 'Rudolph Agricola's *De inventione dialectica libri tres:* A Translation of Selected Chapters.' *Speech Monographs* 34 (1967): 393–422.

Miller, George. 'Stylistic Rhetoric and the Language of God in *Paradise Lost, Book III*.' *Language and Style* 8 (1975): 111–26.

Miller, Perry. *The New England Mind: The Seventeenth Century*. Cambridge, Mass., 1939. Repr. 1982.

Mitchell, William F. *English Pulpit Oratory from Andrewes to Tillotson: A Study of Its Literary Aspects*. London, 1932.

Monfasani, John. *George of Trebizond: A Biography and a Study of His Rhetoric and Logic*. Leiden, 1976.

– 'The Byzantine Rhetorical Tradition and the Renaissance.' In *Renaissance Eloquence: Studies in the Theory and Practice of Renaissance Rhetoric*, ed. James J. Murphy. 174–87. Berkeley, 1983.

Moss, Ann. 'Humanist Education.' In *The Cambridge History of Literary Criticism*. Vol. 3, *The Renaissance*, ed. Glyn P. Norton. 145–54. Cambridge, 1999.

– *Latin Commentaries on Ovid from the Renaissance*. Signal Mountain, 1998.

Murphy, James J. *Rhetoric in the Middle Ages: A History of Rhetorical Theory from Saint Augustine to the Renaissance*. Berkeley, 1974.

Murrin, Michael. 'The Language of Milton's Heaven.' *Modern Philology* 74 (1977): 350–65.

Nelson, Eric. '"True Liberty": Isocrates and Milton's *Areopagitica*.' *Milton Studies* 40 (2001): 201–21.

Nettleship, Richard Lewis. *Lectures on the 'Republic' of Plato*. 2nd ed. London, 1901. Repr. Honolulu, 2003.

Norbrook, David. *Writing the English Republic: Poetry, Rhetoric and Politics, 1627–1660*. Cambridge, 1999.

Normore, Calvin. 'Future Contingents.' In *The Cambridge History of Later Medieval Philosophy*, ed. Norman Kretzmann et al. 338–51. Cambridge, 1983.

O'Donnell, James. *Cassiodorus*. Berkeley, 1979.

Ong, Walter J., S.J. *Ramus, Method, and the Decay of Dialogue: From the Art of Discourse to the Art of Reason*. Cambridge, Mass., 1958. Repr. 1983.

Parker, William R. *Milton: A Biography*. 2 vols. 2nd ed. Rev. version, ed. Gordon Campbell. Oxford, 1996.

– *Milton's Contemporary Reputation: An Essay*. New York, 1940. Repr. 1971.

Patey, Douglas L. *Probability and Literary Form: Philosophic Theory and Literary Practice in the Augustan Age*. Cambridge, 1984.

Patrides, C.A. 'The Godhead in *Paradise Lost*: Dogma or Drama?' In *Bright Essence: Studies in Milton's Theology*. Essays by Jack H. Adamson, William B. Hunter, and C. A. Patrides. 71–7. Salt Lake City, 1971.

– *Milton and the Christian Tradition*. Oxford, 1966.

– '*Paradise Lost* and the Theory of Accommodation.' In *Bright Essence: Studies in Milton's Theology*. Essays by Jack H. Adamson, William B. Hunter, and C.A. Patrides. 159–63. Salt Lake City, 1971.

– *The Phoenix and the Ladder: The Rise and Decline of the Christian View of History*. University of California Publications, English Studies 29. Berkeley, 1964.

Patterson, Annabel. *Hermogenes and the Renaissance: Seven Ideas of Style*. Princeton, 1970.

Pender, Stephen. 'The Open Use of Living: Prudence, Decorum, and the "Square Man."' *Rhetorica* 23 (2005): 363–400.

Pine, M. 'Pietro Pomponazzi and the Medieval Tradition of God's Foreknowledge.' In *Philosophy and Humanism: Essays in Honor of Paul Oskar Kristeller*, ed. Edward P. Mahoney. 100–15. New York, 1976.

Plett, Heinrich F. 'The Place and Function of Style in Renaissance Poetics.' In *Renaissance Eloquence: Studies in the Theory and Practice of Renaissance Rhetoric*, ed. James J. Murphy. 356–75. Berkeley, 1983.

– *Rhetoric and Renaissance Culture*. Berlin, 2004.

Popkin, Richard. *The History of Scepticism from Erasmus to Spinoza*. Berkeley, 1979.

Poppi, Antonino. 'Fate, Fortune, Providence, and Human Freedom.' In *The Cambridge History of Renaissance Philosophy*, ed. Charles B. Schmitt et al. 641–67. Cambridge, 1988.

Rebhorn, Wayne A. *The Emperor of Men's Minds: Literature and the Renaissance Discourse of Rhetoric*. Ithaca, 1995.

Reeves, Charles E. '"Lest Wilfully Transgressing." Raphael's Narration and Knowledge in *Paradise Lost*.' *Milton Studies* 34 (1996): 83–98.

Rex, Richard, ed. *A Reformation Rhetoric: Thomas Swynnerton's 'The Tropes and Figures of Scripture*.' Renaissance Texts from Manuscript 1. Cambridge, 1999.

Rice, Eugene F. *The Renaissance Idea of Wisdom*. Cambridge, 1958.

Rostagni, Augusto. 'A New Chapter in the History of Rhetoric and Sophistry.'

Translated by Phillip Sipiora. In *Rhetoric and* Kairos: *Essays in History, Theory, and Praxis*, ed. Phillip Sipiora and James S. Baumlin. 23–45. Albany, 2002.

Russell, D.A. *Ancient Literary Criticism: The Principal Texts in New Translations*. Edited by D.A. Russell and Michael Winterbottom. Oxford, 1972.

Samuel, Irene. 'Milton on the Province of Rhetoric.' *Milton Studies* 10 (1977): 177–93.

– 'Milton on Style.' *Cornell Library Journal* 9 (1969): 39–58.

– *Plato and Milton*. Ithaca, 1947.

Schmitt, Charles B. *Cicero Scepticus: A Study of the Influence of the Academica in the Renaissance*. The Hague, 1972.

Shapin, Steven, and Simon Schaffer. *Leviathan and the Air-Pump: Hobbes, Boyle, and the Experimental Life*. Princeton, 1985.

Shapiro, Barbara. *Probability and Certainty in Seventeenth-Century England: A Study of the Relationships between Natural Science, Religion, History, Law, and Literature*. Princeton, 1983.

Shuger, Deborah. *Sacred Rhetoric: The Christian Grand Style in the English Renaissance*. Princeton, 1988.

Sipiora, Phillip. 'Introduction: The Ancient Concept of *Kairos*.' In *Rhetoric and Kairos: Essays in History, Theory, and Praxis*, ed. Phillip Sipiora and James S. Baumlin. 1–22. Albany, 2002.

Skinner, Quentin. 'Moral Ambiguity and the Renaissance Art of Eloquence.' In *Visions of Politics, II: Renaissance Virtues*. 264–85. Cambridge, 2002.

– 'Motives, Intentions and Interpretation.' In *Visions of Politics, I: Regarding Method*. 90–102. Cambridge, 2002.

– *Reason and Rhetoric in the Philosophy of Hobbes*. Cambridge, 1996.

– 'The Republican Ideal of Political Liberty.' In *Machiavelli and Republicanism*, ed. Gisela Bock, Quentin Skinner, and Maurizio Viroli. 293–309. Cambridge, 1990.

Sloane, Thomas. *Donne, Milton, and the End of Humanist Rhetoric*. Berkeley, 1984.

Stanwood, P.G., and Heather R. Asals, eds. *John Donne and the Theology of Language*. Columbia, 1986.

Steadman, John. *The Hill and the Labyrinth: Discourse and Certitude in Milton and His Near Contemporaries*. Berkeley, 1984.

– '"Man's First Disobedience": the Causal Structure of the Fall.' *Journal of the History of Ideas* 21 (1960): 180–96.

– *Milton and the Renaissance Hero*. Oxford, 1967.

– 'Milton's Rhetoric: Satan and the "Unjust Discourse."' *Milton Studies* 1 (1969): 67–92.

– '"Semblance of Worth": Pandaemonium and Deliberative Oratory.' In *Milton's Epic Characters: Image and Idol*. 241–63. Chapel Hill, 1959.

Struever, Nancy. *The Language of History in the Renaissance: Rhetoric and Historical Consciousness in Florentine Humanism.* Princeton, 1970.

Thomas, Keith. *Religion and the Decline of Magic: Studies in Popular Beliefs in Sixteenth- and Seventeenth-Century England.* London, 1971.

Thomson, D.F.S. 'The Latinity of Erasmus.' In *Erasmus,* ed. T.A. Dorey. 115–37. London, 1970.

Trinkaus, Charles. *The Poet as Philosopher: Petrarch and the Formation of Renaissance Consciousness.* New Haven, 1979.

Tuve, Rosemond. *Elizabethan and Metaphysical Imagery: Renaissance Poetic and Twentieth-Century Critics.* Chicago, 1947.

Vickers, Brian, ed. *English Science, Bacon to Newton.* Cambridge, 1987.

– *In Defence of Rhetoric.* Oxford, 1987.

– 'The Power of Persuasion: Images of the Orator, Elyot to Shakespeare.' In *Renaissance Eloquence: Studies in the Theory and Practice of Renaissance Rhetoric,* ed. James J. Murphy. 411–35. Berkeley, 1983.

– 'The Recovery of Rhetoric: Petrarch, Erasmus, Perelman.' In *The Recovery of Rhetoric: Persuasive Discourse and Disciplinarity in the Human Sciences,* ed. R.H. Roberts and J.M.M. Good. 25–48. London, 1993.

– 'Rhetoric and Poetics.' In *The Cambridge History of Renaissance Philosophy,* ed. Charles B. Schmitt et al. 715–45. Cambridge, 1988.

– 'Rhetorical and Anti-Rhetorical Tropes: On Writing the History of Elocutio.' *Comparative Criticism* 3 (1981): 105–32.

– 'The Royal Society and English Prose Style: A Reassessment.' In Nancy Struever and Brian Vickers, *Rhetoric and the Pursuit of Truth: Language Change in the Seventeenth and Eighteenth Centuries.* 1–76. Los Angeles, 1985.

Ward, John. *Ciceronian Rhetoric in Treatise, Scholion and Commentary.* Turnhout, 1995.

Weinberg, Bernard. *A History of Literary Criticism in the Italian Renaissance.* 2 vols. Chicago, 1961.

Wittgenstein, Ludwig. *Philosophical Investigations.* Translated by G.E.M. Anscombe. Oxford, 1953. Repr. 1976.

Wittreich, Joseph. '"The Crown of Eloquence": The Figure of the Orator in Milton's Prose Works.' In *Achievements of the Left Hand: Essays on the Prose of John Milton,* ed. Michael Lieb and John T. Shawcross. 3–54. Amherst, 1974.

– 'Milton's Idea of the Orator.' *Milton Quarterly* 6 (1972): 38–40.

Wurtele, Douglas. '"Perswasive Rhetoric": The Techniques of Milton's Archetypal Sophist.' *English Studies in Canada* 3 (1977): 18–33.

Glossary of Rhetorical Figures and Tropes

A fortiori Proving the likelihood of an argument by having it follow another argument that, though true, is even less likely to be the case.

Adynaton A professed inability to express oneself as the subject requires.

Amplificatio (1) A general term for intensifying or augmenting the emotional power of a speech through any of a wide range of techniques; (2) the third of an oration's five parts, which states the arguments for the case (q.v. *partitio* [2], *refutatio*).

Anaphora Beginning successive clauses with the same word.

Anthimeria Switching a word's customary grammatical form, for example, using a noun as a verb ('Lord Angelo dukes it well in his absence' – *Measure for Measure*, III. ii. 91).

Anthropopathia Ascribing human speech to God.

Anthypophora Asking a rhetorical question, then answering it oneself.

Antimetabole Interlaced repetition of two words in the pattern 'x-y-y-x' (see page 110, where the words are 'belly' and 'birthright').

Antonomasia The substitution of a descriptive phrase for a proper name, or vice versa.

Apostrophe Breaking off discourse to address directly some person or thing either present or absent.

Argumentum ad hominem Attacking the character of one's opponent rather than refuting opposing arguments.

Asyndeton The omission of conjunctions between clauses.

Auxesis Words or clauses placed in climactic order.

Climax Ascending in stages to a climactic idea (differentiated from auxesis in that the clauses are of parallel construction).

Conduplicatio Repetition of a word or words in succeeding clauses.

Denumeratio Piling up the details of a general fact or idea.

Distribution A general term for the division of something into its constituents, such as a subject into its adjuncts, for either better understanding the thing under examination (as in Plato's dialectic) or rhetorical amplification (q.v. *divisio, enumeratio, partitio*).

Divisio The division of a genus into its species.

Ekphrasis Vivid description of a setting or location.

Ellipsis The omission of several words in a clause or sentence.

Enumeratio The distribution of a cause into its effects.

Epanalepsis Beginning a clause with the same word that concluded the preceding clause.

Epiphonema Pithy summation of an argument.

Epiplexis Rhetorical question intended to reproach or upbraid.

Erotesis Rhetorical question that strongly implies its own answer.

Hypallage Transferred epithet or change in the ordinary relation of words, as in 'the tents of wickedness' (Psalm 84.10).

Hyperbaton A disordered or unusual arrangement of words or clauses in a sentence.

Hypotyposis A general term for vivid description.

Metonymy The substitution in either direction of cause for effect or a proper name for one of its qualities; or, more generally, reduction (as the corporeal for the spiritual).

Paromoiosis Parallelism of sound between the words of two clauses either approximately or exactly equal in size.

Partitio (1) The division of a whole into its parts; (2) the second of the five parts of an oration, which sets forth what is to be proved (q.v. *amplificatio, refutatio*).

Peristasis Relating the particular circumstances of an event.

Ploce Repetition of a word with a new signification after the intervention of another word or words.

Polyptoton Repetition of a word in a different grammatical form.

Prosopopoeia (1) Attributing human qualities to inanimate things; (2) representing an imaginary or absent person as speaking or acting.

Protrope Exhorting hearers to act by threats or promises.

Refutatio The fourth of the five parts of an oration, which refutes an opponent's arguments (q.v. *amplificatio, partitio*).

Sygkrisis Systematic comparison.

Synecdoche The substitution in either direction of genus for species or whole for part; or, more generally, representation (as an agent for his works).

Index